Lancaster crews of 9 Squadron, Bardney, Lincolnshire, waiting to go out to their aircraft for another night operation, led by the Commanding Officer, W/C Pat Burnett, D.S.O., D.F.C.

(John Moutray photo)

CRITICAL MOMENTS

Profiles of Members of the
Greater Vancouver Branch of the
Aircrew Association

Dedication

SQUADRON LEADER E.H." MAC" McCAFFERY D.F.C., A.F.C.

The profiles which make up this book were in the hands of
the word processor prior to printing, when the life of our friend and comrade
was suddenly cut short. We owe it to his memory that "Critical Moments"
be dedicated to Mac, since he was the prime mover of the project and gave
hours of his time towards its completion.

CO-ORDINATING COMMITTEE

The late E.H. (Mac) McCaffery D.F.C., A.F.C
John Moutray D.F.C., D.F.M.

EDITORIAL COMMITTEE

Stan Lancaster C.D. Chairman
John Gowans D.F.C.
Norm Armstrong D.F.C.
Art Jackson
Tom Colbeck
Ivan Todd
Harry Bray
Roland Bouwman

MARKETING/FINANCE COMMITTEE

Harry J. Hardy D.F.C.,C.D. Chairman

TECHNICAL COMMITTEE

George F.Grant D.S.O.*, D.F.C. Chairman

PHOTOGRAPHY

Ivan J. Scott D.F.C., C.D.

DUST JACKET

Front—John Moutray D.F.C., D.F.M.
Back—Robert J. Banks/Dan C. Ryan
Black and white illustrations—Dan C. Ryan

TYPESETTING

Maggie Edwards

A project of and by the members of the branch, assisted by the New Horizons Program, Health and Welfare, Canada.

Second Printing 1990

ISBN 0-88925-967-4

Printed in Canada

Commendation

All aircrew are united by a special bond and none moreso than wartime aircrew, who shared a unique experience and are justly proud of their contribution to the peace and freedom that the western world enjoys today. From a Canadian perspective, their history of achievements is legion. Their sacrifices must never be forgotten. As a soldier who fought in Europe during the Second World War, I have much reason to remember them with gratitude and admiration.

In the First World War, 21,000 Canadians flew with the Royal Naval Services, the Royal Flying Corps and its successor, the Royal Air Force. Proir to, and in the early stages of the Second World War over 2,000 Canadians migrated to Britain to join the R.A.F. where they served with great distinction. Of these 870 were killed in action and 100 taken prisoner of war. There were approximately 132,000 aircrew graduates from the British Commonwealth Training Plan established in Canada in 1940 through to 1945. Seventy-three thousand of these graduates were members of the Royal Canadian Air Force. Over 40,000, as well as R.C.A.F. permanent force aircrew served overseas. Twenty-four thousand flew with R.A.F. squadrons, the remainder with the 48 Canadian squadrons in service. Thirty-five thousand served with the 40 Canadian squadrons operating on the Pacific and Atlantic Coasts and the West Indies, the 10 Operational Training Units in Canada and the 92 Training Stations of the B.C.A.T.P. in Canada. Casualties of R.C.A.F. aircrew in the Second World War were in excess of 17,000 serving overseas and almost 1,000 in Canada. Additionally, 3,000 were taken prisoners of war and 1,200 disabled. Canadians in the R.A.F. received 630 decorations; those in the R.C.A.F. received approximately 5,000 decorations and were "Mentioned in Despatches" on more than 2,400 occasions.

Aircrew are very conscious of and grateful for the contributions of the ground support services. Without them there would be no airforce. They share fully in the accomplishments of this arm of the service.

The Greater Vancouver Branch of the Aircrew Association is to be commended for its initiative in recording this unique profile. It puts into perpective the variety of roles and experiences and recalls both the courage in times of adversity and the lighter moments that are typical of aircrew in times of war and peace. It records for posterity, a cross-section of aircrew that is the airforce.

August 1988

Honourable George Hees
Minister of Veterans Affairs
Parliament Buildings
Ottawa, Ontario

Introduction

This profile of members of the Greater Vancouver Branch of The Aircrew Association was produced, in response to a number of recommendations made by the members, at a workshop in June, 1987. These recommendations expressed the desire to get to better know fellow members and to recapture the esprit de corps experienced by many. It will, hopefully, also be appreciated by members and friends of the family; aircrews generally, have said very little of their experiences.

A big problem in the early months of planning was to choose a suitable title for the book, but after studying over fifty suggestions, from "Calling Tatlow Two" to "Dicey Do's", the Editorial Committee decided that "Critical Moments" was elastic enough to include humour as well as danger in the written word.

Acknowledgements

Many people are to be thanked for their help in compiling this profile. First, are the members, for their response to requests for accounts of some of their experiences and photographs. It is not easy to publicly talk about oneself. As one respondent wrote, "Enclosed is my effort for the A.C.A. Profile. I found it very difficult to do. I don't think I did anything very outstanding. I did the best job I could and probably one of the major contributions, was my encouragement and support to my fellow crew members."

The Co-ordination and Editorial Committee spent many hours, without remuneration, producing this unique cross-section of aircrew experiences in war time and in time of peace. They have earned our admiration and we thank them.

July 1988   *H.H. Lawrence D.F.C.*
                                         President
                                         Greater Vancouver Branch
                                         Air Crew Association

Contents

A Prophecy

The time will come when thou shalt lift thine eyes
to watch a long drawn battle in the skies
while aged peasants, too amazed for words
stare at the flying fleets of wond'rous birds.
England, so long the mistress of the sea,
where winds and waves confess her sovereignty.
Her ancient triumphs, yet on high shall bear
and reign, the sovereign of the conquered air.

TRANSLATION FROM GRAY'S "LUNA HABITABILIS".
CAMBRIDGE 1797 A.D.

W/C D.G. BELL-IRVING C.D.

PILOT R.C.A.F.

Gordon was born in Havana, Cuba, of Vancouver born parents and attended Prince of Wales Public and Secondary Schools in Vancouver. His post-secondary education was at the Royal Military College, Kingston, Ontario. His hobbies in Vancouver included skiing and boating and his pre-service occupation was that of student.

He joined the R.C.A.F. from the Royal Military College, at Saskatoon in May 1941 and volunteered as pilot. His training included E.F.T.S. at Fort William, S.F.T.S. at Uplands, C.F.S. at Trenton, Ont. and at #4 S.F.T.S. Saskatoon as an instructor. He then went on to 36 Mosquito O.T.U. at Greenwood, Nova Scotia,then in England he went to 60 O.T.U. High Ercall. He then spent some time on 21 Squadron (R.A.F.) with 2 Group Mosquitos from Feb. 1944 to August the same year.

Returning to Canada, he was at 7 O.T.U. Debert, N. S. (an instructor, once more), C.F.S. Trenton, S.F.T.S. Kingston, then 400 Squadron (Aux) Toronto on Vampires '46 - 49. He was then posted to Vancouver at A.D.C. H.Q.12 Group, then from 1954 until 1958 at R.C.A.F. Staff College, Armour Heights, Toronto A.F.H.Q. and wound up his career as C.O. of R.C.A.F. Station Dana, Saskatchewan.

He was mentioned in Despatches and received the '39-45 Star, War Medal, operational wings, C.D. plus Aircrew Europe and France & Germany clasp. His final promotion was to that of W/C. Gordon was honourably discharged at Dana, Sask in August 1964 and pursued a civilian occupation as Insurance Broker and Real Estate agent. He is married to Mary McDonald, daughter of Brig-Gen M.F. McDonald and they have one son two daughters and four grandchildren.

FIRST OP.

They were in the first course to graduate from the Mosquito O.T.U. at

1

Greenwood in the summer of '43. Twelve pilots, mostly Canadian, formerly flying instructors, crewed with freshly graduated R.A.F. navigators. The navigator was a Lancashire lad, Bert Holt. They did some further training at High Ercall in the U.K. and expected to go to intruder squadrons. However, some of them went instead to 140 Wing in 2 Group R.A.F., at that time specializing in daylight low-level bombing with Mk VI fighter-bomber Mosquitoes.

Gordon's first trip in the afternoon of March 2nd, the target a Noball site (VI launching station) in the Pas de Calais, was part of a four pronged "Ramrod" operation involving about 130 aircraft. They were in the final phase of the operation. The formation of four Mossies (they were No.3) went over the channel at wave-top height, crossed the French coast and a little later climbed to about 1500 feet for the run-up to the target for a shallow dive attack. They were spread out in loose line astern so the eleven second delayed action bombs would have time to go off before endangering the aircraft coming up behind.

Then the air was full of red lines and Bofors bursts. They had been taught to porpoise so as to present a difficult target. This he did for dear life. Suddenly there was a very loud bang, the aircraft seemed almost to stop, and went into an uncontrollable diving turn to starboard. Before they hit the ground, with full throttle on the starboard engine, hard rudder, the port throttle closed and about twenty degrees of bank to port they were going in a straight line in the general direction of the target, still with a full bomb load. The simplest way to deal with that part of the problem was to bomb the target and this they did. (The rearward aimed cine camera showed them leaving the target in a straight line but with considerable bank.)

Gradually, the pressure eased, they picked up speed, regained almost normal trim and landed at base with no problem. It transpired that a radio mechanic had forgotten to re-attach the hinged section of armour plating behind the navigator's head. In their state of pre first operation nervousness neither the navigator nor Gordon had noticed this. When they began to porpoise, the large chunk of steel had tripped the cable inflating the two man dinghy which had wrapped around the fin. The dinghy had eventually disintegrated leaving a few shreds of rubber and a large hole in the tail.

At debriefing the leader apologized for climbing earlier than necessary before the target thus exposing all of them to what the old hands confirmed was "intense light flak". He expected a pat on the back for bombing the target under duress, but the crew behind them in the fourth aircraft were furious because they, the green crew, had nearly blown them up by being slow over the target.

The poor erk responsible for their problem was put on a charge, but Gordon never did find out what happened to him.

THE FLUKIEST OP.

They were crossing the channel outbound from the Wash, on England's east coast, at low level, on the night of April 20th, 1944, and shortly after

2

leaving the coast flew over a small convoy protected by balloons. Seeing the balloons above them, Gordon pulled up pretty violently and, feeling that nothing was wrong went on to Quakenbruck and bombed his target. Next morning he was awakened and told to explain to the C.O. why he had not reported a taxying accident. His wing tip had a cable cut through it like a chain saw cut. Thenceforth, they crossed the channel at a more prudent height! The effectiveness of this kind of convoy protection as regards the number of enemy aircraft brought down was poor; it claimed far more friendly aircraft!!

NEATEST OP.

During August 1944, precision bombing attacks were made on buildings known by British Intelligence to house enemy personnel and great care had to be taken not to kill any civilians nearby. The Gestapo barracks at Bonneuil Matours in the corner of the Forest of Mouliere was the target for an attack on Bastille Day and Gordon and his navigator were one of four of 21 Squadron crews in this attack. This raid was in retaliation for the murder of 34 Operation Bulbasket team members on July 7th, near Poitiers under Hitler's "Commando Order". It was later reported that 150 members of the Gestapo were killed in this raid.

Gordon's most exciting operations were bombing and strafing the Wehrmacht at night, under flares in the Falaise Gap in mid-August 1944.

'DeHAVILAND DH-82C TIGER MOTH "4388"

FLYING OFFICER A.G. BOSSLEY

AIR BOMBER R.C.A.F

Alexander Bossley was born in Nelson, B.C., the son of a railroad engineer, and was raised and educated at North Bend, a town located in the Fraser Canyon. Thinking of his father's experience in World War 1, where his father was wounded and gassed at Passchendale but survived Vimy Ridge, he enlisted in the R.C.A.F. as an airframe mechanic two months after his eighteenth birthday in June 1941.

His first three months in service were spent in the Fairbanks Morse building, Vancouver, learning wood and metalwork. He was then posted to the "cattle stalls", of Manning Depot at the C.N.E. in Toronto where short arm inspections and female employees reduced any modesty attitudes.

"BOZ" graduated from St. Thomas as an airframe mechanic B Group. Six months later he remustered into aircrew and within another six months started his aircrew training. I.T.S. at Edmonton; No. 2 B & G at Mossbank, Saskatchewan, and received his wings at No.7 A.O.S., Portage La Praire, Manitoba. In August 1943 he sailed aboard the good ship Queen Elizabeth from Halifax to Greenoch, Scotland.

On one training flight from Penhros, Wales he had visions of being interned by the IRA when their Anson aircraft developed engine trouble and they were forced to land in Ireland. But the Airstation repaired their engine and the crew returned to base without further incident or without even a drink of stout or Irish whiskey to mark the occasion.

Bossley was posted to Stony Cross 299 Squadron where he joined his other aircrew members, then moved to Tistoch (1665 HC) to fly in Stirlings. They were posted first to 190 Squadron, Fairford, Gloucester, then six months later to their base at Great Dunmo.

His Squadron was used for dropping supplies to the underground, towing Horsa gliders, flying in paratroopers and making the occasional bombing run.

Flying north of Lyons on one trip they dropped fifteen paratroopers, including a major, his batman, who had never jumped before, and his dog. A parachute was specially made for the animal. One member of the troop's parachute opened in the plane, he gathered it up, held it in his arms and jumped with the rest of his group.

On "D" Day, operating under the code name TONGA, their plane dropped twenty-four paratroops along with all their supplies. Bossley was especially impressed to witness and see the Armada of ships heading for the Normandy coast.

For operation "Market", September 19th, 1944 their plane towed a Horsa glider, full of troops and supplies to Arnheim, just north of the Niemagen bridge. The first arriving Horsa glider would land at the end of a field and the rest of the gliders would land in behind them.

They returned to Arnheim to drop supplies on September 21st, without any knowledge that a mix-up had occurred and their Squadron did not receive the coverage expected from fighter command. The German Airforce and their 88mm guns on the ground were waiting. The two Stirling Squadrons stationed at Great Dunmo lost seventy percent of their planes on this mission. Bossley's plane flying at 500 feet with little room to recover was hit. His pilot F/O Middleton did a remarkable job pulling out between the ground and under high tension wires. One of the engines was shot up, the prop would not feather and with the trim gone they had a difficult time getting back to base. F/O Middleton was awarded the D.F.C. for his efforts.

Bossley, referring to their last flight as their swan-song, took place on March 24th, 1945. They towed a glider and dropped it east of the Rhine. On this operation, flying under 1,000 feet, airspeed 125 mph they lost four of their aircraft from flak.

Alex was honorably discharged in Vancouver in September, 1945. For his service career he received the Air Bomber Badge, the Air Crew Europe Medal, his Operation Tour Wing and the C.V.S.M. with clasp, also the 39/45 Star, War Medal and Defence Medal.

From 1946 to his retirement Alex was employed with the Canadian Pacific Railway as a conductor. He now lives in Coquitlam with his wife Vivian and spends as much time as possible playing golf.

F/Lt ROLAND BOUWMAN C.D.
NAVIGATOR R.C.A.F.

Rollie was born in Holland and after public school attended John Oliver High School in Vancouver to grade 13. After high school he joined the R.C.A.F. and decided he would like to try out for pilot, but because of clumsiness with the Link Trainer he failed to pass the course. He took full advantage of his grade 13 marks and with some expert wheedling and begging, convinced the instructors at #2 Air Observers School at Edmonton that he would make an excellent Air Observer, not withstanding the fact that most of his higher mathematics were forgotten. He was not too worried about not being a pilot as he considered himself to be a professional loser.

He was nearly overlooked because he was only one pound over the limit for recruits and he was barely able to get two letters to substantiate his existence and also because there were so many applications for the Air Force. He finally asked a former high school teacher, who was now in the R.C.A.F., to put on the pressure. It worked, but only because the R.C.A.F. really did need navigators. From October 1941 when Rollie was 18 years old and he enlisted, to August 1945 he came to the conclusion that he was lucky as well as being a professional loser.

After going through the usual training sessions such as armament, bombing, astro and long range navigation, Rollie graduated with the rank of Pilot Officer and in October 1942, boarded the Queen Elizabeth and sailed for England, ending up at Bournemouth.......and waited. He did not have a chance to fly until March 1943 but that seemed to be the game....waiting. Ultimately he reported to the R.A.F. at Silloth in Cumberland where he flew Wellingtons at O.T.U.. Rollie had wanted to fly Mosquitos as he felt Wellingtons were lower class aircraft and they never did anything interesting...so he thought. The Wellingtons he flew were to be used for torpedo dropping at night, from 50 feet!!

After 32 re-training flights he was sent to #1 Torpedo Training Unit at Turnberry in Scotland where he learned that the exercises were to consist of one plane dropping flares and the second aircraft was to drop torpedoes to hit a ship between the two Wellingtons...at night...at 50 feet!! This kind of conduct was more for Polish airmen than the shy and bashful Bouwman. He found out that bravado was also the name of the game and was shocked to find out as well, that crews flying Beauforts (those funny and tiny planes) would boast and say they had to CLIMB to 50 feet before dropping their torpedoes. Someone was heard to say that dropping torpedoes was the second most dangerous adventure invented by the R.A.F., the absolute worst being the Nickel Raids.

Roland was determined not to ask what they were, but he soon found out. However he was posted to Talbenny for a while and then to #303 Ferry Training Unit at Pembroke Dock where there were lots of "heavy load take-offs" and then one day he and the crew took off for Hara (#3 O.A.D.U.)....he's forgotten what that means...and then after more days of waiting found himself in Fez, Morocco, from where he eventually went to Cairo in September 1943. When they got there they found there were 40 or 50 other Torpedo dropping crews already there, so they had a great party. In the usual way the crew reported to the adjutant and found him to be a very polite officer (R.A.F.) and the crew was very polite in answering his questions about their training, especially as the chances of them having to fly any dangerous missions were slim, since there were so many crews ahead of them. Then the polite R.A.F. officer dropped a bombshell. They were ordered to report to #1 (M.E.) Ferry Command at 22 PTC for "special duties" at El Maza which was 40 km west of the pyramids. "And do what?" they asked. "Nickel Raids" he said. The crew, at this time in their service careers, had no clue what they were, but they were soon enlightened. They were to drop leaflets, the polite R.A.F. officer told them, and their crew was chosen as most of the other crews either had forgotten how to fly, some were missing and others had V.D.

He also told them they would be replacing another Wellington crew as they were shot up and crashed over Crete. When the crew asked the polite R.A.F.officer if the Germans on Crete had many guns they were told they certainly had. German guns, Italian guns, Greek guns and British guns. Rollie's crew was told they would be dropping leaflets on Crete and other islands in the vicinity and that they were to fly at exactly 10,000 feet, no higher, no lower. Apparently, the leaflet load, weighing about one ton and containing 500,000 to 650,000 single leaflets, took about 40 minutes to dump. Two Wellingtons had been lost but no deaths....yet, reported the polite R.A.F.officer. Three planes were to be used at a time and Rollie and his crew had 14 of these flights between the middle of September '43 and the end of October.

During these 39 days the following things happened:

- Everyone contacted GypoGut.
- Wimpy HE 710 burned to the ground when the engine caught fire on starting.
- Nine islands were saturated with leaflets.
- On five occasions the plane was hit, especially over Crete.
- One piece of shrapnel made a 1/2 inch hole in front of the pilot, then out Rollie's left hand sleeve.

On the second trip, Bouwman (navigator) got lost over Turkey and they had to go back to base fully loaded.

On the last trip the flak was so violent, the plane was hit, but no-one knew where. They soon found out it was the fuel tank. One engine quit and they were rapidly losing height. They threw everything moveable out the hatches, guns, ammo, instruments in an effort to keep airborne, but they finally made a bumpy landing in the sea a mile off the Egyptian coast. The plane floated and they all climbed on to the wing, wondering how they were going to swim to shore, when all of a sudden a huge orange thing appeared on the starboard wing and grew to an enormous size and then they realized it was a dingy which had opened automatically as soon as the mechanism was soaked with sea water. Thankfully, they climbed aboard and laboriously paddled to the shore.

Reaching the shore they tried to pull the dinghy in, but found it most difficult until with herculean efforts on the part of all the crew they found that a rope, trailing behind them had been tied to a large cube-shaped bundle, which, when opened proved to hold survival kit, flares, radio, all the comforts of home. They sent out a signal for help and very soon afterwards a truck came along manned by Australian troops who were very angry with the crew, since they had landed on the edge of enemy lines, actually near Mersa Matruh.

Rollie stayed in the Air Force for a year after the war ended and was honorably discharged in June 1946. He attended U.B.C. on an architect course for 4 years and then a law course for 3 years and graduated in law in 1954. For 12 years he was deputy City prosecutor for Vancouver, then 11 years with B.C. Tel as Vice President General Counsel and secretary. On retirement he purchased a duck farm in the Langley area and has recently sold it and now has only window boxes to attend. He is married to Marilyn and has two sons from a former marriage. He was awarded the 1939/45 Star, Italy Star, War Medal, Defence Medal, C.V.S.M. and the C.D.

FL/LT GEORGE BUMSTEAD
OBSERVER R.C.A.F.

George was born at Dauphin, Manitoba and attended elementary and High School there, where he was a violinist member of the High School Concert Orchestra. After school, having obtained his T.Q. Ticket in the Plumbing and Heating industry, he worked for three years in that trade.

He enlisted in the R.C.A.F. in Winnipeg in September of 1940 and applied to serve as an Observer. In order to obtain his navigators O badge, George went through #5 A.O.S., Winnipeg; #3 B.& G. McDonald; #1 A.N.S. Rivers. On graduation he was posted to Ferry Command. His most memorable trip being in Hudson #AE 598. The pilot and w.a.g. were both civilians; it took them fourteen hours and fifty five minutes to cross the pond with a stop at Gander. The civilians returned to Canada, George stayed in the U.K. After an O.T.U. at Upper Heyford he was posted to #420 Squadron at Waddington, flying Hampdens.

After 19 trips on the old "flying pencils" which included visits to some of the hottest spots in Europe; fire bombing Rostock, using 1900 lb H.E. bombs; the first and second Thousand Plane Raid on Cologne and Essen; visits to the Ruhr; the submarine pens at Keil, Brest; several jaunts over Hamburg, Bremen, Wilhelmshaven; and for a change of scenery some long range moonlight cruises to Mannheim and Turin, the squadron was re-equipped with Wellingtons and George was tour ex. by January 1943.

For the next fifteen months George served as an Instructor at #6 Group Heavy Conversion Units. At Wombleton, #s 1666 & 1679, he was promoted to F/Lt as Navigation Officer. He had already served at #s 1659 & 1664 which rather well covered the conversion squadrons.

George volunteered for a second tour and was given the bonus of 30 days special leave to Canada. He didn't waste much time getting back to his girl friend, who soon became his wife, in July 1944. It must have been an all too short honeymoon but it proved to be a lasting marriage. George and Helen have two sons and four grandchildren. One son a high school principal, and the other a Chartered Accountant.

On return to the U.K. he was posted to #424 Squadron but after 5 trips on Halifaxes his second tour was cut short. On their sixth outing over Cologne, Oct 9, 1944, the crew was shot down, ending in the river Rhine. Fortunately they were picked up, only the flight engineer didn't make it. The pilot was detained in hospital to have a leg amputated, George was thrown into solitary confinement at Dulag Luft at Frankfurt for the next 14 days. He was reunited with his crew, after a three day's and night's train ride ordeal—remember that by now German rolling stock was taking a terrific pounding and the chance of getting shot during such a ride becoming an increasing likelihood—they met at Stalag Luft 3 at Sagan (Belaria).

A long three months later, all the prisoners were marched out of Sagan at 5 a.m. to begin the infamous "long march." Rumors were flying; the Russians were within 25 miles of the camp, the war was about to end, Hitler had been killed in a bombing raid. These were all rumour and speculation but the reality of the situation was slim rations, the struggle of weakened bodies through snow and ice, which later turned to rain and mud, the very real threat of attack from the air, for the allied airforces were roaming around Germany shooting at anything that moved, especially men in columns.

Eight days later the column reached Spremberg; here they were loaded and locked into box cars, the same vans from the First World War labelled "8 chevaux or 40 hommes" but this time they held at least 50 men, albeit rather thin specimens. Three days later (the ride was almost worse than the walk), they were unloaded at Luckenwalde, Stalag #3A, some 30 miles south of Berlin. Here they were crowded in with thousands of other prisoners, British, Americans, French, Russian, Italians, Jugoslavians, Czechs and Norwegians. Later a veritable flood of refugees fleeing from the Russians, poured into camp.

For the next two months, as guests of the Reich, rations, when available, were the same as allocated to non military and non essential civilians; two cups of ersatz coffee, one cup of barley soup, one potato and 1/12 of a loaf of bread per man per day. Red Cross parcels had ceased to exist. It was a very long sixty days.

On the 21st of April 1945, the Russian army reached the camp and they were liberated but it took a further month before they were handed over to the Americans. After that it was a rather quick trip back to Canada. George was re-united with Helen in July 1945.

Back in Canada, George started his own plumbing and heating business at Dauphin, Manitoba and continued in that line of work until retirement in 1982. He now has time to watch his grandchildren participate in the sports he so loved at school - hockey, curling, golf, track and field. Sometimes, he even gets around to playing his violin.

On Legion parades he can display the 1939/45 Star, Aircrew Europe, C.V.S.M. and Clasp, M.I.D.(2), the War Medal and Defence Medal and of course an ops wing.

FLYING OFFICER NORMAN ARMSTRONG
D.F.C.

PILOT R.C.A.F.

Norm Armstrong was born in Summerland, B.C. in 1920. He attended The MacDonald Elementary School for eight years in Summerland and the Summerland High School for four years, graduating in 1938. West Summerland at that time was a small town with a population of 1100 people, situated in the Okanagan where the major industry was fruit growing. His chief sporting activities were playing softball, hiking, tennis and skating. For spare time work, Norm was employed in various jobs, as a grocery clerk, in a fruit packing plant, and doing carpentry. He planned to enter the College of Optometry in Toronto when the necessary funds were available.

Early in 1941 he made application to join the R.C.A.F., and on May 21st he was called to report to Vancouver to enlist and left the same night by train for Manning Pool at Brandon, Manitoba. After six weeks of basic training - drill, route marches, polishing brass, haircuts etc. he was transferred to the R.C.A.F. Equipment Depot in Winnipeg for a session of Guard Duty. From there he was posted to #4 Initial Training School at Edmonton for a month of Ground Schooling which was the first step towards becoming Aircrew and where he learned to wear the white flash in his cap with pride.

Armstrong began his flying training on Tiger Moths at Boundary Bay (B.C.)E.F.T.S. The last ten days of the course Norman spent in sick bay with a severe case of the 'flu. As a sidelight, after the war the hospital was moved to Langley and Norman served on the Hospital Board for several terms. From Boundary Bay he was posted to #1 S.F.T.S. Claresholm, Alberta, training on Ansons and Cessnas. Following the Wings Parade and Embarkation Leave, he was off to Halifax and onto the "Capetown Castle" for a nine day voyage to Liverpool. Then on to Bournemouth for a nine week spell with the Loyal Lancashire Regiment, in Norfolk.

Norm's first U.K. posting was to an Advanced Flying unit at Grantham, Lincs., where he mastered the intricacies of the Airspeed Oxford and from there he was selected to attend a General Reconnaisance Course at Harrogate. At this stage, each graduate was asked to indicate his preference of aircraft which he would like to fly, Norm's choice was Sunderlands, but to no avail. Instead he was posted to Limavady, in Northern Ireland, #7 O.T.U. where they flew Wellingtons "1C"s, a far cry from Sunderlands. However it was a Coastal Command Training Course, so at least part of Norm's wishes were fulfilled. Each pilot was given the opportunity of selecting his own crew of five members, a co-pilot, navigator and three wireless-cum-radar operator W.A.G.'s. Of the five selected, two were New Zealanders and three were Canadians, all of whom were very compatible except for the two from down under who had little respect for each other. The best thing about Limavady was the great improvement in the food.

On completion of the O.T.U. course, Norm's crew was assigned a new Wellington and they were posted to 179 Squadron, a Coastal Command station at Gibraltar, however, before they left England they were transferred to 172 Squadron stationed at Chivenor, North Devon, and they were to be there for an eighteen month tour. The 172 Squadron was the first to be equipped with the Leigh Light, a unit with a million candlepower that could be lowered out of the belly and which focussed on a U-Boat that had been located by the radar. The "Wimpy" was also equipped with a radio altimeter that enabled it to descend to 50 feet above the water before the "Light"was turned on so the U-Boat was taken by surprise without time to begin firing.

After thirty one Bay of Biscay sorties, the Armstrong crew and five others from Chivenor were detached from the squadron to Terceria, one of the Azores Islands, to begin patrols in search of U-Boats. The crew were stationed at Gibraltar for a few weeks before the landing strip on Terceria was made ready for landing. Under an Agreement some 600 years before, Portugal had granted the Government of the U.K. the right to make use of the island.

In November 1943 while on temporary assignment to R.A.F. North Front, Gibraltar, Norm and his crew and aircraft were assigned to provide an advance escort for a Naval Force proceeding eastward in the Mediterranean. They flew back and forth ahead of the lead vessels in the force for seven or eight hours, scouring the sea for enemy ships. When it was time to leave the flotilla, the Wellington had been instructed to fly lower and signal that they were leaving. H.M.S. Renown was the largest vessel in the convoy and the crew speculated that Prime Minister Churchill must be aboard, and one member was certain that he could see cigar smoke rising from the "Big Boat"..!

12

A week or so after the escort duty, Norm wrote a letter to his parents and mentioned the cigar smoke incident without using names. When his parents received the letter some time later, fully seventy five per cent of it had been cut out and all that remained were a few incidental words. Which went to prove that:

1) Censoring your own mail didn't pay and
2) Cigar smoke will give you away every time.

In early December, the six crews were established in tents on the Island and began their search for U-Boats of which there were plenty, and in addition they periodically did escort duty for the odd convoy. In five weeks, Armstrong's crew had attacked four U-Boats. In the last encounter on January 13th 1944 they were carrying out a patrol ahead of an Escort Group in Wellington L172. They were 400 miles north-east of the Azores flying at night, at 1500 feet when the Radar Operator picked up a contact ten miles ahead. Norm flew into a position "down moon" descending to 800 feet and sighted a U-Boat 2 1/2 miles ahead. He pushed the stick forward and dived straight into attack from the port beam. There was a bright moon shining that night and so it was not necessary to use the Leigh Light. Norm dropped three depth charges and the Front Gunner raked the deck of the U-Boat with machine gun fire. The rear gunner, who also opened fire, saw the first depth charge explode close to the port side of the U-Boat and the second charge exploded with a brilliant blue flash, indicating that it had exploded on hitting the vessel. Norm circled to port intending to drop the remaining charges, but a cloud obscured the moon and he had to make another circle. This time he sighted the U-Boat again and he made another attack, the stern of the U-Boat was submerged and the bow was well clear of the water. The front gunner had again raked the deck with gunfire and the U-Boat replied with what was estimated to be a single round of cannon-fire which destroyed the rear turret and hit the rear gunner in the left arm and leg.

By chance an American destroyer was some distance away and picked up the German crew some hours later. The next day, Coastal Command received a message that the destroyer had picked up the crew but it was 120 miles north of the actual position of the attack. It was another 48 hours before a second message was received that the American vessel had made an error of 120 miles in their report. It was finally straightened out and Norm's crew was credited with a 'known sunk!' Unfortunately the Rear Gunner had his leg amputated as a result of his injuries. Coastal Command's review analysis was that it was "a very skillful and successful attack resulting in a "known sunk" except for------" The German Admiralty assessment blamed lack of success of "U 231 on the commanding officer, Kaptanleutnant Wolfgang Wenzel, "a rabid and stupid Nazi" who tried to commit suicide by shooting himself in the mouth. He missed again, however, for the bullet lodged in the back of his neck and he explained that he had a sore throat.

Even with a crew of fairly compatible natures there are times when an occasional rift will develop and it takes more than wisdom to maintain peace and harmony. Norm was at one time faced with the problem of dealing with an incompetent crew member. The man was six foot three and was very awkward. He stayed up until all hours of the night and then stayed in bed until someone came and would literally have to pull him out of bed. He was competent at his wireless and radar trade but once at his duty-position in the aircraft he would stretch his long legs into the aisle and go to sleep. Since he always removed his helmet, he wouldn't hear any messages over the intercom. Trip after trip he would follow the same routine and shaking him or kicking him would be of no avail. Norm regularly reported him to the C.O. and just as regularly the C.O. gave him the same reply -"You're the Captain - deal with it yourself". As the other crew members became frustrated and angry it was obvious that something had to be done. The C.O.'s response was simple, "You lay a charge of incompetence and I will send him to the A.V.M. at Group". Norm followed the order and off went the crew member with an armed guard. The A.V.M. gave the recalcitrant airman a "blast" and gave him time to ponder his unacceptable actions, in the "glasshouse". Norman, who is normally a pleasant and friendly chap found this a difficult but necessary task that had to be done.

In October of 1943, Norman became engaged to Miss Kathleen Giardelli, a pay accounts clerk in the W.A.A.F., and they were married in September 1944, after Norm had returned to Chivenor from the Azores, at Englefield Green, Surrey, and fortunately they were able to return to Canada on the same ship.

Following his discharge in Vancouver, Norman entered U.B.C. for first year Arts, and in 1946 he was enrolled in the College of Optometry in Toronto and graduated in 1949, eleven years and many experiences after making his decision to make Optometry his career. He opened a practise in Oliver, B.C. and after four years, moved to Langley where he began thirty years of practice, retiring in 1983. Kay and Norm have three children, Geraldine, Trevor and Mariane and three grandchildren. Geraldine is a Nurse and Trevor and Mariane are both lawyers.

Norm received the D.F.C. -Immediate, and earned the 39/45 Star, the Italy Star, Atlantic Star, the CVSM and clasp and the War Medal.

He was discharged from the R.C.A.F. on August 23rd 1945 at R.C.A.F. Headquarters, Jericho Beach, Vancouver.

F/O EDWARD SANDFORD CHAMBERS D.F.C.
BOMB AIMER R.C.A.F.

"Ted" Chambers is a native Albertan, born in Edmonton, who moved with his family at an early age to Vancouver where he attended Lord Selkirk School and Vancouver Technical School. He enjoyed sports in his youth, soccer and softball being his main interests. At this time he also became an aviation fan, little suspecting the adventures in this field that he was soon to share, with so many other youths of his age in the skies over Europe. After graduation, Edward joined the staff of the B.C. Electric Railway Co. and on September 16th, 1942 he joined the R.C.A.F. at Vancouver, B.C. and started his service in Edmonton Manning Pool, thence to I.T.S. in Saskatoon, E.F.T.S. in Prince Albert, Paulson B.& G. School and A.O.S. at Portage la Prairie. He was posted overseas in January, 1944.

From the embarkation depot at Halifax, Ted's journey overseas was routed by a troop train known as "The Canadian Main Special" which was to take the draft to New York City harbour and all the airmen were cautioned not to get lost or to miss the train; one authority warned "If you miss the troopship at New York you will be considered as deserters unless real illness is the reason." Ted did not leave the train until they arrived at Albany, the capital of New York state, when he decided to disembark to buy some lipstick, silk stockings and such luxury items that were difficult to obtain in England, so he set out to find a store that carried the items he wanted. By the time he had located a store, had made his purchases and returned to the railway station, the Canadian Main Special had departed for New York. As he stood by the tracks pondering his future and the chances of being a deserter, another airman, P.O. West, whom he knew from I.T.S. also showed up; both found the truth in the old adage that misery loves company.

The local passenger agent put the two men on the next train for New York City and hours later they arrived at the famous Grand Central Station. The other train with the main draft, arrived at Weehauken Station in Jersey City and those airmen crossed the river by ferry, carrying their gear, and marched up to Pier 84 where the "Aquitania" was berthed. Ted and P.O. West however were more fortunate; they were met at the station by a corporal from the R.C.A.F. Transit Depot who took them by taxi up Broadway and the Great White Way up to the ship where their gear was already waiting. They struggled up the gangplank and were much relieved to rejoin their fellow airmen.

Ted and his crew flew their first operational sortie on the night of September 23rd 1944; the target was the marshalling yards at Nuess, six miles west of Dusseldorf. They took off from Kirmington, Lincs, their home airfield, with a bomb load consisting of eight one thousand pound medium case, four one thousand pound semi armour piercing, and four five hundred pound medium case aerial bombs. In addition to the bombs, they carried "Nickels" of propaganda leaflets and "window".....(small bundles of metal foil) which the Bomb Aimer pushed out through a tube built into the side of the aircraft. The many strips of foil were spread out by the slipstream from the aircraft. The enemy radar would try to pick up each of the hundreds of pieces of foil and would become overloaded and unable to direct the anti-aircraft fire, night fighters and searchlights to the aircraft. Everyone in the bomber stream was collectively shielded by it; many aircrew will remember "windowing" with warmth and affection.

The take off was smooth and uneventful and old W "William" and crew climbed in a "radius of Action" until they reached their planned height and set course on the first leg of their first mission at nineteen nineteen hours. There was a good tight bomber stream across the English countryside and, at twilight as they crossed the coast at Clacton-on-Sea, two of the aircraft collided and both bomb loads and petrol exploded in one great blast, and the planes, locked together in a fiery ball, fell straight to earth. Fourteen men died in an instant of time. As they pressed forward on their flight, all wondered which of their comrades had lost their lives in this spectacular manner.

After this incident, the crew continued on course without further incident and arrived at the target about twenty one eighteen hours and started their bombing run. Dusseldorf and Nuess were mostly covered by cloud but Edward could make out some details on the ground and identified a green and a red TI on opposite sides of the main fire at the target. A red TI glowed in the centre of this fire and indicated the aiming point, and Edward released the bombs at twenty one twenty two hours.

As Ted pressed the bomb release, Gerry Reid the rear-gunner yelled "Corkscrew, starboard, Paul" and Paul Saunders, the pilot, took the evasive action called for, turning starboard and diving to start the corkscrew action. As the aircraft dived to the right, Ted floated for a moment then came down on his belly as the plane turned to port and started a climb. He did not have time to get into the front turret to fire at the fighter which he identified as a

16

Focke Wolfe one ninety, after a flare illuminated the area. The mid upper gunner fired at the attacker first as it passed by on the starboard side. Luckily the aircraft was not hit but the tracer bullets passed unpleasantly close.

W "William" corkscrewed out of the target zone and set course for base. They were in the first three to land and at debriefing learned that the two aircraft that collided were from their squadron. It was an exciting first mission and an experience from which they learned a lot that would help them during the balance of their tour of operations.

The seventh operation of the crew of W "William" is one that remains fixed in Ted's memories. They took off at sixteen hundred hours, October 23rd from their base at Kirmington. The bomb load totalled eleven thousand and eighty pounds to be delivered to the Krupp Works in Essen, and included one four thousand pounder (the famous cookie) and the remainder were thirteen cans of thermite filled incendiaries. The weather was poor all the way to the target and there was ten tenths cloud at the target. The target was marked by Wanganui which was an incendiary marker from which stars of an assortment of colours dripped. The colour in use for this raid was red. Old W "William" couldn't climb above seventeen thousand five hundred feet so Ted had to bomb practically on top of the Wanganui. He released the bombs at nineteen forty seven hours and started the single and salvo routine to ensure that there were no hang-ups when a heavy blow jarred the aircraft. Everyone was confused for a moment then someone said over the intercom that a large bomb had fallen from above and had dropped through the starboard wing. It went through the starboard main plane, just missing the number three fuel tank and to add to their troubles the port inner engine packed up. After some discussion they decided to land at Manston where there was a long runway for use in emergencies, rather than to risk returning to base. On examining the aircraft after they landed they saw a hole about four feet by one and one half feet and concluded that this must have been made by a thousand pounder. Ted recalls the return trip to the squadron by rail and subway through London wearing their flying suits and sheepskin lined boots and carrying their parachutes and flying gear.

Ted's posting while he was in England were to number three (O) A.F.U., Halfpenny Green, Worcs., Number eighty three O.T.U. Peplow, Salop., Number sixteen hundred fifty H.C.U., Lindholme, Yorkshire and Number 166 Squadron, Kirmington, Lincs. He flew in Tiger Moths, Anson, Bolingbroke, Wellingtons, Halifaxes and Lancasters. He served in England from January 1944 to January 1945, and completed one tour of operations of 30 trips. He was awarded the D.F.C. and has earned the 1939-45 Star, the France/Germany Star, the Defence Medal, War Medal, and C.D. Medal. After the war he was employed with B.C. Hydro and obtained his B.A.(English Major) in 1981. He also served with the Irish Fusiliers of Canada (Vancouver Regiment) for twelve years. Ted is a bachelor.

F/O JAMES S. CLARK D.F.M.
WOP/AG R.A.F.

Jim was born in Perth, Scotland and after the usual stint at public school attended the High School at Tayport, Fifeshire, Scotland, where he enjoyed soccer and athletics and later on, golfing.

He was a payroll clerk with a jute manufacturing company in Dundee for 4 years prior to enlistment in the R.A.F. on November 11, 1941 at Padgate, Lancs. He was posted to No 4 Radio School where he had 26 hours in Proctors (single engine aircraft) and Dominies (twin engine). He then went to #10 Advanced Flying Unit for 36 hours in Ansons, followed by 86 hours in Wellingtons at No 15 O.T.U.

Jim then went on conversion course #1663 flying in Halifax aircraft (59 hours) and ultimately joined #77 Squadron in Sept. 1943, a Halifax squadron and completed 12 operations with the same crew (as Wireless Operator/Air Gunner)

After the accident, related following, he flew as spare W/Op with different crews until the end of op's tour. He was promoted to Pilot Officer, August 28th, 1944 and to Flying Officer on 24th February 1945. His medals include the D.F.M., 1939/45 Star, Aircrew Europe Star, War Medal, and Defence Medal. He was discharged on September 10th, 1946 at R.A.F. Hednesford, England.

Jim joined the Civil Service on discharge and emigrated to Canada in May 1953 and held purchasing and administration positions in both Montreal and Vancouver until retirement. Jim is married, has one married daughter and two grandsons.

A HAIR BREADTH ESCAPE

On the morning of December 9th, 1943 Jim's captain was detailed to carry out a Fighter Affiliation exercise with the full crew, of which Jim was the radio operator. This was over an airfield in Yorkshire, England.

They took off and climbed to 8,000 feet to make contact with the fighter, and the exercise began. The skipper was strapped in, but it was optional for the rest of the crew. It turned out later that all but the bomb aimer and Jim were strapped in.

The third attack the fighter made was from the port bow so the captain dived to port, to counteract the attack, on instructions given by the air bomber who was in the nose. On learning that the fighter had broken off the attack to starboard, the captain tried to bring the plane out of its dive but it seemed to shudder and then turn over as Jim was held rigid in his seat and they lost height very rapidly.

The "G" pressure must have decreased, because after hearing the skipper call out to abandon the aircraft, Jim was able to grab his parachute pack as he knelt by the escape hatch. One clip went on, but the other would not, probably due to his haste. He decided to leave it and open the hatch and after a short struggle managed to get the escape hatch open and the other clip fastened to his harness.

Somehow he got his legs through the hatch and dropped into space, but he must have pulled the rip cord almost immediately as suddenly there was a terrific jerk and he found himself swinging back and forth below the large canopy of silk. He had no flying helmet so it must have been discarded after getting the "abandon aircraft" order.

Jim must have been very close to the ground when he dropped out as it seemed no time at all until he had to pull on the rigging lines of the 'chute and make a knees up and roll-over-landing in a farmer's field.

He remembers looking down at where the plane had crashed on a hillside and seeing another parachute further down the valley; as it transpired later, the air-bomber had abandoned the aircraft just after Jim, and was lucky to get clear, before the aircraft crashed with the other five members of the crew still inside.

On October 22nd, 1943, Jim's aircraft, a Halifax, was detailed for an operation to Kassel. Their route was a three leg one over the North Sea, before crossing the enemy coast, where, on arrival, the navigator discovered they were twenty minutes late.

A vote was taken by the captain on whether or not they should "press on" or turn back to base. As they were so far behind the main stream they would have been at a great disadvantage if they arrived so late over the target.

The majority vote was that they should turn back to base, bringing back their bomb load. The next day an intense investigation of the navigator's log failed to produce any error and it was established that one or more of the bombs had magnetized the compass which resulted in a course error of 13 degrees on each leg of the North Sea.

This situation could well have accounted for other aircraft arriving late over their targets, on other operations, and being shot down.

The crew's useless flying time was three hours and forty minutes and, of course, did not count as an operation.

F/O H.M.(TONY) CRAVEN
R.C.A.F. AIR BOMBER

Tony Craven was born in England in 1923. In 1929 the family moved to Canada and settled in a small town, Castor, Alberta. While there, Tony attended school, learned to skate, play hockey, baseball, ride horses, shoot trap and hunt. In 1937 the family moved to Burnaby, Vancouver, where he attended Burnaby South High School. At the end of his final year in 1942, Tony and four of his friends joined the Air Force and went to the Edmonton Manning Depot and then on to I.T.S. at Saskatoon. After Saskatoon two of them went on to pilot training, two for air bombers, and one for air gunner training.

Tony's first experience in flying was at Mossbank Bombing and Gunnery School, where he and another student were sent up in a Fairey Battle for a camera gun exercise. This is where the students get into the turret, and shoot at another aircraft with camera guns. However, when it came to Tony's turn, clouds of smoke began pouring out from the engine cowling just like were seen in the movies of air battles. The pilot indicated to the students to take up crash positions, braced against the main spar, as he was going to try to make it back to base, but might have to crash land. The pilot made a diving turn and after what seemed to be forever, landed at the airfield, wheels down, cross wind on the grass, to be greeted by fire engines, and ambulances. The pilot was taken immediately to hospital in the ambulance. It turned out that a glycol line (engine coolant) had broken and poured antifreeze on to the hot manifold of the engine causing the smoke. The pilot had got the glycol in his eyes and had done a miraculous job of landing the plane, as his vision was blurred from the glycol. Not the best way for two students who had not flown before, to be introduced to aircrew. As is the custom, the students were required to fly again right away, and actually did three more trips that day.

From Mossbank the course was posted to Air Observers School at Winnipeg and upon graduation, Tony received his Commission and the rank of Pilot Officer. During his embarkation leave he was reunited with Frank Dolter, one of those whom he had joined up with a year earlier. They travelled to Halifax and spent a few days together, before Frank was posted overseas. That was the last time the two friends were together as Frank was killed in the spring of 1944 in a bombing raid over Germany.

Shortly after Frank was posted, Tony sailed on the "Louis Pasteur" for England. During the voyage he amassed a fortune of $250.00, playing Black Jack. In England he was posted to #15 Operational Training Unit, Harwell, where he was crewed up with two other Canadians, Cliff McDowell (navigator), Bill Johnson (rear gunner), and two Englishmen, Art Boswell (pilot) and Duncan Gillies (wireless operator). After O.T.U. they were posted to the Middle East and flew a new Wellington to #40 Squadron in Foggia, Italy. While on the squadron, the crew was involved in raids designed to cripple the German war effort in Italy, southern Germany and the Balkans. This was done by bombing shipping, marshalling yards, oil refineries, and airfields. They were to bomb anything that would hinder the supply of essentials to the German Army and later to impede their retreat.

There were many raids #40 Squadron participated in, which hastened the German army's retreat out of Italy and the Balkans. Two very productive raids were when they mined the Danube. This could only be done on clear full moon nights as the planes had to go down to twenty feet over the river. The first one was on May 31, 1944 near Noui Sad. Noui Sad was the headquarters of the Yugoslavian army. Unfortunately, due to an error, Tony's crew turned on to the river downstream from Noui Sad, instead of upstream. They soon found this out when the rear gunner announced there was a balloon above them on the starboard side. Shortly after this, the aircraft hit a balloon cable which sheared off the tip of the starboard wing. The pilot was able to maintain flight, and they found their section of river and made their run. In these runs the bomb aimer sits in the front turret and times the drop from a particular land mark for the mines on board, which weighed 1000 pounds each. He is in the front turret so that he can operate the guns and attempt to shoot out the search light of light anti-aircraft batteries along the bank of the river, while the rear gunner is doing the same from his position. Once the mines had been dropped, the pilot opened the throttles and climbed out of the valley as soon as possible. After gaining a safe distance from the target area the pilot inspected the aircraft for possible damage, and found that it had been hit rather seriously. A light anti-aircraft shell had come through the port side of the Wellington and had nearly severed the elevator control rod. This rod was made of hollow tubing and three-quarters of it had been shot away within five inches of one of the brackets, which held it to the fuselage. This meant it was impossible to put a splint on it, as this would interfere with the rod's movement through the block in the bracket. The bracket could not be removed as this would put even greater strain on the metal that still remained at the damaged section of the rod. It was decided that Tony would hold the damaged rod in his hands so as to only allow horizontal movement. Bill, the gunner, was to leave his turret after they crossed the enemy coast, and stand by the elevator balance bar. If the rod looked like it was going to break, Bill was to hold the balance bar steady while the others bailed out, and then bail out himself. Fortunately, the control bar held and the plane landed safely at base. To this day the pilot has the damaged section of the control rod beside the Distinguished Flying Cross he was awarded for this trip. The crew completed another eighteen trips, thirty-seven in total, including another mining of the Danube near Belgrade.

One operation #40 Squadron went on, was a diversion raid into southern France. It was designed to divert the attention of the Germans away from a daring attack by the French Maquis on a prison to free their members who were being tortured there. Since the target was beyond the range of the Wellington the squadron was required to land at an American base in Sardinia to refuel. While this was being done the American Sergeant in charge of the refuelling leaned his elbow against the fuselage. Since the Wellington had a geodetic frame covered with canvas, his elbow went in a little. He turned to one of the other ground crew and said "This Goddam plane is made out of rags." After that the Wellingtons in Italy were known as "Rag Bombers."

After the tour was completed, Tony's crew were posted individually to different places. Bill and Tony were sent back to Canada for a rest, to be crewed up again and posted to the Far East. When he arrived home in the spring of 1945, Tony was told there was a surplus of aircrew graduating from flying school and that he could have his discharge.

Tony Craven was discharged from the R.C.A.F. as F/O in February 1945. He attended U.B.C. for one year and then became a Certified General Accountant. He held the position of Assistant Treasurer at U.B.C. when retired. His medals include 39/45 Star, Italian Star, C.V.S.M., War Medal, Defence Medal, and Ops Wing.

Tony is married to Pat and has three children.

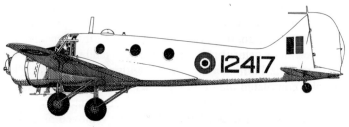

AVRO ANSON MK Ⅴ 12417 RCAF

F/O JOHN DELALLA D.F.C.
AIR GUNNER R.C.A.F.

John P. Delalla was born in Vancouver, B.C. and grew up in South Vancouver area of the city. He received his Public School education at Sir Alexander McKenzie school, and Secondary education at John Oliver High. He was active in all sports with a preference for baseball.

John became interested in aviation at an early age and on most summer weekends would ride his bicycle to Vancouver Municipal Airport. He joined the Air Force on August 13th, 1941 at the age of 18, spent a few weeks at Brandon Manning Depot, a few months at Guard Duty in Dauphin, Manitoba, and was posted to #2 Wireless School, Calgary, Alberta.

Upon graduation on September 10, 1942 he was posted to #8 Bombing and Gunnery School, Lethbridge, Alberta, received his Air Gunners Wing on October 12, 1942, was posted to England, and arrived there on November 10, 1942. John took additional wireless and gunnery training at #6 Advanced Flying Unit, Staverton, and on February 15, 1943 was posted to #22 Operational Training Unit, Gaydon, where he became "crewed up".

The crew was posted to #432 Squadron, 6 Group, Skipton-on-Swale, Yorkshire, and began operational flying. They were then posted to #424 Squadron, North Africa, where they completed the balance of their tour of operations. John was screened, and he instructed for eight months. In September 1944 he was repatriated to Canada for one month's aircrew leave, and at the end of his leave returned to England.

John became a spare and flew as an Air Gunner with five different crews. He was then posted to #427 Squadron, Leeming, Yorkshire, where he was crewed up with Flying Officer Danny Kaye who had lost his mid-upper gunner. John completed the balance of his second tour of operations with Danny.

Total number of sorties completed - 46.

He received an honourable discharge in Vancouver, B.C. on August 15, 1945. John was the recipient of the Operational Wings and Bar, Distinguished Flying Cross, France and Germany Star, Italy Star, 39/45 Star, Defence Medal, the Canadian Volunteer Service Medal and the War Medal. His rank at discharge was Flying Officer.

Following the cessation of hostilities, John worked as a sales representative for various companies. In 1954 he became a licensed Real Estate Agent. John and his wife, Doreen were married in 1958. In 1965 he joined the Properties Division of the City of Vancouver, and in 1966 received accreditation in the Appraisal Institute of Canada. In 1981 John was promoted to the position of Assistant Supervisor and held that position until his retirement on October 31, 1987.

On February 15, 1943 John's newly formed crew was posted to #22 O.T.U., Gaydon, Yorkshire, and on February 21, 1943 made their inaugural training flight. The aircraft was the famous Wellington Mk III Bomber. Affectionately known as "Wimpy" because of its resemblance to the Popeye cartoon character "J. Wellington Wimpy".

They became airborne at 20:15 hours, and upon approach to their first night landing, he suddenly became aware that the aircraft had lost flying speed and was sinking. Moments later the aircraft impacted heavily on to the runway, collapsing the undercarriage, and immediately burst into flames.

Normal access to and from the "Wimpy" is through a hatch situated on the underside of the aircraft just aft of its nose; as a result of the crashlanding however, this avenue of escape was impossible, because the underside of the aircraft was resting on the runway.

The secondary escape route, a hatch situated above the cockpit had jammed as a result of the crashlanding and they were effectively trapped in the burning aircraft, loaded with gasoline and ammunition. One possibility for escape remained; this was the astro-dome, a plastic bubble situated on the top side of the fuselage, about mid way, its size approximately two feet in diameter and for the most part, used by navigators when taking sextant shots.

John's thoughts were two fold:
- If it's jammed, his luck has run out.
- If it's *not* jammed, can they escape before the aircraft explodes?

By this time, perhaps only a few moments following impact, the starboard engine and wing were engulfed in flames, and night was day.

Four spring loaded-toggle bolts secure the astro-dome in place. He tried to release the back two toggle-bolts but they wouldn't budge. Fighting panic he noticed that someone had permanently wired the toggle-bolts in the closed position. He desperately tried the front toggles; they released and the astro-dome opened.

Still fighting to remain calm, he endeavoured to escape through the opening but without success. The parachute buckles on his harness had jammed against the aircraft. He tried to release the jammed buckles but failed, because the skipper was trying to force him through the opening. He then kicked him, released the jammed buckles, and jumped to the ground. The skipper followed seconds later. The other occupant of the aircraft, the rear gunner, had escaped through his turret doors minutes before.

John's log book indicates that their total time airborne was fifteen minutes. It also indicates that they were airborne the following night.

John's crew was posted to 432 Squadron, Skipton-on-Swale, Yorkshire, on May 16, 1943 to begin their tour of operations. This was to be their second raid, and they were flying the Wellington Mk III bomber.

The excerpt from his log book indicated the following:

Date: May 29, 1943
Take-off time: 22:40 hours
Flying time: 5 hours, 30 minutes
Bomb load: 1-4,000 bomb (called a cookie)
Target: Wuppertal (Elberfeld)

Wuppertal is situated in the heart of the "Ruhr". The Ruhr valley was called "Happy Valley" by Bomber Command Aircrew because it was heavily defended by night fighters and hundreds of flak guns. In addition, the west side of the valley was illuminated by two belts of searchlights. The belts were approximately fifty miles apart and contained many hundreds of mobile searchlights. Searchlights were usually in cones (similar to an inverted ice-cream cone) across an aircraft's line of flight. Each cone consisted of banks of 15, 20 or more lights.

In early 1943, Bomber Command operational strategy was rudimentary, and air tactics, at best, were hit and miss. (no pun intended). This was to change for the better, with the advent of sophisticated radio and visual aids to navigation, the formation of a Pathfinder Force, and the implementation of master bombers.

Briefly, Pathfinder aircraft illuminate the target, moments prior to the arrival of the Main Bomber force, and the Master Bomber (invariably circling the target at a lower level), directs the bombaimers to aim at specific illuminators or pinpoints.

In those days, Bomber Command invariably crossed the Dutch coast between Amsterdam and Rotterdam. John's crew made a serious navigational error on return from the target and were many miles south of the intended track. They inadvertently flew directly over Dunkirk and became coned by large numbers of searchlights. A very terrifying experience in that the interior of the aircraft became brighter than day, and they were blinded by the intense brightness and candlepower of the lights.

The skipper immediately commenced violent evasive action in a futile attempt to escape. The searchlights followed each gyration with apparent ease. In desperation, he pushed the control column forward sending the aircraft into a screaming dive from 21,000 feet, and they escaped out to sea. During these violent manoeuvers, they were constantly subjected to intensive flak activity.

John's log book simply states the "Wimpy" had been struck eleven times by flak and sustained damage. It also states that action time over Dunkirk was ten minutes.

They had become lost and thoroughly disoriented. Because of this, and poor weather conditions, they failed to realize they had crossed the British coastline. They also neglected to activate the I.F.F., and were immediately fired on by British anti-aircraft gunners. By this time they were low on fuel and compelled to land as quickly as possible.

They used the Very pistol and fired the call sign of the night and the gunners ceased firing. The navigator believed they were somewhere over England because of their time in the air, but was not too convincing, however, they spotted an airfield a few moments later and decided it was preferable to stay with the aircraft rather than bailing out into the night.

They landed on metal meshing which had been placed over an undulating grass field. Previously all their landings had been on concrete runways. Because of fatigue, and disorientation, it tended to affirm their suspicions that they had landed in France and were about to become prisoners of war. They made preparations to destroy the aircraft. A ground crew type greeted them in the thickest Scottish brogue imaginable. They would not allow him to enter the aircraft because they thought he was a German.

It took considerable convincing on his part, to assure them that they had landed in England. They noticed his R.A.F. uniform and felt both relief and embarrassment.

The airfield was the famous horseracing track "Newmarket".

John was then posted to 420 Squadron, Tholthorpe, Yorkshire on November 12, 1944 to begin a second tour of operations. They were flying the four engine Halifax Mk III Bomber. A few days prior to flying with his newly formed crew, who incidently had also completed one tour of operations, he came down with a severe head cold and was temporarily grounded from flying. The crew, with his replacement, flew the first trip of their second tour and failed to return. Ironically even to this day he seldom catches a cold.

On a squadron, aircrew without a crew are known as "spares" whose duties specifically are to replace aircrew in another crew, on a temporary basis. His first raid as a spare was on the night of November 21, 1944, the target being "Castrop Rauxel". The hydraulics became unserviceable, in that the crew could not raise the undercarriage. They flew around aimlessly for two hours, in order to burn off fuel and thereby reduce weight for landing, then returned to base. Not a good beginning.

Four sorties were completed rather uneventfully, and the fifth was scheduled for "Osnabruck", on December 6, 1944.

They became airborne at 15:13 hours and headed on the first leg to Osnabruck; unfortunately that old nemesis hydraulic failure compelled them to return to base. The undercarriage collapsed on landing because of the combined weight of the bomb load, and fuel. Fortunately the aircraft did not explode, and they got the hell out of there fast. The aircraft was written off.

His last operational sortie at 420 Squadron was on the night of January 6, 1945; the target was "Frankfurt". John was scheduled to fly the following trip with the same crew but was informed he had been posted to 427 Squadron "Leeming" effective immediately. The crew with his replacement failed to return from that raid!

The "Battle of the Bulge" had been raging for days in the German Ardennes area, in what was to be Hitler's last effort towards staving off defeat. For one week the R.A.F. had been unable to assist the allied ground forces, because England, and the western portion of Europe were engulfed in fog.

On December 24, 1944, the weather finally broke and John woke up to a bright sunny day. Not surprisingly he was notified that operations were scheduled. In fact, in addition to Bomber Command, the tactical airforce, consisting of medium range bombers, and Fighter Command, were also scheduled for operational duty in support of the beleaguered ground forces.

At briefing they were notified the target was "Dusseldorf" (another Happy Valley Raid). He was to fly "spare" as mid-upper gunner in a Halifax Mk III four engine bomber. Take off was 12:00 hours, and the trip lasted 5:35 hours.

The route to the target was fairly uneventful, but on approach to the target, flak was intense. They were hit by flak over the target and their aircraft suffered severe damage. His log book indicates the aircraft sustained 23 holes of varying sizes. Because of the damage, they were unable to return to base and therefore diverted to a small satellite aerodrome in the southern part of England called "Langham". They were to remain there three days. That night they were billeted in what must have been a beautiful estate prior to the war. As with many other estates it had been requisitioned for use by the armed services.

He woke up in the morning to an overcast rainy Christmas Day, away from base, and with a crew he had only met prior to briefing on December 24th. He was feeling very lonely and out of place. The crew tried to be friendly, particularly in view of their ordeal over Dusseldorf, but he missed the camaraderie of his own crew.

At supper time, the station commander reluctantly informed them that they had turkey sufficient for staff personnel only. Their Christmas dinner consisted of spam, potatoes, the forgettable brussel sprouts, and no dessert.

Later, the officer's lounge opened; unfortunately however, they had no money to buy beer or spirits. Bomber Command policy dictated that because of the probability of being shot down, aircrew were not to carry money, wallets, cinema ticket stubs, letters, or anything which could benefit the German intelligence service, in determining the various squadrons involved in a specific raid.

During the course of the evening, the lounge became filled to capacity and all were dressed in their finery. They, of course, were still in their battle dress and flying boots. The C.O. graciously supplied them with free liquor.

On December 28th they returned to base. Upon arrival they were surprised to learn that the crew had been reported missing in action. The adjutant at "Langham" had apparently failed to notify the squadron of the diversion to their station on the 24th.

To compound the situation, John's brother who at the time was in the army, stationed near the town of Horsham, had arrived on the squadron to spend Christmas with him. He was informed their aircraft had failed to return and was presumed to be missing in action.

It was a most memorable Christmas.

WING COMMANDER L.J. ANDERSON D.F.C.
PILOT R.A.F

L.J.'Andy Anderson' was born in Moose Jaw, Saskatchewan, attending Elementary and Secondary schools there, and later graduated from the Moose Jaw Junior College on a second year Arts and Science program. During his younger days in Moose Jaw, Andy was a Y.M.C.A. leader, played High School football, participated in track and hockey, and did rifle shooting. He had various jobs as a youth, including that of an 'Oiler' in a power plant. In 1938, Anderson and his partner Roy Holtom, an ex-Mountie caught a cattle boat to England where Andy joined the R.A.F. with a short service commission.

In October 1938, Andy (Len) Anderson reported to #8 EFTS at Woodley Aerodrome near Reading, learning to fly the Miles Hawk and Magister. In January 1939, he was posted to #4 FTS in Abu Sueir, Egypt, training on Hawker biplanes. Later in August, Andy went to Air Intelligence in Cairo. From Nov'39 to Jan'41 he served with #70 Squadron, flying passengers and cargo to Palestine, Baghdad, and Khartoum. He was wounded on his third mission in a Wellington and off flying for six months. He then took fighter training at #71 (F) OTU at Ismailia. Andy, now an F/O, was posted in August to #33 Squadron, a fighter unit in the Western Desert where he completed 57 missions. He trained new fighter pilots at #128 Squadron in West Africa during the early part of 1942. He was made Flt. Commander and Deputy CFI at #1 (F) OTU at Bagotville, Quebec in July 1942, returning to twin engine a/c in May '43. After completing a couple of months refresher training at #34 OTU at Pennfield Ridge in New Brunswick, Andy took tactical training on the B-25 Mitchell at Bicester, Oxon, in the U.K. Now a Squadron Leader, Anderson was posted to #114 Squadron in Italy in January '44, flying Bostons. He completed 70 missions there and served as Flight Commander. Promoted to Wing Commander in 1945 he became O.C. Flying at #75 OTU at Shallufa in Egypt, and later was posted to HQ #45 Group, of Transport Command in Montreal, after a short Staff College course in England.

During his operations as a fighter pilot in Egypt, an enemy force of nine Ju 88's, six Me 110's and three Me 109's made an attack on the Giarabob Oasis, and the R.A.F. had only three minutes warning. With only three serviceable Hurricanes available, Anderson was sent out with two other pilots to meet the onslaught, acting as leader. One of his pilots broke off, instead of remaining in formation, and chased the Me 109's. He was shot down and killed. The other pilot saw the six Me 110's below racing in for a shootup of the airfield just bombed by the Ju 88's. He dived on the formation and chased them but without success. Anderson chose to go after the Junkers aircraft, and clumbed to 12,000 feet. Three times he dived into the formation, saw his fire strike the enemy, but with no apparent effects. Meanwhile his Hurricane was severely damaged by the Ju 88's, and as he dived to port, oil and glycol streamed through his cockpit. He immediately shut off his engine to prevent a fire and decided to attempt gliding back to his base. Anderson tried to slide his hood back to get air, but eventually had to break the perspex of the hood. He approached Giarabub at about 3000 feet hoping to land on the escarpment above the Oasis. While skidding along at fair speed, dodging boulders, he went off a fifty foot cliff and stopped with his aircraft standing on its propeller. Anderson sustained a deep cut under his right eye as well as other minor cuts and bruises. While being attended to by the MO he learned that one pilot and three airmen had been killed. He was given five days off and shortly thereafter intercepted a Recce Me 110 and shot it down.

Later in January 1942, Anderson was assigned to go on a special long range operation, a reconnaissance of out-of-contact British tanks engaged by Rommel's tanks at Bir Nofilia. When possible, and without risk to themselves, the pilots had a secondary objective of strafing targets before returning. Rommel's tank force was entrenched in and around El Aghelia. #33 Squadron was then at Antelat, and Anderson was asked to lead the six long range Hurricanes. They flew low over the bay to a wadi (fiord) and as his formation was sweeping up over the cliffs at the end of the fiord Anderson saw a motor transport refuelling and all aircraft went in to strafe the targets. Three vehicles were left in flames and others were damaged. The aircraft then turned and flew low over a nearby airfield firing at aircraft parked on the field, but no fires were seen. On their arrival back at Antelat the pilots found that the whole area had endured torrential rains, and that only a short strip of the runway was still out of the water. Anderson's companions landed safely and moved to the driest end. Anderson using full flaps and breaks just stopped his aircraft a couple of feet short of another aircraft, and it wound up standing on its nose. On January 18th, a signal was received from the AOC congratulating Anderson for the successful mission. The CO of the squadron was later advised that because of the airfield raid, twenty-five Me 109's had to be moved back from the front to protect the area.

In August 1944 Andy Anderson was to experience a strange incident which he vows is the truth. He was returning to base near Naples, and was flying over the Mediterranean after having bombed a gun position on the south coast of France near Cannes. Anderson had had a very close friend, an American pilot, Lance Wade, who came to #33 Squadron in 1941. Wade had risen to command #145 Squadron and at the time of his death, in a Spitfire accident in 1944, was a Wing Commander with a D.S.O., D.F.C (with 2 bars), and 25 confirmed kills. Anderson, on leaving his target area was taking evasive action from the enemy fighters, when suddenly he saw the image of Lance Wade's face appear before him on the right side of the cockpit at eye level. He recognised immediately his tanned skin, dark eyes, drooping black moustache, and expression. Andy then heard a voice shout, "ANDY! HARD LEFT---DIVE, DIVE!" He heard once more, "HARD, HARD, I SAID!" Andy stood his aircraft on its port wing, rammed open the throttle and fell away and down. An aircraft then shot by very close to him on the same track he had been flying on, and disappeared into the cloud cover. Andy thought he had seen a black cross and the unmistakeable shape of the tail assembly of a Ju 88. At that point Wade's image vanished, as Andy came out of his diving turn and back on track, heading for base. His turret gunner on R/T asked him how he knew the Junkers was behind him as he himself saw it as it passed by. Anderson said he would explain later. A little later after landing, the two of them concluded that 'earthly beings know nothing of another world that exists out there.'

Andy Anderson was discharged in April 1948 in Montreal, and accepted a position as Station Manager, Atlantic Region, for T.C.A. After holding positions in other companies, Anderson attended U.B.C. from 1962 to 1966, and completed a Bachelor of Education Degree. He completed his 5th year in Education during the Summer Session of 1970, and taught Mathematics and Science in West Vancouver until his retirement due to ill health in 1979.

He married Margaret McConnachie in Arvida P.Q. in 1943, and has three sons. He now resides in West Vancouver alone as his wife died on December 25, 1988.

Andy was awarded the D.F.C., the Defence Medal, the Africa Star, the Italy Star, the War Medal and the 1939-45 Star.

F/LT CLIFFORD DICKINSON
AIR BOMBER R.A.F.

Clifford Dickinson was born in Sheffield, England and completed his schooling in Sheffield Halls of learning. He attended Broom Hill Council School, High Storrs Grammar School, Sheffield Technical College and Sheffield University. He was a Wolf Cub, Boy Scout and Rover Scout, being a member of 26th Saint Marks Group, Sheffield, and his sports activities included tennis and water polo and he joined the Sheffield Otters Water Polo Club and the Brincliffe Tennis Club to follow these pursuits. He first became interested in flying as a schoolboy and had his first flight in an Avro 504 which was one of the airplanes of Sir Allan Cobham's Flying Circus. This was in 1932 when flying was still a novelty that not many people had experienced. Clifford was a keen model aircraft builder, both solid scale and flying models and he was the fifth Scout in Sheffield and District to obtain his Airman's badge.

His second flight was in 1938 in a DeHavilland Rapide. Flying was one of his main interests at this time and he wanted to make his career in the Royal Air Force. His parents however, persuaded him to accept an apprenticeship for electrical engineering with a well known English company. At the outbread of World War II, he volunteered for flying duties with the R.A.F. but was turned down as he was in a "Reserved Occupation" and it wasn't until January 1942 that he was "Dereserved" and he applied to the R.A.F., passed his tests and was sworn in on February 8th 1942.

Clifford's first flying training was when he joined the Sheffield University Air Squadron where he had some lectures and parades and also some dual instruction on DH Gipsy Moths. He was called up to Air Crew Receiving Centre on April 10th, 1942 and at Fairoaks Aircrew Grading School he solo'd on DH 82A Tiger Moths and after 20 hours instruction he was graded "Pilot." On account of his height Clifford had to use cushions so he could

31

reach the rudder bars properly. After a course on engines at St Athans, he was posted to Canada to train under the Commonwealth Flying Training Scheme on March 18, 1943. He was posted to the Flying Training School at Stanley, Nova Scotia where he flew in Fleet Finch Aircraft. Once again Clifford had trouble reaching the pedals and he was not allowed to use cushions so the powers that be decreed that he would not be a pilot after three and one half hours flying; he was a very disappointed airman. Determined to be Aircrew, he remustered to BombAimer and after training at No. 4 Bombing and Gunnery School at Fingal, Ontario, Clifford graduated on October 29, 1943 and was commissioned on November 1, 1943. He returned to England aboard the R.M.S. Aquitania.

Clifford's operational training on his returning to England included postings to No. 2 (O) A.F.U. at Millom, No. 18 O.T.U. at Finningley where he was crewed up with Skipper F/O Bert Atkinson, Navigator P/O Allan Brand, Gunner Sgt. Jock Gallagher and WOP Sgt. Ken Bourke. From Finningley the crew participated in two Diversion Raids to the Dutch Coast and one leaflet raid to Ouistreham, just before D Day. Diversion raids involved a major force of O.T.U. crews flying to Europe to attract the attention of the German night fighters. While the Main Force of Bombers would head a short time later for the actual target over a different route, the fighters were distracted by the Diversion Force, which upon reaching the coast, would abruptly alter course and return to base leaving the fighters miles distant from the attacking bomber force. From O.T.U., Clifford was posted to No. 1667 Heavy Conversion Unit at Sandtoft and then to No. 12 Squadron at Wickenby. While Clifford was on compassionate leave attending his father's funeral, his skipper failed to return from a second dickey trip and the surviving crew was sent back to 1656 H.C.U. to pick up a new skipper, Geoff Dury and a new Gunner, Ken Strange. The new crew was then posted to 153 Squadron where they did their first operational trip on November 11, 1944 and after two more trips they were transferred to 150 Squadron where they completed their tour on April 25, 1945 with a raid on the S.S. Military Barracks at Berchtesgaden which was a good target with which to end their tour.

Clifford recalls that his worst experience on ops was the first trip over Dortmund, when they ran into heavy flak which left many holes in the fuselage, and also in the Elsan Toilet, one could say that the aircraft was flying very high. On a trip over Ulm, a near collision with another Lancaster caused a flurry of excitement. Over two other targets, Chemnitz on February 14, 1945 and Kassel, on March 8, 1945, they were chased out of the target area by fighters with the consolation that on the last occasion they "winged" a JU 88. The most interesting flight while they were on the squadron was when they flew Air Commodore Cozens when he was filming the approach shot for what is now Video Night Bombers.

When their tour was completed, the Skipper, Navigator and W.O.P. were posted to 78 Squadron where they converted to DC 3 Dakotas and were to be engaged in glider towing and dropping troops and material; their ultimate destination was to be Burma.

An overseas posting meant that everyone involved had to have a medical check, and it was during this check that the medics found out that Clifford was colour blind and should not have been in aircrew. Actually the whole crew was medically unfit; in spite of this, in true Service tradition, they were sent on their way and flew with twenty erks on board, bound for India. They were not destined to complete the trip however. While they were crossing the Mediterranean, the atomic bomb was dropped so their flight was cut short at Cairo. 78 Squadron was seconded to 216 Group to fly passengers and mail up and down the Mediterranean but before the crew could savour this change of pace from operational flying, their medical records caught up with them and they were all four grounded. Clifford ended his service career as Officer in Charge of Passenger and Freight at the terminal at El Adem, near Tobruk.

Clifford was repatriated to Britain and demobbed at Hednesford on November 14, 1946. He was awarded the 1939/45 Star, France & Germany Star, the War Medal 1939/45 and the Defence Medal.

After the war, he returned to his pre-war employer to complete his apprenticeship but was not happy with conditions in England and migrated to Canada in March 1956 where he joined a well known consulting engineer in the pulp and paper industry in Vancouver, where he remained until 1983 when he retired. He has resided in West Vancouver since 1969. He is married to Jean and has two sons and three grandchildren.

VICKERS WELLINGTON MC.Z1572 44 19 MOOSE SQN R.C.A.F.

F/LT MURRAY A. EDWORTHY
PILOT R.C.A.F.

Murray A. Edworthy was born in Gladstone, Manitoba. He began his education at Star City Elementary School in Star City Saskatchewan and later, enrolled in Star City High School. He attended the University of Saskatchewan in Saskatoon, followed by training at the McGill Medical School, in Montreal.

While living in Star City, his extra curricular activities included skiing, curling and hiking. In addition, he took violin lessons and played in the high school and Sunday School orchestras. Murray also was a member of the Star City Boys' Band, playing the E Flat Bass Tuba.

Before enlisting in the Air Force, Edworthy worked in the Star City Pharmacy for a year as a pharmacist's apprentice, through the University of Saskatchewan. He joined the R.C.A.F. in June of 1937 as a boy apprentice at age 17 in Regina.

His first posting was to the Technical Training School at Trenton, Ontario for one year and from there, he was transferred to Jericho Beach station in Vancouver. In 1937 Murray was given "leave-without-pay" to attend University for a year, following which, he was back in the airforce assigned to Western Air Command. He was posted to #4 B.R. Squadron at Ucluelet, where he was the Corporal in charge of Motor Transport.

His next posting was to North Brandon and in the fall of 1941 he remustered to aircrew. Murray had achieved the rank of Flight Sergeant in Motor Transport, when he re-mustered and was reduced to A.C.2. He took his elementary training at High River, Alberta, training on Tiger Moths. From High River, he moved south to #15 Service Flying School at Claresholm, where he mastered the Avro Anson and the Cessna Crane. Here, Murray received his 'wings' and his Pilot Officer's Commission.

Edworthy was posted to the Flying Instructors Schools at Trenton and Arnprior (Elementary) and Prince Albert, Sask. (Service). He taught flying for two years and then was posted overseas to Advanced Flying Training on Airspeed Oxfords at Little Rissington. Following A.F.U. he then went to O.T.U. at Wellesbourne and the satellite Gaydon, where he began training on Wellingtons. Here he was 'crewed up' and then posted to a Heavy Conv. Unit on Lancasters at Wombleton in Yorkshire.

Murray and his crew were assigned to two bombing missions over Europe but before any more took place, the war was ended. The crew returned to Canada and were assigned to serve in the Pacific theatre, but before they saw action, the Japanese war ended as mentioned.

Murray returned to "school" after the Japanese war ended - first to complete his Bachelor of Arts at the University of Saskatchewan - and then to enroll at Medical School at McGill University in Montreal. During his terms of Medical Undergraduate training, he worked as a Medical Officer's Assistant for four summers at St. Hubert, Quebec; at the Institute of Aviation Medicine in Toronto and two summers at Namio Air Port in Edmonton. In the summer and fall of 1954, Murray served as Medical Officer at Zweibrucken in Germany.

Dr. Edworthy began General Practice in Medicine in Hamilton, Ontario, then in Manchester, England, Zweibrucken, Germany and in New Westminster, B.C. until his retirement in 1986.

In 1949 Murray had married Ann MacGillvery - they had four children, two boys and two girls plus 8 grandchildren. Ann died in 1977 and Murray married G.Thelma Perry (a widow with six children) Combination (both his and hers) 18 grandchildren!!!

While instructing at #6 E.F.T.S. at Prince Albert, Murray and two other pilots volunteered to take three Tiger Moths to Winnipeg for repair, together with three students. The February day was clear, cold and sunny, but the wind began to increase and gas was getting low, as the three Tigers were heading into ever increasing head winds.

Murray was watching out for landing fields as the gas gauges were going down and they were flying about 500 - 800 feet above sea level, when Murray's motor coughed and he had to make a forced landing. Two other Tiger Moths followed in. The field in which they landed had been roughly ploughed and was covered with drifting snow. Murray rented a horse and sledge from a nearby farmer and drove about four miles to the nearest phone, called the C.O. at Yorkton S.F.T.S., their first destination, and informed him that the field was not fit for a Cessna to land on, so they sent out a barrel of gasoline by truck. They divided the gasoline into three parts and took off successfully.

The wind was, by this time, getting stronger and soon Murray's motor coughed again, so he cut off the throttle and looked down to see rocks, trees and a churchyard. Somehow all three managed to land safely, in the churchyard (the dead centre of town). Two Cessnas were sent out, to shepherd the

Tiger Moths into Yorkton, but Murray's plane was too cold and it wouldn't start, as the weather was 20 degrees below zero.

Murray agreed to fly the Tiger out of the churchyard, if the ground crew could get it started, so they built a fire under the engine (in a tent) and soon the engine fired. Murray then asked the ground crew to go out towards the church and chase away any cows that might be on the take-off path. With the brakes on tight, and full throttle, he released the brakes and hobbled across the snowy churchyard.

In was, by this time, quite dark and the Tiger Moth had no lights, but using the barely visible church as a point of reference and horizon, with some bad flying, he skidded around the church and rose up behind it, gaining height fairly rapidly. The moon came out and it was then clear flying to Yorkton airfield, which was in darkness, but the runways were fairly clear and Murray was able to land safely and taxied into a hangar. The threatening storm materialized and the three pilots were grounded for two days.

After appearing before the C.O. to explain their misadventure, the three of them took off for Winnipeg. The Saskatchewan landscape, after the severe snowstorm, consisted of miles and miles of white drifts, with roads and even fence posts buried. The three instructors had decided to take a short cut across the frozen snowy landscape and follow the Yorkton C.O.'s advice to fly to Dauphin, Manitoba, refuel, then go on to Neepawa and so on to Winnipeg, using the railway tracks instead of radar. They landed without further mishap and left the planes at Steveston Airport repair depot.

It was a good day for flying, a cool March day in Prince Albert, Saskatchewan. One of Murray's students was having some trouble getting out of spins, so Edworthy took him up in a Tiger to get in some more practice. They did spins from a straight climb, from a tight turn and incipient spins and were of course, tightly strapped in their seats.

After about an hour of practice, they let down from 6,000 feet and began to fly towards the Prince Albert airport, but on the way, Murray decided to practice a forced landing, so he reached down and cut off the gasoline supply to the Tiger's motor. It stopped and Murray instructed the student to set the plane down somewhere; he had already noticed a field which was moderately flat, wet and icy, but clear of snow. After some coaching, the student prepared to land there and commenced the forced landing procedure to approach the field. Murray turned on the gasoline supply as they approached the field and the exercise went well until the student landed the plane about 40 feet in the air and it stalled!

The right wing dropped and caught in the soft wet ground and immediately Murray called "I have it." and opened the throttle, kicking the rudder as he did so. The wing came up and the left wing dug into the ground. The motor now caught and the aircraft cartwheeled across the field. Edworthy cut off the throttle with a surprise exclamation "J.C." as the plane teetered on its nose. He thought "At least the rudder is O.K!", at which time the plane fell on its back, wheels in the air. George Rex's aircraft was somewhat bent!

Both Edworthy and his student were O.K., in fact Murray's flying glasses remained in place as they hung upside down in the Tiger.

Murray possesses no medals, as he did not apply for them from Ottawa, but it appears he would be entitled to the 1939/45 Star, C.V.S.M. and Clasp, War Medal and Defence Medal.

F/O D. CRAIG FERGUSSON
NAVIGATOR R.C.A.F.

"Lew" Fergusson was born in Vancouver the 27th of March 1921, D.Craig Fergusson. Although he attended several schools in Vancouver, including Prince of Wales, Lew spent quite a bit of his school days at Pender Island. Maybe it was the island influence that got him his first jobs; commercial fishing and in the now defunct industry of whaling.

On April 4th, 1942 he left the ocean for the sky, joining the R.C.A.F. as a Navigator. From Vancouver he was shipped to Edmonton Manning pool then on to #6 B & G at Lethbridge, flying in Fairey Battles. Next stop #2 I.T.S. Regina followed by a stint on Ansons. They must have been the Mk I's as Lew has firm memories of "winding up the bloody wheels."

On graduation, it was off to England on the good ship "Andes" wearing his new sergeant's stripes. January 1943 found him at A.F.U. at Morton Valence and Staverton. He did his O.T.U. at Honeybourne, on Whitleys; Conversion Unit at Croft, on Halleys, and was finally posted to 433 Squadron at Skipton-on-Swale, flying Hally 3's.

One of his early trips, he remembers more vividly for the return, rather than the op. Coming home to Skipton-on-Swale through heavy rain, they were down to about 400 feet, groping their way towards base; according to "Gee" all was well and Lew reported to his skipper Bid Meldrum, "Right over base now." Bid's reply was "Oh yes, I see the perimeter lights." Lew packed up Gee and got ready to land.

The touchdown was uneventful but when pilot Meldrum asked the tower for taxi instructions, tower came back with, "We can't see you; blink your lights." This they did; still no contact, so they fired a Very cartridge. That brought action in the form of a 1/2 ton truck and an enquiry, "Who are you?"

Bid said, "Never mind who I am, tell me WHERE I am." You're at Dishforth, was the rather startling reply. They had been in the Dishforth circuit while talking to the Skipton tower. They knew they would be in for a razzing on their return to base.

Fortunately for them they were not the only squadron members to get into the wrong circuit, for very shortly they were joined by a crew skippered by a very senior driver.

Lew's flying came to an abrupt end on the night of February 24th., 1944 when he was shot down over Schweinfurt. From then on he was a P.O.W. until his successful escape effort April 7th., 1945. In Lew's words - "The Deutchers started to march us out of Fallingbostel, heading us in the general direction of Lubick."

The first night out they were counting them and herding them into a big barn for the night. It was almost dark, and on the spur of the moment, George Fielding, who was Mulvaney's pilot (See co-incidences) and Lew ducked behind the barn door. They then sneaked around the back of the barn and laid low until all was quiet, then took off.

Well, next morning, the Goons counted the Kriegies as they came out of the barn to make sure that no-one hid inside. Of course they were two bodies short, so they put them all back in the barn and brought them all out again - typical Goon procedure, with the usual Kriegie co-operation and cat calls. Four hours later, having forked out all the hay and bayonetted every crack in the place, they gave up. George and Lew got back to England on April 17th after ten days of fun and games while getting through to Allied territory.

It had always been his ambition to be in Piccadilly on V.E. Day and Lew made it.

Lew got back to Vancouver where he was discharged 28th August 1945. It took him a little time to get around to it, but in June, 1948, he married Nancy Pearce. He and Nancy have three daughters. Lew supported the family for 30 years, working in the marketing division of Shell, Canada. Lately the Fergussons retired to Cobble Hill.

Lew's story would not be complete without a look at the parallel airforce career of his friend Mulvaney. These two did not know one another prior to joining up, but they both joined up in April 1942. Both were posted to Edmonton Manning Pool, together; #6 B & G, together; #2 I.T.S., together; #3 A.O.S., together; United Kingdom, together; A.F.U., together; O.T.U., together; Conversion Unit, together; 433 Squadron, together; and were shot down the SAME NIGHT, OVER THE SAME TARGET, Schweinfurt, IN SEPARATE AIRCRAFT.

They were both sent to Dulag Luft, although they didn't see one another. Next to Stalag Luft #6, Heydekrug, East Prussia, where they ended up in the same hut. Next, the "twins" were sent to Stalag 357, Turun, Poland, relocated to Stalag 357, Falling Bostel in Germany. Although they did not escape together, they both returned to Canada on the "Louis Pasteur", together; arrived home together in Vancouver.

There Mulvaney got married. Lew, of course, was his best man and to this day doesn't see why he was not welcomed on the honeymoon. After all, he had known the bride before Mulvaney.

When the Fergussons retired to Vancouver Island it didn't take the Mulvaney's long to follow. What a wealth of experiences they have to share. Lew's medals include the 1939/45 Star, Aircrew Europe Star, Defence Medal, C.V.S.M. with Clasp and the Victory Medal.

F/O WILLIAM G. (BUFF) FORRER
BOMB AIMER R.C.A.F.

Bill or (Buff) as he was sometimes called in the Air Force, was born in the East end of Vancouver and received his education at Lord Nelson Elementary and Vancouver Technical Schools.

Shortly after his 18th birthday, he applied for aircrew, but was turned down as Junior Matric was the basic requirement and he hadn't quite completed grade 12. It was suggested that he join the army and then if and when standards for entry into the R.C.A.F. were lowered, he could transfer. Once in the army, however, there seemed to be no way out and so he tried by other means to get into the service he longed for. Two years later and after several escapades, the army decided they could do without William G. Forrer and allowed him to enter the R.C.A.F., whose standards had apparently been lowered somewhat.

"Buff" reported to Manning Depot in November 1942 and was also at I.T.W. in the same city. E.F.T.S. followed at Prince Albert, but only briefly, as it seemed everyone wanted to be a pilot and if students did not grasp the intricacies of the Tiger Moth immediately, it was washout time. His ground loops were works of art, but in order to assure victory over the Boche, another trade was suggested to him and he chose that of bomb aimer, receiving his wings and a commission at Rivers, Manitoba.

Posted overseas, he eventually crewed up and arrived at Leeming, Yorkshire, on 427 Squadron. By this time the war was winding down, but he managed to get in 18 ops, most of which were routine but some, exciting. On their 6th op. they were credited with shooting down one fighter over Worms, Germany; their previous sortie had seen the bomb doors jam, while on op. no. 7, the Gee caught fire, the cookie would not release and they landed with it dangling in the bomb bay. On sortie no. 12, half the roof was blown off and the flight engineer badly wounded, but later on, he thankfully recovered.

Buff was discharged in September 1945, in Vancouver and after a series of different jobs, became a journeyman floor layer, until retirement in 1987. He is married to Florence and has a son and a daughter. His medals include the 1939/45 Star, War Medal, Defence Medal, C.V.S.M. and France/Germany Star.

Buff was the bomb aimer in Danny Kayes' crew, stationed at #427 Squadron, 6 Group, Leeming, Yorkshire. They were notified that they were on the "Battle Order" for a raid scheduled that day, March 25, 1945. The navigator grumbled about this being their 4th trip in four days. He and Buff went to their respective briefings on bomb load release sequencing, bomb sight settings, routes, heights, winds, etc; and the rest of the crew went with Danny to check out the "kite". At briefing, the crew was informed that the target was "Hanover". Take-off was 05:10 hours, and bombing height over the target would be 17,500 feet. On daylight raids, Bomber Command Aircraft flew in what was known as a "gaggle". This was a unique development in bombing tactics, which allowed a maximum amount of time. Each bomber would fit into the stream in accordance with its assigned altitude. In a gaggle, all aircraft fly in a comparatively tight grouping, but each navigator ran his own plot, and each bomb aimer bombed on target markers, rather than on instructions from a formation leader as in the U.S.A.A.F.

In flight, the bomber force resembled a swarm of hundreds of aircraft strung out for 10 to 12 miles, and varying in height by approximately 5,000 feet. Theoretically, this type of formation provided the German flak gunners with a constantly changing target. The skipper climbed to 18,000 feet and did a shallow dive to 17,500. Visibility en route was unlimited. Buff armed the bombs and entered the appropriate sequencing.

On approach to the target, there was a curtain of flak ahead, which appeared more ominous in daytime, because of the lingering visible black puffs. The allied bombers were flying into a "box barrage". This was a system whereby the German gunners would concentrate their fire at the approximate height and heading of the bomber stream. Bombers were compelled to virtually fly through a wall of steel.

A second method and one equally as devastating to the aircrew of Bomber Command, was called "predicted flak". Specifically, German flak gunners would attempt to electronically calculate the exact location of a singular bomber. This was accomplished by the gunners determining the altitude, heading, ground speed, and wind drift of a bomber, then firing a number of shells at the precise point in the sky occupied by the bomber at that moment. This procedure was repeated until the bomber force passed out of range.

On run in to the target, Buff ordered the Skipper to open bomb doors, then went through his usual ritual, "Left, left ... left, left ... hold it skip, steady ... steady ... bombs gone, let's get the hell out of here."

Shortly after leaving the target area, Buff felt the aircraft give a series of shudders, roll left, and then dive vertically. The shudders were the result of the kite being hit by predicted flak, and the roll was caused by the flight engineer, being hit by shrapnel and thrown against Danny. Danny regained control of the aircraft and informed the crew that the flight engineer had been hit. Blood was spurting from a wound to his right shoulder and he was in shock. The starboard inner engine which took the brunt of the flak burst, sustained damage and Danny feathered the propellor. (Feathering is accomplished by turning the propellor blades into the wind, thereby reducing drag.) The cockpit was filled with broken plexiglass and other debris; confusion was further compounded by the rush of wind entering the cockpit, through a gaping hole in the windshield.

One Mustang from the fighter escort, noting their difficulties, formated on them, until they reached the "bomb line". This was an imaginary line which represented the front line of the advancing allied armies, and was a point upon which the allied airforces were not allowed to bomb for fear of hitting their own troops. It was also a point of safety for bombers flying home.

The engineer was semi-conscious,lying on his left side on the floor. Someone had given him a shot of morphine and there was a debate as to whether it was advisable to land at the closest aerodrome, or return to the familiar surroundings of home base. The morphine had taken effect and he appeared to be resting comfortably, so they opted for home. Once they passed the bomb line, Buff opened a parachute and wrapped it around him, and John Delalla vacated his turret to assist Danny.

Upon returning to base, Danny was instructed to land immediately and taxi directly to the hangar area. Medical officers and attendants were waiting on the tarmac. The engineer was attended to in the aircraft, then taken away in an ambulance. A weeks leave was requested by the Squadron Commander and approved by the Base Commander, but his operation flying days were over. Total flying time to Hanover and return, six hours, fifteen minutes. - It seemed longer.

The crew had recently converted to Lancaster bombers and on March 11, 1945 were informed that operations were scheduled for Essen, Ruhr Valley, with a bomb load of 1 x 4,000 lb bomb (cookie), 6 x 1,000 lb bombs and 2 x 500 lb bombs.

They had been airborne approximately one hour and thirty minutes, when Buff detected smoke inside the brand new aircraft. He immediately informed Danny, the skipper, who ordered a search of the aircraft by the crew, in order to locate the source of the smoke. The engines were functioning normally and Buff deduced the problem had to be electrical, or hydraulics; unfortunately, the crew were unable to locate the source of the problem. In view of the dense acrid smoke and its unknown source, the skipper ordered - "prepare to abandon aircraft". At that moment, the navigator noted that his "Gee" equipment was on fire. The order to bail out was quickly rescinded and the fire was extinguished.

In wartime, Gee was a highly secret visual aid to navigation, which used a cathode tube. (Similar to today's T.V. tube.) In order to prevent the equipment from falling into enemy hands, it was armed with a detonator. The detonator was activated, during flights over enemy territory. In this instance it had inadvertently become activated resulting in an explosion and dense black smoke. The remainder of the journey to the target, went without incident, and Buff released the bomb load on Essen. He then noticed with alarm, that the cookie had failed to release and was hung up in the bomb bay.

Buff went through the usual procedures and drills in an attempt to release the 4,000 lb. bomb, but to no avail. On the return flight, they flew to an area over the North Sea specifically set aside for such situations. Buff again went through his check list. The skipper dived and climbed and dived again in an attempt to dislodge the cookie, but without success. Buff, and his mid-upper gunner, then took turns trying to chop through the floor of the aircraft. After much frustration and consumption of time, they conceded defeat.

The crew then proceeded to home base, Leeming, Yorks; and their Wireless Operator radioed base, informed them of their dilemma, and received permission to land. This was contrary to policy, whereby a crew would invariably be ordered to head the aircraft out to sea and then bail out. - An exploding 4,000 bomb can devastate a large area. Buff surmised that because the Lancaster was brand new, the Station Commander felt there was a reasonable chance for a safe landing. The skipper greased the kite in!

In wartime, superstition was prevalent among Aircrew of Bomber Command. Most Aircrew types possessed talismans, and diligently carried out certain rituals in an attempt to appease Lady Luck; for example, some would not consider taking off on a raid without first urinating on the tail wheel of their aircraft. Many wore St.Christopher medals, some of whom were not even Catholic. A number of Aircrew carried all variety of mascots, anything to hopefully ward off evil spirits.

On March 24th, 1945, Buff's crew was scheduled to bomb "Bottrop" a Benzol plant situated in the Ruhr Valley. Buff's rear gunner was being disciplined for wearing bizarre clothing and unfortunately would not be making the trip with the crew. The Gunner had become "real operational" since the night in late February 1945, when he got a confirmed kill on an ME 109 over Worms.

Bomber types felt confident, flying as a crew and some became uncomfortable if they had to replace one of their members with a spare; it must also be noted however, that flying as a spare was a very unenviable undertaking. A spare usually became a loner, with no close companionship. One usually became a spare as a result of losing his own crew. A spare would invariably only meet the crew he was to fly with, at briefing.

The replacement rear gunner had recently returned to operational duty, after spending many months in hospital as a result of a plane crash. Some members of the crew, for some unknown reason, thought the spare was "jinxed". Buff disagreed and thought they should give the guy a chance.

Over the target, the aircraft was hit by flak and the rear gunner sustained a slight wound to his arm. Whether the spare was a jinx or not, was never resolved, because shortly thereafter, their regular rear gunner returned to the crew. Buff thought the 'jinx' concern, by a few of the crew was merely superstition; the crew noted, however, that he always urinated on the tail wheel of the aircraft prior to taking off on an operation!

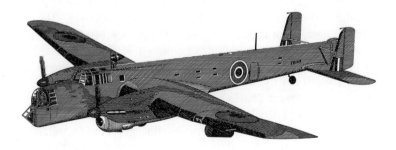

ARMSTRONG WHITWORTH WHITLEY Mk V T4149

F/LT (BOB) R.J. BANKS
BOMBAIMER R.C.A.F.

Robert J. (Bob) Banks was born in East Vancouver in 1923. He was the youngest of four children. He attended public school and Vancouver Technical High School, graduating in 1941. He was a member of the Seaforth Highlanders Cadet Battalion for three years. In the meantime he found a job as a proofreader in a print shop, earning 9 dollars a week. At this time, the shop printed various papers, among them, the "New Canadian", the Nisei Japanese newspaper.

In the fall of 1942, he decided to get some more education, so he obtained his senior matriculation and entered U.B.C. as a second year student. At this point he signed up with the Canadian Scottish Regiment, to go at the end of term, however, early in 1943, Bob joined the Royal Canadian Volunteer Reserve and celebrated his 20th birthday as a brand new sailor. A life on the ocean wave beckoned, full of adventure and a chance to win the war single-handed.

From Vancouver he went to H.M.C.S. York in Toronto, for basic seamanship training and was soon on an Officer's Training Course. He was then posted to the new, huge H.M.C.S. Cornwallis in Deep Brook, Nova Scotia, for advanced training, which included gunnery training, on a beautiful grey and polished brass 4.7 gun. It was here that he got his first close look at a war plane, a Westland Lysander from the nearby Shearwater base. He also spotted a few Blackburn Sharks. Towards the end of the course, Bob was sent to H.M.C.S. Red Deer, a Bangor class minesweeper, on escort duty, from North Sydney, Nova Scotia to Port-au-Basques, Newfoundland.

One day, three Hurricanes flew past the ship at about 100 feet off the surface, a living recruiting poster for seasick sailors, to join the R.C.A.F. Later, one night, the fuelling jetty in Sydney Harbour was destroyed by fire;

mooring lines had to be cut with axes to set the ships free. Banks was on shore leave and saw his ship slowly backing out, paint burning furiously all along her length ... an unsettling sight ... but as it turned out, she was not badly damaged.

The day arrived when Bob was sent ashore, to sit before the Officer's Selection Board. He was asked a question pertaining to current affairs. "If the United States, with all her resources, withdrew from the war, what would happen?" Banks promptly shot back "I think we'd lose, sir." This caused consternation and confusion and the interview was terminated. Instead of rising to the rank of Sub-Lieutenant, Ordinary Seaman Banks was now promoted to Able-Seaman. It was suggested, rather testily, that he could re-apply for a commission in six months, or request a discharge, so October that year found ex-A.B. Banks back in Vancouver, and, remembering those Hurricanes, he applied and joined the R.C.A.F. and was promptly sent to Manning Depot in Edmonton.

After preliminary tests, Banks was off to Gimli, Manitoba, as Deferred Aircrew and it was here that he took his first flight in an Avro Anson, on night instrument flying, doing circuits and bumps; he found to his relief and joy that he liked flying.

At I.T.S. Regina, where he studied diligently, he found he had two left feet, asked to be posted to pilot training (for those Hurricanes) but was told in no uncertain terms that he would be lucky to get Bomb Aimer. So off he went to No 2 B & G Mossbank, where among other things such as training, he earned extra pocket money, drawing strip maps and posters for fellow students.

On a low level exercise one day, the starboard engine spewed blue flames and Banks, as student navigator, feared the worst and was only prevented from jumping out, by his fear of heights ... and parachutes.

Finally, the much coveted propeller was sewn on his sleeve and he and the rest of the course were off to #5 A.O.S. Winnipeg, Manitoba. Bob had found to his dismay that seasickness wasn't half as bad as airsickness; there was no rail to run to and it was difficult cleaning up the bombsight afterwards. On graduation, Bob was promoted to P/O.

By this time, things were winding down in Europe and aircrew bods were becoming too plentiful, so he was now sent to Aircrew Graduates Training School at Calgary, to get some Commando/Survival training, while he waited hopefully to go to O.T.U. at Boundary Bay, B.C. as, with everyone else, he had signed up for the Pacific Theatre.

In December 1944 he was given 30 days leave and told to wait until called, but on December 22nd he was released and transferred to Class E Primary Reserve. In the spring and summer of 1945, Bob worked as a stager at Vancouver shipyards, on the conversion of "M.S. Menethseus" from a freighter to a fully-equipped "Rest and Recreation" Vessel, for servicemen in the Pacific. She was completely refurbished, with theatres, casinos and a complete brewery. By the time she was finished, the war was over!

Banks then attended the Vancouver School of Art, taking a course in graphic art. There he met his future wife, Elma, who was also a student. He left art school in 1947 and was married in Humboldt, Sask. They returned to Vancouver and have managed to make a living in art. The Banks have two sons, Rory and Jeffrey and have two grandsons and two grand daughters.

F/O ROBERT G.C. HADAWAY
PILOT R.A.F.V.R.

Born in Folkestone, Kent, England, Bob Hadaway, after receiving his Public School education, attended Art School and then Rowancroft College in Exeter, Devonshire. He played cricket, soccer, rugby and participated in boxing, wrestling, ju-jitsu, rowing, swimming and lifesaving. He played professional soccer for Exeter United for three years and rowed for Exeter University against Oxford and Cambridge at Henley in 1930 and 1931.

Bob joined the Maidstone Borough Police in February 1933, and was promoted to Sergeant six years later. He qualified as an Air Raid Precautions Officer, and a German Bomb Disposal Officer, during the Battle of Britain, in charge of the Civilian Control Room at Maidstone, Kent Township.

In September 1942, Bob Hadaway enlisted in the R.A.F.V.R., and was posted to I.T.W. in St Andrews, Scotland. In October 1943 he was sent to #31 E.F.T.S. at Dewinton in Alberta, and received his wings at #36 S.F.T.S. in Penhold, Alberta, and earned a commission. Bob took his O.T.U. course at Comox, B.C. in preparation for operations in Burma on C47's. Later he was posted to India, completing courses there, in Glider Towing, DZ Dropping and Paratroop Dropping. In May 1945 he was posted to #215 Squadron at Imphal, attached to Combat Command Task Forces in S.E. Asia Command. Number 215 Squadron had bases for Operations at Imphal, Chittagong and Hmawbi, but crews flew from various other locations, according to the mission or duty assigned, sometimes supplying forward troops, moving fighter squadrons, personnel, or dropping secret agents. Bob Hadaway was a pilot on one of these crews.

During the final night drops, whilst on temporary duty at Paratroop Dropping Unit, R.A.F.Station, Chaklala, in June 1945, sticks of 20 - 25 paratroops were carried on exercise runs in Dakota aircraft C47's. To save time, and yet achieve the number of flights scheduled, crews were allowed to take over an aircraft previously flown by another crew, immediately preceding them on the basis of verbal reporting of the aircraft's condition. The aircraft was dispersed at the end of the airstrip, with its engines left running. With crews interchanged, a fresh stick of paratroops was loaded, and the aircraft continued its runs to the assigned DZ. On one occasion, Hadaway's crew was scheduled for the final three lifts, in an exercise commencing at 0300 hours. Two flight crews had flown the aircraft preceding this turn. The crew just relieved, reported the aircraft serviceable. Twenty Paratroops were loaded and ready for the first drop, as the aircraft started its take-off. Halfway down the runway it became apparent the aircraft could not make its takeoff speed, and it began to labour violently, with unusual vibrations throughout its fuselage. The airstrip was short and darkness made it difficult to judge the distance remaining. Throttles were slammed through the gate for maximum power, and the aircraft lifted hesitantly, unsteadily, and faltered in its climb. It was obvious something was drastically wrong. Although conditions were hazardous an immediate landing was necessary. At three hundred feet, the aircraft levelled out and "Maydayed" the Tower for immediate landing, receiving clearance. When down and dispersed, with passengers unloaded, the crew took a careful look at their aircraft. The tips of all propeller blades were bent back some ten inches towards the wings. The props had obviously been in contact with the ground on a previous takeoff, after its wheels had been retracted. The person responsible was suitably dealt with!!

During July 1945, while based at Imphal, in India, Hadaway was scheduled to fly R.A.F. Fighter personnel from 'Dum Dum' airport, Calcutta, to Tanjore near Madras. On one of these trips he combined an additional duty by flying an aircraft (C47) from base to the Service Maintenance Depot at Dum Dum and exchange it for one coming off a major inspection and ready for return to the squadron. Having taken over the aircraft and having collected twenty-four passengers, he took off for Madras, flying south inside the coastline. This took the aircraft over a mountain range and a climb from eight thousand feet to fourteen thousand was necessary. During the climb, the starboard engine over-heated badly and had to be closed down, necessitating the return to the nearest R.A.F. station at Cuttack, where the C47 could be serviced.

During the lunch period, the senior NCO, a flight sergeant i/c maintenance, came to see Hadaway. He produced a large clump of cotton waste, about the size of a football, which had been found in the base of the engine nacelle, lodged in the airscoop. It was burnt to a crisp and when removed from the engine was still a mass of hot cinders. He could not understand why the engine had not caught fire. The waste had been left there in error by a member of the maintenance unit at Dum Dum.

After the Japanese campaign collapsed in August 1945 and the repatriation of P.O.W.s was completed, Transport Command took on the task of supplying new locations for our Armed Forces further east, in order to proceed with occupation. On one of these trips, flying unescorted from Bankok to Saigon, Indo-China, Hadaway and crew flew with a twelve thousand pound load of fuel in sixty drums for the purpose of building a military fuel dump at Saigon Airport. They experienced an incident which was long to be remembered.

During the early morning, they had been flying between layers of ten-tenths strata cloud at twelve thousand feet. Conditions were stable, but the ground was not often visible and the navigator needed a 'fix', in order to maintain an accurate DR plot. The pilot changed course and a break in the clouds revealed the southern tip of a lake below. Suddenly, to their surprise, they saw two black spots rising swiftly from the ground to meet them. Below was a camouflaged Japanese Military airfield. The navigator shouted, "Bandits - dive for the clouds!" The Japanese forces below had not laid down their arms and were still at war. The C47 was put into a steep dive to starboard, seeking cloud cover. As the aircraft eased up, to enter the cloud, shadows passed by in a flash, on their port side and a thunderous noise close by, signalled the passing of the enemy aircraft. Hadaway's plane had lost seven thousand feet. Two of the drums in the cargo compartment had torn away and were rolling free, until the navigator and wireless operator secured them. The aircraft stayed in the cloud, until the crew felt free from the fighters. The radio operator, who had been intent on his work and had little knowledge of what had happened, finally asked the navigator "What was that all about, just then?"

During the monsoon season, flying was difficult and treacherous. Crews were advised by more experienced crews, to fly the Ti-Nyabo Ravine in the clear, from Huthi, where the entrance was identifiable to Kawkareik, and then west over the River Gyaing to Moulmein and out to sea. This route was to be used as an alternative in bad weather. Hadaway had done this on two previous occasions, not knowing he would do so again. He was attempting to cross the lower Siam-Burma border at eight thousand feet, when conditions in clouds made it impossible. He climbed in a spiral manner, looking for a break in the cloud formation, without success. At fifteen thousand feet he let down on a reciprocal course to try the ravine. He reached the one thousand foot level in the clear. A gentlemen's agreement ensured traffic would fly only one way, as an exit to the sea. The cloud base was very low, so Hadaway entered the river valley north of Hnohng Pla Hlai, and let down to four hundred feet. Ahead, was the Ti-Nyabo Ravine, lost in a heavy rainstorm. There could be no turning back and all the crew knew they could not lose sight of the ground or river. As they approached the gorge at the narrowest width of three hundred yards, heavy rain and sleet reduced forward visibility to practically zero. The cloud base forced the aircraft to fly even lower. The river, being in full flood, at this narrow point was boiling, with torrents of white water improving the visibility. At one moment, Hadaway was so close to the mountain, he thought the end was near.

The jagged walls of the ravine, rose vertically from the river on the port side and had to be avoided at all costs. He stayed clear, by favouring error in the starboard side, where the terrain swept more gently away, providing more leeway. He kept the river under the port wing, turning and twisting with the flow, being buffeted by strong winds and experiencing heavy turbulence. With the aircraft yawing and slipping, he literally was fighting the controls to stay in position. The rain eventually lightened, and visibility improved and the crew could see more of the canyon. Before long, the valley ahead took on more space, the canyon walls opened up and the city of Kawkareik became visible. The worst was over and Hadaway flew to Moulmein and out to sea, much relieved.

The significance of his decision to fly the ravine, became evident, when later, he heard that his was one of a few aircraft that had returned to their bases. Many had been lost that day in the violent weather. The following morning, the crew learned that the friend who had persuaded them to fly the ravine was himself missing.

Bob Hadaway was discharged in November 1945 and was awarded the 1939/45 Star, the Burma Star, the Defence Medal, the 1939/45 War Medal, General service medal with clasp, (S.E.Asia). He had completed seventy-five missions.

Bob returned to police duties at the Kent County Constabulary, H.Q.R.S., Maidstone, Kent, in January 1946. He resigned in March 1948 and emigrated to Canada, being employed by the Hudsons Bay Company from 1948 to 1979, Bob was General Manager, Regional Distribution Centre, Lake City Industrial Park, in Burnaby, B.C. From 1953 until 1959, Bob was a member of the R.C.A.F. #443 Squadron, Sea Island, serving as a Flying Instructor. He later became a BCIT Qualified Methods Time Measurement and Productions Analyst and a Life Member of Canadian Materials Handling and Distribution Society. He is also a life member of the International Materials Management Society.

Robert Hadaway is married to Joan Deslauriers and resides in Surrey, B.C.

F/O J. BERNARD HAWLEY
NAVIGATOR R.C.A.F.

Bern was born at Port Haney, B.C. and attended Haney Central School, followed by MacLean High School. He enjoyed an active outdoor life, which included such sports as hunting, fishing, hiking, sailing, camping and lacrosse.

Prior to joining the service, he worked with Canada Car & Foundry, also Handley-Page Hampden Construction, in Montreal. While there, he trained with the Black Watch RHR of Canada. Later he was with Boeing Aircraft, then Canso Tool and Jig Engine Installation at Sea Island. With this experience among aircraft, it was second nature to join the R.C.A.F., which he did in August 1942, at Vancouver. He chose to try out as a navigator.

He was posted to #7 A.O.S. Portage la Prairie and graduated in October 1943, then went to #1 (O) A.F.U. Wigtown, Scotland, graduating in May 1944. Another bout of training saw him at #24 O.T.U. Honeybourne, where he graduated in September that year, to be followed by a month at #1666 H.C.U. Wombleton. Finally he was posted to 424 Squadron, Skipton, Yorks, where he started his tour with the rank of W/O.

Bern's crew, were known as the "Kid crew" as the skipper turned 21 years of age before they finished their tour. The bomb aimer turned 20 and Bern was even OLDER. The rest of the crew were teenagers. Bern was awarded the 1939/45 Star, France/Germany Star, War Medal , Defence Medal as well as the C.V.S.M. with clasp and also Ops Wing.

While at Portage la Prairie, Bern met and married Murriel, a Vancouver girl (1943) and they have two sons, two daughters and nine grandchildren. Seven of them are boys and great soccer players!

After the war, Bern took a special course, in Fishery Resource Management, was appointed Inspector of Fisheries, Mission City (1947), District Supervisor at Kitimat (1966), Manager of Central Coastal Division, Vancouver (1970), Manager, Regulations and Enforcement, Dept. of Fisheries & Oceans for B.C. and Yukon and retired in 1979. He then acted as Consultant in matters pertaining to the Fisheries component of Native Land Claims in Western Arctic, also the History of the establishment of Indian Fishing reserves in B.C. and the determination of their boundaries.

Anyone who has been on Ops. knows about guns and flak, searchlights and fighter planes. This is about an operation with none of these elements, but it concerns Bern's trip to Dresden with a bit of confidence because, being the Navigator, he still has his chart, log and photo-flash picture of the trip.

His airplot started at 2113 on February 13, 1945. They flew south from Skipton, and as they had done so often in the past, turned south-east over Reading. He logged "nav. lights out" as they crossed the coast near Eastbourne and turned eastward just south of Abbeville. The planes passed a safe distance south of Darmstadt and by one o'clock in the morning were able to start working their way north-east; then east, past Chemnitz and on to Dresden, with a time on target of 0132. The Bomb Aimer logged air positions and gee fixes. The Navigator used the H2S as required. It was a good system and they were able to keep on time and track. However, Dresden was indeed a surprise! No searchlights, no flak, no fighters ... no lights of any description ... and most startling of all, not another aircraft of any type anywhere. Just that beautiful city laid out below them. What had gone wrong? A quick check of watches, showed that the navigator's watch had gained twenty minutes!

The reason? The Navigator and Bomb Aimer were seated side-by-side in the MK I Lanc. The Bomb Aimer logged air positions and Gee fixes every six minutes. The Navigator changed the R.F. units as required, took his H2S fixes and did the plotting. They both used the Navigator's watch and the Navigator took whatever information he required off the Bomb Aimer's log.

At their briefing that evening, they were instructed to fasten the wristwatch to the table between them with thumb tacks so they would not have to shuffle through the charts and papers on the desk looking for the watch ... or such was the theory.

The vibrations through the desk caused the Navigator's watch to gain twenty minutes. Their plane arrived over Dresden all alone and lonely. Opposition was not a problem. Thank God it was not Hamburg! No wonder the Flight Engineer had been complaining as the Navigator urged the Pilot to increase his air speed along the route, in order to keep up with the speeding timepiece!

To kill time until "H" hour, the crew orbited the city eight times, looking for a choice spot on which to drop their bombs and incendiaries. Eventually, the Master Bomber arrived and marked the target, which was not the spot *they* had chosen. However, they successfully bombed what they perceived to be a very vital target, ending up with an 1,100-yard error from the briefed target. The pilot was able to listen to the Master bomber (Alan Emmott, a member of the A.C.A. Vancouver branch) using V.H.F. for the first time.

No regrets, however, for the *Daily Mirror* saw fit to include a mention of this brave(?) crew in the paper's report on the destruction of Dresden.

It is not commonly known that on flights to Dresden, at this time, since it was so far east and only about 40 miles from the Polish border, where the Russians were driving towards the city, aircrew carried square-shaped placards with words of greeting in Russian, in case they were shot down. It was felt they had a better chance of survival if they crashed or parachuted in Russian occupied territory, than into Germany itself. The placards were hung over their heads like the old sandwich boards, seen often in the streets of London. Fortunately, none of Bern's crew had to use them.

On April 25th 1945, 424 Squadron mounted its last raid against Germany, and F/O Hawley tells about it as he remembers.

The purpose of the raid, was to destroy coastal batteries on Wangerooge Island. Some high level people, decided to employ a new tactic and fly the bombers in a "gaggle" as in geese, behind a lead aircraft in a daylight attack. Now most people know, that a gaggle of geese is something seen in a barnyard at feeding time, and on the ground, not in the air. Geese have enough knowledge of flying to know that a gaggle, does not work in the air. In 1945, the leaders did not consider this. Although the aircraft were assigned specific heights at which to fly, the general instruction was to follow as closely as possible, behind the leader. The concept was that the turbulence caused by so many four-engine bombers, would make it extremely difficult for enemy fighters to attack successfully.

However, not only were the aircraft flying in the gaggle, subjected to the turbulence, from the adjacent bombers, but for some reason, the lead aircraft flew at too slow an air speed, to permit the following aircraft to maintain stability. The results were predictable.

First, a Halifax fell off into another Halifax and seven parachutes floated out from each of them! Minutes later, a Lancaster fell off into another Lancaster and fourteen more chutes floated down to the icy waters of the North Sea. The weather was absolutely clear that afternoon, as Bern watched twenty-eight fine, young men in their Mae Wests, splash about in the numbing waters for a few minutes ... then they floated ... unmoving. Flak was slight over the target and it is supposed the raid was termed a success. However, the sight of those 24 Canadians and 4 British airmen dying on that beautiful afternoon is not one which Bern Hawley will ever forget. Yes indeed, war is hell! But there were lighter sides, as he recalls:-

On joining the R.C.A.F., good health and High School graduation were required. Boys short on education, took advantage of the "Wet Pee", Wartime Education Training Programme.

Those men with High School graduation, were summoned to downtown Vancouver's Royal Bank Building. Here, they sat on benches, waiting for their medicals. Their first encounter with urinalysis. "Doc, I can't!" "Well, go out and have a couple of beers and hurry back" were the instructions.

Eventually, Bern arrived in Britain and was introduced to Pub Life. Out the back to do it against a wall, where others had been doing the same for five hundred years!

Then to ops. and always before take-off, the crew had to urinate on the port tire. The nervous pee. Very important to morale.

Their WAG, with a true Canadian taste for beer and a tired bladder, scrounged a length of hose and a funnel, designed to permit him to urinate into the "window chute", thus saving a trip back to the Elsan.

Back from the pub, and called for an unexpected op., at 21,000 feet, the WAG (still with beer in his gut) had to go in a hurry. A chance to try out his new "modification". Down the chute window and out along the belly of the aircraft it flowed. The Tail Gunner had also modified *his* turret by removing a panel to permit greater visibility. The slip stream carried the liquid back to him and through the opening into his face! The resultant scream on the inter-com was enough to make the Pilot start a "Corkscrew Port".

Some of the liquid seeped into the bomb bay and froze. When it came time to release the bombs, some of the releases were frozen. After some "bunting" of the aircraft over the target, it was decided that all of the load had shaken loose and the bomb bay doors were closed. Lucky to survive that one, with only slight flak damage!

Returning to an emergency airdrome, the Pilot landed the aircraft on and off the runway, finally coming to a stop well off to one side. The Flight Engineer cracked open the bomb bay doors and ran a ruler up through the crack to see of all bombs were gone. One 1,000 pounder was still in the bomb bay! It had been released when the aircraft landed hard enough to break the grip of the ice on the rack and had fallen down onto the doors. Needless to say, the crew wasted no time in leaving the aircraft. So much for modifications!!!

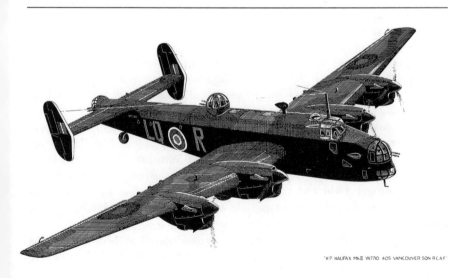

HP HALIFAX Mk II W7710 405 VANCOUVER SQN RCAF

F/LT R. BRUCE HUTCHINSON C.D.
OBSERVER R.C.A.F.

Bruce Hutchinson was born in Melville, Sask., and attended Biggar Public School and Albert Public School, Saskatoon. His secondary school education was continued at Nutana Collegiate, Saskatoon, while his post secondary education was at the College of Pharmacy, University of Saskatchewan, in Saskatoon.

He lived at Biggar until age eleven, where he was active in cubs, while his hobbies included hockey and golf. From that tender age, he graduated to scouting in Saskatoon, still retaining a keen interest in golf, but he soon got into curling and softball.

He took an apprenticeship in Pharmacy, in Saskatoon and in August 1941 joined the R.C.A.F., showing a preference for aircrew. In October 1942, Bruce graduated from # 7 O.A.S. Portage-la-Prairie, with his Observer's wing, being commissioned on his graduation. He was then posted to #8 B.& G. Lethbridge as Course Control Officer, with some instructing in bombing. July 1943 saw him promoted to F/O and shipped overseas to A.F.U. West Freugh, Staffordshire, thence to 100 Squadron, 1 Group in May 1944. He completed 20 sorties, then was posted to 582 Squadron P.F.F. His crew position was Navigator II and Radar/Gee Operator. Bruce was promoted to Fl/Lt in October 1944 and completed 22 sorties with that squadron, then posted back to Canada on leave. He was discharged in March 1945 at Regina.

After the war, he worked as a graduate pharmacist in Moose Jaw and Vanguard, Saskatchewan and in January 1955 he rejoined the R.C.A.F. as a pharmacist and retired as Fl/Lt. in December 1967. He then worked for Woodwards and Shopper's Drug Mart, until his final retirement in 1985. He was married to Gladys, a former R.C.A.F., W.D. in 1943 and they have 4 children, a daughter and three sons.

Bruce feels that his training, instructing and operational experiences could be classed as "a piece of cake" (or pieces of cake) compared to those of other aircrew, even though he had 42 "ops" altogether.

He was air bomber with 100 Squadron, 1 Group, Waltham, near Grimsby, Lincolnshire and records that his first trip to Tergnier was made in a severe thunder and lightning storm, which he felt was quite a show for a beginner. This was in May 1944 and in June, on a trip to Foret de Cerisy they encountered a Junkers 88, but due mainly to the rear gunner's evasive "patter" and the skipper's ability to follow, no damage was done to their aircraft, although they recorded possible damage to the Ju 88. A week later, on their first daylight trip to Le Havre, Bruce counted at least 50 Lancasters around them and he wondered about night ops, when there were possibly the same number and maybe more, around them.

Their longest trip was a circuitous route to Revigny, taking 9 hours and 20 minutes, only to have the mission abandoned and then diverted, on return to England. In August 1944, Bruce transferred to 582 Squadron, 8 Group, at Little Staughton in Bedfordshire, on which squadron he had 22 ops, flying as nav.II.

His first trip with Pathfinder Force, was a daylight to Falaise and due to an error in marking, they almost bombed Canadian troops. Fortunately, the error was corrected before any damage was done. On August 11th, on a trip to Castrop Rauxel, they had to make a second run over the target and as a result the perspex in front of Bruce was shattered by flak. Fortunately he had just moved back, to check his maps and he was not hit. The next day on a trip to Frankfurt, they had to eliminate one leg of the planned route, in order to make up time. Their aircraft was hit by our own troops, before being identified by I.F.F. and the colours of the day. Bruce was operating H2S and Gee Box and they were doing a blind bombing, using time and distance.

The Nav. 11 differed with the Nav. 1 as to where they were, the pilot agreeing with the Nav. 1, only to have their flares and bombs dropped on time, but 20 miles short. Unknown to them at the time, the electrical circuit to the bombsight had been hit and the next day, on a trip to Osnabruck, the bombsight was discovered to be u/s. However, they bombed, using the lead aircraft as guides, and dropped slightly ahead of them. The main result was a good photo of the "cookie" exploding.

His last trip was on November 18th, 1944, to Munster, which was uneventful and he was subsequently posted back to Canada, on leave and discharged in March 1945. He earned the 1939/45 Star, France and Germany Star, Defence Medal, C.V.S.M. and clasp, War Medal, P.F.F. Badge and the Canadian Forces Decoration.

F/LT GEORGE LAING D.F.C. AND BAR
PILOT R.C.A.F.

George was born at Durban, Manitoba and after finishing high school there, in June 1941, joined the R.C.A.F. on the 5th of July 1941. After joining up, he was assigned to a leave without pay status until September 1st 1941. In September, he reported to Winnipeg and was sent to Manning Depot in Brandon. From "Tent City" in the exhibition grounds, he left Brandon for Paulson, just out of Dauphin and again put in a "hold" position. This unit was referred to as Paulson Holding Unit. He spent about 2 months in Paulson, then was posted to No. 10 S.F.T.S., Dauphin, to do guard duty.

His pilot training finally commenced at No. 7 Initial Training School in Saskatoon, then to No.19 Elementary Flying School in Virden and he received his wings at Yorkton No. 11 Service Flying Training School in October 1942. He was posted overseas immediately and arrived in England on November 6th, 1942.

After a very short stay at the Bournemouth Reception Centre, he was posted to an Advanced Flying Unit, at Church Lawford, then to No. 29 Operational Training Unit at North Luffenham and then on to No. 1660 Conversion Unit at Swinderby.

George was posted to 57 Squadron, Bomber Command, R.A.F., at East Kirkby and commenced flying operational flights over enemy territory. He completed a tour of operations with 57 Squadron; 10 of those trips were to Berlin, in what was known as the Battle of Berlin. Of the 27 pilots on the squadron, 17 of them were Canadians. He was awarded the Distinguished Flying Cross on the 13th sortie and the citation reads as follows:

"One night in December, 1943, this officer was the pilot of an aircraft detailed to attack Berlin. Although engine trouble developed on the outward journey Flight Lieutenant Laing continued to the target and bombed it. He afterwards flew safely to base although two of the aircraft's engines were out of action. Flight Lieutenant Laing has participated in many sorties and has always displayed praiseworthy skill, courage and determination."

After a short rest period, his crew joined the Pathfinder Force (P.F.F.) in 97 Squadron, R.A.F. He joined Squadrons 83, 627 and 617 to become the Marker Squadrons for 5 Bomber Command, on special targets and when needed, flew Pathfinder Force with the main force of Bomber Command.

In the early afternoon of April 9th 1944, 3 special crews of 57 Squadron were briefed by a very high ranking British Naval Officer and George's Commanding Officer, W/C Bill Fisher. Generally the raid was to mine Danzig Bay and the ship canal into the ports of Konigsburg and Pallau.

The route was out over Denmark, Sweden, south-east over Bornholm Island to Hal Point in the Gulf of Danzig and then east to Konigsburg. The three aircraft arrived for the run in line astern. Laing's aircraft was number 3 and just after the run in was begun, an enemy fighter was spotted at 5 o'clock high. The mid-upper gunner suggested that they stay level and ignore the fighter and try to get it to attack from below. This strategy was successful as the fighter flew into the ground. For this action the gunner received the D.F.C., as a Warrant Officer ... a high honour.

All the aircraft dropped their mines at a very low level, (below 1,000 feet), right into the built up area of the docks. "Butcher" Harris, in his book, "Bomber Offensive", says the raid was such a success, that the canal and bay were closed for 13 and 15 days respectively. This greatly assisted the U.S.S.R. spring advance into East Prussia.

Laing's crew was also on a raid to the city of Konigsburg in August that year, when 134,000 people were made homeless. That raid's bombing time was ten hours and only 3 aircraft of 5 Group went missing.

Twenty years later, in discussion with a female Fighter Control Officer of the Luftwaffe, who happened to be in Konigsburg the night of April 9th, she said that was the day, when she realized for the first time, that the war was going bad for Germany. She also confirmed the port being blocked for two weeks, as she was two weeks late in shipping out on leave, to her home in Hamburg. During the attack, she watched from her hostel window and literally had a bird's eye view as she was actually above the aircraft themselves.

George's crew were very fortunate, in never having been too badly shot up and they always returned safely. The crew flew a total of 384 operations. It has been said that pilots received the most decorations, but this is questionable, as noted below in Laing's crew:

Pilot	George H. Laing	D.F.C. & Bar	R.C.A.F.	F/Lt
Nav	Roy Davis	D.F.C.	R.A.F.	F/Lt
B/A	Geoff King	D.F.C.	R.A.F.	F/Lt
W.O.P.	Vincent Day	D.F.M., M.I.D.	R.A.F.	W.O.1
Eng.	Jock Burns	D.F.M.	R.A.F.	W.O.1
R/G	D. Polson	D.F.C. & Bar D.F.M.	R.A.F.	F/Lt
M.U.G.	Frank Green	D.F.C.	R.A.A.F.	W.O.1

Upon completion of his second tour of operations, George was awarded a Bar to his D.F.C.

He returned to Canada in November 1944 and served on many Canadian stations; Rockcliffe, MacDonald, Rivers, Mountain View, Trenton, Boundary Bay, Comox and Greenwood. He was honourably discharged from the R.C.A.F. in April 1946.

He joined Trans Canada Airlines on the 2nd of July, 1946 in Winnipeg and was assigned to the Canadian Government Trans Atlantic Service in Montreal. In April 1947, C.G.T.A.S. became T.C.A.'s Overseas Service. He remained on the trans-Atlantic service until 1953 as a co-pilot on DC 4's and was promoted to Captain on DC 3's in Moncton, N.B. in May, 1955. He returned to the Montreal base at that time and remained there until September 1978, when he transferred to Vancouver.

On the Vancouver base, he flew B-747's mainly to Europe and charter flights to Honolulu. In September and October 1982, Air Canada had a contract with Royal Air Maroc to fly "hajis" (Moslem pilgrims) to Mecca. They were based in Casablanca and flew the pilgrims to Jedda, Saudi Arabia the first month; the second month he flew them back to Morocco. George did the last landing of his flying career on the 21st of October 1982, landing at Mohammed V Airport, Casablanca.

So, after starting with the R.C.A.F., then the R.A.F., T.C.A., A.C., he finished doing a Royal Air Moroc flight in the Air Canada 747 and with just over 30,000 flying hours.

George has flown 23 types of military and civilian aircraft - in T.C.A. Air Canada he flew the DC 4, DC 3, North Star, Vanguard, DC8, L-1011 and the B 747.

He was a member of the Canadian Airline Pilots Association (CALPA) and attended conferences for a number of years of the International Airline Pilots Association (IFALPA) and for two years served as a Regional Vice-President. In 1978 he was awarded the Scroll of Merit by IFALPA for his work with the Federation.

George and his wife Bernice have lived in Matsqui, B.C. in the Fraser Valley, since 1978.

SHORT STIRLING · No. 1651 CONVERSION UNIT R.A.F.

F/LT HARRY BRAY
PILOT R.C.A.F.

Harry Bray was born at Exeter, Ontario and attended Blyth Public School, then the high school at Blyth, Clinton Collegiate. His post secondary education included English II and Calculus by correspondence in service from Queen's University while his vocational subsequently included D.V.A. courses, Business of Farming in Canada, Spanish and German at night school as well as various writing courses.

Harry's family moved to various locations, Saulte Ste Marie, London, Blyth and Kitchener where his dad worked for the C.B. of Commerce at the time of the '29 crash and was subsequently moved back to Blyth.

Harry played hockey, E flat alto sax. in a band and various other groups as well as basketball, baseball and football. His mother insisted on him having 5 years of piano lessons and he joined the church choir because of a young lady who also belonged. He now sings with the Langley First Capital Chorus of the Society for the Preservation and Encouragement of Barber Shop Quartet Singing in America.

Prior to the war Harry worked as a farm laborer, electrician's assistant ("mainly" he says "driving holes through old, thick, stone foundations and drilling holes in rock hard old rafters, while lying on his back among the cobwebs in old attics.") When he got his call to "join up" he left a dull old ratchet drill half-way through a rafter.. and it could be there still!!

He actually went to enlist in June 1940 but was not called until October that year. He and a buddy drove their beaten up 4 cylinder Henderson motorbike some 400 miles to Ottawa for both these meetings with the King's representatives.

Harry decided he'd like to become a pilot/navigator, a rare hybrid, spawned in the early days and the only qualifications for which appeared to be high marks in navigation. He earned pilot's wings and was sent to G.R. course at Pat Bay but on posting to 8 B.R. Squadron at North Sydney, found that he was a NAVIGATOR and did not get back to "driving" until eight months later.

He did E.F.T.S at Malton civilian flying club, service Saskatoon, Ansons, Harvards and Cessna Cranes and then gained his pilot's wings in May 1941. From there he did O.T.U. at Pat Bay where he flew a collection of aircraft such as Norsemen, Deltas, Lockheed 10's and 12's as well as Beechcraft until he was posted to #8 BR Sidney, N.S. in October that year as Pilot Officer. The Squadron then moved to Vancouver on Dec 26 and the last stragglers flew in early March.

When the Japanese were approaching Alaska they were hastily moved north to Anchorage where for the next 8 months they did the bulk of the coastal patrols from Nome to Yakutat and other delightful spots in the far north. They came back to Canada in February '43 and were re-equipped with Venturas where Harry was kicked out of the squadron by the new C.O. and ended as Chief controller of Sea Island, but he finally talked his way back to flying. Then he was posted to O.T.U. Boundary Bay on Libs in May 1944, as F/Lt but lost his S.Ldr on posting. His tour in the far east included Salooni and the Cocus Islands, where he was when "the bomb" was dropped.

His medals and decorations were The Atlantic Star, Burma Star, Pacific Star and two tours of ops with ops wing and bar, also the Defence and War medals. He was honourably discharged at Jericho Beach, Vancouver on Feb 26th 1946.

After the war, he started charter air services out of Kamloops B.C. with F/Lt Bob Marcou and his bombaimer F/O Peter Hunting D.F.C. until they were bought out by Central B.C. Airservices 1st April 1950, which company eventually grew to become Pacific Western Airlines. Harry's company started with an open cockpit Cirrus Moth on floats (circa 1927) and ended on jets.

He also ranched for a while, built houses, sold mutual funds, fished commercially, had a few articles published, went for a year to British Honduras on a tourist development project, got married four times and divorced thrice, tried to do a lot of living...his autobiography is stalled at page 144. He now works, some times as a deckhand for son James on his whale-watching charter boat at Tofino. A sister, Lorna, flies commercially, including helicopters.

#1 EXPERIENCE

One very cold winter day Harry was on Honour guard duty where the squadron was going to be inspected by the then Governor-General Hon. Vincent Massey. All the "erks" knew he was important because of his famous film star brother Raymond Massey. Harry's issue shirts were at least two sizes too large for his small frame and the below zero weather further shrunk his neck.

When the great man arrived almost an hour late, all the lads were somewhat chilled and shrunken. The Governor-General couldn't have enjoyed the cold much, although he was barely out in it, making fast inspections, until he and the party were walking directly behind Harry.

There was an ominous pause in the crisp sound of feet on snow, a longer pause...then "Pull in your neck, son, you look like a turtle!"

The next day the store wallas found some shirts in Harry's size.

#2 EXPERIENCE

There were two crews at Nome, Alaska, housed in double walled tents heated by a small inverted funnel of a stove. The tents were always burning down or becoming untenable from coal gas. They were also infested with rats which ran over their faces at night.

Christmas 1942 and 42 degrees below zero and a solidly frozen package arrived from his home, which upon inspection contained among other things a tin of lobster which had frozen and burst, and Harry was about to throw it out when someone thought of a great idea.

The lads heaved the tin under the tent floor of the other crew and for several days and nights the rats left them in peace. Harry wrote to his mother saying how much her package had meant to him, but he did not give details.

#3 EXPERIENCE

Once the European War was over, Harry's squadron at the time, #356 was inundated with high ranking officers in Group who knew nothing about how to fight their particular war. The squadron was sent out against a reported build up of Japanese twin engine bombers, which had been seen on the south coast of Sumatra, near Benkelen.

The new "Brains Trust" insisted that they fly the whole way at no more than 100 feet to "baffle the radar" (which was actually non-existent). Now it was very difficult to locate an aerodrome at tree top height and the Japanese let them fly around while they loaded up everything they had, then rolled back a jungle on wheels and sent up fighters.

At 25,000 feet, where they should have been they were more than a match for the Tonys, but at the present tree-top level, it was a much different story. Harry and his crew located the twin engine bombers and went in to drop their string. The co-pilot was luckily in the bomb bay making sure that the doors stayed open. Harry was alone in the cockpit.

Suddenly...the whole instrument panel was tattooed by machine gun fire and Harry knew he was dead!! He just had to move and parts would fall off!! They took a .5 on the nose and a burst through the navigation compartment killed Jock, their navigator, instantly!!

Somehow, the frequency of the machine gun bullets that had come up from behind, through the bomb bay, had miraculously spaced the shots around his arms and not through his body, as it seemed to be the only route.

No 2 engine was on fire, but the crew extinguished it, but had to restart it later as fuel was insufficient for the long haul (900 nautical miles) back to the Cocus. Several of the tanks were leaking, the nav. compartment was a shambles and most of the radio was dead.

The bomb-aimer, Pete Hunting set up shop in the wireless compartment and somehow Len MacDonald the W/AG got one radio to work and managed to get Q.D.Ms from base.

Pete got a field D.F.C.(the only one given in S.E.A.C. according to Harry's belief) and the next day Jock was buried. A week later the "bomb" was dropped.

In 1986, on a visit to the far east, Harry found out just how the Japanese had made suckers out of them for the twin engined bombers were dummies made of wood and bamboo, while the Japanese themselves had leaked the intelligence on the "build up."

F/O GORDON F. LARSEN
PILOT R.C.A.F.

Gordon was born in North Vancouver in 1923 and after the usual public schooling, graduated from North Vancouver High School in June 1941. His first and only job, prior to joining the R.C.A.F. was as an office clerk/typist and receptionist for B.C. Marine Engineers and Shipbuilders Ltd.

He joined the R.C.A.F. in October 1942, when he was 19 and went to Manning Depot in Edmonton, where it was minus 60 degrees F that winter. While there, he was assigned to the Precision Squad, consisting of 28 young men who did precision drill with rifles, usually in a drill hall and at times in front of the public. The drill instructor was very good to the boys. He would take them out on a route march into Edmonton on a Saturday morning and then tell them to break off outside the gate... for a day off!

He took his I.T.S. at Saskatoon, Sask. and then on to E.F.T.S. at Virden, Man. on Tiger Moths. He returned to Saskatoon for S.F.T.S. on Cessna Cranes, where he received his P/O rank and wings. He sailed overseas on the "H.M.S. Andes" from Halifax to Liverpool - they played "Take it Easy" continually on the P.A. system - a good choice.

He spent a short time at Bournemouth and then to Church Lawford for familiarization training on Oxfords. He had his 21st birthday there, quite an occasion. He was sent to Montrose, Scotland to take Flying Instructor Training, but Gordon couldn't instruct, talk and fly at the same time. Next, he went to O.T.U. on "Wellingtons" at Kinloss, Scotland, where he also picked up a crew. He then went to Conversion Unit at Marston Moor and flew Halifax Bombers. He had one more night flight to do, when V.E.Day came, so he volunteered for the Far East war against the Japanese, therefore he had to train on Lancaster Bombers, going to Bottesford for that course.

He was then sent back to Canada in transit to the Far East, on board the "H.M.S. Duchess of Richmond". Half way across the Atlantic it was V.J.Day. What a welcome they had, as they were the first C.P.R. ship to arrive in Quebec City, after the war was over. He then proceeded home to Vancouver where he was discharged with rank of F/O from the Airforce, almost 3 years to the day since he joined up.

#19 E.F.T.S. VIRDEN, MANITOBA - TIGER MOTH - AUGUST 1943

One night, while doing "Circuits & Bumps" (they used two circuits, one left and one right), Gord was using the right turn circuit this night; when he was on his final approach at approximately 400 feet up, he saw this dark shape coming straight at him. He put the nose down and this other Tiger Moth went over him with about 20' clearance; he had been on the left turn circuit and misjudged his landing and not thinking, he did a right turn into his flight path; he never did find out who it was.

#4 S.F.T.S. SASKATOON, SASK.—CESSNA CRANE—NOV. 1943

This was the day he found out the difference between Wooden Props and Metal CS Props. This was actually his day to begin formation flying. His instructor was in a plane with wooden props, his had CS props. Gord was told to start off before he reached takeoff, and did just that, his plane caught up to the instructor's by the time he was just airborne; he had to do a steep turn to the right almost at ground level, pulled up the nose of the plane and shot skyward like a rocket - needless to say formation flying was not too close after that!

#19 O.T.U., KINLOSS, SCOTLAND—WELLINGTON—OCTOBER 1944

One day at about 8000 feet over the airfield, he was flying toward a cloud formation when, as he was about 500 feet from the cloud, a Spitfire came out of the cloud, heading precisely at him. He immediately pushed the nose down, the Spitfire went up, his crew seated in the rear of the plane, headed up toward the topside of the fuselage, both motors stopped and the Wimpey headed down. All was well, very shortly, when the motors came back to life and Gordon headed back up.

STILL AT KINLOSS, SCOTLAND

Gordon was returning from a daylight practice bombing session with his crew. The practice had gone very well except that one bomb had "Hung up". They arrived back at the airfield and taxied into the dispersal bay. The crew all got out and were waiting for Gord beside the plane. He was climbing down the ladder at the nose of the aircraft, looking towards the rear, when all of a sudden right in front of him, the "BOMB" that had hung up, dropped on the tarmac - no bang!

Gordon was demobbed in October 1945 and returned to his old firm as officer clerk for a year. He was married to Peggy in February 1946 and they have a son and daughter, John and Ann. In September 1946 Gordon joined Canada Customs as a Customs Officer and was with them until he retired as a Customs Superintendent in October 1981.

W/O STAN J. LILBURN
WIRELESS AIRGUNNER R.A.F.

Stan Lilburn was born in London, England, on April 18th, 1922, attending Public School at Blackheath Road, Greenwich, and Secondary School at Brockley County Grammar School, where he participated in soccer, cricket and tennis as a youth. Before the war Stan's occupation was in the building trades.

After living through the Battle of Britain and the London blitz, Stan volunteered for aircrew, and was accepted and introduced to the R.A.F. at Padgate. After initial Ground Wireless Training at Blackpool and Yatesbury, he had a stint on the ground at Silloth, Cumberland, and then more Wireless at Madly. He completed his Air Gunnery Course in February 1943 at #3 A.G.S. at Mona, the Isle of Anglesey in N. Wales. He finally arrived at #21 O.T.U., Moreton-in-the-Marsh, Enstone, training on Wellingtons. After crewing up and completing his training, Stan found out that he was posted overseas. In July, 1943 he was sent to #150 Squadron, R.A.F., at Kairouan, via Gibraltar in a new 'Wimpey' and did operations with that unit until January 1944, completing a tour of 35 trips.

During the time Stan was on 150 Squadron, it changed locations twice, once to Oodna, Tunisia, and then Cerignola, Italy. For their 33rd. op., Stan's crew was selected (?) for a low level operation on the night of November 13th 1943. (No one was superstitious). The crew had a replacement pilot and the target was a bridge at Nice in the south of France. The bomb load consisted of one 4,000 lb bomb with an eleven second delay and it was to be dropped from 500 feet.

Because of the distance involved, they took off from base at Kairouan in Tunisia, with the bomb on board, landed at Tunis, about 100 miles away, where they refuelled to capacity, then took off for Nice, flying over Sardinia, which was now in Allied hands.

On reaching and identifying the target, the bomb was dropped from the required height and they flew away as fast as possible in the Wimpey, with all the crew counting up to eleven. After reaching twenty, without hearing any "crump" or similar expected sound, they realized that the bomb had not gone off for some reason, and that in all probability, it would never go off. Naturally, very disappointed, especially after a trip of over 500 miles, the pilot turned round and circled the target to take photos, which, in all probability scared the local population. After taking the pictures, they set course for North Africa, but as they were flying down the coast of Corsica, it became evident that they were either running out of fuel, or the fuel gauges were not functioning properly.

By the time they reached the northern tip of Sardinia, there was a possibility of an early morning swim in the "saltchuck", so Stan commenced to send out S.O.S.s. They finally landed at Cagliari in Sardinia, where the landing was not the best they had ever done. Leaving the Wimpey at the 'drome, they completed the last leg by D.C.3 to Tunis and then back to the squadron. This was the longest trip of Stan's flying career (8 hours and 50 minutes) and to quote one of World War II's well-known sayings:- "Was your journey really necessary?" The crew never did learn why the bomb failed to explode.

Living in tents, was a little different from England, and the crew missed the eggs and bacon. On December 29th, 1943 while Stan was in Cerignola, he applied for a 48 hour pass and set off hitch-hiking, to find his brother, who was in the 8th Army (Desert Rats). After going through Foggia, and across Italy, he went up the Adriatic coast where he finally located him. His brother was in the R.A.S.C. and wangled a place on a convoy going back to Foggia. Here, the two brothers spent a 1943 New Year's Eve together. Needless to say, spirits were high and also plentiful that night. The next day, "hung over" Stan, arrived back at the Squadron.

On completion of his tour in December 1943, Stan was posted back to England, on compassionate grounds. The first leg of the trip was pleasant, flying from Foggia, Italy to Algiers, via Naples and Tunis, arriving there on January 8th, 1944. There, his fortune changed and he continued his journey on a ship in a very slow convoy and after 17 days and nights, sleeping in a hammock, he was very glad to see Greenock from the side of the ship.

In February 1944, Stan was posted to #11 O.T.U. as a flying instructor in Wellingtons at Westcott Oakley. In May 1945, he was posted to H.C.U. North Luffenham on Lancasters. On completing the course he was posted to #75 N.Z. Squadron, but the war ended so he finished up at Cranwell, at the No. 1 Radio School. Stan was discharged in November, 1945 and was awarded the 1939/45 Star, the Italy Star, the Defence Medal and the War Medal.

Returning to civilian life, Stan found a career in Advertising, and also enjoyed a couple of years as a semi-pro soccer player. He emigrated to Canada in April 1957 and settled in Vancouver, working for various advertising agencies.

Stan is now retired and living in Vancouver with his wife Diane. Stan has two children from a previous marriage, Roy and Patricia, and one granddaughter, Crystal. His spare time is taken up by playing tennis and trying to improve his photography skills.

MK IIA SUPERMARINE SPITFIRE P7923 No 411 (F) SQUADRON R.C.A.F.
BASED AT DIGBY, LINCS - SUMMER 1941

F/LT ROY MACKENZIE D.F.C.

PILOT R.C.A.F.

Roy was born at the little town of Eyebrow, Saskatchewan and attended public schools at Regina and Vancouver. Secondary school education was at Scott Collegiate, Regina and he then went to Balfour Technical School in the same city. During his school years, Roy was active in baseball, hockey, soccer and track.

In 1937 he worked with B.A. Oil in Regina and was there for two years, until in June 1939, he joined the R.C.A.F. as a clerk Group C. By November 1941 he was promoted to Flight Sergeant Group A when he remustered to aircrew a month later. In January 1942 he was posted to #4 I.T.S. Edmonton, then to #16 E.F.T.S. Edmonton, flying Tiger Moths.

Roy graduated from #4 S.F.T.S. Saskatoon on September 11, 1942 and of the 62 graduating, eleven Sgt.Pilots were posted to the embarkation depot (Y depot) at Halifax. They left for England on November 5, 1942 on the "Queen Elizabeth" and after five days on the Atlantic, arrived at Greenock, Scotland. The food on board was excellent, two meals per day, approximately 16,000 on board. In first class cabins with 14 other pilots. Due to demand Sgt. MacKenzie (#4149) spent only eight days in Bournemouth, the R.C.A.F. reception centre, and was posted to Advanced Flying Unit in Scotland flying Oxfords, a twin engine aircraft similar to a Cessna. Two months later, February 15, 1943, with another 80 hours flying time, he was posted to #23 O.T.U. Pershore, near Worcester in England for operational training on Wellington MK III's - twin engine aircraft. The engines were Bristol Hercules 1600 h.p. radial engines, probably the best radial engine manufactured in the world. They were extremely powerful and reliable.

Forty five days later, with 80 more flying hours, Sgt. MacKenzie and his crew consisting of a Navigator, Bomb Aimer, WAG and Rear Gunner, were

67

posted to 420 Squadron, Middleton St George, England, to commence operations flying over Germany. This crew was one of four out of the 16 crews who trained at Pershore to be sent to a Wimpey squadron. The other 12 were sent to a Conversion Unit for training on Halifaxes. He thinks it was fate that sent him to Wellington squadron as three of the four crews survived. With 400 hours of flying to his credit, Sgt. MacKenzie was now ready for operations against the enemy.

On April 16th he was detailed as Second Pilot with PO Morton on a seven hour trip to Mannheim. It was like daylight over Mannheim with all the searchlights and the sky was full of flak. Sgt. MacKenzie could not believe that they would go through such a terrifying sight ahead. However, Morton dropped the bombs on the marshalling yards and the trip back was uneventful.

On April 26 Sgt. Roy and crew, were briefed to bomb the marshalling yards in Duisberg - in the Ruhr, known as Happy Valley. Take off was 11:45 pm with light cloud. They climbed on track over the North Sea to 19,500', putting on oxygen masks at 10,000'. The masses of searchlights brightened the sky like daylight. Far below they saw a four engine aircraft coned by the lights - probably a Stirling. Flying straight and level on the bombing run, Jackson dropped the 4000 pound bomb on the red flares marking the target. Suddenly the world seemed to come to an end as there was a "Bang" and the port engine was on fire. "I think I was paralysed for a few seconds", MacKenzie said later and then he pushed the fire extinguisher button, feathered the prop and shut off the engine. Unbelievably, the fire went out, as they turned off the target to the starboard. He increased the revs and throttle to the starboard engine as they headed back on a course of 300 degrees.

They began to lose height rapidly after losing the engine but figured they would hold height at 3000'. He called off the altitude to the crew - "nineteen, eighteen, seventeen thousand" as they proceeded west at 3000' and were still going down as he increased the power on the one engine. By now it was obvious that the prop had not feathered. One of the crew suggested bailing out but the pilot was sure it would fly them back and he wasn't interested in bailing out. The sky was lighter now and at 500' they were holding altitude at climbing revs and boost. They could see ground occasionally, and water ahead. Searchlights came on ahead but did a large circle and missed them. They soon crossed what they thought was the Dutch coast and headed west at 250' over the water. By now, using the engine at full power occasionally, to hold altitude, they had used a lot of petrol. The navigator, P/O Frank Lenihan, didn't think they would make England, so they sent an SOS with an estimated position of ditching in the North Sea. MacPherson wanted to use the code but MacKenzie said "use plain language". He lit a cigarette - thought they might get wet; he had never smoked before while flying.

Finally they saw the coast of England coming up and two Beaufighters flew by, showing them the way. The gas tanks had all read empty for a while, including the nascelle tank - 75 gallons. They crossed the coast and not far inland saw an airdrome. Jackson started pumping the wheels down as they came in for a landing. At the last minute it was evident the aerodrome was under construction, so he pulled up over the bulldozers and landed on the grass beyond. The wheels collapsed as they slid over the grass, through a fence, over a road, came to a stop and switched everything off. They were back, but Roy's friend Earl Newburg and his crew did not return and they were listed as missing after air operations.

The squadron was transferred with 424 and 435 squadrons to Tunisia for the Sicilian and Italian campaigns. Later, they flew from Lands End to Ras El Mar in French Morocco losing 10% of the squadron to Junkers 88's over the Bay of Biscay. Roy did 37 more trips over Sicily and Italy, bombing railway yards, bridges and aerodromes. On October 5th, 1943 he did his last trip, bombing Grosetto Aerodrome in Italy (near Rome), returned to England and became an instructor at 22 O.T.U. Gaydon.

Roy earned the D.F.C., the 1939/45 Star, Italy Star, Aircrew Europe Star, Defence Medal, War Medal and the C.V.S.M and Bar and was honourably discharged on June 23rd, 1945.

In civvy street once more, he became a sales representative for Canada Roof Products in Vancouver and Calgary and also for Peace River Glass in Vancouver. In May 1945 he married Maude, his present wife who was a radio operator with the B.C.A.T.P. They have two children, a boy and a girl, and three grandchildren.

"NOORDUYN NORSEMAN "2486"

SQD/LDR E.H.McCAFFERY D.F.C.,A.F.C.
NAVIGATOR R.C.A.F.

Elmer H."Mac" McCaffery was born in Winnipeg, Manitoba and raised on a farm in the Miami district of southern Manitoba. He attended the Opewaka Rural Public School, Miami High School and the Collegiate at Manitou. One of his delights in his early teens was the training of a pacer (horse) and showing carriage horses at agricultural fairs.

Max was employed as a salesman in Winnipeg by a Manufacturer's agent of National brand confections, when war broke out in 1939. He married in October that year and joined the R.C.A.F. on October 28th 1940. He was posted to #2 Manning Depot at Brandon, Manitoba for the traditional military training and then to R.A.F. Station Penhold, Alberta for guard duty.

On Jan. 24th 1941, while washing floors he received a telegram announcing the birth of a son, but the Officer Commanding denied him compassionate leave. Mac understood the reason why not, when two days later he was posted to #2 Initial Training School at Regina, Saskatchewan. From I.T.S. Mac was posted to #5 Air Observer School in Winnipeg.

The Air Observer training embraced navigation, wireless operation, bombing and gunnery, which was a carry over from World War I. The advent of four engines and faster and larger twin engine aircraft dictated more specialization, and the "Flying O" was replaced in 1943 by the "NavB" and straight "Nav". Upon completion of the course in Winnipeg, Mac received his wings and promotion to the rank of sergeant.

On conclusion of his astro-navigation course at #1 Astro-Nav school at Rivers, Man., he received his commission as pilot officer and was one of fifteen selected to navigate U.S.A. Lend-Lease Hudson Venturas from Dorval, Quebec to Prestwick, Scotland, via Gander, Newfoundland.

Crewed up with R.C.A.F. pilot F/Lt McChalski and civilian wireless operator McKercher, they flew to Gander and grounded for four days due to bad weather. On September 26th, 1941, the three "Macs"took off for Prestwick at 21.39 hrs G.M.T. The flight plan called for ten hours. Drift readings and astro navigation using a single shot marine sextant were the main aids to dead reckoning navigation, and at the point of no return, severe icing was experienced and the pilot descended to one hundred feet. The cold front was some five hundred miles west of that forecast.

It should be noted the aerial sextant takes 40 readings or so over one minute and averages them to compensate for the "yaw" of the aircraft. Single sextant readings on the North Star continually showed the latitude of the aircraft to be considerably south of the planned track. Understandably the pilot was reluctant to depart from the flight plan when presented with a revised course. However, Mac's creditability was somewhat restored when they reached the Irish coast less than three miles from the projected landfall.

They encountered cloud down to the deck over the Irish Sea, but thanks to the wireless operator they reached Prestwick, landing through broken cloud. Flying time was twelve hours and twenty minutes and the fuel tank read "empty." It was later learned that two of the aircraft which took off that night went missing.

Posted from the Holding Unit at Bournemouth, Hants, England to #22 Operational Training Unit at Wellesbourne and Atherston-on-Stour, near Stratford-on-Avon, Mac was crewed up with R.C.A.F. pilot P/O Hal. Miles, co-pilot Sgt. Wiseman, W/Op Sgt. Frank Mitchell, R.A.F. rear gunner Sgt. Bert Wright on A Wellington. Sgt. Wiseman was killed on a training exercise and was not replaced as Bomber Command (Europe) at this time dispensed with the second pilot.

Mac was then posted to #1651 Stirling Conversion Unit in April 1942 where P/O. Bill McAlpine and Engineer Sgt. Paul Curtis joined the crew. Sgt. Scotty Goodall joined the crew at #15 R.A.F. Squadron, 3 Group on their seventh operation. Up to that time Mac had done the bombing, starting with the first 1,000 bomber raid on May 30th on Cologne, Germany.

A 1,000 bomber raid planned for Hamburg on July 28th ended in a fiasco due to weather. All bomber groups except 36 group cancelled out. Severe icing was experienced and on reaching the target maneuverability of the aircraft was seriously restricted. Mac's aircraft was twice caught in searchlights, the second time for eleven minutes and was severely bounced around by flak.

Things were looking rather grim when the silence was broken by the mid-upper gunner's Lancashire voice over the intercom. "I say skipper shall I give the B.....s a burst?" "Hell, yes" the pilot replied, "But save some for the night-fighters if we get out of this lot." This broke the tension and eventually the bomb-aimer jettisoned the incendiary bombs south-west of Kiel from a height of 4,000 feet. On arrival at base, the ground crew said there were fifty three holes in the Stirling "T" W7585, from anti-aircraft flak. Twenty-six of the ninety Stirlings reached Hamburg and returned safely, the others returned early or went missing.

Mac was appointed Squadron Navigation Officer after seventeen operations, but carried on with his crew. The day after this appointment, August 27th 1942, the crew was on the battle order for a raid on Nuremburg. As they crossed the coast at Abbeville, they had a run in with a night fighter and lost a starboard engine; shortly after, it became evident the Germans had succeeded in jamming the main Navigational aid "Gee". That left map reading and astro navigation.

The first landmark visible through the haze was the Rhine River. Either they were a few miles north of track, or more than forty miles south. A decision was made that they were north of track and they altered course accordingly. On E.T.A. on target they could see the Autobahn, canal and railroad. This was NOT Nuremburg. They bombed the marshalling yards and headed out on the planned south-westerly route.

Astro shots through the broken cloud indicated they were considerably south of track and this was confirmed when they came upon the northern end of lake Constance. The flight engineer advised that petrol was running low. The pilot asked for orientation of their location and outlined the drill for "bailing out", commenting "What a helluva way to make a living!"

Just then the second engine quit and Mac was asked up to the cockpit to lend a hand in controlling the aircraft. Then..... they saw the coast ahead, twenty two miles from Manston and as they approached, the pilot asked for permission to come straight in. The flare path turned out to be a row of Spitfires of a Polish squadron set on fire earlier by a bomber aircraft in distress swerving off the runway. Mac's Stirling stopped in front of a hangar and the crew had no sooner evacuated the aircraft, with the pilot stretched out on the ground exhausted, when another Stirling came in over top and crashed into the hangar. Amazingly no-one was seriously hurt.

Ten bomber aircraft landed at Manston that night, all in trouble. Reviewing the charts, logs and photographs the next day, it was concluded the crews had bombed Augsburg!! What a way for a new Squadron Navigation Officer to start out; the reversal of winds and the early loss of an engine were given as his excuse!!

The crew completed their tour of thirty trips in October 1942. During that time they had twentysix cancellations or recalls due to weather and two due to mechanical failure. Mac observed that on reflection his crew was probably typical of many. They held various jobs before "joining up" and had fresh memories of the depression and probably experienced an average number of "shaky-do's" due to night fighters, anti-aircraft flak and weather. The W/Op got them out of trouble many times on the way back to England, in adverse weather conditions; the pilot showed his skills time and time again; the mid-upper gunner and rear gunner were credited with shooting down an Me 109 and a Ju 88 after the latter had strafed their aircraft from nose to tail with no-one wounded.

Mac carried on as squadron Navigation officer doing a couple of trips with the 24 year old commanding officer. One of these trips was a leaflet raid on Marseille announcing the arrival of the American Army in North Africa. They lost an engine over western France in a brush with a night fighter. The mid-upper gunner, the squadron gunnery officer and a noted pre-war author, suggested that if they were in trouble, he had a villa near Angers and knew many of the local population who would look after them if they had to bail out!!

In December 1942 Mac was posted to #7 Pathfinder squadron as Station Navigation Officer with the rank of Squadron Leader. In March 1943 he was posted to 36 Group Headquarters as Group Navigation officer. He was repatriated to Canada in time to spend Christmas 1943 with his wife Fern, son and family. He was then appointed Chief Navigation Instructor of #5 O.T.U., Boundary Bay, B.C. where crews were being trained for the war in the Pacific.

Mac was honorably discharged in Vancouver on October 15th 1945. During his service career he was awarded the Distinguished Flying Cross, the Air Force Cross, the R.C.A.F. operational wings and was mentioned in despatches. He was recipient of the 1939-45 Star, (Air)Europe Star, Canadian Volunteer Medal with clasp, the Defence Medal and the 1939-45 medal with oak leaf.

Mac's post war vocations were divided evenly between sales/sales management of the distribution of plumbing, heating, oil and gas equipment and accessories and that of executive director of a major trade contractor association in B.C. The latter involved working with Labour, Government, design authorities and the public on behalf of the contractors, initiating and directing management training and liaison with the construction community.

He represented the employers of the construction industry, was on the Provincial Apprenticeship Board, the Occupational Training Council, college and Trade Advisory Boards for a number of years.

A second son was born in 1948 but was killed in an accident in 1979. He has two grandsons and two sisters; his late brother Edgar did a tour plus in Bomber Command as a mid-upper gunner.

FAIRCHILD M-62A-4 CORNELL Mk II "10738"

F/LT HAROLD HOPE
PILOT R.C.A.F.

Harold was born in Vancouver, B.C. and attended his grade schools from 1 to 8 in that city, as well as Port Alberni and Armstrong, while high school was also at Armstrong. He followed this with two years at U.B.C. and he served as a jeweller and watch maker before the war, joining the R.C.A.F. in Vancouver during 1941.

His choice in flying trade was to be a pilot and he went through the usual I.T.W., E.F.T.S., S.F.T.S. etc. at various stations, including Regina, Virden, Dauphin, Summerside, then after going overseas, was variously at Kidlington, Conningsby, East Fortune, and Port Ellen, then overseas in another direction, to Morocco, Algiers, followed by Cairo, India and finally Burma.

He flew in a wide type of aircraft, beginning with the Tiger Moth then the Crane, Anson, Harvard, Oxford, Cornell, L5, Chipmunk, Beaufort, Beaufighter and the D.C.3.

He was married to Irene Morris on September 3rd, 1943 and they have three children, Graham, Jacqueline and Roger.

Harold's final rank was that of Flight Lieutenant and he holds the following medals: 1939/45 Star, Burma Star, War and Defence Medals, as well as the C.V.S.M. and clasp. On his demobilization in October 1945 at Vancouver, he became a broker and financial consultant and he says he's going to retire one of these days.

In his spare time he has constructed an Anson aircraft which he flew as recently as March 31st 1989, on the 60th anniversary of the R.C.A.F. at Chilliwack, B.C.

On March 20th, 1944, Flt/Sgt Harold Hope and his navigator, Sgt.Jack Pettifer, an Englishman from Birmingham, set out on an operational sortie in company with three other Beaufighters. The target was a Japanese training camp at Lemyata, near Henzada on the Irrawaddy River, thirty miles north of Rangoon. The leader of the exercise was an Australian Flying Officer, with several sorties to his credit.

The duration of the flight from home base, a jungle strip near Chittagong, was beyond the range of the four aircraft, so a refuelling stop was arranged at the remote strip of Ramu, ten miles inland from Cox's Bazaar. Take off time was set for 15:30 hours, to be over the target by dusk.

On arrival at Ramu, one of the other pilots placed his aircraft u/s, with the complaint that his starboard engine was consuming an excessive amount of fuel, and his intercom was non-functional. Since Hope was the junior pilot on this operation, the leader decided that the crew of the u/s aircraft should trade with Hope and Pettifer, while they returned to base with the unserviceable Beau.

However, Hope and Pettifer decided differently, and when the other three departed they also took off in the u/s aircraft, and followed at a reasonable distance. These flights were done at low level so it would be difficult to be seen. (It was because of this type of operation that the Japanese referred to the Beaufighters as "Whispering Death".)

Finally the camp came into sight and the excitement began. Each aircraft made three attacks without loss, as only small arms were visible, but no anti-aircraft guns. During one attack Hope spotted another Beaufighter coming towards him at a great rate, at an angle that would make it impossible for the pilot to see that he was heading for a collision. To avoid the inevitable, Hope went lower ... and lower, until he was just touching the tree tops ... while the other passed three or four feet overhead - a close call!

All aircraft broke off and headed home independently, with orders to attack road and rail traffic when available. Several attacks were made, but as it was now becoming quite dark, all crews decided to head for base. The other three arrived safely, but Hope and his excessive fuel consumption and no intercom ran into difficulty. With his navigator standing immediately behind him shouting directions in his ear, and each searching for the flare path of their base, they noted that the fuel warning lights had been on for almost 20 minutes.

Suddenly, Hope spotted the flares of the landing strip about a mile off to the left. An immediate turn to port with a straight in approach was attempted, but luck faded and Hope and Pettifer were forced to set down about a half mile short of the base. Fuel may have run out, but not luck at this moment. They ended up in the middle of one of those large water holes where the Indians bathed themselves and washed their water buffalo.

Debriefing was a combination of scolding and praise - the scolding for not obeying orders and returning to base from Ramu, and praise for carrying on under some difficulty. Hope had his own Beaufighter - G for George, returned to him for future use.

On March 11th, 1945 F/O Hope and W/O Pettifer had orders to patrol the Irrawaddy River from Hanzada south to the Gulf of Martaban. This type of operation, known as a "rhubarb", where a single aircraft, in this case a Beaufighter, armed with four 20 mm cannons, six machine guns and eight rockets, flew at low level, picking off river traffic that appeared to be carrying enemy personnel or provisions. These flights became relatively routine, but always most exhilarating and on this occasion more than thirty river craft were attacked. It was never known if real military supplies were demolished or if innocent civilians suffered from these efforts. The excitement built up, due to the closeness of the main concentration of Japanese aerodromes situated in the general area of Rangoon.

In this instance, further excitement developed when Hope and Pettifer were on their return to home base.

Some thirty miles north west of Henzada in enemy held territory, Hope spotted a Spitfire on the ground in a large paddy field. The pilot, an English Pilot Officer, was standing beside his aircraft. When he realized he had been spotted, he set about to let the Beau crew know it would be safe to attempt a landing. As Hope circled around to determine if the rescue was practical, the Spit pilot ran the length of the field indicating the best direction and approach, all the while waving that it would be safe to land.

What should have been done was to mark the spot and by wireless send a message to base to have an L5 make the pickup, but Hope decided it could be accomplished after remembering he had twice landed on a short field, used by Swordfish. The landing was made successfully and the Spit pilot wasted no time in climbing aboard. The young pilot was from a squadron based on the coast of Burma, about fifty miles north of Akyab. On arrival there, it became evident that the strip was considerably shorter than those used for aircraft that weighed in excess of ten tons, with an approach speed of 110 knots and a landing speed of ninety. However, with a controlled precautionary approach, and applying all the braking power available, the landing was successful and another pilot was happy to be home.

Now the trick was to get out again! Several irks cut into the bush at the takeoff point and pushed the Beaufighter back at least fifty feet, to allow for more take off run. Then it was decided that two irks would lay on the elevator, while Hope ran up to about 70% power. On a signal from Pettifer, who was in the capola looking aft, they jumped clear and Hope throttled toward full power. At a point about three-fourths of the runway length, Hope was able to lift off, raise the wheels and turn starboard, out to sea to avoid hitting the trees at the end. As it turned out, all went well and three more men were safely home again.

If ever in the future, Hope could meet up with his rescued pilot friend, it would certainly be great reason for a well deserved pint in a London pub!

F/LT CHARLES (CHUCK) APPLETON D.F.C.
PILOT R.C.A.F.

Charles A. (Chuck) Appleton was born in Cambridge, England where he attended St. Faith's Preparatory School and Leys Public School, where he played soccer, rugby and tennis. His interests weren't all in sports as he was a keen observer of wildlife and always liked to do woodworking.

He came to Canada and settled in Toronto shortly before the Second World War started in September 1939. There he finished his formal education, completing grade thirteen at Harbord Collegiate. He joined the 48th Highlands NPAM while working at the Imperial Bank, but early in 1941 enlisted in the R.C.A.F., and June of that year found him at Manning Depot and I.T.S. Toronto.

At #10 E.F.T.S. at Mount Hope he learned to fly Fleet Finches, then to Dunnville S.F.T.S. on Harvards where he earned his pilot's wings. He then proceeded to Central Flying School, Trenton and 16 S.F.T.S. Hagersville as an instructor on Ansons. He received his commission in February 1943 and was recategorized as a B2 instructor. After a year of instructing he was posted overseas in July 1943. He passed through A.F.U. at Perton and Wheaton Aston before reaching O.T.U. at Wellesbourne Mountford where he crewed up and commenced flying Wellingtons.

CO of Wellesbourne was the renowned G/C Willie Tait who told all new pilots they had now stopped flying toy aeroplanes. The new crew consisted of F/O Murray Dobson Nav; F/O Norm McEwen B/A; WO2's Roland Wallace and Harold Edwards, Gunners; and Vic Swimmings, WAG.

After O.T.U. he and his crew spent two miserable weeks under control of the British Army on a battle course at Dalton while on their way to 1659 Heavy Conversion Unit at Topcliffe and their introduction to Halifax Mk II's. At Topcliffe the crew was joined by a very young Flight Engineer, Terry Hobbs, who had been originally trained for Stirlings while at St. Athans. Norm McEwen had to be replaced as B/A by Ernie Dickson on medical grounds.

The crew had an experience that they would long remember; an experience that taught them the importance of good crew discipline and would possibly save their lives on later trips. At the Heavy Conversion Units, Halifax Mk II's, with Merlin engines, were used for training purposes. Chuck and his crew were on their initial check-out for night flying with a screened pilot and an additional trainee pilot. During take-offs the port inner engine had been throwing trails of sparks, but when questioned, the screened pilot told Chuck "Not to worry and that they do that all the time." Who could argue with a pilot with a tour under his belt? On the first solo circuit, the constant speed unit of the port engine failed, and with a high pitched scream the tachometer wound right off the clock as the prop went into full fine pitch. Flames began pouring out and feathering action was initiated followed by actuation of the fire extinguishers. The fire was brought under control but to Chuck's surprise the aircraft did not swing when the port inner was feathered. A quick check of the tachometers showed that the rev counter on both the port and the starboard inner engines were registering zero--they had two engines out, at night and at only 1,000'!! With climbing power on the two outers, the aircraft was still losing height. Chuck called the tower for a possible down-wind landing, if this became necessary. Not only were they losing height but the gyro instruments, deprived of the inner engines' vacuum pumps, were beginning to topple, and spin. The only visual cue left in that black night was the flarepath somewhere behind the aircraft. It was finally determined that another crew member had taken upon himself to feather the problem engine, but had inadvertently selected the wrong one. The starboard inner was restarted immediately and the aircraft climbed back to circuit height and the subsequent 3 engine landing was uneventful. Later it was determined that the port inner never did feather properly. It had seized, but fortunately the fire had abated. Chuck and his crew learned a great deal from this experience that resulted in a firmer crew discipline, which would stand them in good stead in the future.

Early in 1944 the crew was posted to 433 Squadron at Skipton-on-Swale. One of the crew's "ops" was "D" Day, the night of June 5/6, 1944, when a load of bombs was dropped on the German defenses a few hours before the landing craft arrived on the beaches.

Impressive as the invasion must have been, it is a trip some time later to Stuttgart on the night of July 25/26, 1944, that stands out most clearly in Chuck's memory. Here is the story in his own words:

"As crews who flew Halifax III's will recall, the hydraulic system (Messier) was designed in such a way that the jacks operated hydraulically in one direction only, with fluid being forced onto an accumulator, thus storing the energy as air pressure, for the actuation of the jacks in the reverse direction. Thus, lowering the U/C and flaps and opening the bomb doors were really done pneumatically.

It was essential that various levers be returned to neutral after actuation in order to avoid possible excessive build up of pressure in the accumulator. The U/C had a special feature in the form of manually operated up locks; in the event pressure was lost, then the gear could be held up until required for landing and at that time would be dropped by gravity. On this trip to Stuttgart, I neglected to return the bomb door lever to the neutral position after closing the bomb doors following the bomb run. This was an easy omission in view of all the other things needing attention, as the target area was vacated. Normally a relief valve should have bypassed the excess pressure. But it failed to function on this occasion.

Shortly after leaving the target there was a tremendous bang back near the rest position, as the accumulator exploded due to the excess pressure which the relief valve had failed to bypass. At first, of course, we thought that we had been hit, but the aircraft was flying normally and all the crew were accounted for. Upon further inspection, however, by the F/E, it was found that hydraulic fluid had sprayed from one end of the aircraft to the other. It was nearly impossible to move around as everything was so slippery. The F/E was only able to move a limited amount of window from the rest position. Since all hydraulic fluid and pressure had now been lost, we realized that once the gear was dropped for landing it would be down to stay and there would be no flaps available. Unfortunately, we were diverted that night but had no problems with the flapless landing at a strange aerodrome. Next day we had to return to base all the way, with the gear down and with no flap or bomb door movement available.

What only the F/E knew at the time was that any mixture of oil and oxygen is highly volatile and that the dripping hydraulic fluid down on the oxygen bottles stored near his position, presented a highly hazardous situation, should even the smallest of oxygen leaks occur. Obviously, the bottles and connections were tight, for we survived to tell the tale. One can only imagine the anxiety suffered by the F/E as he sat on his secret all the way back to the UK - not wanting to add to the stress on the rest of the crew".

It was not only the operational trips that could prove risky. An air test with the Flight Commander nearly ended in disaster for him.

On a trip to Aachen on May 24th, 1944, Chuck had been assigned an altitude of about 21,000 feet but was unable to coax "A Able" to that height. Upon reporting this to the Flight Commander on his return, he was rebuffed by a challenge in the form of a 5 pound bet that the aircraft could easily have reached the assigned altitude. A flight test was arranged for the next day and since there would be no bomb load on board, a height of 26,000 feet was agreed upon.

As Chuck was taxiing out the next morning with the Flight Commander and the F/C's crew on board, the F/C ordered Chuck back to the rest position as he wanted his own Bomb Aimer to do the take off. Presumably, he had done this before, as there were no dual controls in the operational aircraft. How would he cope with the tendency of the Hally to swing to starboard on take off? How could an F/O argue with an S/L anyway? The take off scared the devil out of everybody in the aircraft and on the ground. From the rest position, all Chuck could see was grass going by the small window and hear the S/L screaming instructions to his B/A, while trying at the same time to juggle the throttles and operate the control column from a standing position. Somehow the aircraft miraculously staggered into the air, having missed the control tower by mere feet. By this time Chuck didn't care whether they reached 26,000 feet, just as long as the S/L was going to let him land the aircraft. It took over two hours to nurse "A Able" to 26,000 feet but the S/L declared that he had won his bet. Even if the test was less that fair, Chuck didn't mind as long as he got to land the A/C. He paid up thankful to be alive.

The S/L was subsequently posted to another squadron where he was killed along with a different crew and another crew in a second aircraft. The two Halifaxes collided while the aircraft were in formation. The S/L was allegedly found in the rear turret from which he was trying to take pictures while a member of his crew was attempting to fly the aircraft!

Chuck was to meet the original bomb aimer at the 1982 Allied Air Force Reunion in Toronto. His first words on meeting Chuck for the first time in nearly forty years were, "You're the one I nearly killed once, aren't you?" He said that that occasion was the first and only take off he had ever attempted and he had no more wanted to do it than did anyone else. It was the F/C's idea. In all, Chuck and his crew did 35 trips and must have done a creditable job for both he and his navigator Murray Dobson were awarded D.F.C.'s.

For his rest tour Chuck was posted back to Topcliffe as a screened pilot. While he had been completing a tour of operations, the H.C.U. had been re-equipped with Lancaster Mk I's and III's and although he flew them until the end of hostilities, he still kept faithful to his first love, the old Hally III.

During his time at Topcliffe he served as instructor and base test pilot. He completed the Junior Commanders' Course at Cranwell, Bomber Command Tactics Course at Ingham, Lincs, a Bristol Aero-Engines Course at Bristol, Offensive Support Wing Course at Old Sarum and started a Test Pilot's Course at Woodford and Baginton when the war ended. Had the Japanese not surrendered he would have been on his way to the Far East for a second tour.

He remained with the R.C.A.F. until 1948 when he joined the Federal Department of Transport as a Civil Aviation Inspector. He served in the Toronto and Winnipeg Regions, developing new navigation aids and landing systems, also inspecting and licensing private airports. In 1960 he was transferred to HQ in Ottawa, and became Superintendent of Airways in 1970. He took early retirement in 1975 after 35 years of government service.

Shortly after retiring, Chuck and his wife, Hazel, moved to Peterborough, Ontario where they had a family cottage. Their two sons and six grandchildren all living in the Vancouver area proved to be an even greater pull, so in 1987 they moved to the West Coast to join them and are currently living in Burnaby.

In addition to a newly acquired hobby of wood carving, Chuck's interests include duplicate bridge, the Aircrew Association, the R.C.A.F. Association and are directed toward keeping the four surviving crew members (Navigator Murray Dobson, Ottawa; Bomb Aimer Ernie Dickson, Mississauga; Terry Hobbs, Chester, England) in close touch. What nostalgic memories they must share.

F/LT GEORGE H.K.BEGG D.F.C.
PILOT R.C.A.F.

George Begg was born in Vancouver. He obtained his elementary education at Van Horne Public School and took secondary Matric at the Vancouver Technical School. Later he was a student at U.B.C., for three years, studying Market and Sales.

The Begg residence was at #82 East 50th Avenue which was conveniently located by the Langara Golf Course where George became a caddie. Later he took up rowing and a membership in the Vancouver Rowing Club. His preservice occupation involved an apprenticeship with B.C. Telephone Supplies.

Begg tried to join the R.C.A.F. in 1941; after being processed he attended the Seaview Enlistment School prior to enlisting in January of 1942. As a L.A.C.he trained at the E.F.T.S. at High River, Alberta, flying Tiger Moths - then moved to S.F.T.S. at Calgary mastering Cessna Cranes. On graduation there, he was promoted to Pilot Officer and assigned to #34 O.T.U. at Pennfield Ridge in New Brunswick to train on Venturas and then to #1 O.T.U. at Baggotville in Quebec.

George sailed from Halifax to England and spent some time at Bournemouth and Sidmouth before being posted to Hartford Bridge for a period on Flying Control. He was promoted to Flying Officer and on to #18 A.F.U. at Church Lawford for training on Oxfords. From there he went to Bramcote in Staffordshire for training on #1513 Beam Approach course. The next assignments were to O.T.U.s on Wellingtons at Ossington and Gamston in Nottingham. Begg got his introduction to four engined Halifax bombers at Dishforth followed by a session on Lancaster X's at Dishforth #6 L.F.S.

George and his crew joined #419 Squadron at Middleton-St.George in Durham and from there, they made 16 trips—all but one over Germany.

After the 16th trip the crew was requested to volunteer for Pathfinders and went to Warboys in Bedfordshire and completed their training. They were posted to #405 Sqd. at Gransden and on to operations. At #405 Squadron the crew started at the bottom as "sprogs" and worked their way up to completing one trip as Deputy Master Bomber on a daylight mission. In late May of 1945 the crew left Gransden Lodge as a squadron to go to Linton-on-Ouse in Yorkshire in preparation to fly to Canada, where they were based at Greenwood, N.S. and became part of the Tiger Force due to become part of the offensive in the Pacific. George remains thankful to this day for his navigator's Dead Reckoning and for his crew who refused to panic under serious situations.

George Begg's problems began when he was at #34 O.T.U.. On a single engine landing, he got cut off by another aircraft, taking off, creating too much turbulence and he lost control and had to pull up the undercarriage to miss a tank car of gasoline. For this he got a Blue endorsement in his log book!

On another occasion, flying on a single-engine aircraft, the engine failed and he had to "hit the silk" and WON. In this event he learned one important lesson - that being to have the parachute harness snug and properly positioned.

Two weeks later on another night flight, two thirds of the runway lights failed leaving only the far end of the strip illuminated and, with the fog closing in, he had no alternative but to come down. In doing so he knocked the starboard Oleo leg off on a runway obstruction. With only one wheel and leg locked he careened into the darkness. Result! he was charged with a bad landing and had his Blue Endorsement entered again.

The worst operation of the 36 while on Sqd. 419 was his 16th and also it was their 4th trip in 90 hours. It was the worst flying weather they had ever encountered with icing, stratus cloud to 8,000 feet and cumulus to 23,000' all the way from base to their target at Osnabruck.

George's crew was twenty minutes late in take-off and, forty minutes out, the port inner constant speed unit began to surge from full fine to full course pitch. The problem was partially overcome by running the engine at half throttle and full coarse pitch. Once in the target area, preparing for the bombing run the flight engineer advised that the starboard outer was heating up very rapidly. The bomb doors were opened ready for the drop when the flight engineer again reported that the starboard outer was off the clock followed by "the engine is on fire". The bomb aimer was giving instructions for the run-in and George cut the throttle and called for the petrol to be shut off to the starboard-outer then cut the mags switches off. Then the flight engineer was called to feather the prop and, on doing so, the whole electrical system blew out leaving no intercom., no navigation work light, no radio etc. The starboard outer prop did not feather so he had to push the gravenor button for engine foam.

Because of the situation with no intercom. etc., and with the bomb doors open, the pilot pulled the jettison toggle and closed the doors to hold height. The navigator was asked for a D.R. course to get over their own lines in France. With no communication in or out and once more over friendly territory, they set course for Manston in preference to crossing the North Sea on two good engines and one at half-power - and the starboard engine-outer windmilling. Their route to Manston was in 10/10 cloud when the plane hit a severe cold front and the starboard inner engine iced up and lost. With more power on the port outer and full rudder, with airspeed just off stalling, they proceeded in a long slow let-down. When they finally broke the cloud, there was Manston in the distance ahead. With the colors of the day and reds from the Very pistol they flashed the Amber runway and began the S.I. for the landing.

In February of 1945, Black Mike McEwen (A.O.C. of 6 Group) commended the crew for their co-operation and discipline in assisting in getting the aircraft safely back to England. For this George received a Green endorsement in his Log Book.

George Begg was awarded the Distinguished Flying Cross and given a Permanent Pathfinder Operational Wing. He also holds the '39/45 Star, France/Germany Star, Defence Medal, War Medal and C.S.V.M.. George was discharged Sept. 15th, 1945.

In March of 1951 he was called up to train on Chipmunks at the Vancouver Airport for the Vancouver Aero Club. Later he was transferred to Montreal to continue the Course until 1956.

George married a school chum, Janet Adkins, and they had one daughter, two sons and two grandchildren. His wife passed away in 1979.

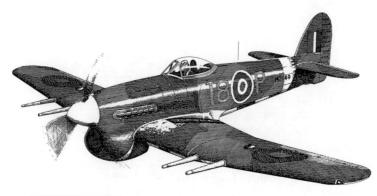

HAWKER TYPHOON MkIB MPI49
NO. 440 (FB) SQDN. R.C.A.F.

SQUADRON LEADER K.W. BROWN C.G.M., C.D.
and Bar
PILOT R.C.A.F.

Kenneth William Brown was born in Moose Jaw, Sask. in 1920, the last of seven children. From the beginning, his life was full of pitfalls. By the age of four, among other things, he had broken his collar-bone, by five he was nearly drowned, by six he managed to be in front of a hydrogen explosion where he received a face full of glass, almost losing his left eye. At age seven he was shot at by a deranged war intern; unfortunately, his school chum standing behind, caught the full blast.

Ken managed to scrape through public school and stumbled through high school and the Dominion Aeronautical School. He was active in the Y.M.C.A., participating in Gymnastics and basketball. He also played tennis, hockey and golf. Prior to joining the R.C.A.F. he worked with a survey crew during the construction of the Moose Jaw air base.

In 1941 he received his pilot's wings and was almost immediately posted overseas.

During the Second World War, Ken Brown was one of thousands of Canadian aircrew who were attached to the R.A.F.. His crew was made up of 4 R.A.F. and 3 R.C.A.F. types, destined to fly in Bomber Command.

It was during one operational tour that he had the fortune to serve with four members of the R.A.F. who were awarded the Victoria Cross.

Ken finished OTU the latter part of September 1942 and was posted to St. Eval, Cornwall, England where he joined Coastal Command in its struggle to prevent the German U-Boats from sinking allied ships. Ken's crew probably made several U-Boats crash dive when their tired old Whitley appeared in their vicinity of the Bay of Biscay, however they were soon posted to Bomber Command where they converted to Manchesters and Lancasters. The Manchester was a joy to fly but like the Whitley, its performance on one engine was

84

rather exciting. Needless to say the crew was overjoyed when they converted to Lancasters. It was near the end of the conversion course when a rather cocky young F/Lt. instructor named Mick Martin was to instruct the crew in fighter affiliation. With a Spitfire aircraft to assimilate attacks he demonstrated how it was possible to avoid the fighter. On completing the exercise he removed himself from the pilot's seat and said "Well, young fellow let's see what you can do". In jest Ken replied "Anything you can do so can I." That was their first meeting, but they would see a great deal more of each other, on Mick's way to becoming a legend in the R.A.F.

Having acquired a grand total of 25 flying hours on the course, the crew was posted to #44 (Rhodesian) Sqdn. commanded by W/C John W. Nettleton V.C., who had been awarded this most prestigious honour for leading a low level bombing attack on Augsburg.

Ken's crew experienced the terror of the word Ruhr, being "coned" by searchlights, damaged by the post graduate gunners of Essen and sweating from sheer terror.

When "Ops" were on, as each crew member entered the briefing room he would turn his head sharply to see the designated target. One particular night it was BERLIN, and each gut filled with fumes, as it wouldn't be easy...it never was. At the end of the briefing the Wing Commander advised Ken to report to his office. He was not the type to give one the "old boy" routine, so he was anxious to find out just what was in store for him. The C.O's opening remarks were,"Brown, you have been selected to join a new squadron being formed at Scampton." It was the last thing Ken expected but he asked the C.O. "Sir, I would prefer to finish my tour here as our crew is just settling in and I don't think our limited experience would be of much benefit to a new squadron."

The C.O. with the sobriety of the Sphinx, informed Ken that "this is a name posting" and he could do nothing about it. Ken wondered who had chosen his name and remembered the night they came back from a raid on St. Nazaire and extolled the fact that it was the proverbial "piece of cake", the easiest raid they had been on. The Winco remarked that the target was "a carpet of fire" and Ken recalls that if looks could have killed, his cake would have been burned. The Winco continued to say that Ken's crew were to be the backbone of the new squadron and set the standards for the new crews.

Berlin was warm even though it was March and the defenses gave them their usual high calibre reception. They identified the target, but the P.F.F. markers were not down, so they circled only to see them dropped some 7 to 17 miles from the target.(Bomber Command War Diaries, p371). However Ken's crew bombed the target and returned to base in their aerated aircraft and received the usual reward of ... one egg for breakfast. The crew was able to catch a few hours sleep before packing their kitbags and at the appointed hour climbed aboard an open air transport and headed for Scampton. Ken met W/C Nettleton three months later at Scampton. He was talking to G/Capt Ernie McNab in the mess and seemed surprised to see him. Ken learned from him that only one crew was still alive among the crews who were there when he left the squadron.

On the night of July 12/13, 1943, W/Commander Nettleton's Lancaster was shot down by a German night-fighter, over the channel, while returning from Turin. He and his crew all perished.

On their arrival at Scampton they were allotted married quarters which in peace time would have housed an airman's family. As the crew were all N.C.O.'s and having settled who would be up and who downstairs, and stashed their gear, they met other aircrews who were also wondering "what was up?" Rumours started and as more aircrews arrived they discovered that many were wearing D.F.C. and D.F.M. ribbons and they soon realized that there were a great many experienced aircrew and that this was to be no ordinary squadron. Ken's Cockney wireless op. remarked, "Skip, if we're the backbone of this outfit, then we must be near the ass end." Yes, they were the sprogs among the elite group and in the minds of them all was one question, which would not be answered until May 15th, 1943.

There were four Canadian pilots in the squadron, three N.C.O.'s and one P/O. There was also an American whom the Winco found amusing, and as the word got out that W/Cdr Guy Gibson's favourite types were not Canadians, perhaps the American might act as a buffer since he was in the R.C.A.F.. It wasn't long before one of the Canadian crews were shipped out. A few days later as Ken's crew were crowding through the crew room door, Ken ended up last and closed it. The W/C told him to report to his office after briefing...his first encounter with Guy Gibson. When he arrived in the office he was surprised to find he was on a charge for being late for briefing. He thought the W/C was joking, but soon realized that this was not so. The charge was read out and he pleaded "guilty". The W/C asked Ken if he would accept his punishment and when Ken answered in the affirmative, Gibson ordered him to wash all the windows in the briefing room...inside and out! Why the lesson in humility? He never found out but this would not be the last time Ken felt the brunt of the Winco's wrath.

Then came the raids on the dams!! Three of the dams in the highly defended area of the Ruhr were considered primary targets for 617 Squadron's bombers, the Mohne, the Sorpe, and the Eder. The Mohne and the Sorpe were responsible for 75% of the available water being held back in the Ruhr valley. The Eder dam was a source of hydroelectric power with a capacity of some 200 million tons of water. Ken was pilot of F Freddie which had trouble finding the dam due to heavy mist, but Ken dropped down low and released incendiaries which lit up the area. His bomb aimer Sgt Oncia was enabled to place their bomb accurately on the target, although the dam still remained standing and it was later found that it was immune to the Wallis bomb because of its structure.

After the dams raid the Winco's attitude towards Ken changed appreciably and he invited Ken to join him in a night out with some of the others in Nottingham. Incidently, Ken was the only Canadian pilot to survive the dams raid and 617 Squadron.

Ken's third Officer Commanding was Group Captain Cheshire who had taken a demotion in rank to take over 617 Squadron.

On the night of 12/13, Feb 1944 Ken and his crew took off for Anthear Viaduct, a single line railway viaduct between France and Italy which the Germans were using to supply their forces at Anzio. Ten Lancs. from 617 Squadron were used.

The sides of the valley were very steep and the target well defended. Cheshire and Mick Martin were the first to arrive at the target area and they found that visibility was just fair in the dim light. Ken heard Martin ask Cheshire to provide fire cover and the transmission was loud and clear and as an aircraft passed Ken outbound, he assumed this was Martin. It was a tactic commonly used where the lead aircraft would try to draw the flak by firing its guns, while the second plane carried out the attack in its shadow, so to speak. The Winco acknowledged Mick's request with "O.K. Mick", but his transmission was weaker than Mick's. Ken then saw an aircraft turning away from the target just as the flak guns commenced firing and Mick's aircraft was badly shot up, his bomb aimer being killed while both Mick and his flight engineer were wounded in the legs. The aircraft sustained unbelievable damage but Mick was able to land at a small American airstrip on Corsica. The rest of the aircraft completed the bombing of the target with heavy hearts and great determination and returned safely to base, except for a Canadian pilot and his crew.

Ken was angry at what he had witnessed the night before and in an interview with the wingco blamed him for what had happened to Mick. Ken's words were emotional and bitter, but the wingco did not rebuke him, nor did he try to defend his actions.

In his book, *Cheshire V C*, page 111, which is very revealing, Cheshire compares his own run-in with Martin's, declaring harshly, and with scant respect for his five subsequent lone attacks, that he had lost his nerve; it had never happened to him before. This admission from a man with the highest awards his country could bestow on him is the mark of this man, for in Ken's opinion G/C Cheshire V.C., D.S.O. & 2 bars, D.F.C., was and is the bravest of the brave.

Ken then went to Lancaster Finishing School, supposedly to instruct for three months, but Canadian H.Q. denied him his chance to fly operationally again.

After demobilization, Ken joined the Winter Experiment. Here he flew a variety of aircraft including the Lanc, the Hally, Hudson, Ventura, Mossie, Lib, Lincoln, Hastings, North Star, Spit, Mustang, Meteor, Vampire and Hornet. It was at Edmonton where he flew with the first jet aerobatic formation display team. Before leaving the unit in July 1949, he purchased a surplus Spitfire and entered it in the Cleveland Air, but as he had no previous close circuit racing experience he allowed another pilot to fly the Spit. It placed third.

Ken transferred to the staff of the Officer's school in Toronto and a year later was transferred to Trenton to take command of the Search and Rescue Unit and the Air Armament Flight. His other activities are much too numerous to be included in this profile. Suffice it to say he has flown over 40 types of aircraft and logged over 8,000 flying hours. His decorations and medals include

C.G.M., C.D. and Bar, 39-45 Star, France/Germany, Italy, C.V.S.M and Bar, War and Defence medals. He married Beryl Blackband in 1945 and has four sons and one daughter and today lives in White Rock enjoying tennis and golf.
Born of the sun, chastised by war, beleaguered by faith, endeared by luck.

ACTING W/C
HENRY (HANK) NORMAN BURROWS
PILOT R.C.A.F.

Hank Burrows was born in Stewartstown, Tyrone County, Northern Ireland on August 2nd, 1915. He emigrated to Toronto, Canada during the depression of 1929, receiving his elementary and secondary schooling there. Later he attended Central Tech., in Toronto where he took an aeronautical course. During his youth Hank was involved in model aircraft building and flying, representing Canada at several International Model Flying contests.

During the year 1935-36, Hank was a member of #10 R.C.A.F.(NP) Squadron, but in 1937 resigned and worked his way over to England on a cattle boat and joined the R.A.F with a Short Service Commission. He completed his Elementary Flying at Feltan Air Park (Hanworth) on Blackburn B.2's. From there Hank went to the R.A.F. Depot at Uxbridge, and then was posted to #11 F.T.S. at Wittering, flying Hawker Audex and Hawker Harts. At the beginning of 1938 he was posted to #4 Group and #215 Bomber Squadron flying Handley Page Harrows and Vickers Wellingtons. Later in the year the squadron moved to Honington in #3 Group and Burrows remained with the squadron until the outbreak of war the following year. Burrows was then posted to Bomber Command HQ as an assistant to S/L T. Chilton in the Navigation branch before being sent to the Royal Aircraft Establishment at Farnborough to test navigational aids.

With an invasion threat in 1940, Burrows became attached to #214 Squadron at Stradishall, flying Wellingtons. From Stradishall he was posted to Air Ministry as O.R. 3A in the Operational Requirements Department, under W/C Ted Chilton. Later he was sent to #31 Air Navigational School at Port Albert, Ontario, Canada. Returning to Bournemouth, England, Burrows became C.O. of the training school there. Twelve months later he was posted to Air Ministry taking an Air Sea Rescue course at Blackpool. This resulted in a posting to HQ Middle East Command in Cairo where he was placed in command of Air Sea Rescue and Accident Investigations. He remained there at HQ.ME in Cairo from 1943 to 1945 when he received a compassionate posting back to the U.K. to get married before being discharged.

While at Stradishall in 1940, Burrows witnessed several crashes of aircraft taking off or returning from operations. On one occasion as an aircraft was taking off for Malta and the Middle East, it swung off the runway and crashed into one of the hangars. The groundcrew (including a Padre Harrison) rushed to the crash and managed to get all the crew out safely before the aircraft exploded. On another occasion an aircraft returning from operations crashed at the end of the runway and caught fire.

Padre Harrison was again observed rushing into the wreckage to rescue some of the crew. He was awarded the George Medal for his gallant effort.

During his posting to Air Staff at Air Ministry in London, Burrows lunched frequently at Naronies Bar just off Trafalgar Square. This bar was visited by Naval Officers who were on special duty as members of an expert bomb disposal team. On one occasion Burrows observed an officer making a telephone call and then walking to the bar, ordering a tall drink and then leaving in a hurry. He had responded to a call about a land mine that had come down and was lying in the middle of Charing Cross Bridge. He had taken a healthy drink to steady his nerves before proceeding to the bridge where he was successful in defusing the mine. It was later learned that he had been awarded the George Medal for his brave deed.

Burrows was discharged from the RAF in 1945 and received the following medals: 1939-45 Star, the Aircrew Europe Star, the Defense Medal, the 1939-45 Victory Medal and the Bomber Command Aircrew Medal.

Hank Burrows returned to Canada with his English bride and joined the Domtar organization as a sales representative. He remained with that company until his retirement in 1980. He now resides in Sardis, B.C.

F/LT E.A. (TED) ALLAN, D.F.C., C.D.

PILOT R.A.F. & R.C.A.F.

Ted was born in Edmonton, February 2nd, 1915 and lived there until he completed high school. He got started in the flying business when he was fourteen years old, working during the summers and weekends as an apprentice air engineer, for Western Canada Airways. Many years later, his teacher was his engineer on two occasions, on the first of which they ferried a Liberator across the Atlantic with radar parts for D Day.

Besides learning to be an engineer, Ted also took flying lessons at the Edmonton Flying Club and did his first solo in 1931 at 16. He and his family then left Edmonton, to live in Ottawa and he immediately joined the Ottawa Flying Club and carried on with his flying, intermittently, as he was then taking pre-medicine, at the University of Western Ontario, in London.

In 1938 Ted joined the R.A.F., travelling to England with other recruits on the "S.S.Askania". By this time he had both his private and limited commercial licenses. He was first posted to #11 E.F.T.S. in Perth, Scotland (similar to the future Commonwealth Air Training Plan), then he went to #9 S.F.T.S. at Hullavington in Wiltshire. Here he won his wings and in January was commissioned.

Following this he went to a bombing and gunnery school at Warmwell, Dorset, then to 8 Squadron, a Fairey Battle unit at Boscombe Down. After two posting cancellations, he was sent to a Ferry pool, operating out of Hucknell, where he tested and delivered aircraft all over the country, until the end of 1939. The pool then moved to France where, for the remaining months of the "phoney war", he delivered aircraft to Rheims, Lille and Seclin. When the German blitz began in 1940, he was posted to No 4 Ferry pool in Cardiff, Wales, but he had hardly arrived, when he was returned to France to join a squadron, flying Battles.

This squadron was soon wiped out and everyone had to make it back to England by whatever means they could. Ted found a Blenheim that was unserviceable and had been abandoned, but with the help of the ground crew, he made it flyable and took off for England, with everyone he could cram on board (about 12 people). He was almost immediately sent back to France with an Anson, carrying a demolition crew, who were to blow up ammunition dumps and bridges, before the Germans could get to them.

While there, he and his crew of two, found an abandoned NAAFI depot loaded with all sorts of goodies. One of his boys stocked up with cigarettes, the other found about $ 3500 (in pounds of course), which he brought back to England, but had to hand in. Ted found whisky and loaded his parachute bag with Haig's Dimple, which he *didn't* turn in, and this greatly improved his war in those trying times.

Safely back and finished with France, he was then sent to Central Flying School at Upavon, Wilts, where he qualified as an instructor, being posted to 12 S.F.T.S. at Grantham, where he taught flying until 1941. He was then posted back to Canada to 33 S.F.T.S. Carberry, Manitoba and for a year, taught student pilots on the Harvard and Anson. He was promoted to Flight Lieutenant in September that year and was made Flight Commander in 39 S.F.T.S. at Swift Current, Saskatchewan, then the unit was moved to the Calgary Municipal Airport, where he again taught on the Harvard.

In March 1943, before being posted back to England, he took part in a bond drive, with "Buzz" Beurling, spending a month with him in Moncton, awaiting a ship to take them overseas. Back in England, he went to a Wellington O.T.U. for a course on transport flying and was subsequently returned to Canada to 45 Group in Montreal, where he again became an instructor.

In the winter of 1943 and part of 1944, he was based in Nassau, Bahamas as a 45 Group instructor, often doing overseas trips himself. On one, he delivered a Liberator to Accra and was then ordered to proceed to Lagos. The captain of the B.O.A.C. Boeing C314B Flying Boat, carrying an important purchasing mission, had been taken ill and Ted was instructed to act as co-pilot on the flight west. The aircraft carried two complete crews on board, for the very long ocean crossing and Ted enjoyed flying the big boat. Later in 1944, the R.A.F. transferred Ted back to England, to be the training officer at No. 246 squadron, a V.I.P. transport unit flying Libs. This squadron carried all the most important people - Churchill and his close advisors. Thus, Ted attended the Yalta Conference, flying Field Marshall Hastings and other high ranking officers, from London to Malta and to Saki, the airport for Yalta.

In January 1945, Ted transferred over to the R.C.A.F., but stayed with 246 squadron until No 426 squadron R.C.A.F. was formed late in the year, where he was again the training officer. In January 1946, everything wound down and he returned to Canada again, this time to civilian life. He retired in March that year, after six years of flying many types of aircraft, often under harrowing circumstances.

Back in civilian life, Ted immediately applied to TCA (Air Canada now) but was rejected because of his age, all of 31, but in June that year, he met Grant McConachie, had a chat with him and was hired and started with C.P.Air the next month. He began his flying with C.P. out of Edmonton, to the Yukon and to Fairbanks, Alaska.

In 1948, during the severe Fraser River flood, he transferred to Vancouver, flying the domestic routes to Fort St. John, Sandspit and Calgary. He was made Captain in 1950 and flew the same routes as a reserve captain, until 1953, when he was moved to Montreal. Six months later however, he was back in the west, to Vancouver, where, except for a four month stint flying relief in Winnipeg, he stayed. Later, he was able to hold a position on the overseas routes.

In his airline career, Ted has flown the Lodestar, DC 3, DC 4, DC 6, the Britannia and the DC 8. He made his last trip on March 29th, 1969 and was grounded medically, with rheumatoid arthritis. Ted figures he has amassed a total time of around 30,000 hours in the air and has flown 143 types. He recalls, that at the beginning of World War II, the British Government impounded all civilian aircraft that were in the country, and there were many different kinds, some whose names are lost in history. Ever hear of a Hendy Heck? Ted has flown one. Or a 4 engine DeHavilland 86B? He's flown one of those too!

Ted was married to Eileen Jones in May 1941 and they have one daughter and one grand-son. He holds an Honorary Life Membership in the Air Force Officers' Association in Vancouver, is a keen coin collector, stamp collector, a model aircraft builder and despite a derisive snort from his wife—a gardener.

He holds the D.F.C., 1939/45 Star, C.V.S.M. and Clasp, War Medal and Defence Medal and also the C.D.

CONSOLIDATED LIBERATOR MK Ⅴ 600 - No. 10(BR) SQUADRON R.C.A.F.
GANDER NFLD. - SUMMER 1943

F/O EBER RICHARD IRWIN CARRUTHERS
PILOT R.C.A.F.

Eber was born in 1920 at Portage la Prairie, Manitoba, a son of the manse, his father being a United Church Minister back east. Eber's education was in Manitoba as were his first two years at Brandon Normal School. Between 1939 and 1941 he taught school at Dand, Manitoba, then at Lady Hubble Public School.

Joining the R.C.A.F. in December 1941, he was first posted to E.F.T.S. in Brantford, Ontario, graduating as a pilot on February 5th 1943. Three months later, Eber was posted overseas to A.F.U., R.A.F. Station Shawbury, Shropshire, where he was assessed "above average" at 1534 B.A.T.School. His next move was to Flying Instructor School at Upavon, Wilts, graduating as a Flying Instructor (Single and multi-engines). In fairly quick succession he was at #11 (P) A.F.U. at R.A.F. Condover, #1 Beam Approach School R.A.F. Watchfield, then #1524 B.A.T. flight R.A.F. Newton, Nottinghamshire.

Still on the move, Eber was transferred to #16 O.T.U., R.A.F. Upper Heyford/Barford St. Johns, (this was a Mosquito High Level Bombing School). Finally he was posted to 571 Squadron at R.A.F. Oakington, 8 Group, Mosquito Light Night Striking Force. Later he volunteered as Mosquito pilot, for service in the Far Eastern Theatre. Eber was honourably discharged from the R.C.A.F. in 1945 after hostilities ceased.

After the war, he attended the University of Winnipeg and then graduated as a Chemical Engineer from McGill University in 1949. In all, Flying Officer Carruthers made some 600 training flights with over 200 student pilots. His medals include the 1939/45 Star, the France/Germany Star, C.V.S.M. and Bar, the War and Defence Medals.

Many pilots experience a real thrill, by flying at high speed, on low level cross country flights. The flash of the houses and roads under the nose of the aircraft, the accurate gauging of aircraft height above ground - or high tension wires, gives an exhilaration never savoured by land locked humans. Map reading at low level becomes a real challenge, because the student pilot is not allowed to climb to 1,000 feet, to find his location. He must learn to stay close to the ground for the protection it can give, if or when an enemy aircraft is on his tail. Also he must find his way back to base before his fuel runs out.

One day, Eber took a recently arrived student pilot on a low level high speed flight in a twin engine Oxford II - the standard training aircraft. When he told the student to turn left onto another course, a slight downdraft and a shudder throughout the aircraft signalled danger. The port wing tip had hit a tree!! There was a gaping hole in the leading edge of the wing. Suddenly, unexpected questions arose -- could the aircraft be flown back to base? was there some structural damage to the wing? would it fold up as soon as a turn was made? Gingerly, Carruthers took over the controls, and flying straight and level, back to base, put the aircraft down gently. Safe once more!!

The proximity of 16 (P) A.F.U. to the rolling hills of Wrexham, Wales, made it necessary to climb directly after take off. This was especially important in the many night flights, when dark clouds hung low over the airfield, obscuring the horizon. On the other hand, the low clouds afforded good protection against marauding enemy fighters. These training conditions were harbingers of the weather and terrain, which many student pilots would experience, when on full scale operations.

One dark, horizonless night, at Wrexham, Eber took a student for his first night flying in Great Britain. Shortly after the aircraft was airborne, the starboard engine failed. This necessitated hard left rudder, dipping the port wing a little, holding the aircraft straight and then applying full throttle to the port engine.

Carruthers vividly remembers glancing down at the runway - not enough room left to abort the take-off - no choice but to try a single engine circuit from 100 feet. Holding a steady take-off pattern, Eber told the student to radio "Mayday" to the control tower and request permission to make a cross wind landing. At 200 feet, he could see there was a chance for success; after a climbing turn onto the downwind leg of the circuit, the aircraft was at 800 feet - the danger had passed, it was now time for the descent and they were high enough to cut the port engine and attempt a glide landing. It was so smooth that all three wheels kissed the runway together! Sweet Mother Earth!

Now what to do? Not the time to stop. He must restore the confidence of the shaky student pilot! Carruthers immediately signed out another aircraft and took off again for the assigned flying lesson, with the student.

After the war ended, Eber was honourably discharged in August 1945 and availed himself of the Canadian Government post war veteran's assistance, by attending McGill, as mentioned earlier in the narrative and then he joined the British American Oil Company in 1949. After 18 months, he joined Asbestos Corporation Ltd., in charge of friction material manufacture.

In 1955 he went to the Johns Manville Research Division in New Jersey, U.S.A. and in 1962 returned to Asbestos Corp. as Technical Director, in which capacity he served until his retirement in May 1986.

His first marriage ended in divorce and he had three children, John Graham, Peter Hugh and Margaret Alice Louise. In 1971 he remarried and he and his wife, Norma Margaret, a previous University Nursing teacher, reside in Langley, B.C.

F/LT. J.B.(Barry) CHASTER
PILOT R.C.A.F.

Barry Chaster was born in Duncan, B.C. in 1921. Shortly after he started school, at Duncan Elementary, the great depression hit. Since he was the oldest in a family of eight children, it must have been a challenging time for the whole family but Barry remembers these years as being truly happy ones. He loved outdoor life, the fine fishing and hunting that Vancouver Island had to offer. In Duncan high school Barry was active in Basketball, Tennis, Golf, Soccer, Rugby, Softball and Lacrosse and still had time for studies.

Jobs were not easy to come by, but he managed to work as a clerk in a shoe store and as a logger in the local mill.

Although he was a member of the 3rd. Btn. of The Canadian Scottish Reg. as a reservist, Barry enlisted in the R.C.A.F. in February 1941 as a pilot. From Brandon he went to I.T.S. Regina, then E.F.T.S. in Fort William, #11

S.F.T.S., Yorkton and on to Montrose, Scotland for a stint of training on Masters and Hurricanes, then next to #1576 B.A.T., Middleton-St.-George on Oxfords and finally to O.T.U. Finningly, Yorkshire, leaving fighters, to Ansons and Wellingtons. Number 25 O.T.U. was moved to Bircotes, Yorkshire, where he took part in the 1,000 plane raid on Essen. Barry was getting to be a multi type pilot and added to his list, Manchesters and Lancasters, when posted to #83 Sqdn., Scampton, Lincs, where he flew ops. on Bordeaux, France.

Another posting to #207 Sqdn., Bottesford/Swindesby broadened his range to ops. along the Danish and Swedish coasts, and to Wismer. Number 207 moved to Langar, Notts., from here they raided LeCrueset, northern Italy, and were in on the 1000 plane raid to Bremen. In all, 14 more op trips were added to his log book while with #207.

Repatriation did not stop Barry adding to aircraft types, nor for that matter to his rank, having been progressively, Sgt., F/Sgt., W.O.1, W.O.2, P.O., F.O., and finally Fl/Lt.

Aircraft types were more of a random addition than a progression. Until demob July 18th 1947, Barry touched many bases; #8 B.G. Lethbridge - Ansons, Bolingbrokes, Harvards, Lysanders; #12 Communication Squad. Rockcliffe-Electras, Beechcraft, Dakotas, Grumman Goose, Lodestar; 165 Squad. Sea Island - Gliders, Lodestars, C60's; while at Uplands there were no new types. At #412 Communications Rockcliffe, he added Chipmunks and other marks of Beechcraft. While there he managed to fly with G/C Louis Leigh to the United Nations San Francisco conference (1945) where he met the then Prime Minister, Mackenzie King. Barry's medals were 1939/45 Star, Aircrew Europe, C.V.S.M. and clasp and the War and Defence Medals.

This social whirl must have palled, for soon, Barry was back in civvy street attending U.B.C. where he earned a degree in Architecture and a Masters in planning; the city of Vancouver was glad to get his services, where he remained as town planner until retirement in 1985.

He now has more time to spend with his wife, Kae, visit his two children Jolayne and Randy also grandchildren, Michael and Christine, and to reminisce with his two sisters Ruth and Joyce who were also in the wartime R.C.A.F. A brother, Ray, also served in the R.C.A.F. but has since passed on.

The most memorable event in Barry's flying history was the night (Jan 3rd, 1943) when he was shot down on an experimental raid on Essen. Twenty Lancasters - 10 from his squadron (207) and 10 from another squadron, were to bomb flares set by Mosquito Pathfinders over target at 20,000 feet. The weather was to be $9/10$ths over-cast. But with high winds, it cleared. They dropped their bombs practically in the flares (Mosquitos were using a new homing navigational device, H2S) and they were immediately coned by search lights. After violent evasive action, they escaped the search-lights and proceeded for home. However they picked up a night fighter flown by a veteran German Ace, Manfred Meurer, who had shot down 69 aircraft before being killed himself in 1944. He attacked them three times but the first shot by cannon on an upward firing gun was the killer. It knocked a big hole in the fuselage midships. They dropped to 15,000 feet, when he attacked them again, knocking out the starboard motors. Barry gave the order to bail out, but the forward hatch was jammed. The Flight Engineer handed him his chest pack and retired to the rear, along with the Bomb Aimer. He decided to see if he could make it to England, but the fighter attacked again, right up the middle and the plane started to roll at 5000 feet.

Barry opened the small window along-side his seat, pulled the rip cord and shoved the parachute and his head out the window. It might be noted that there are only about 6 inches between the port inner prop and the fuselage. When he came to, he was drifting down in his chute, not properly done up, with a hole in the chute. He could see a plane burning on the ground. He had perspex in his head and was bleeding a little.

He landed rather heavily in an open field, picked up his chute, and headed for the woods. He buried the chute, checked his wounds and started walking away from his landing spot as lights were coming across the field toward him. It started to snow and it was cool in only a battledress, so he put his handkerchief over his cut head and his service cap on with straps under his chin.

Near morning, after scrambling over fallen logs and deep underbrush, he again came to open country, somewhere south east of Roermond, Holland. He went into a barn, got a little sleep and then approached a farmer. He told him in English that the Germans were billeted next door and that he couldn't help, but gave him an old overcoat, and with his escape kit which he always had tucked in his battledress tunic, he set out in a north west direction heading for the coast, or so he thought. He walked for several hours, visited a church, no food or wine, so he dug up a mangel, in case he really got hungry. He hid under a bridge for an hour or so, then said "To hell with it" and started walking again. Approaching a city - Roermond - and a bridge across the Meuse River, he walked over the bridge and gave the guard the deaf-dumb sign and he let him through. He walked on through or along the fields and approached a farmer in a cart, but he was afraid to help. Near dusk, he approached another barn on a farm. Much ado over his appearance - - later, three men came to the barn -- one was the Chief of Police for that sector. They took him into the farmhouse and the ladies fussed over him with food, hotwater bottles etc. and he had a good sleep. He drove in the Police Chief's car to the Holland/Belgium border and stayed in a house 1000 or 2000 yards from the border. Anna Van Horne recalls his stay, as he was the first airman she helped - after that she helped a thousand more people, for which she later received a medal. Barry met her when he returned to Holland/Belgium in 1987, - his first visit back to Europe since 1943, with his Bombaimer, John Banfield R.A.F., who lives in Kent, England.

He left Anna's that night and walked over the border and was met by a friend with bicycles, and they biked for a while, then got on a tram. Arriving at Liege, Belgium, he stayed there with a storekeeper and was treated by a doctor who removed perspex from his head with the aid of cognac. He was overseen by a chap named Joseph Heenan, who claimed he was a spy - having deserted the Belgian army. He also visited him in 1987 in Brussels. (He told Barry he was part of the famous Comete Line, but at that time, the Germans had infiltrated the network and the Line was collapsing, both behind and in front of him. Two weeks after he left Liege for Brussels by train, he was captured and spent 28 months in Dachau, one of the worst Nazi prison camps. He was one of the few who survived and is still living.) In Liege they were going to fly Barry out by Lysander but because of the breakdown sent him on.

He had stayed in Brussels for about 2 weeks with a Mrs. Paulisen (now deceased) and in a separate house, with two women (E. Warnon and E. Leigois), whom he also visited in '87. They also spent 24 months as Nazi prisoners.

These people and others who helped them really risked their lives and are among the bravest people he has ever known. There were not many of them in 1943, who put their lives on the line for airmen. One other whom he missed on his 1987 visit, was a man known as "Joseph", whose real name is Albert Greindel and believed to be a Baron and was also known as NEMO. As the Comete Line was broken down, he escorted Barry all the way to Spain. He went by train from Brussels to Paris where he actually met Albert, collected 2 Americans in Paris and proceeded on to Bayonne. Nightfall he caught a train for the Pyrenees and got off at the Spanish border in no-mans-land. They climbed the mountains all night and arrived at a mountain cabin where other guides picked them up after a meal of eggs, with cafe-au-lait that tasted good, especially after the mangel!

Headed for civilization - another long walk - they were met by a taxi and headed for Portugal. However, they were caught by the Spanish Police and put in jail in Elazondo. It snowed that night again, no windows in jail just bars. So he paid the taxi driver and they were escorted to a better jail in Pamplona. Menu - soup twice a day. Seven in one cell, built for one man. One American, 2 Czechs, Joseph, 1 Belgian, 1 Englishman and Barry. The two Czechs played in the prison band and for this they got meat in their soup.(They had escaped from the "Organization de Tote" in France.) Three weeks later the British Military Attache got Joseph, the American and Barry out of the prison.

He drove to Madrid - said goodbye to Joseph and the American and took the train to Gibraltar, stayed a week, then took a ship to Britain. The irony of that, was that the convoy was attacked and one ship was sunk. He returned to Britain and after a few months was repatriated to Canada.

PILOT OFFICER THOMAS S. COLBECK
AIR BOMBER R.C.A.F.

Thomas Colbeck was born in Dauphin, Manitoba and his parents, like many before and after, heard the siren song of the West Coast and moved to Vancouver in 1932. Tom grew up in the east end and attended Tecumseh and Charles Dickens public schools and King Edward high school, and enjoyed playing basketball, softball, tennis and fishing. Prior to enlisting Tom worked for the Hudson's Bay Store in Vancouver. He took a pre-enlistment course for air frame mechanics at Vancouver technical school and joined the Air Force in July 1941.

Tom was an "A" group Rigger/L.A.C. when he re-mustered to air crew in 1942 and was posted to #7 I.T.S. Saskatoon which included R.A.F. and Polish airmen at that time. From Saskatoon he was posted to #7 B.& G. at Paulson, Manitoba and then to #1 A.O.S. at Malton, Ontario where he graduated to Sergeant Air Bomber in August 1943. After graduating he was posted overseas on the "Queen Mary" and went to #1 (0) A.F.U. at Wigtown, Scotland which started his training in preparation to being posted to an operational squadron. After A.F.U. he took his O.T.U. at #84 O.T.U. Desborough and Harrington, then followed a commando course and conversion course at #1657 conversion unit and a short time at #3 O.F.S., Feltwell. Finally in May 1944 the crew was posted to #514 squadron at Waterbeach, Suffolk, and they were to report on June 30th after a period of leave.

An incident which Tom recalls, occurred while the crew was on a cross country at O.T.U. and they were flying about 12,000 feet, when the pilot, Jack Hannesson of Vancouver stated that he could hear music, to which Tom replied "Heavenly Music?" and Jack said "Yes". None of the rest of the crew heard the music and everyone laughed. Jack was killed in a mid air collision a short time later. On recounting the story with some U.S.A.F. aircrew Tom found that they had had the same experience. This is the type of incident which gave rise to the fact that aircrew are inclined to be a superstitious lot.

On their arrival at No. 514 squadron, the crew found that they were scheduled to go on a daylight operation to Villers Bocage, France; their aircraft was to be "P" for Peter. There was little time for pre flight preparation and when they were shuttled to their aircraft for take-off, it had not had an air test and the armourers had run into problems and had not yet completed bombing up. With only seconds to go before take-off, the armourers finished their work and the crew climbed aboard, taxied to the runway and took off on their first operational sortie.

The formation was to assemble over Luton but unfortunately "P" Peter arrived late and no other aircraft were visible so the skipper headed for the south coast to catch up and join the formation at a designated point on the coast. The rear gunner spotted a group of bombers approaching from the rear so the pilot turned to formate on the group to identify the squadron and approached them from their starboard side. Tom reported that a Lancaster was closing in on them and the pilot elected to dive under this aircraft to avoid a collision. Unfortunately there was another Lancaster slightly below the first one and it was necessary to dive even more steeply in order to miss this one. As they passed under the second "Lanc" there was a hell of a crashing, grinding noise as the tailplane of the second aircraft crashed into the cockpit of "P" Peter, instantly killing the pilot, Jack Hannesson, and the flight engineer. Tom's parachute had been moved from its regular spot by the armourers while they were setting the switches on the panel and when he reached for it after the collision, it was a bit of a shock to find that it wasn't there; however he reached into the turret and located it and managed to get one hook attached to the harness. Tom remembered not being able to get off the floor and the next minute he was falling through the air with debris from the aircraft. His parachute was rotating in the air, unopened, and held by only one hook and he managed to pull it towards himself so he could reach the ring and open the parachute. When the chute opened Tom's flying boots fell off along with his maps and foreign money and he floated barefoot to the ground. Fortunately his parachute caught in an apple tree and his fall ended about two feet from the ground. An excited Englishman ran up shouting "Are you theirs or ours?", and on learning that he was a Canadian, invited him in for a cup of tea and to meet his wife and daughter. Tom was then rushed to the King Edward VII Sanatorium where he met his wireless operator, Bert Brown, who was less fortunate and was hung up painfully in a tree about 30 feet from the ground. Tom suffered only minor scratches and bruises as he was thrown from the plane and Bert received a cut which the doctor stitched up while Bert was anesthetized by brandy in the absence of the usual anesthetic. The others in the crew never got out of the aircraft (Jack Hannesson was promoted to Pilot Officer posthumously one week after the crash) and were all killed.

Upon returning to duty, Tom was posted to No. 90 squadron at Tuddenham, Suffolk and was crewed up with an R.A.F. crew who had seen the collision; they were amazed that anyone got out alive. The rear gunner of the other plane was killed when his turret collided with the cockpit, the pilot ordered the rest of the crew to bail out and then courageously landed his plane with the badly damaged rudder and tailplane.

August 9th, 1944 is the date of another memorable experience in Tom's wartime career in the R.C.A.F. The new crew piloted by Flying Officer Tony Cooper was on an operational sortie to Engles, France, with fourteen one thousand pound bombs on board, their aircraft was Lancaster "U" for Uncle. This was considered to be a "milk run" and after successfully bombing their target, as they were nearing the French coast on their return to base, they were hit by flak. The bombaimer's compartment was a mess, Tom's intercom was shot in half, the camera had been hit and pieces of shrapnel were sticking all around in the nose section. It was later ascertained that there were over forty holes in the nose section and gas tanks. Tom's guardian angel looked after him again and he didn't receive so much as a scratch. They were flying at five thousand feet when they were hit and the pilot reacting swiftly, put the nose down to increase speed and to get away from the coast. He told the crew of his plan but Tom's intercom was out of commission so he did not know what was happening, all he could see was the North Sea approaching at a rapid rate. He grabbed his parachute, unfortunately by the rip cord and the chute released into the bombaimers compartment. He gathered up the chute and hooked it on to the harness and jettisoned one part of the escape hatch and was on his way out when a hand grabbed him and restrained him from leaving through the hatch. They were diverted to Mildenhall and needless to say they appreciated the tot of rum they were given during the interrogation.

Tom prided himself on his bombing skills ever since bombing school and an incident on a daylight raid in September showed that he had the courage of his convictions. His crew was ahead of him in operations completed and Tom had to do an extra trip to catch up and he was chosen to fill in with another crew whose pilot was a Squadron Leader. The operation was to soften up the Germans who were surrounded at Lehavre by the British and Canadian armies but who would not surrender. They were the lead bombers on the target. On the bombing approach, Tom set the wind direction and lined up the target in the bombsight and gave a course correction which the pilot tried to change. Tom stood his ground and stated that he was in charge at this stage and continued on his corrected course. The pilot threatened that something drastic would happen to Tom if he fouled up the bombing run. When they returned to base and the picture showed a perfect hit, Tom felt a certain satisfaction that he had carried out his duties according to his standards, even in the absence of an acknowledgement or apology from the Squadron Leader.

The longest operational trip that Tom made was on the night of August 22nd, 1944 when the target was Stettin, Germany. The bomber force left in daylight and the route followed a course over the north sea, across Norway and Sweden then to approach the target from the north. Sweden did not have a blackout and was lit up like a Christmas tree; shots were fired at the aircraft but somehow none found their mark. When they arrived over the target, the city was burning furiously and Tom's crew dropped their bombs and headed for home. The flight engineer reported that they were low on fuel when they were approaching the English coast and when they reached base, it was fogged in with a ceiling of under 300 feet and they were diverted to Newmarket. As they let down over Newmarket, again through very low cloud, they nearly hit a church steeple and again they were diverted to Mildenhall. The pilot requested permission to land immediately as they were practically out of fuel, and the tower gave the green light. The pilot made a good landing and they just got to the end of the runway when the fuel ran out. The trip had taken ten hours and fifteen minutes and they had burned two thousand one hundred and fifty gallons of gas. Once again the crew enjoyed a hell of a nice toddy of rum at the interrogation.

Tom's tour of operation included a lot of invasion support, dropping dummy parachutists over Utrecht to help the allied parachutists. A lingering memory is on returning from Lisieux, France on the morning of the invasion, seeing what looked like whitecaps on the channel but which in reality were masses of boats; it was an unbelievable sight. Tom earned the 1939-45 Star, Aircrew Europe Star, Defence Medal, Canadian Volunteer Service Medal and bar, and the War Medal.

Sometimes Canadians didn't get along with some R.A.F. officers and the converse was equally true; Tom's C.O. on 90 Squadron was in the latter group. Tom applied three times for a commission but the C.O. wouldn't let him see even the adjutant. After he had finished his tour of operations, Tom was repatriated to Canada, and was up before a board who asked why he had never applied for a commission. Tom related his past efforts and of the attitude of the C.O.. The board said that they knew of the officer and Tom was granted his commission at that meeting. He volunteered for a second tour but was told that they had enough air crew and Tom received his discharge on February 15th, 1945.

After his discharge, Tom joined the Vancouver Fire Department and retired as District Chief after thirty six years of service in 1982. He married Mary Davies in 1950 and they have three sons, two daughters and nine grandchildren.

S/LDR R.V.(RON) DARNBROUGH, C.D.
AIR GUNNER R.C.A.F.

Ron was born in Victoria, B.C. but grew up in Vancouver and took his schooling there. He attended Lord Kitchener Elementary School, Point Grey Junior High and Lord Byng High Schools. He was active in sports and played Canadian football for Lord Byng High School. After school he joined C.P. Airlines in their repair depot at Sea Island as an aircraft fitter.

In 1942 he decided to enlist, and joined the R.C.A.F. as an Airgunner. From the Recruiting Depot in Vancouver, he was posted to No.3 Manning Depot in Edmonton and then to No.3 Bombing and Gunnery School at McDonald, graduating as a Sergeant Air Gunner in July 1943 and in August 1943 he was crewed up at 1659 Heavy Conversion Unit at Topcliffe, Yorkshire. On September 15th, 1943, he flew on his first operation with 429 Squadron, Leeming, Yorkshire, only one month after leaving Canada. He completed four trips with 429 squadron and then the crew was transferred to 433 squadron and carried out thirty three more sorties from that station.

He was screened and received his commission in July 1944 and was transferred back to 1659 Heavy Conversion Unit at Topcliffe, doing fighter affiliation training with sprog crews, which, Ron said, "scared the hell out of me, most of the time". After four months he was posted to "Dalton-on-Ouse", where he took an Instructors Course and did so well, that he was sent to the 6 Group Instructors School as an instructor. This ended his flying career with 6 Group; he remained at Dalton, until he was posted back home to Canada, via the Repat Depot in Warrington. Back in Canada he ended up at 24 O.T.U. Boundary Bay near Vancouver, where they flew Liberators and B-25's and was there when the war ended. He was demobbed in Vancouver in 1945.

Three members of Ron's first crew, completed their tours before Ron had done the required number of sorties and Ron relates how he became crewed up with his second crew. After his pilot was screened, the crew was given a week's leave, which Ron spent in London. Returning to the squadron, Ron became a "spare gunner" and as such, flew one trip with a Warrant Officer Major to a buzz bomb site; it was a piece of cake. When they got back to base, it was daylight and as they circled the airfield they saw a strange sight on the field. There was a Hallybag on one of the runways and there was another Hally resting on top of it.

These aircraft had been scheduled to fly on the operation and were the last two in the line of aircraft marshalled ready for take-off; they were to have been the last two to take-off. As the first of them was preparing to leave, the wind changed and they were instructed to taxi down the runway and take-off from the far end. As they taxied down the runway, someone gave the second aircraft a "green" and the plane started to roll. About half way down the runway, aircraft number two caught up with aircraft number one and slid up the fuselage as far as the mid upper turret. There was not enough of a jar to set off any of the bombs and there was no fire. The rear gunner of the bottom aircraft was killed but no other crew members were injured. The skipper of the bottom aircraft was F/O Hank Wright. Ron contacted Hank the next day and joined the crew to replace his former tail gunner.

Ron did nine trips with this crew, one ending in a belly landing. Their tenth trip was a memorable one for Ron, the target being Stuttgart. They lined up on the runway for take-off. It was daylight, and they got the green. Ron was sitting in the rest position and was plugged in to the intercom, (he always liked to know what was happening), Hank opened the throttles and they started to roll, the tail came up and they started to become airborne. Suddenly, the aircraft swung hard to port and they were on the grass, off the runway and bouncing across the infield. Ron could hear the bombs rattling on the shackles, when Hank said "Christ we've had it". What the crew members inside the aircraft did not know, was that there was a pretty good fire burning along the port wing. The aircraft came to a stop, still in one piece, and everyone made a very rapid exit, then ran to a nearby ditch in record time. Just as they jumped into the ditch the fire got to a gas tank or to a bomb and there was a very big bang. There was nothing left of the aircraft but two wing tips and the tail turret. No one was hurt, although they were all put in the hospital for the night, and the next morning they were all screened. Ron was told that his commission had come through the night before and he was given a week's leave and on his return, was transferred to Topcliffe as an instructor. Ron likes to claim that his tour ended with a bang!!

On returning from his leave, Ron was to experience another strange occurrence. He arrived back from leave, a brand new P/O and got cleared and ready to leave for his new posting at Topcliffe. He went to the M.T. section to ask about transport, where he was greeted by a corporal who advised him that there was no transport available, as it was being used for "M" Day; the King was coming to the station that day and they had to be ready for him. Ron checked with the Adjutant and was told that he was cleared and didn't belong to the station any more and that he had better hit the road and walk over to Topcliffe; so down the road he went, with his full marching gear, gas mask, tin hat and webbing, his kit bag over his shoulder, heading in the direction of the roundabout at Thirsk station. When he was about three quarters of the way to Thirsk, he saw two motorcycles coming, in front of a very large car with a large pennant. He realized that he was about to meet the KING on a one to one basis. He faced the road, dropped his kit bag and hoisted what he thought was a presentable colonial salute. The King waved, the Queen waved, the driver waved and Ron picked up his kit and continued on his way to Thirsk!

He arrived at Topcliffe about 4 p.m. and found his way to the Officer's Mess. It was a typical Mess, with an entrance lobby about thirty feet square. In the lobby, two fellows were standing with tennis racquets and circling the lobby near the ceiling was a bat. The fellows tried to knock it down, without much luck, as the bat veered around them each time they took a swing. Ron also noticed that the two guys were a little bit stoned. It seems that the King had been to the Station, distributing gongs, before he left for Skipton, Leeming and other points, and a party had started as soon as he had left.

A corporal took Ron upstairs to his room. Topcliffe was a permanent station and a room with hot water heating was a pleasant contrast to the cold Nissen Hut at Skipton. He found a couple of friends and spent his first night at the station, very pleasantly. In the morning he got up to shave and found a door opening off his room, which led to a spectacular bathroom, white tile and chrome and very clean. As he finished shaving, another fellow came into the room through another door and passed the time of day, saying "See you at breakfast" as he left. Ron noticed his jacket as he left, it had four rings, a D.S.O. and a D.F.C. Later in the day the connecting door from Ron's room had been locked!!

After Ron was discharged in 1945, he spent about six years as a salesman. During this time he married his wife, Betty and they had a son. In 1948 he joined the R.C.A.F. Reserve with a fighter squadron (442, P51's and Harvards). Since they couldn't find an armament officer, Ron took over. In due course, the squadron became a Wing, adding another squadron. They got the first jets (Vampires) and added a radar unit, a medical unit and an intelligence unit. About this time, the Korean war became hotter and there was a bad prang in Quebec, which wiped out several Air Defence Command Staff. One thing led to another and Ron was asked if he would come back in the regular force. It meant dropping his rank to Flying Officer and he was sent on course after course, on things like radar gunsights, fire control systems, rockets and later into missiles. He spent about seven years in experimental work, with the Central Experimental and Proving Establishment and was moved to Cold Lake, Alberta with the Air Armament Evaluation Detachment. He got checked out as a rear seat occupant in the position normally filled by a Nav.A/I, but since he was checked out on all armament and fire control systems, in the all weather fighters, it worked out well, because he was the Project Control Officer on some of the rocket and gun work. Here he was, at thirty years of age, flying in jets. He finally retired as Squadron Leader in Vancouver in 1971.

Ron was awarded the 1939/45 Star, Aircrew Europe Star and France/ Germany Clasp, Defence Medal, C.V.S.M. and Clasp, War Medal, Canadian Forces Decoration and the R.C.A.F. Operational Wing.

After being discharged in 1971, Ron and Betty moved back to the west coast, where both their parents lived. They have lived there ever since and Ron is managing an apartment block.

SQUADRON LEADER J.R. GOWANS, D.F.C.,C.D.
PILOT R.C.A.F.

John Gowans was the fourth son of Mr. & Mrs. Wm. Gowans of Grand Forks, B.C. The family also had four girls, two of the boys and one sister were to serve their country on active service overseas. Bill joined the Canadian Navy on September 9, 1939, while Geraldine joined the Canadian Army Medical Corps as a nurse. John, the youngest son, was to join the Royal Canadian Air Force.

John received his early education in Grand Forks, completing his Elementary and Secondary schooling there. He obtained his Senior Matriculation in New Westminster and completed a year at the University of Washington in Seattle, before attending Normal School in Victoria.

Following his graduation from Normal School in the summer of 1941, John enlisted in the R.C.A.F., and was immediately posted to Toronto Man-

106

ning Depot. From the "cattle stalls" at the C.N.E. it was a quick trip to I.T.S. at Belleville and then a posting to Portage la Prairie for flying training on Tiger Moths. Finally it was a move to Yorkton for twin engine training on Cessna Cranes. Gowans received his wings on July 26, 1942 and was next posted to #31 G.R. School at Charlottetown before going overseas.

He had been selected for flying boat training on Catalinas and a Captain's course, so was posted to #131 O.T.U. in Killadeas in Northern Ireland. On completion of the course he was sent to F.T.U. in Stranraer, Scotland. Gowans and his crew went to Beaumaris in Wales to pick up a new Catalina, FP 282, and returned to F.T.U. to prepare it for operations.

On March 18th, 1943, the crew was finally posted to their squadron, #413 R.C.A.F. Squadron in Ceylon and left Stranraer on March 26th for Plymouth as the first step of the journey. Being "in transit", the aircraft was not allowed to be armed and after leaving Gibraltar the aircraft had to fly south of the desert war and east across the breadth of Africa over the desert area to the Nile, a distance of almost 2000 miles. As the Catalina approached Cairo fuel was very low, and Gowans decided to land at Alexandria.

As the aircraft was touching down in the harbour at Alexandria one engine cut out for want of fuel - the trip had taken twenty hours. Gowans then cut the one still running engine and requested help from a thirty foot Navy m.v. for towing the Catalina to a mooring buoy. The H.M.S. Harpoon's skipper misjudged the speed of the boat and crashed into the starboard wing-tip float, bending it severely. What a day! No gas and now a broken float! It was eventually necessary for the aircraft to fly with floats down to Cairo, locate a repair unit, to become serviceable. The delay took ten days.

Leaving Egypt, Gowans and his crew flew to Lake Habbaniya in Mesopotamia (Iraq), then to Basra, landing on the Euphrates river. Finally the crew was off to Karachi in India and then on to Koggala Lake in southern Ceylon and #413 Squadron. The flight from Stranraer in Scotland to the Squadron's base had taken twenty six days and an elapsed flying time of ninety eight hours.

At the Koggala base the crew were given two days to have their Catalina FP282 checked out, and do some air tests before making their first operational trip. In April 1942 S/L Len Birchall of the Squadron had become the "Saviour of Ceylon" by sighting and reporting the position, course, and speed of the Japanese invasion fleet before being shot down. A similar attempt to invade was suspected during April 1943. Gowans' first trip on operations was to make an "anti-invasion search" for enemy naval units that were thought to be in the Malacca Straits off Sumatra. The trip was made through a monsoon storm without incident and took over twenty hours.

Gowans and his crew flew convoy escort patrols, anti invasion searches, and air sea rescue missions over the vast expanses of the Indian Ocean, and the Bay of Bengal, in all types of weather, including the monsoons - from bases in Ceylon, and India, as well as from many tropical coral atolls such as the Maldivian Islands, Seychelles, Mauritius, and Diego Garcia. On some islands no maintenance was provided and crews were responsible for their own minor repairs and overhauls. Refuelling took many hours at bases where four gallon "Jerry" cans were the only available supply. However long their trips might have been, the crew had to refuel their Catalina before getting a much needed rest. The key word was "monotony". Crews from the North Atlantic were unhappy to find themselves shunted to this "Indian Ocean Backwater".

On one of Gowans patrols he and his crew were involved in a rescue operation for the tortured survivors of the JEAN NICOLET, an American merchant vessel, in what has been called the worst atrocity at sea in W.W.2. Torpedoed American seamen were made to run the 'gauntlet' atop the Japanese U-Boat between rows of enemy sailors who struck them with iron bars, tools and wrenches, and then bayonetted them into the shark infested waters. Gowans operator had picked up the Mayday signal while on a patrol elsewhere and so Gowans altered course for the position given. As the Catalina hove into sight the submarine quickly submerged leaving the survivors awash on the deck. Every seaman had been beaten. Eighty seamen were lost, while twenty three were saved.

It is to be noted that the U-Boat Captain Arizume later in the war became a Flotilla Commander, and afraid of postwar crime trials committed "hari kari" and was reportedly buried at sea.

Doug Stewart, the second pilot in Gowans crew, visited the twenty three survivors rescued, at an island hospital later, and was thrilled and amazed to find that the last survivor picked up was Jack Van Ness, a pal of his from his Hollyburn Ski Club days in Vancouver years before.

On November 3rd, 1943, while escorting a convoy in the Nine Degree Channel off the southwest coast of India, Gowans was ordered to provide extra cover to a straggler that had some troops aboard. At about 10:30 p.m. in the early evening moonlight he headed astern of the convoy, when suddenly A.S.V. contact was made four miles from a submarine, which soon became visible in the moon's wake as being fully surfaced and moving rapidly towards the straggler. Gowans moved in to attack from a height of fifty feet and was met by heavy gun fire from the U-Boat. The submarine suddenly turned at right angles out of the moon's wake into the darkness. Gowans turned about and attacked a second time. This time the submarine headed up the moon's wake and an attack was made from the quarter with depth charges. The submarine was seen to be sinking at a great angle as darkness closed in. Heavy 20 mm gunfire from the U-Boat had damaged the elevator and rudder controls so Gowans requested immediate relief. None was forthcoming, so the Catalina stayed with the convoy continuing to give it cover throughout the rest of the night and morning until a fuel shortage required it to land at Cochin before returning to the Koggala base. The convoy was molested no further. The night's escort patrol had lasted over eighteen hours. Gowans was later awarded the D.F.C. for the attack.

By August 12th, 1944, Gowans had completed over 1,790 hours, 1,442 of

108

them on Catalinas while overseas, with 1,009 hours operational and a completed tour. He had flown eighty patrols with forty eight of them over fifteen hours in duration. Following his tour Gowans was made Flight Commander of the Squadron with the rank of Squadron Leader. In January 1945 the squadron was posted to England - Gowans arrived back home in Grand Forks in April.

In September 1945 he entered the University of British Columbia at the third year level and in June 1947 graduated with a degree in Mathematics and Chemistry. He started teaching at the Senior Secondary School in Kelowna that fall. In July 1948 John married Mary Henderson, who also served in the R.C.A.F. They have three children, two boys and a girl.

During his teaching in Kelowna John was active in coaching track and basketball. He was President of the Kelowna Kinsmen Club and in 1953 became District Secretary of the Association of Kinsmen Clubs of B.C.. He was Secretary-Manager of the Kelowna Regatta for one year. In 1959 he moved his family to the coast and obtained a teaching position in the Coquitlam School District. He became principal of the Montgomery Junior Secondary School in 1964, and in 1967 accepted the principalship of the Terry Fox Senior Secondary School in Port Coquitlam and served in that capacity until he retired in 1980 after suffering a heart attack.

Retirement activities include water colour painting and involvement in Legion activities at West Point Grey Branch No.142. He is past President and a Life Member of that Branch. John remained active on reserve strength of the R.C.A.F., serving on the Recruiting Office in Vancouver during the summer months for thirteen years and was awarded the C.D. for his service. John's other medals include the '39-45 Star, CVSM & Bar, Defence Medal and War medal.

He and Mary now spend their summers at their camp at Christina Lake near Grand Forks.

SHORT SUNDERLAND MK III EK591
No 422 (GR) SQUADRON
BASED AT ST. ANGELO, NORTHERN IRELAND
NOVEMBER 1943

F/O L.R.G. DENT D.F.C.

BOMB AIMER R.C.A.F.

Another bumper crop of boys arrived in the early and mid-twenties of the twentieth century.

Amongst these were two boys in one of the multiplying families of Dents. The first one arrived in Regina about 1922 and the other one in Liskard, Ontario in 1924.

The parents named the oldest one Gilbert and the next one Ronald, but if you asked Ronald what was his first recollection, he would say it was Limerick, Saskatchewan, with jack rabbits, shotgun shells, snow and flat country. His hobbies in sport included racquet ball, tennis and golf.

From there they moved to Orillia, Ontario with a big house, two cars, a maid, making maple syrup and his first year of school.

Then there was a change in the financial affairs of men, resulting in a move to Port Sydney, Muskoka, Ontario, to live for six years in a house owned by someone else. High school started in Huntsville, then Bracebridge, Ontario, and then to Orono, Ontario, followed by his first real job in an advertising agency in Toronto.

By now it was 1942, Ron was eighteen and everyone was going, so he enlisted in the Air Force in Hamilton, Ontario.

Manning depot Toronto and thousands of men was a new experience for Ronald whose brother was already overseas as an air frame mechanic.

Somewhere along the line some nameless and faceless sergeant tried to teach this bag of (unmentionable) tied in the middle, how to march and march he did.

Bombing and gunnery at Jarvis was a step up from trying to hit ground-hogs with a rusty .22, and just as difficult.

Thinking about arriving in Chatham, New Brunswick in the middle of winter, just for the fun of riding around at night in a very drafty Anson and you will know why learning to drink Seagrams V.O. and gingerale was one of the pastimes.

But it didn't help, the sextant was just too much for this farm boy and the thought of long patrols over the Atlantic as a navigator resulted in the option to go back to bombing and gunnery as a bomb aimer.

Somewhere along the line, brother Gilbert went missing over the Kattegat, after switching to Air Crew.

This was 1943 and a real travel year for Ronald, first Halifax, then Bournemouth, then some other places in the middle of England with more Ansons.

One night Ronald had his faith tested in his R.A.F. pilot after the port engine just stopped running and the pilot complained he couldn't hold altitude. Wheels up, down they all came, over the outer circle, pitch black and "clang clang" as the metal props bent back.

Ron didn't realize, when everything got suddenly very quiet with no lights of any kind to give any reference, that the aircraft was still moving. After ordering two other unfortunates out of the hatch he went out and fell on his face as the tail plane just kissed over the top of his head, still rolling down the runway, (the plane not his head). The first man out didn't come to for a few minutes and it was probably just as well that he couldn't remember where he was, otherwise he might have been very annoyed at Ronald for telling him to get out.

Finally crewing up, and his first raid in a Wimpy from O.T.U. on September 3, 1943.

This trip did not work out very well at all, one bomb hung up, photoflash never went off, then back over England one engine quit, wouldn't feather, started sparking and the fire extinguisher didn't work.

When the navigator jumped,so did Ron, facing forward, parachute wrong way round and now it was his turn for amnesia. After he was half way out and his boots blew off, the next thing he knew was when he woke up on the ground with a very sore neck.

His debriefing came in Oxford Head and Spine Hospital where he learned that he and the navigator were the only two who got out. After convalescent hospital, a lonely few days at some nameless station before a new crew at his second O.T.U. As fate would have it, Ronald, as a result, avoided the murderous winter of 1943-44.

By this time he had also married one of the nurses from the convalescent hospital and was spending a good part of his time off the base, which may explain why he didn't know any of his squadron mates too well.

By the time it was up to twelve or thirteen trips he and his crew qualified for a brand new aircraft, "Q for Queenie", which his pilot Orendorf promptly took up, and feathered three engines to see if it would still fly.

Sometime later, when on daylight raids on flying bomb sites, it was on the bomb run that for the first time he saw flak close enough to see the orange hearts. "Skipper they're shooting at us" he shouted. Orendorf soothingly replied "No, they're just putting up a barrage". BANG, RATTLE, BANG, RATTLE, BANG, RATTLE, it was time to dump the load and check for damage. He was amazed that gasoline could pour out of the wing of an aircraft without catching fire and just a little uneasy at having to limp back at low speed with all these smoking stragglers and no fighter protection.

Ford Emergency 'Drome was a real bounce, first on one wheel and then on one plus a flat tire. After this large four engine aircraft finished wobbling off the runway, seven figures scattered in seven directions.

After a memorable high-low split poker game in the Sergeant's mess when Ronald was holding a sure win tight (so he thought) someone else had the temerity to pick up both the high and low pot with a bicycle 1,2,3,4,5, of spades.

Then when Ronald was offered a commission no one thought to inform him that they did not play poker in the officer's mess, only bridge, otherwise further consideration may have been given before accepting the commission. As it happened on one memorable game Ron won six shillings from Frank Covert the Halifax lawyer, and his little twisted mind thought that if he could best a lawyer at bridge then perhaps that would be a good line of work for him.

Somehow or other after this, there were gaps in between trips and when the last trip came up everyone was a little rusty including the navigator. On the way in to the target, since they were early, the situation called for a five minute dogleg north then five minutes back to track. Somehow or other instead of turning on back to track they just kept on the same direction as the dog leg back and ended up coned over the Ruhr.

This was not their first time up stage front, coned in a blaze of light that shone all through the aircraft, but happily it was their last.

The thought has always occurred to Ron afterwards, that when the searchlights came on, the compelling thing to do was to take a bow. After all it was theatre, the theatre of war. Ron was awarded the D.F.C., 39/45 Star, France/Germany Star, Defence Medal, War Medal and C.S.V.M.

Arriving home safely the young Ronald attended U.B.C. Law School, graduated and two more marriages and eight children later is still practicing away.

F/O ROLAND ENOS D.F.C.
BOMB AIMER R.C.A.F.

Roland Enos was born in Montreal, Que. He attended school at St. Dominic's elementary School and, for his secondary education, went to Sir George Williams High School. He majored in Commerce at Vocational.

Growing up in Montreal, Roland's sport activities centred on softball and hockey. Prior to joining the R.C.A.F. in 1942 he worked as an order clerk. During his training, under the Commonwealth Air Training Plan, and following Basic Training, he flew in Anson and Bolingbroke aircraft, completing that experience in July of 1943.

In August of '43 he was posted to England and continued his training for 'operations' on Ansons, Wellingtons and Halifax's, then was posted to #425 Squadron in May of 1944. Roland flew on 35 sorties over Europe in a five month period, finishing in September, during which time he received a promotion to Pilot Officer.

P.O. Enos was posted back to Canada wearing the Distinguished Flying Cross. Back 'home' he served as Liason Officer for Air Cadets and held that post until he was discharged from the R.C.A.F. in June of 1946 with the rank of Flying Officer.

After his discharge, Roland attended university, taking first year Commerce. Subsequently he worked as a supervisor and office manager, with an industrial firm.

From 1946 to 1956 he served as C.O. of #96 Air Cadet Squadron.

Roland and his wife, Betty, have two sons - David and Gregory; three daughters - Veronica, Beverley, and Susan - and six grandchildren. He received six decorations and medals - the D.F.C., Volunteer Service Medal, 1939/45 Star and clasp and Operational Wings, War Medal and Defence Medal.

Roland was posted to #425 Alouette Squadron, part of #6 R.C.A.F. Bomber Group, stationed in Yorkshire. Immediately arriving at R.C.A.F. Station Tholthorpe, the crew, consisting of two officers and five sergeants, were billeted together in one corner of a Nissen hut. They were promptly informed by another crew member living in the same hut, and puffing on his long stemmed pipe (Austrian type), that Enos' crew were sleeping in the "Coffin Corner". They were told they wouldn't last long on the squadron as previous crews in their corner went for a "Burton" soon after arriving on the station. A very sobering thought, as one could imagine. Ironically, this particular crew member met his end on his very last sortie over enemy territory two months later. Needless to say, his cherry wood pipe was collected as a souvenir on their first day. Much to Roland's dismay the pipe was handed over to him. On his first leave he gave the pipe to his future "father-in-law" as a memento which, after hearing the story, he dubiously accepted. However, he felt uncomfortable with it and returned it to Roland, when he completed his tour.

OPS ON BORG LEOPOLD

After briefing, their crew was told "The target for tonight is a Military Hospital, housing German Officers, convalescing from the Eastern Front. Your objective is to stop them from returning to active duty, thereby helping our ally, Russia. It will also allow the N.C.O.s to vent their frustration against officers in general". Being extremely naive, they were shocked to hear this. The crews were conditioned by the newspapers and news-reels, that they only bombed "military targets". But they surmised that all is fair in war.

The Halifax was loaded with 16 - 500 lb. bombs and they were given E.T.A. on target, heading, air speed and height, together with met. forecast and a pep talk from the W/C. It was then time for the R.C. Padre to hear confessions and give Holy Communion, as they were largely an R.C. group. Then they were despatched to their various "kites" in the dispersal area, awaiting the time to "scramble", to get in line for take off. This was a well defended target. Imagine flying 2 1/2 hours in complete darkness and then suddenly on "the Bomb run" to the target, all hell breaking loose! Bombers immediately forward and to the port and starboard were being shot down in flames and Rolands crew tried to concentrate on hitting the designated flares over the target while they were expecting to go down next. It was a successful mission, as shown in the target pictures taken by another crew on the same raid. The crew was very happy to get back to 'home base' for eggs and chips!

A night raid to Stuttgart started off normally at 21.15 hours, on July 25th, 1944. It was only at E.T.A. on target that the crew realized something was amiss. There was 7/10 cloud cover. The captain, F/O Dargis, requested pin-point reading from the Bomb Aimer. It was found that the plane was near the German-Swiss frontier. The navigator was upset with this pin-point reading, as it intimated that he had made a navigational error, which was not the case as it will be proven later, however, the captain confirmed the pin-point from his abbreviated map. It was decided to drop the bombs live over Germany before setting course for home base. As the bombs fell, a Junkers 88 fighter was spotted on the port side, heading towards the #425 Halifax. They altered course into Swiss air space and headed towards home, enduring some inaccurate Swiss flak whilst the German flew a parallel course over German territory, until it was lost in the clouds. Checking the fuel tanks, it was found there was insufficient to reach base. Permission was sought to land at R.A.F. Stationford, in the south of England, and at daybreak the aircraft landed safely.

Another mission, this time to Hamburg, proved to be the toughest target during the whole of Roland's tour of operations. Hamburg was very well defended by many batteries of searchlights and powerful Ack Ack guns. The flak was so intensive that one could easily walk on it, with German fighters operating on the perimeter of the city. A major effort was called for by #6 Group, so all available aircraft and crews were present at the 'briefing' for the all important raid. The Enos crew was assigned to a Halifax "U", whereas the Halifax "K" they used, on the previous Stuttgart raid, was assigned to the crew of the lad who smoked the cherrywood pipe. Unfortunately, the latter crew failed to return from this sortie. it was therefore surmised that both the Gyro and Magnetic compasses in the Halifax "K" were unserviceable.

Another major effort to Hamburg was called for by No. 6 Bomber Command on the same target as the night before. On this particular night, the weather at home base was deteriorating rapidly - but they all scrambled to their aircraft; Enos had one of those inexplicable premonitions that he wouldn't be coming back from this sortie. Imagine his elation when the raid was aborted at the last minute, due to poor visibility at base!

F/LT ART COY
PILOT R.C.A.F.

Art Coy was born in North Vancouver, B.C. He received his schooling there, graduating from North Vancouver High in 1935. He was active in sports, favouring badminton, tennis, basketball, swimming and skiing. He was also active in youth organizations, usually associated with the church.

Prior to joining the R.C.A.F. in January 1942, he worked as a Mint Craftsman, Royal Canadian Mint, Vancouver branch, melting and purifying gold shipments for assay, before shipping it to Ottawa.

He was accepted for pilot training and released from his job in January, 1942, and took all his training in Alberta, receiving his wings February 5th, 1943, and was immediately posted to Instructor's School, Vulcan, Alberta, then to MacLeod, to instruct on Ansons for a year and ten months.

Although instructing was repetitious and often routine, there were moments that remain unforgettable.

As a means of testing a student's ability to read instruments and react to them, Art would place him "Under the Hood" at a safe altitude, tell him to close his eyes while Art placed the plane in an "unusual position" (usually nearing a stall and with one wing low) then he would call "You have control" and let the student recover.

On one occasion he watched the student's hands grasp the wheel (his head was under the hood so not visible). He moved the wheel a couple of times then dropped his hands to his lap. Art took control and asked why he was not attempting to fly the plane. He lifted the hood immediately and a very red, irate face appeared, as he said "But Sir, you told me to close my eyes!!!"

Yet somehow, we still won the war!

In July, 1944, Art was posted to #5 O.T.U. at Boundary Bay and Abbotsford, "crewed up" there and, after a stay in Bournemouth, a flight to

116

Karachi, then Bombay, and a long tedious train trip across India, ending at Jessore, 75 miles north-east of Calcutta, joined 357 Squadron, R.A.F. Special Duties.

Over the whole tour of 372 hours, the crew averaged 15 1/2 hours per trip, between the first on March 13th, 1945 and the last from Minneriya in Ceylon, on July 3rd, 1945. The shortest trip took 6 1/2 hours and the longest twenty-two hours, fifty-five minutes, having flown 3729 air-miles in that time, at an altitude of 500 feet over water.

There was one memorable trip to a valley, code named "Hebrides", in the mountains of Northern Malaya, south of a small town named Yala.

The clouds usually sat right on the hill tops and made any approach from higher level very difficult, so the proposed new route was from a pin-point at Khota Bharu, an old airport east of the hills, which had been heavily damaged by the Japanese, earlier.

From there and remaining below the cloud level, they found a pass through the hills into a fairly wide valley, which proved to be their dropping zone.

On the ground, small fires blazed in a neat triangle, plus a "T" of old parachute strips, indicating wind direction, and a letter "K" flashed by a very excited looking man on the ground below. Also on the ground were more white strips spelling out the letters "F" "O" "O", easily interpreted as "FOOD", probably the strips for "D" had been used to make the "T".

Apparently these men had been starving for some time, due partly to the proximity of the enemy and to the low clouds which seemed always to be covering the surrounding hills which ranged from 2500 to 5000 feet and prevented preceding crews from letting down safely. Wireless reports over the past months had indicated their condition, the latest request for food had started with "Reduced to eating our shoes".

Art's plane had entered from the east end of the valley and his bomb-aimer, George McGregor, noted a small river to the west, which showed on the map as running out of the valley, then turning north into another valley toward Yala. They checked this rather warily and found it made an easy route out. On subsequent trips to "Hebrides" they used that little river valley as their entry and were able to stay below the clouds and out of trouble.

Since the threat of enemy action was, at that point, being discounted, they often travelled in brilliant moonlight, skirting individual storms where they could see the rain beside them. On two occasions they saw what they felt would have been a rainbow but with no colour, only different shades of grey. It was actually a long arc and exactly as a rainbow would have been during the daylight, but without colour.

At this point they were informed that the length of tour was increased to 400 hours, so in June, three trips, and July, one trip more completed the tour. The Squadron headquarters was now at Minneriya and China Bay in Ceylon, flying across the Indian Ocean to Sumatra and Malaya, probably safer, but not as interesting as the north to south runs from Jessore, average time about 20 hours per trip.

No reference to 357 Squadron would be complete without a tribute to the ground crews, whose record was second to none; their ability was never doubted and crews flew with complete confidence that the planes were always in top repair and capable of any long trip. They and the Pratt and Whitney Wasp engines they serviced deserve a great deal of credit for the many successful trips carried out over long distances by the squadron members.

Navigators were by far the busiest crew members and deserve the greatest credit for their efforts.

On June 14th, 1945, Art was told to take one of two old Liberators to Cawnpore, carrying extra crews, so that they could pick up newer Liberators with more time left on them. The two old Libs. were in the BZ class, almost antique from their point of view. However, each had over 20 hours left so were considered safe to use. They had most of the equipment and instruments, but significantly, as it turned out, no fire extinguishers in the engines.

Two and a half crews were put in each plane and travelled to Cawnpore without incident, only to find no planes ready for the return. It was hot at Jessore but one could sweat at least. At Cawnpore it was 120 degrees, with no shade, and the sweat dried so quickly it stayed on the skin as salt. When Art got into the pilot's seat, he touched the back of his arm against the metal of the seat and actually burned the skin, leaving a brown mark.

Since there were no replacement aircraft, they were told to return in the old BZ's. The other crews left first and found that they had no compasses working, ran into a violent storm and finally landed at Dum Dum (Calcutta).

Ray Jorgenson, Second Pilot, started the engines with some difficulty and by the time they reached the runway, the engines had overheated so were shut down to cool. They were restarted, after a time, found that #4 was very close to overheating but they left quickly, feeling that they could get up, open cowls and cool off.

They were about 15 minutes out when they could see #4 smoking heavily so feathered and turned back, realizing they had no way of putting out a fire. Art could not hold altitude on three engines but, checking with the fellows at the rear, discovered all the old armour plating and other parts were stacked there. As a result they scattered Liberator parts over that area of India until he was able to hold altitude at 1500 feet and, as the fire appeared out, made their way back to Cawnpore without further incident.

It turned out that #4 engine had "blown a pot",so was not to fly again.

They spent a very uncomfortable night at Cawnpore and, fortunately, were able to locate a replacement in the morning, this time in the KH class, in fact it only had 73 hours flying time to date. They could have it, provided Art test flew it, as they did not have a test pilot available.

He took it up for one circuit and landed, taxied back to sign papers and had to shut down to cool engines before leaving again. Only then did he receive the news that testing was not encouraged at noon, due to the excessive heat and the last time anyone did test at noon, they exploded at about 500 feet and all were killed. It was too late to complain, so they silently filed out and flew home.

On another occasion they were sent on a trip, likely to take at least 22 hours and had to pass through the intertropical front, about 200 miles of broken cloud and rain, on the way to Sumatra, where they turned across the Malay Peninsula, past Kuala Lumpur to the Kota Tinggi area about 35 miles north of Singapore.

In the intertropical front one actually flew between separate clouds from which rain was pouring into the Andaman Sea below. These downpours were so distinctly separated that a wing could be put into one and the rest would still be in sunshine, while that wing was being soaked.

The policy was to avoid going directly into these downpours as the lift could be affected by the probable temperature change. Certainly the visibility would be cut down for the time spent inside, so the course was altered slightly to avoid actually passing through and was corrected later as required.

A pinpoint would be picked up at Sumatra anyway.

A new First Pilot was aboard for this trip, for familiarization so provided an opportunity for Art to leave his seat and relax for a time on the flight deck behind the seat and below where the mid-upper gun turret had been. At this stage of the war, it had been decided that range could be increased if the plane was lightened, so, along with nose guns, belly guns, waist guns, and ammunition, the mid-upper turret had been removed and replaced rather roughly with a metal cover.

Art had dozed off briefly, when he was awakened by water dripping on his face, so he stepped up to the cockpit to investigate. What he saw was startling; the instruments indicated an altitude nearing 100 feet and loss of altitude over 500 feet a minute — down! They were completely within a downpour.

He hollered "pull up", reached past the throttles to knock the automatic pilot off and pulled back on the wheel. At this point both pilots in the seats pulled back on the wheel so were over-controlling.

He hollered "Level out" and they forced the wheel back to normal while setting the mixtures to "Full Rich" in order to use the throttles to better advantage, and were able to stop the downward drop, but he will never know how close to the water they actually came.

That was the first and last time that Art left his seat on any of those low level trips. The visiting pilot said he was amazed that he could see the water so clearly in that downpour. He was lucky that he didn't get a much closer look!

In any event, it is safe to say that they had survived a rather "dicey situation", probably due to a drop of water.

Art's medals include the Burma Star, 39/45 Star, Canadian Volunteer Service Medal & Bar, War Medal and the Defence Medal. He was discharged in February 1946 in Vancouver.

After the war he attended various night school courses relating to electricity, sales and management and joined B.C. Telephone Co. in September 1946 and was with that firm until he retired in 1980 as a supervisor of installations and repairs.

Art was married to Margaret Currie of North Vancouver, B.C. in 1947 and they have two daughters and one son, all married. They now have five grandchildren with #6 due before this book is published.

F/LT ALVIN P. FAST D.F.M.
WAG R.C.A.F.

Al Fast was born in the town of Laird, Saskatchewan. He began his schooling at Rosthern Elementary and, on completion, he moved to Rosthern Secondary School for his high schooling. Sports were the major activity which Alvin enjoyed.

On completion of his schooling, he went to work as a farm labourer and, by 1941 had moved to Langley, B.C. With the second world war well under way, Alvin volunteered for aircrew in the R.C.A.F., when a mobile recruiting unit visited Langley. It was four months later, when he was called to Saskatoon, to take his oath of allegiance and then off the next morning to Manning Pool in Toronto. His first posting was to Camp Borden, for a session of guard duty. From there he went to Guelph, Ont. for a twenty week course in No.4 Wireless School, followed by flying instruction on Tiger Moths and Norsemen. Having been assigned Wireless Operator and Air Gunner, he next went to Fingal Bombing and Gunnery School, from December 1941 to January 1942. He was promoted to Sergeant and posted overseas.

On arrival in England, Alvin spent some time in Bournemouth and soon was posted to #1 Wireless School at Cranwell, followed by assignment to #26

O.T.U. at Wing and Tring in Buckinghamshire where he was crewed up with English airmen. They began their ops on Wellington 1C's with 150 Squadron at Snaith in #1 Group. His pilot was killed flying with another crew for familiarization. With a new pilot his crew flew 7 operations from Snaith and then moved to Kirmington, Lincs, from whence they did six more ops, two of which were daylight trips to Essen and Emden. Al was promoted to Flt/Sgt., in November of 1942 and was posted to #156 P.P.F. Squadron in December. After four more ops, now on Wellington III's, his crew was split up.

Alvin joined a Canadian pilot, Flight Sergeant Horan, and moved onto Lancasters and continued through to April 23rd, 1943 when Horan finished his tour and a new pilot replaced him, a New Zealander, Flt.Lt. Mandeno, who had done a tour in Whitleys. In August of 1943, Al received two promotions, first to W.O.2 then W.O.1, and in September he was promoted to Pilot Officer, which had been effective in July!! He did his last op to Berlin on August 31st and eleven days later he was married to Helen MacLachlan at Warboys, Huntingdonshire. Helen was a Scottish W.A.A.F. on 156 Squadron. Alvin was assigned to #21 O.T.U. in September, stationed at Morton-in-the-Marsh until February 1944, when he was transferred to a Canadian unit at Pershore and then to Wellsbourne and Warrington Repat. Centre and then back to Canada on the "Queen Elizabeth".

Back in Canada, he was assigned to the Calgary Wireless School, where he took courses on release legislation by the R.C.A.F. and by D.V.A. Following his courses he went to Regina and helped to open and close #7 Release Centre. In 1946, now a Flight Lieutenant, Alvin Fast took his discharge from the R.C.A.F. at Calgary Release Centre.

Alvin's tour of duty from October 1942 to August 31st of 1943 involved a number of experiences of different character. His first trip was to lay mines off the coast at Brest, at a prescribed height of 700 feet, when they were attacked by a flak battery and the skipper dived to 300 feet.

The longest trip of his tour was to bomb the city of Turin, crossing France, seeing the lights of Berne, Switzerland, and across the Alps that were bathed in brilliant moonlight and on to bomb their target. They landed in time for an 8:30 a.m. breakfast, nine and a half hours after take off.

On one trip to bomb Berlin, their aircraft was picked up by a masterbeam, so bright they could see to read a newspaper at 19,000 feet. Alvin was in the astro-dome and had the presence of mind to reach down, switch the I.F.F. off and when the masterbeam went out, they proceeded to bomb the target.

In June of 1943, his crew had two trips, when their plane was damaged by German fighters. The first involved a diversion operation to Munster, during which, they were attacked by a fighter and the mid-upper gunner was hit in the hand but kept firing. The second was on a trip to Cologne and, again, attacked by a German aircraft. He hit the port inner engine and all the oil drained out. The mid-upper gunner on this trip was the Squadron Gunnery Leader and his first remark at de-briefing was "I could not believe the closing speed of our attacker."

Another sortie was to the Krupp Motor Works at Essen, where they were attacking from the north and the crew saw two Lancasters and a Mosquito caught in one search light cone and two more Lancs caught in another. As far as he could see, Alvin noted that all six got away.

On one trip to bomb Pilsen, flying over France at 3,000 feet, one of the squadron's aircraft caught on fire over Metz. Al's crew were able to count six parachutes before the plane crashed. The crash lit up a small village and they could see, quite clearly, the streets, the church, the town square and the trains moving about the railroad yards - a real hive of activity.

A highlight of Alvin's time in service in England was being invited to the investiture at Buckingham Palace to receive his D.F.M. from His Majesty King George VI.

Al paid great compliments and thanks to all the ground crews of #150 and #156 Squadrons for their dedication and expertise in keeping the aircraft in top condition.

The decorations and medals he received were the D.F.M., 1939/45 Star, Aircrew Europe Star, Defence Medal, C.V.S.N. and Bar, Victory Medal, P.F.F. Badge and Canadian Tour Wings and Bar.

Al was discharged from the R.C.A.F. in January 1946 at Calgary, Alberta and in civilian life became a butcher and owned a meat freezing plant. Helen and Alvin have three sons, Harry, Richard and Melvin and three grandchildren.

W.O.1 LYLE FLEMING
R.C.A.F.- PILOT

Lyle Fleming was born in Notch Hill, B.C. He received his Elementary and Secondary schooling at Revelstoke, and was raised there, playing most team sports in his youth. After School Graduation, Lyle worked as a "Finisher" in a paper mill at Ocean Falls, B.C.

Lyle enlisted in the R.C.A.F. in October 1942, as a pilot, and was posted to #3 Manning Depot in Edmonton, Alberta. His flying training began at High River on Cornells. After completing his Service Flying at Vulcan on Anson II's, Lyle was sent to Pat Bay, B.C., for O.T.U. on Expediters, and a Captain's course in Dakotas. He was posted to England for three weeks, and then was flown to Cairo, with an immediate posting to #267 Squadron, at Bari, Italy. His duties there, involved trips all over the Mediterranean area, (supply dropping, evacuating wounded, taking blood to the front lines, etc.) At the outbreak of Civil War in Greece, in the fall of 1944, between the Communists and Royalists, the Squadron was designated to supply the British contingent in Athens. Eventually, the airport there, was the only area in British hands.

Many Squadrons were later slated to go to the Far East, and as a result, some Canadian crews were broken up. A few went intact to #216 Squadron in Cairo, while other Canadians were posted all over the Middle East. Lyle was posted to Athens, to set up a briefing room. The airport to the west, was captured and the personnel there were instructed to remove all insignia and to turn in their paybooks. Unfortunately, the faded parts where wings and stripes were attached, could not be hidden. Luckily, after being under seige at the airport for two weeks a truce was signed.

Unknown to Fleming, the planning for the Yalta conference was being held and Athens was the last stop on the way. He was directed to get maps, but all the information arriving, was labelled "for Officers' eyes only". However, a week before the Delegation arrived, an officer was sent in to take over, and Fleming was relieved of much responsibility.

Shortly after VE Day, Lyle was requested to set up an establishment at Salonika. He refused the assignment, and was immediately posted to the Far East. While en route through Cairo, Lyle was advised that he would be sent home for thirty days leave, and was sent to an H.C.U. at Bilbeis on the Canal. He was flown back to the U.K. and landed in Dorset. On arriving in London, Lyle found that he was in the middle of VJ Day celebrations. He soon located a few of his old buddies from his training days and they convinced him, that he should sign up with the Occupational Airforce. He did so, and crewed up with a veteran from #435 Squadron in India. He flew as a co-pilot out of Odenham, on trips to Hamburg, Cologne, Berlin,and Vienna. In that city the crew was not allowed to leave their hotel, and were guarded by Russians with Tommy guns.(the equivalent)

Fleming then found that he was a member of one of several crews, that were loaned to British Overseas Airways to re-activate their pre-war routes. After an intense instrument course, he was sent to Croydon and assigned to the London - Athens run. It was a four day trip, with overnight stops at Rome, both ways, and at Athens. On one occasion, the crew picked up three newly created Cardinals, including one from Canada.

Being one of the last W/O 1 aircrews left in Europe, Lyle and his buddy, were detailed to march in the Victory Parade in London. It proved to be a highlight of his Airforce career. Lyle Fleming was discharged in August 1946 at Jericho Beach in Vancouver. He was awarded the 1939/45 Star, the Italy Star, the C.V.S.M. and the Victory Medal.

Following his discharge, Lyle was employed by the Department of Transport in 1948 as a Meteorological Technician. In 1961 he left that employment and took one year of teacher training at the University of Victoria. He had been attending summer schools for eleven years and had received a degree in 1958. He became a school principal in Prince George, serving from 1964 until his retirement in 1984. Lyle Fleming married Irene in 1975 and now resides in White Rock, B.C.

SHORT STIRLING · No. 1651 CONVERSION UNIT R.A.F.

F/O STAN LANCASTER C.D.

NAVIGATOR R.A.F.

Stan was born at Gateshead, County Durham, England in 1916 and at age five the family moved to Sunderland. He attended Hendon Boy's School and won a scholarship to attend Bede Collegiate Boy's Secondary School, Sunderland.

Stan joined the staff of The Royal London Mutual Insurance Society as office clerk. During that time his family moved to Welwyn Garden City, as work was opening up there, and there was a mass migration from the north country and from Wales, but Stan stayed on in Sunderland for almost two years before parental pressure forced him to go south. He there became accountant for Beiersdorf Ltd (makers of Nivea Creme) and it was here he met his future wife, Gaye Shopland.

His sport was badminton and he played for the county of Hertford before the war. He was called up on June 11th 1940, going to Cardington. After a week or so at Cardington, Stan was posted late one night to Morecambe where the usual square bashing and rifle firing took place.

Then followed almost six months at Binbrook, Lincolnshire as u/t S.P doing bomb dump guard and checking airmen's buttons. It was here that 12 and 142 squadron were based, flying Fairey Battles.

The police course at Uxbridge followed in December and Stan was chosen to be an instructor, especially since he had done two years as a special constable before "joining up".

After an exciting experience with a prisoner, Stan remustered to aircrew and went down to St. John's Wood in London for a week or so, then to I.T.W. Newquay, as course leader. Then he spent several weeks at Burnaston, near Derby, trying to get in his twelve hours on Tiger Moths. He failed to pass as pilot and was posted to Heaton Park, Manchester to await a draft to either South Africa or Canada.

He sailed to New York on the "Queen Elizabeth" (93,000 tons) thence by train to Mountain View, Ont. where he did among other things gunnery and bombing and then was posted to #31 B & G School at Charlottetown, P.E.I. He was again the course leader throughout the navigation course and took the entire wings parade leading up to the presentation. That one day, Stan had three ranks, corporal, sergeant, on receiving his N.B. wing and later in the day, Pilot Officer.

A G.R. course in Summerside followed and once again there was a decision to be made ... to Boundary Bay or Nassau. Unfortunately decisions are not made by the individual and Nassau was the next destination. Stan says if he had gone to Boundary Bay he most likely would have emigrated straight to B.C. in 1947 instead of 1977.

Then the entire course was called in for posting briefing and it was announced that they were all going to Britain. However "one crew is going to Ceylon" said the "announcer".

Stan's crew, pilot Lyn Pryce, a New Zealander with Ray Lassiter the co-navigator, flew a brand new Liberator KN 820 from St John, Quebec to India via The Azores, Rabat Sale, Castel Benito, Lydda, Shaibah, Karachi and Allahabad. There they handed over the Lib and took trains to Madras, then train ferry to Ceylon and ended up at Kankesanturai near Jaffna on 203 squadron (Coastal).

Flights went daily to the Cocos Islands, 1500 miles south east and mid-way between Ceylon and Australia, carrying medical supplies, which were then flown to Sumatra and dropped to troops fighting there. Stan was in Ceylon when the "bomb" dropped and later the squadron flew daily to Singapore to bring back repatriated prisoners of war. One of the things which amazed the crews on reaching Singapore was the stores filled with goods of all kinds, such as cigarettes, watches, fountain pens and cameras.

Early in December 1945 the crew went on leave and Stan was just enjoying wearing "blues" up in the hills, when an urgent signal came from the squadron telling him to report back at once. It turned out to be repatriation (Group 27) but Stan waited at K.K.S. for two weeks, then at Worli (Bombay) for another 3 weeks before finally boarding the "Ile de France" bound for England via the Cape, and after a month at sea finally reached Southampton early in January '46. Medals earned were Burma Star, Defence Medal, War Medal and C.D.

Stan received his grey pin-stripe suit on Jan 12th at Hednesford, Staffs and bade farewell to the "old firm" after serving five years and seven months. On reaching his home in Welwyn Garden City he saw his daughter, Diana age 16 months, for the first time. Then followed 22 months with his prior employers, until October 1947 when he emigrated to Toronto. During the past year he had organized a branch of the Royal Air Forces Association in Welwyn Garden City.

He flew alone in a Skymaster to Toronto at the end of October, was employed by his firm's agents there for two months and after meeting his wife and daughter at New York, they went to Charlottetown, where they stayed for over nine and a half years.

He was active in many organizations, became P.E.I Badminton Singles, Doubles and Mixed champion in 1949,50 and 51. He also joined #5 Signals Regiment Reserve Army, with rank of Lieutenant and found time to organize and direct the Charlottetown Male Voice Choir. A second daughter, Patricia, was born in 1950.

After a year and a half with an insurance company he joined the staff of Wells Organization, Church fundraisers and was with them for six years. Stan was invited to join a similar organization at United Church Headquarters and again the travelling took place, for over four years, until in 1967 he decided to form his own one man company and he limited his geographic field of operations so he could be home each night. In the meantime, in 1957 he and his family moved to Peterboro, then to Mississauga and finally on a trip to B.C., just "to look", in 1976, they saw a house they liked in Mission, put a down payment on it and moved west in 1977.

In 1981 Stan and his wife bought a house in Langley, the children having "flown the nest" in 1967 and 1971 and presenting them with three grandchildren, Zenija Esmits and Sarah and Michael Bragg. Stan has continued with fundraising consultancy and he says he expects to retire one of these days.

On joining up June 11th 1940, the only aircrew trade immediately available was airgunner and as Stan was six feet one and a half inches, he settled for Service Police as he had done 18 months volunteer work as a "Special Constable" in Welwyn Garden City, Herts. Later, at a Radar station near Barrow in Furness he had to escort a 6' 4" prisoner to Wing Headquarters in Liverpool as he had broken "open arrest" and he was put in close arrest as he was considered dangerous.

As the personnel were all billeted out, a clothing vehicle used to come at infrequent intervals, when those who needed new clothing etc., were supplied with it. The very day the vehicle arrived the C.O. decided Stan should take the prisoner to Wing in the truck and after lunch they all boarded it. The driver and the clothing corporal in the front seat and the prisoner and escort sitting among the used clothing in the back. It was a bitterly cold and snowy day in December and they tied the tarp down at the back of the truck so that the snow would not sweep in and make things even more uncomfortable.

After an hour or so, the prisoner asked Stan if he could stand up and stamp his feet around as he was very cold. Stan gave him permission and watched him jump up and down for ten minutes until suddenly he sprang on top of the already half frozen S.P. Of course he had the advantage of being on top and having some blood circulation and he managed to loop a portion of the tarp's ropes round Stan's left wrist and to a strut, and using the elbow as a lever he exerted pressure upwards until Stan thought his arm would break. In fact the prisoner said if he didn't stop struggling he would break his arm.

So Stan stopped struggling and was relieved of his Smith and Wesson 45, which was in his holster and loaded with 5 rounds, and then he was ordered to sit up on the bales of clothing just behind the cab of the vehicle. A few minutes later the truck began to slow down and immediately the gun was stuck in Stan's ribs and the prisoner ... no longer a prisoner ... put a dirty shirt over his hand to cover the gun if one of the lads from the front came around. Fortunately no-one did and the truck began to pull away again. Stan was ordered to throw over the wallet and comb belonging to the ex-prisoner and he undid the tarp, climbed onto the tailboard and when the truck slowed to round a corner ... coincidently in the city of Lancaster ... the prisoner dropped off in the thick snow.

Stan yelled and banged on the cab with an old pair of boots and the driver finally stopped and came around to see what the trouble was. They tried to trace the prisoner through snow prints, but he had run through a house, whose door was open and out the back and they lost the trail. The only thing to do now was to inform the civilian police that a dangerous airman was on the loose armed with a loaded gun.

Arriving at Wing, Stan was given first aid treatment for his badly bruised left wrist and his C.O. was told that in future if there was a prisoner to be escorted, there should be two S.P's.

About a month later, on a rumour that the late prisoner had been seen in Barrow, Stan and another police sergeant drove around the town calling in NAAFI's, Institutes and finally the YMCA. They managed to arrest him, put handcuffs on him and escorted him to the city police station. On searching him the police found a diary with a number of German names and addresses, but Stan was never able to learn if he was a spy or not, for a couple of weeks later he re-mustered to Aircrew! Stan ... not the prisoner!

On Stan's first flight at Oakes Field, Nassau in a B25 Mitchell and with a brand new crew, the pilot of which was flying a B25 for the first time, everything went well on the exercise over the blue waters of the Caribbean, and after about 5 hours the Station Chief Flying Instructor who was checking out the pilot, told Stan to put his charts away and to give him a course for base.

A short time later they spotted the Island and having put his charts away, Stan stood just behind the two pilots and watched as they prepared to land.

Stan noticed that the instructor was covering a dial with his hand, as the pilot was attempting his first B25 landing and he was curious to know what he was doing that for. His gaze wandered around the controls and then suddenly he was horrified to see that the red handle for the undercart was still in the "up" position. Very timidly, Stan touched the instructor's arm to point this out to him, but it didn't seem to worry the C.F.I. as he brushed Stan's arm away and the aircraft kept getting lower and lower, until it was level with the palm tree branches along the sides of the runway.

The two comics were still intent on having the Mitchell make a nice smooth landing, which Stan didn't think was at all possible, unless something was done about it. This time, with a judo chop to the muscles of the instructor's right arm, Stan bent his mouth to the C.F.I's ear and yelled "Undercart! Undercart!"

With that, and no questions asked, the C.F.I knocked the pilot's hands off

128

the controls, opened wide the throttles and hauled back on the column, and according to Flying Control afterwards, they cleared the deck with the ground a foot from the propellers.

They had been yelling "Mayday Mayday, Fox George Fox George" but the pilots had everything on "intercom" instead of "Liaison" and so they heard nothing. The C.F.I levelled off at about 2,000 feet, handed the controls over to the pilot then turned round, shook Stan's hand and said "Thanks pal ... Thanks pal".

A fairly smooth landing was accomplished, the C.F.I jumped out and told the pilot he was satisfied with him and to take it up again. Stan said to the new pilot that if he would fly the aircraft, he, Stan, would see to it that the undercart was lowered ... and it was so!

P/O GERALD H. GIBBENS
NAVIGATOR R.C.A.F.

Gerald Henry Gibbens was born in Vancouver on May 20th, 1916. He attended Lord Tennyson Elementary School and Kitsilano Junior and Senior High School. Gerry was very active in local sports; tennis, badminton and softball. He worked in a local fur store as a retail merchant from 1936 to December 1939, then joined the Hudsons Bay Fur dept. in Vancouver in 1940 and remained there until enlistment in the R.C.A.F. in June 1942.

Gerry was posted to Edmonton, Manning Depot in July 1942. (Nice warm weather.) In Edmonton he attended I.T.S. and A.O.S. training and on Nov. 23rd, 1942, he graduated as a Sgt. Navigator. Then on to Y Depot for posting overseas. He finally left for England, via Halifax, arriving in Liverpool on May 24th, the Queen's birthday.

The trip overseas was uneventful and the convoy made it OK with limited losses. Upon arriving in Bournemouth and being billeted, he met with a few friends who took him on a tour of the park, where a day before, a FW 190, low flying, shot up and bombed the place leaving many park visitors dead and maimed. It was his first taste of real war damage.

After many frustrating weeks, a posting finally came through, for a course of map reading at No.13 S.F.T.S. at Shellingford near Oxford. When he arrived, he found out the aircraft they were to fly in was a Tiger Moth.

Gerry's next posting was to Dumfries, for a month of advanced navigation in August 1943. The weather was so bad, they could hardly get in eight hours of daylight flying and only about six hours of night flying. They did attend several funerals of aircrew trainees, mostly Canadians, killed in crashes, due to the horrendous weather.

His next posting was to No. 82 O.T.U. near Newmarket, Suffolk. Here a crew was made up; five Englishmen, one Irishman, and Gerry, a Canadian. There were the usual bombing, gunnery and navigational exercises. On one of the local cross country trips, Gerry's plane broke cloud cover at ten thousand feet, but unfortunately the wireless set became unserviceable. Here they were, at eleven thousand feet in the pitch darkness of night and no moon. The pilot decided they would continue on the trip rather than return to base. The wireless operator did his best to get the radio in operation, but to no avail. Luckily the Met report was good, with little or no wind. After reaching the turning point at Lands End and returning to base area, the pilot descended through the cloud cover. Upon breaking out at eight hundred feet, the airport was sighted slightly to starboard. Gerry's plots and courses as navigator were bang on, coupled with the pilot maintaining constant airspeed and a steady course direction. Needless to say the tension was very high indeed. The popular saying, "It's better to be lucky than good" certainly applied in this case. O.T.U. training for Gerry, finished at the end of November, and the new posting was to 1657 Conversion Unit at Stradishal.

On the evening of July 16/17, Gerry made his first operational trip to Sterkade in the Ruhr valley, a good beginning, as no enemy or flak were seen. Things changed on Gerry's fifth trip. The target was Kiel, north of Hamburg. On this trip, no bombs were carried, only anti-jamming tinsel; therefore it was not required to fly over the target area. Gerry gave the pilot a new course to steer when they were approaching the target, where they were immediately hit by flak. Evasive action by corkscrewing was implemented, still on the old course. When the error was noticed, it was discovered they were heading deeper into Germany! A new course was quickly given. This trip was the first time Gerry used a new navigational aid called A.P.I. (Air Position Indicator) which gave the longitude and latitude position in the air. Upon inspection of the plane the next morning, fourteen medium to fairly large holes were counted. Luckily none were serious.

The night of August 25/26, 1944 was a night that Gerry will always remember. The target was the Opel car factory at Russelheim, near Frankfurt in the Ruhr valley. The trip from England to near the target area was quiet, except for never-ending search lights which kept the crew alert. When they were on the final approach to the target, a FW 190 got a burst of cannon away and knocked out the intercom and set the inner starboard engine on fire. The pilot could not put the fire out and gave the order to bail out, which had to be passed to the crew by word of mouth. Four members of the crew did not survive. Three bodies were identified and buried in Germany, the other could not be found; his name is listed at the Runnymede Memorial. Gerry came down by parachute, still clutching the D ring, and could see the target in flames and his aircraft finally explode when it hit the ground. Gerry floated down and nearing the trees, German voices were heard, then a tree top seen, and then a hard landing which injured his back. He was left in an almost helpless position. An older German was by his side immediately, and with his aid and compassion, Gerry was taken to the local police station. After a short identification process, Gerry was taken to a basement prison cell. Shortly afterwards, four of his crew joined him in the cell. The next day all were handed over to the local Luftwaffe, who treated their injuries as best they could. The next day, a Sunday, all were escorted through Frankfort to the main interrogation centre for British and American Airmen.

Gerry was very surprised to find that the German interrogator knew their exact route to and from the target, the pilot's name, type of plane, the rest of the crew's names and even the name of the squadron C.O. But Gerry stuck to name, rank and serial number only, which earned him a trip back to solitary confinement. One more interrogation and one more trip back to solitary and Gerry was on his way, Sept. 1st to new quarters, destination unknown. About midnight, a large number of American and British airmen were herded into a rail car marked "Forty men or eight horses" - markings unchanged from the First World War. Three days later they arrived at Luft 7 in Upper Silesia. They were surprised to find the 700 or more prisoners there, were well tanned and healthy; a condition which was to change soon, as rations were cut and there was much talk of a move, which came on the 19th of January 1945; they were to march to a new camp.

Many of the prisoners started out with all their possessions including musical instruments, extra shoes (a far more practical choice) but a lot was abandoned on the way. Overnight stops in bombed out buildings, stables, sheds and much reduced rations took toll of baggage and men. Twenty one days and 256 kilometers later, they arrived at the severely overcrowded camp at Luckenwalde, where conditions and food were appalling. Gerry recalls each day of the march, as a dreadful experience, being so cold, tired and hungry, 24 hours of each day. The march usually started at 8.00 p.m. and went on through the night to dawn. Those who could not continue, were picked up by the medics at the end of the line. By January 29th they were approaching Standorf (now in East Germany), the weather was bitterly cold;

about midnight a blizzard started. The road was clogged with refugees who, like the P.O.W's had to dodge army vehicles. A staff car skidded and struck Gerry, knocking him down, but he was judged able to march. Several days later Gerry's ankle was scalded when a tin of boiling water spilled from its perch on the camp fire, and Gerry was sent to the rear for transport.

Transportation was by a charcoal burning tractor, pulling three carts, loaded with those unable to walk. At each hill the carts were unhitched and pulled up the hill individually and re-joined again, again and again. Four days later, the column finally reached Luckenwald where Gerry was to remain, until May 8th 1945. Although the first Russians entered camp 19th April, they were not allowed to go home, being now prisoners of the Russians.

On the march, the warmest billets the prisoners encountered, were horse stalls, cow barns or any other animal shelters, but these too had their hazards. One night Gerry lay down in a feed trough in a horse barn; the horse did not like the intrusion and kept nipping at him. Gerry moved to the cow barn where he fell asleep, exhausted, only to be awakened by a steer astride him urinating over his great coat. At least it was warm!

At six a.m. on V.E. Day, about forty happy prisoners broke out of camp and were met by two lorries waiting to take them to the Americans at Magdeburg. The Russians denied them the use of roads to the Elbe River until the early evening. After much Vodka and celebrations, they were allowed to get to the quayside across the river from Magdeburg. The Americans came across on a landing craft and took them to freedom.

Gerry returned to Vancouver and civilian life, September 20th, 1945. He married Mary in 1951, returned to the retail trade, furs and furniture, and he and Mary managed to raise two daughters Marion and Margaret, one of them making the Gibbens proud grandparents.

On Remembrance Day, Gerry wears the 1939/45 Star, Aircrew Europe Star, as well as the Defence and War Medal, and the C.V.S.M. though it is doubtful if his Pilot Officer's uniform still fits.

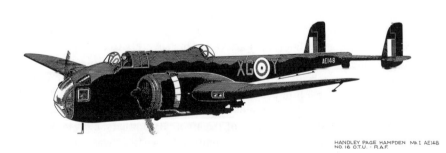

HANDLEY PAGE HAMPDEN MK I AE148
NO. 16 O.T.U. - R.A.F.

132

F/LT STAN D. GOOK D.F.M., C.D.
WAG R.A.F.

Stan was born at Brentwood, Essex, England and attended Essex County Council schools there, then went to Brentwood Grammar School,after which he attended night school at Watford, Herts and graduated as an Associate of the Grocers' Institute (A.G.I.) London. At school he played cricket and soccer and was interested in motor cycles from age 12 and rode them from age 15 on. At age 16, he was sent to Watford by his father, who was a master grocer, to be an apprentice in the grocery trade. He returned to Brentwood to help him in the business, but his father died in 1934 and Stan managed the business for his mother, until he joined the R.A.F. in 1939.

On March 29, 1939 Stan Gook bought a book for two shillings by Nigel Tangye, called "Teach Yourself to Fly". The next day he found out that there was no chance to join the "Civil Air Guard" as there was a waiting list of thousands. On that same day he filled in a form to join the Volunteer Air Reserve and took it to the Labour Exchange.

On April 1st, 1939 he made a note in his diary, "The R.A.F. is 21-years-old today." On April 26th, another note, "conscription for those between 20 and 21." Being 24, Stan was in a hurry to get into the R.A.F. aircrew, and excited at the prospect of flying - the best choice, in his opinion. On April 27th, he completed the application form to join up and had it endorsed by the headmaster of Brentford School, a bank manager and the butcher next door. He mailed it off that day.

Stan was interviewed on May 5th at Westcliffe Town Centre, England by the V.A.R., where the selection committee made him WOP/AG. He had some training in morse code and basic armament at The Town Centre and had his first passenger flight in an Anson aircraft from Rochford aerodrome, courtesy of R.A.F.V.R. On November 9th, 1939 Stan was called up and attended basic training at Felixstowe. One night there was a big bang that shook the brick barrack block. It was a mine which sank a destroyer as it entered the waterway to Harwich Harbour. While there, a Barrage Balloon unit moved into the area, mostly manned by W.A.A.F.'s, who flew their silver coloured balloons to protect the sea plane base.

From January 13th, 1940 to August 24th, 1940 Stan received radio training at electrical and wireless schools at Hamble and Cranwell, with a five-week break at Hornchurch on ground defence.

While there, an R.A.F. Hampden bomber was brought down by A.A. guns early on the morning of May 22nd. The crew failed to give the necessary signals and were probably off course or lost; no one was killed. Stan took his air gunner course in South Wales at 7 B.G.S. in four weeks, ending September 21st, 1940. He got his Sergeant's stripes at 7s/6d per day. Training was in Fairey Battle and Whitley aircraft. He took further training at #10 T.U. Abingdon, near Oxford, on Anson and Whitley aircraft, learned to do wireless inspections, had further signals and armament instruction and flew as a tail gunner and wireless operator on local and cross-country trips, some by day, some by night during October and November 1940.

On December 9th, 1940 Stan reported to #10 Sqdn. #4 Group of Bomber Command at Leeming in Yorkshire, flying Whitley aircraft. He flew with a crew, the captain of which was a Pilot Officer. His first operation, as tail gunner, was a "nursery" to Boulogne. Two more trips with the same crew, then on to a crew whose pilot was a Sgt. Unfortunately, the pilot and crew he flew with in his first operations were killed when the pilot forgot to take the control locks off and crashed on take-off.

With the Sgt. pilot and crew they were sent to Linton-on-Ouse to convert onto Halifax I aircraft of 76 Squadron, moving to Middleton-St-George on May 25th, 1941, a new base. Stan flew with a variety of crews, seven different pilots, one of whom was a French-Canadian, Sgt. Paul Morin from Montreal. On his second trip with Morin he was tail gunner over enemy territory. The target was Stettin (now Gdynia). The target was bombed, then the aircraft was coned by searchlights. Paul gyrated around the sky for what seemed like a minute or two, then a voice came over the intercom, "How do I get out of here?" Stan called from the rear turret, "Go north, go north!" The aircraft was soon over the Baltic Sea and heading for home. Stan received the Distinguished Flying Medal for this action.

On October 12th, 1941 Sgt. Morin and crew bombed Nurnberg. Paul misjudged the landing on return to base and on the third bounce the port undercarriage collapsed and they slewed off the runway. The navigator, who dropped the bombs, yelled over the intercom, "We've got a five hundred pound bomb hung up," and they vacated the aircraft in a big hurry! The bomb was well secured so all were safe on "terra firma." The endurance record for 76 Squadron was broken on that trip at 8 hours 55 minutes.

On December 30th, 1941 Stan took part in a daylight raid by squadrons of Halifax aircraft on the docks at Brest where the two German cruisers were. The bombers were screened by R.A.F. fighters and there was some A.A. fire.

The bombers, flying in formation, seemed a bit dicey but most made it to the base in St. Eval, Cornwall.

In March and April, 1942 he took part in three raids on the Von Tirpitz in Trondheim fjord. The aircraft were carrying 4,000 lb. bombs. He ended his tour with the three 1000 bomber raids, Cologne, Essen and Bremen, except for his final raid in a Halifax piloted by Sgt. Harwood on Bremen on June 25th, 1942. Of the four Sgt. pilots Stan flew with, one went missing and later was confirmed a prisoner. The others all got commissioned to Pilot Officer.

Stan became a F/Sgt. early in 1942 and P/O in late summer when he reported to #1658 Halifax Conversion Unit at Riccal in Yorkshire as WOP/AG instructor. He got his pilot's course through and left Riccal on May 25th, 1943. After I.T.W. on the south coast of England, Stan reported to #26 E.F.T.S. on September 1st, 1943 flying Tiger Moth aircraft. He left for pilot training in Canada and flew Cornell aircraft at 34 E.F.T.S. Assiniboia, Sask. from December 1st, 1943 to January 28th, 1944.

In March, 1944 he reported to #9 S.F.T.S. in Centralia, Ont. and flew Anson Mk II aircraft until October, 1944, an extended course, due to less losses than expected, in the invasion of Europe in June 1944. He received his wings at Centralia along with five other R.A.F. ex-WOP/AG's including George Rickart who is also a member of the Greater Vancouver A.C.A.

Stan returned to the U.K. in December 1944. All of the returning aircrew were classified redundant, which he found very depressing. He volunteered to be a glider pilot and was posted to an army unit on Salisbury Plain for combat training, but returned to pilot training at #18 A.F.U. at Snitterfield in March,1945, flying Oxford aircraft. Also at #3 A.F.U. at South Cierney and at each of these units was posted away to "Beam Approach Schools" for training.

Stan was demobilized from South Cierney in November, 1945. He worked as a lathe operator, making engine parts for an Australian firm in the U.K. but found it hard to settle down. He applied to rejoin the R.A.F. before his demob. leave ended and became a catering officer. He landed in Egypt in May 1946, posted to Lydda air base in Palestine where he was responsible for feeding up to 1,200 people with the help of R.A.F. and native cooks. Stan slept with a gun under his pillow every night, while there and had a pistol in a holster on his person during the daylight hours. Being area catering officer, he rode a motorcycle, another love in his life, to visit other units to report if conditions were satisfactory.

Stan returned to a snowy and frozen England in time for his 32nd birthday in February and was finally demobilized in March 1947.

He spent a year at a Ford garage, reconditioning tractor engines. When the Labour government in England made conditions intolerable, he emigrated to Canada with his wife and three children on "R.M.S. Aquitania", landing at Halifax, Nova Scotia on June 1st 1948. The family travelled by rail as far as Sicamous, B.C. It was the year the Fraser River broke the dikes at Hatzic. They flew from Penticton airport on a C.P. Air D.C.3 to Vancouver to complete the journey.

Stan did a variety of jobs, until joining the R.C.A.F. at 40 years of age. He became an airframe technician and worked on Harvards and Expeditor aircraft at Penhold, Alberta. He was honourably released at 50 years of age in 1965.

Stan says that his wife, Doris, supported him 100 per cent during the trying times and took good care of the children when he was away from home. He adds, "We couldn't have done it without them."

Stan's decorations and medals include the D.F.M., 1939/45 Star, Aircrew Europe, War Medal, Defence Medal and the Canadian Forces Decoration (C.D.)

GR/CAPT. GEORGE GRANT D.S.O & BAR, D.F.C.
PILOT R.A.F.

George was born in Ottawa, May 31st 1916 and attended Ottawa Public School, then went to Lisgar Collegiate Institute. He had no secondary or vocational education. He was brought up in a normal middle-class family in urban surroundings and was active in sports, particularly Canadian football, basketball, track and field, also badminton. After completion of high school, George followed road building construction in Ontario, Quebec and New Brunswick until the end of 1938.

Believing that war with Germany was inevitable and being ineligible for the R.C.A.F., George and a friend sailed from Montreal on March 17th, 1939 with the aim of joining the R.A.F. and becoming pilots. They presented their applications on arrival in London and in keeping with the story of the day, were judged to have the right number of eyes and sufficiently warm, to be accepted right away.

George, through the benevolence of the Air Force, was posted to No.4 E. &

R.F.T.S., Brough, E. Yorks., for pre-course training, which consisted of attending lectures and signing the daily attendance sheet. This lasted for three weeks and on May first he began elementary flying training on Magister aircraft. R.A.F. Uxbridge was next. Then to No. 8 F.T.S.Montrose, Scotland, for service flying training on Oxford aircraft. He got his wings in early October and completed the course in mid-December 1939 having earned a distinguished pass.

While there, in November, George got a graphic illustration of the effect of frost on the wings of an aircraft. The planes for the senior course were lined up for take-off, having spent the night outside. The first aircraft rolled down the take-off run with its nose well in the air and squashed to a belly-up landing on the adjacent golf course. The next one went down the runway in a similar fashion and came to a halt squashed against two planes of the junior term. The third, carrying an instructor named Dawson and two pupils, staggered over the perimeter and cleanly took out a brick signal box on the railway. By this time, signal lights were flashing and the remaining aircraft taxied back in. Fortunately, there were no injuries, but a most startled railway signaller had seen his signal box disappear before his eyes, to be replaced by a rather untidy looking Oxford aircraft and three frightened looking Air Force Officers.

The upshot of the affair, was a note that appeared on the notice board the next morning viz: "Flying Oxfords white with frost, Nearly Dawson's life was cost. But wasn't that an inspiration, For curing chronic constipation."

Grant was next posted to N & R School, Thorney Island for Coastal Command training. That finished in mid-March '40 and he was posted to 612 Sqdn Dyce, Scotland to fly Ansons on convoy escorts and North Sea patrols in Coastal Command. In June, George was sent to the Air Navigation School St. Athans, Wales for an advanced Air Navigation (Astro) course.

Grant returned to Scotland and after just three days was again posted to the south of England to Blind Approach Training and Development Unit, Boscombe Down, Hants, for special duties. This unit had been expanded to have eight blind-approach trained pilots and eight astro-trained navigators (of which Grant was one) and sundry wireless and signal types. The special duty was to monitor a system of blind bombing beams that the Germans had developed and were about to put into operation. The unit also was to judge the effectiveness of the jamming countermeasures and to test any enemy receivers that were recovered from shot-down German bombers.

In addition, it was possible to predict reasonably accurately where an attack was likely to take place by plotting the location of the beam on the ground and relating it to a known source. A further projection was to mount a series of bombing attacks on the transmitters flying backwards down the enemy beams. The object was to prevent the German bomber pilots from getting an accurate track before they encountered jamming. These raids were carried out initially in Whitleys and later in Wellingtons and included formation flying at night with the hope of increasing the accuracy. Although tracking was fairly accurate, ranging was a problem and was finally solved by

Telecommunications Research Establishment who developed a ranging device. The next progression was the practice of the enemy turning off his beams when he expected to be attacked. Consequently a beam was developed for us known as a Baillie Beam.

As a result, the first, but crude Allied beam blind bombing system was born. How effective it was to be was proven in a trial operational effort called Operation Trinity. This consisted of installing the equipment in Stirling aircraft of 7 and 15 sqdns and bombing the battleships Schoenhorst and Gneisneau in Brest harbour. The beam flying was done by the pilots from 109 sqdn, with the regular Stirling pilots doing the take-offs and landings.

The results were sufficiently impressive to cause a further change to 109 sqdn. In Feb '42 the unit was moved to Tempsford and reorganized. 109 sqdn was to continue to develop "Oboe" (as the system was now called) and a new unit called #1473 Flight was formed to take responsibility for the beam investigation and jamming functions. This unit was to be detached to Upper Heyford and commanded by Grant who was promoted to Sqdn. Ldr. He had recently been awarded the D.F.C. for his efforts on beam bombing and on Trinity.

Grant stayed with 1473 Flight until April '43 by which time it had moved to Hurn.

In April 1943, Grant applied to return to 109 Squadron, but instead, ended up at No. 156 Squadron in P.F.F. on Lancasters. On an operation early in their tour, the squadron was detailed to bomb a target in Italy and because it was a bright moonlight night, the tactics were to cross the enemy coast high up and then to descend to ground level across France and climb over the Alps and remain high over the target. The return was to be done the same way in reverse. The trip was uneventful and went as planned, until about half way back on the return journey. The moon was bright and the ground and the surrounding houses and built-up areas were clearly visible. The crew were relaxed and were flying on automatic pilot, when suddenly a searchlight came on right in front, straight into their faces and others joined from the sides. Light anti-aircraft fire came up from all sides. Grant called for full power from the Engineer and jerked the auto-pilot out, at the same time giving the right rudder a vicious kick. Immediately, his right leg seemed to go numb and he thought he had been hit, but realised that he had to get out of there right away and any wound would have to be attended to later. The smell of cordite was very strong and he thought his gunners were firing at the searchlights. When the aircraft finally cleared the area, the skipper asked the gunners how many lights they had got and both replied that they hadn't fired a shot. Grant's "wound" turned out to have happened because in jamming on right rudder he had driven the adjustable pedal to the limit of its travel and over extended his leg, which was only stiff for a few days. The aircraft though, suffered quite extensively and was judged to be beyond the capabilities of the local unit to repair. It was never learned what defended area they had blundered over.

George finished his tour in November 1943, on completion of which, he was awarded the D.S.O.

Next, he was posted to No. 8 Group H.Q. as Tactics Officer on the Staff of A.V.M. Bennett, which post he held until May 1944. He was then, finally, sent to 109 Squadron at Little Staughton as Squadron Commander. He was made a Group Captain there and at the finish of his appointment was awarded a bar to his D.S.O.

In early December of 1944, he was posted to R.A.F. Graveley as Station Commander. His tenure there was until October 1945, at which time he returned to the rank of Wing Commander and was posted to the Central Bomber Establishment at Marham as a member of the Tactics Wing. This unit was to preserve the techniques of bombing, developed during the war and was to be concerned with future developments and operational requirements.

Grant was sent to the R.A.F. Staff College, Bulstrode, in October 1946 and completed the course in March 1947. Air Ministry Operational Training was the next stop, where he stayed until December 1947. He moved to Bomber Operations, also in Air Ministry, and was further reduced in rank to substantive Squadron Leader from January 1st, 1948. The further reduction in rank, he was told, was because he had not yet become 32 years of age!!

Being unwilling to stay on in the Air Force at this level, and under these conditions, he retired prematurely, at his own request, on compassionate grounds and returned to Canada with his wife and three children.

On retirement, the Air Force granted him his rank of Group Captain and besides repatriating him and his family to "anywhere of their choice in Canada", gave him one day's leave for every month he had been out of Canada, since the start of the war, at the pay of Wing Commander. When his leave ended in April, 1949, his service had covered ten years.

George was the recipient of the Distinguished Service Order, a bar to the D.S.O., the Distinguished Flying Cross, 1939/45 Star, Aircrew Europe Star, France and Germany Star, Victory Medal, War Service Medal and Defence Medal. He completed his service in Vancouver in April 1949 and worked in the Heavy Construction industry and allied businesses until 1974, then went into cattle farming and gravel supplying in the Fraser Valley. His wife, Peggy, is English born and at the time of their marriage was a member of the W.A.A.F. at Boscombe Down. Their family consists of six boys and two girls, three of the children were born in England, the other five in Canada.

P/O EDGAR C.HONEY
AIR GUNNER R.C.A.F.

Edgar Honey was born in Cornwall, England, and came to Canada when he was five years old, with his parents in 1926. He attended public school at Glenora, near Duncan B.C. and finished Grade 9 at Chu-Chua School in the Kamloops area of British Columbia. During his youth he enjoyed hunting, fishing, camping out and woodworking. He worked on farms, sawmills and for the Canadian National Railway, before joining the R.C.A.F. in Vancouver on January 2nd, 1941.

After joining, Ed was sent to Manning Depot in Edmonton, Alberta, then to Jericho and Boundary Bay, B.C. for initial training and graduated from No. 3 B & G School, McDonald, Manitoba, taking his training in Fairey Battles. He completed his training on Halifax bombers in the U.K. and was posted to 77 Squadron, Elvington, York, England.

He made one trip in a Whitley Bomber on a Nickel raid over France, before making his first trip in a Halifax Bomber, May 23rd, 1943 with pilot Bill Hallem over Germany. Everything went routine 'till trip 14, over Hamburg,when they were shot up quite badly, one engine being knocked out, but they dropped their bombs and got back to base. On their 23rd, and last trip, September 27, 1943 their four engine Halifax was shot down over Hanover. Ground fire had taken out their ailerons on the wings of the aircraft and they had to skid around with the rudder, when separated from the rest of the flight, off course; they were picked up in a cone of searchlights. Further ground fire made a direct hit. The far engine went, the next engine burst into flames and when the paint caught fire their pilot ordered: "Sorry chaps, but tonight you will have to bail out and walk home." All seven crew members survived.

Mid-upper Gunner Edgar Honey took some flak in a leg while still in the plane, but managed to get out of his bubble. He took more flak in his back on the way down in his parachute. He was unconscious and woke up in a
140

German Military Hospital. Ed spent four months in the Delmenhorst Hospital where he got several blood transfusions and the flak removed from his back. Then he was taken to Stalag 4B P.O.W. camp and held until liberated by the Russians in April, 1945.

With three other chaps they walked seventy miles to the American lines to be flown to Brussels, Belgium and then to Bournemouth, England.

Forty-one years later, in 1984, Pilot Bill Hallam visited Canada to see Ed and a former prison room-mate. They had not seen each other since the night their plane went down. At their re-union Bill recalled parachuting into a field and walking to what he thought was a farmhouse, that turned out to be a German Army Barracks. He was captured and spent the rest of the war in Stalag 3, Room 23, Block 109. It was in this room where all the final briefings were held for "The Great Escape". Hallem was not chosen to be one of the escapers, because he was too much of a new boy in camp. Of the 126 escapers that got out, 76 made it to freedom, 50 were recaptured and executed.

Honey was discharged in Vancouver, B.C., August 28, 1945. He was awarded the Defence Medal, 1939/45 Star, Victory Medal and the Canadian Volunteer Medal and Clasp and also the Aircrew Europe Star.

After service, Ed worked in sawmills, did construction work, then for thirty years worked for the Provincial Government as a cook at Oakalla. He retired in 1977. His first wife, Gwen was killed in an auto accident in 1961 and his second wife, Ann, died of cancer in 1976. He has two daughters. In 1985 Ed visited Bill Hallam and his family on their cattle ranch in Zimbabwe, Africa.

Ed is now living in Coquitlam, B.C. enjoying his boyhood hobbies, doing woodworking in his basement and fishing during the summer months!

"NOORDUYN NORSEMAN "2486"

F/LT HARRY JAMES HARDY D.F.C.,C.D.
PILOT R.C.A.F.

Harry Hardy was born in Virden, Manitoba, and his early years there were followed by subsequent residence in the town of Timmins in Northern Ontario.

His Elementary education began at Holy Family School in Timmins and thence to the High School and Vocational School. He specialized in drafting and on completion he was employed as a draftsman for the period of one year.

Harry's chief interest as a young man centered around three activities - fishing, hunting and taxidermy. With World War 2 underway he went to Toronto Manning Pool in November of 1941 and enlisted in the R.C.A.F. After basic training he was posted to #9 Elementary Flying School at St. Catharines, Ontario, where he was introduced to the "mighty" Tiger Moth. Unlike the majority of his fellow pilots who saw service on a couple of training aircraft, and one or two operational planes, Harry became qualified on nine different aeroplanes. At #6 Service Training School at Yorkton, Sask. he trained on Cessna Cranes and received his "wings" following which he went to #123 squadron at Debert, N.S., where he flew Lysanders. From Debert he moved to the opposite end of Canada, to #163 squadron and was introduced to Bolingbrokes, Hurricanes, Kittihawks and Harvards.

On leaving Vancouver, Harry made his way to England and joined #61 O.T.U. at Rednal, where he flew Spitfires. From #61, it was up to Bonnie Scotland and #3 Tactical Exercise Unit and Hurricanes followed by a spell on Typhoons. A spell at Bognor Regis (#83 Group Support Unit) preceded his move into operations with #440 Squadron operating from Cruelly, France, then to Brussels, Belgium and then to Eindhoven in Holland.

Harry's final posting was to #83 G.S.U., again where he was engaged in flying Typhoons and Spitfires to the front line.

142

During his months of operational flying Harry Hardy had four shaky encounters that he would long remember.

In April of 1944 he and another Spitfire pilot were practicing air-to-air combat. Harry was flying in front when he lowered his flaps in a turn, causing his partner to overshoot him and the other "Spit" flew into his, causing it to disintegrate! There he was, left strapped to his seat but with no aircraft around him. He was flying at 6,000 feet, so he had lots of time (and presence of mind) to get rid of the seat and open his parachute. They both landed — unhurt!

Then came the 6th of September of '44 when his squadron of 9 Typhoons was moving from Amiens to Brussels. It was late in the afternoon, getting dark and raining, when Harry heard his C.O. ask the Flight Commander if he knew where they were - the answer was negative. The C.O. told them all to pick a field and get down in it - they were running out of fuel and they were lost! The nine Typhoons all landed without anyone being injured.

On Christmas day in 1944 the Squadron of Canadians were sent south from Holland to help the Americans who were holding the Germans in the Ardennes. There was a layer of snow on the ground and it was possible to see where the German tanks had driven into clumps of trees when they saw the Typhoons arriving. Harry attacked a tank and, as he went over, one of the tanks began firing at him and shot part of his tail off. With both hands on the stick and using full rudder he was able to fly back to Holland, where he bailed out. Harry landed in an Army camp and, after being treated royally, he was driven back to Eindhoven - unscathed in the incident.

Three months later Harry was bombing and strafing a train at Appelhusen when his bomb racks were hit by flack but the shell did not explode and, apart from a hole in the wing, there was no damage.

In recognition of his service during four years in the R.C.A.F. Harry Hardy received eight decorations. The D.F.C., the 39-45 Star, the France & Germany Star, the Defence Medal, C.V.S.Medal with Clasp, the War Medal, the Normandy Medal and C.D.

Discharge from the service occurred where he had enlisted - Toronto Manning Pool - in 1945. He went to work as a draftsman for sixteen years, being promoted to a Project Engineer and then to Engineering Supervisor for eighteen years.

From 1954 to 1963, Harry was a member of #443 Squadron Reserve at Sea Island.

Harry Hardy was married in Vancouver in November of 1943 and he and his wife Hazel have two daughters, Roberta and Christine, and now they have eight grandchildren, two boys and six girls.

F/O JOHN C. HOY D.F.C.

AIR BOMBER R.C.A.F.

John C. Hoy was born in Saskatoon, Saskatchewan. There, he attended Pleasant Hill Public School, Bedford Road Collegiate, Saskatoon Technical School and completed an advanced general insurance course. During his school years, he enjoyed all sports, was a newspaper delivery boy and after completing his education, sold general insurance. He joined the R.C.A.F. in Winnipeg in January, 1942.

For his training as an Air Bomber, he took his I.T.S. and A.O.S. at Regina and B. & G. at Mossbank, Saskatchewan. Sent to England to Millom, Cumberland, he took his A.F.U. on Ansons and then to Lossiemouth for his O.T.U. on Wellingtons.

John was posted to the Royal Air Force, Number 158 Squadron flying Halifax aircraft on Bomber Command in the European theatre.

The citation for John Hoy's award of the Distinguished Flying Cross reads in part - "On one occasion took part in a raid on Stuttgart. When nearing the target area, heavy anti-aircraft fire was encountered. A shell burst beneath the aircraft, which was thrown on its back by the force of the explosion, coupled with the violent effect of the slip stream. Considerable height was lost before the pilot regained control. When course was resumed, although badly shaken, P/O Hoy directed the bombing run with great coolness and the target was successfully attacked".

But on another flight, his crew received a less prestigious decoration. Their aircraft had just come off a minor inspection, had not been air tested and no-one had noticed the pitot tube had been disconnected. As their aircraft was taking off, on an operation flight, Hoy advised the pilot there was no airspeed showing. A quick decision was made to abandon the trip. The aircraft hit the end of the runway, took a couple of long grass hopper leaps, the nose fell off from the impacts, and the crew and the rest of the plane came

144

to rest in the airfield sewage lagoon. John's reaction was, this time they were showered in something other than glory!!

After completing his operational tour of 36 sorties, John was sent on a war bond tour of Canadians on attachment in England. His group sold about one million dollars in bonds.

In addition to his D.F.C., Hoy was the recipient of the 1939/45 Star, War Medal, France and Germany Bar, Aircrew Europe Star, Operational Wing and Defence Medal and the C.V.S.M. and clasp.

After his discharge in July 1945, he resumed working with the same insurance company he worked with before the war and continued with them for the next 46 years. Since retiring he is involved as a volunteer, working with the Mentally Handicapped Society.

John was married in 1941 to Eleanor. They now live in Surrey, B.C. and have three sons and six grandchildren.

F/O ARTHUR H. JACKSON
PILOT R.C.A.F.

Art Jackson was born in Moose Jaw, Saskatchewan in 1917 and shortly after he moved to a farm south of Moose Jaw. It was here where he started school in a one room prairie school house. After a year of school, the family moved to Winnipeg for a short time then to Swift Current and finally to Vancouver, in 1925. He continued his public schooling at General Wolfe, McDonald, and Laura Secord schools and afterwards attended Kitsilano Junior, Senior High, and King Edward High Schools, graduating with his Senior Matriculation. He enjoyed swimming, tennis, hiking and skiing and took good advantage of the proximity of the beaches and mountains which provided the opportunity to enjoy these sports. After graduation from high school he worked at various odd jobs and eventually articled to a firm of Chartered Accountants and after completing his Intermediate Exam, he applied to join the R.C.A.F. in August 1940 and was called up in February, 1941, for training as a pilot.

On the first morning at Brandon Manning Pool at 05:30 hours reveille, with hundreds of sleepy eyed neophyte aviators standing in line waiting to shave, Art wondered what he had volunteered himself into. As the days passed, the camaraderie and the wisecracks eased the change from civvy street to the Airforce Routine and the stay became quite bearable, even enjoyable. Guard Duty at Saskatoon and Initial Training School at Regina followed and a lucky break to be posted to Elementary Flying School (No.8) at Sea Island in Vancouver. His memories of E.F.T.S. include hitting his own slipstream after coming out of a loop for the first time, heading in an inverted position for the Gulf of Georgia after messing up a slow roll, the marvelous command of profanity demonstrated by the C.F.I. when he made a sloppy recovery from some aerobatic manoeuver, the flap that followed when some intent young pilot with a long red ribbon attached to his rudder indicating that it was his first solo landing, cutting out T.C.A. and forcing it go around again.

After Sea Island, Art was posted to Number 3 S.F.T.S. at Calgary, getting his wings on November 7, 1941. After two weeks embarkation leave he reported to Halifax and sailed for England the day after Pearl Harbour on the "Californian", an armed merchantman, accompanied by two of the First World War four stacker destroyers that started United States aid to Britain, which both broke down by the time they were half way over. The crossing took two weeks on the cold Atlantic; in cramped quarters it wasn't exactly a luxury cruise.

Arriving in England after a period of a month in Bournemouth and Hastings, Art was posted to Number 1511 B.A.T. Flight at Upwood to practice flying on the beam and then to Number 3 S.F.T.S.(A.F.U.) South Cerney on Oxfords. In April he was posted to Number 16 O.T.U., Upper Heyford on Hampdens. The station was just changing to Wellingtons (1C's) and his was the first course to go on the Wimpeys. Half way through the course, Art and his crew were posted along with five others to North Luffenham, Number 29 O.T.U. From North Luffenham Art's crew was posted to 425 Squadron in September and did the usual familiarization night circuits and cross countries and he did his first second dicky trip to Cologne. On one of the day cross countries, the navigator had completed all of his exercises and Art decided to do some unauthorized low flying during the course of which they flew through a tree, a piece of which he still has among his mementos. The damage to the aircraft was chiefly a broken port propeller and shattered windshield which made it difficult to fly, and they landed at the first available airdrome. They were picked up the next day and flown back to base. The operations list of the squadron for the previous day had been drawn up while the crew was on the cross country, and unknown to Art he had been scheduled to do his final second dickey trip with a crew who had failed to return from the operation. As he was away from the squadron that night, he was still alive but was about to have dealings with the brass. It was over a month before he was brought up on a charge, during which time he had completed four sorties and during which his name was not included at pay parade. The crew completed twenty trips over Europe which included "gardening" at Lorient, St. Nazaire, Scharnhorn and two to Hamburg, Essen, Duisburg, Stuttgart, Mannheim etc. In May 1943 the Squadron was sent to Tunisia to lend support in the invasion of Sicily and Italy, and the crew completed fifteen more sorties in that theatre.

On a mining trip to Lorient, one of their first trips, the Rear Gunner and Wireless Op. were both on sick parade and were replaced by spares. The target area was socked in and following orders they were returning with the two mines, and continued flying under the cloud base towards the English Coast. Everything went smoothly until the navigator reported that the Gee was not working and the wireless op reported that he could not get any fixes. By this time the cloud base was down to one thousand feet and they were practically at the coast. Art climbed into the clouds to gain some altitude and headed in a north easterly direction until they got things sorted out, and soon heard the balloon squeakers from Plymouth gradually increase in volume. They turned 180 degrees to get clear of the balloons and more signals came over the earphones indicating another balloon barrage. By this time the main fuel tanks had run dry and the nacelle tanks had been turned on and there was about half an hour's petrol supply left, and their options were becoming limited. The Navigator suggested finding the Channel and ditching, the Rear Gunner said "let's hit the silk". Art decided that he would back on the north easterly direction and hope for a break. They flew back and climbed hoping to clear the balloon barrage at Plymouth and had reached an altitude of twenty nine hundred feet when the squeakers began to subside. Shortly, a small break in the clouds revealed an airfield, where they landed with barely enough petrol to taxi to the dispersal point. There were no hard feelings after this trip and they flew together for over thirty more operations.

Art was posted as an O.T.U. instructor at Number 82 O.T.U., Gamston and one day as flying was down except for a couple of air-tests, Art and another instructor were talking about parachute jumping and decided to do one of their air tests together, and to draw lots to see which one would fly the plane and which one was to jump. Art drew the ticket to fly! Jumping was not permitted except in case of emergency, so they cooked up a story that the escape hatch blew open and Ward stepped down to close it and fell out. At the flight office they made everything look casual as if nothing untoward was planned, such as asking "Are you going to wear your chute, Jacko?" Art replied "Yeah, I guess I will." "I will too then" he answered. They took off and when they got to a position where their unscientific calculations told them that he should land in the centre of the airfield, he stepped down and opened the hatch, and was gone. Art watched as he swung back and forth drifting to earth over a forest, a field, an ammunition dump, finally disappearing in the middle of another forest area, about two miles from the airfield. That afternoon in the mess, the Group Captain asked what happened and accepted their explanation with his tongue in his cheek, "That's a good story", he said.

From Stratford, Art was posted to the Repat Depot at Warrington and arrived home just over three years from the time he left Canada. After some leave, he was posted to C.F.S. at Trenton on an O.T.U. Instructors Course and then to Number 5 O.T.U. at Boundary Bay and finally to Gimli, on B25's. His last flight in the Air Force was from Gimli to Moose Jaw where the aircraft were to have their last resting place. It was a beautiful fall day and the trip took exactly two hours at fifty feet. Art received the 1939/45 Star, Italy Star, Air Crew Europe Star, C.V.S.M. and Clasp, Defence Medal and Operational Wings. He was discharged in Vancouver as a Flying Officer on October 19, 1945.

After the war, he continued in the accounting field in commerce and for a mining company in South America. He completed his C.A. degree and opened his own office, retiring in 1984. He is married and he and his wife Leona have one son and three grandchildren.

S/LDR J.A. (JACK) REYNOLDS D.F.C. & Bar
PILOT R.C.A.F.

Jack Reynolds was born in Regina, Saskatchewan. His education began in the Lakeview Elementary School and from there, he took his secondary schooling at Regina Central Collegiate.

He was brought up in an urban environment and his most popular leisure activities were swimming, golf, and bridge. On completion of his schooling, Jack was employed as a clerk, by the General Insurance Company. From insurance, he switched to Industrial Acceptance Corporation, in general office duties.

In the fall of 1940 Reynolds joined the R.C.A.F. at London, Ontario, with the expectation of mustering as a pilot. His first posting was to Manning Depot in Toronto and from there, to guard duty at Dunville, Ontario. His first training

148

assignment took him back to Toronto for I.T.S. Jack began flying training on Fleet Finches at Crumbin, Ontario, followed by #5 S.F.T.S. at Brantford on twin engine Ansons. He was moved to the Maritimes, first at #31 G.R.S. Charlottetown, P.E.I.

In preparation for posting overseas, the crew assembled at #31 O.T.U. Debert, N.S. where they became adapted to Hudsons. The Reynolds crew was one of the first Canadian, trained to fly the Atlantic, setting out from Dorval to Prestwick in a Hudson, that had just arrived from California.

The winter weather was appalling, inadequate M.E.T. information had been given and their radio went u/s just beyond the point of no return, so they had to depend on celestial navigation for landfall.

The pre-flight briefing stressed the need for good communication at destination but, having no radio, Jack decided to land at the first available R.A.F. Station in Northern Ireland. The welcome was very casual and the briefing to their final destination at Prestwick, was very off-hand. "Maintain fifteen hundred feet, wheels down and don't look hostile."

A posting to #7 O.T.U. at Limavady in Northern Ireland, to become qualified on Wellingtons, followed by preparation for transit to Malta and action in the Mediterranean, signalled the beginning of an exciting tour for Jack Reynolds and his crew.

Because of the losses flying across the Mediterranean, the R.A.F. decided to pioneer a route through central Africa. Reynolds and company were briefed to fly Gibraltar, Gambia, Freetown, Zakoradi, Lagos. A fortunate private 'pub' briefing with an ex Imperial Airways briefing officer, offered some options to the "official route" that allowed better amenities.

As a result of the "briefing", they landed at a Firestone Plantation in Nigeria and a Pan Am base in Accra, where the P.X.'s were stocked with full American super-market supplies. The crew suffered some sabotage in Gibraltar (sea water had been added to the petrol), but they staggered on to Lagos, where the aircraft was completely checked.

En route from Cairo to Malta, Jack's navigator came down with malaria and dysentery and had to be hospitalized at El Adem, Libya, also, the crew was held up with a bad engine and departed five days later, complete with a new navigator. The Reynolds' arrival in Malta was classed a 'wipe-out!' Landing down wind into a bomb shelter with considerable damage to their pride and to their plane but WITHOUT a crack in any of the cases of Dawes Black Horse they were bringing to the troops!

The new crew joined #69 Squadron, which was a queer grab-bag. The C.O.'s plane was a Spitfire, plus a reconnaissance flight of Baltimores and Marylands, plus an air-sea rescue Walrus and a flight of Wellingtons. The main job was to strafe the German shipping supply lines to Africa. Daylight ops belonged to the Beauforts while the Wellingtons took over at night.

Tactics involved four cross-over patrols each night, covering Italian ports, Greek ports and routes to Africa. Patrol aircraft with A.S.V. had 10 to 12 hours endurance and carried loads of flares. Sightings were radioed to base and the rest of the flight took off to do battle, armed with two torpedoes. When the flight was ready to attack, the patrol plane dropped flares parallel to the convoy's route and the run-in was made. The 'fish' were dropped at 90 feet and a 1000 yards from the target. Despite primitive equipment, the squadron had great success and helped to prevent fuel and armaments from reaching Rommell. Life on Malta was hectic, lots of enemy action and lack of food, sleep, fuel and spares, but the tour passed quickly because of the continual action, (up to 95 hours per month).

After Jack Reynolds returned to England from Malta, he was granted a month leave, back in Canada, which he enjoyed at home in Winnipeg. On returning to the theatre of war, Jack was assigned to #489 Squadron at Leuchers, Scotland and began his second tour, which also was on anti-shipping, torpedoes and rockets, activities mainly along the Norwegian and Dutch coasts.

The first 'flap' was just after joining #489 (a New Zealand squadron), when the "Tirpitz" was rumoured to be breaking out of Trondheim. Every coastal strike squadron was assembled around John O'Groats, for a panic joint effort. Generally, the squadrons didn't have the range for the round trip, so the Navy was scheduled to lay on a picket of ships, about 150 miles from the Shetlands to fish survivors out of the 'drink' when their fuel gave out! Fortunately the Tirpitz came down with mechanical problems and stayed until the Lancasters finished her off some months later.

Tactics had become quite sophisticated and the crews enjoyed real success. One entry in Jack's log book, showed an attack on a convoy of fourteen ships on the Dutch coast, nine of which were sunk. Number 489 Squadron formed a Wing of #455 Squadron (R.A.A.F.) and were based in Leuchars, Scotland, at Langham in Norfolk and finally at Dallachy, back in Scotland. Jack Reynold's second tour wound up in December of 1944 and he was posted to the Torpedo Training Unit at Turnberry, where he waited out the *end*!

He was discharged in Calgary in January 1946. His awards were the Defence Medal, D.F.C. and Bar, the 1939/45 Star, the Africa Star and Clasp and the Atlantic Star and Clasp and the Victory Medal. Jack and Dorothy were married in 1948 in Edmonton, where he was employed with Industrial Acceptance Corp. and moved around to Lethbridge, Regina and Calgary as branch manager. Subsequently, he was branch manager for Imperial Investments and later with Canadian Kenworth as Sales and Regional Manager. He retired in 1982. Jack and Dorothy have two daughters and one son and also six grandchildren.

F/LT HAROLD H. LAWRENCE D.F.C.

BOMB AIMER R.A.F.

Harold (Laurie) H. Lawrence was born, 30 July 1919, in Shanghai, China. He was educated at Shanghai Public School and St.Frances Xaviers College where he matriculated. He later attended Henry Lester Technical Institute, whilst serving an apprenticeship with the Shanghai Gas Co, which he almost completed, before joining the R.A.F. late in the year 1940. He reported to the British Consulate and was sent to London via the Cape, a journey which took several months instead of the 28 days it would have taken had the Suez route been used.

On the 18th May 1941, after an intensive medical, he was accepted for aircrew training as a navigator. First posting was to #10 I.T.W. Scarborough and then on to Canada and #5 Air Observer's School, Winnipeg, flying in Ansons. Next #7 B.& G. followed by #1 Advanced Navigation School at Rivers, Manitoba. On graduation Laurie was posted to Ferry Command, Dorval, ostensibly to crew an aircraft across the Atlantic, but the supply of aircrew exceeded the demand and much to his chagrin, Laurie returned to the U.K. by boat.

At Bournemouth he volunteered to join 166 squadron as a bomb aimer and was again sent to an O.T.U.. He flew his first op with Bomber Command, against Essen on the 5th. March 1943 and again to the same target on the 12th. At that time 166 squadron was at R.A.F. Kirminton, Lincs. These raids marked the beginning of the Battle of the Ruhr. He completed his first tour of operations in Aug. 1943, having bombed targets at Duisberg, Mannheim, Dusseldorf, Wuppertal, Krefeld and Cologne, amongst many others.

He was promoted to P/O and posted to #21 O.T.U. as an instructor, where he remained until May 1944.

In June 1944, having requested a posting to an operational unit, he was sent to #1652 Conversion Unit and Halifaxes. He completed his second tour of operations with 102 Squadron, Pocklington, Yorks. This tour was carried out after D Day and the sorties were more varied. Attacks were made on V1 and V2 sites, railway marshalling yards, submarine pens and also in direct support of the army, like the bombing of the forward positions of the enemy troops at Caen and the delivery of loaded petrol cans to an airfield near Brussels. His second tour was completed 6th Oct. 1944 and while on leave he was informed that H.M. King George had seen fit to award him an immediate D.F.C.

Laurie was posted to R.A.F.School of Administration and later sent to Bangalore, India, where he joined 904 wing as Adjutant. The war with Japan was over and the wing was sent to Kemajoran airfield, at what was then Batavia, in Java. This unit was amongst the first allied troops landing on the island.

Prior to his return to the U.K. for demobilization, he was sent as Senior Admin. Officer to an airfield construction squadron, which was at the time, expanding the runways at Kai Tak, Hongkong. He was later granted a permanent commission, retiring from the R.A.F. in 1962, but not before flying Meteor NF II and Gloster Javelin fighters, as well as a tour each, on Lincoln and Canberra aircraft. The last campaign in which he was actively involved was with 39 Squadron Meteor NF II's in 1956, in Cyprus against Egypt.

In addition to the D.F.C., he holds the 1939/45 Star, Aircrew Europe, France and Germany Stars, Defence Medal, Victory Medal and General Service Medal with two clasps.

Laurie married his wife Jean, in 1951 and they have two sons Roger and Mark. His brother George was a pilot in the R.C.A.F. and served with 415 Squadron. He was later reported missing in 1943 in India.

After F/Lt. Lawrence retired from the R.A.F. he emigrated from the U.K. to Canada, where he worked in sales, business systems and computers, finally retiring in 1985.

Laurie has been very active in the Aircrew Association and is a past president of the Vancouver branch; the first to be formed in Canada.

One of his most memorable wartime trips was in March 1943. The crew was detailed to carry out a mine laying sortie to drop two 2000 lb mines off the Dutch coast, in the channel off the Friesian Islands.

The weather that day was bad, with an extremely low ceiling and conditions expected to be marginal for their return. The possibility of the operation being scrubbed was quite high; ironically, the crew was hoping that it would be a "go" as the sortie was considered a gift, but nevertheless, contributed to the completion of a tour. The Wellington had reached the operational area, flying at 600 feet over the sea, just below a thin sheet of low cloud and must have presented a silhouette to any observer below. The navigator, an Australian called Lumby, had fixed his position on Gee and the aircraft was turned in on course for the drop. Laurie was lying down in the bomb aimer's position, arming the mines and setting the length of stick.

He had just ordered "Bomb Doors Open" as they were approaching the dropping point when suddenly, several streams of tracers seemed to erupt from the surface of the sea. Paddy, the pilot, reacted immediately, by throwing the aircraft into a sharp diving turn to avoid being hit. The aircraft, luckily, did not sustain any damage but the mines had not been dropped. There was no alternative but to go through the same procedure, although it was realized, that a flak ship was anchored near the dropping zone. On the second attempt, the bomb doors were opened and the mines had been re- leased from the aircraft, when all hell broke loose. A searchlight flashed on, several streams of tracer fire of different colours sailed upwards and simulta- neously, blue white flashes erupted in the fuselage. The rear gunner, Geoff, had opened fire and succeeded in hitting the searchlight and all firing from the enemy ceased. Joe, the wireless operator, who had been keeping a look out for enemy fighters from the astrodome, shouted that he had been hit.

It naturally became Laurie's job to render first aid, as he was the one who could best be spared. Joe, by this time, was lying on his stomach over the main spar; he appeared to have sustained a hit at the back of his thigh; further investigation showed that he had been hit with an explosive shell which had gouged a hole sufficiently large to hold a large orange. The wound was filled with a shell dressing, bandaged and morphine administered, then a tourniquet was applied.

Joe was suffering from shock and complained of the cold despite the fact that he was lying on, and covered with five leather flying jackets, trousers and battle dress blouses that the whole crew had volunteered. They them- selves were flying in shirt sleeves. It was extremely cold, but he was made as comfortable as possible in the navigator's cabin while the navigator stood on his seat to do his navigation. The tourniquet was released at intervals and some two hours later, the aircraft landed at base, R.A.F. Kirmington, Lincs. Joe was taken to hospital and he survived the ordeal, but never returned to the crew. He now walks with a limp.

The aircraft sustained considerable damage, having been hit at the root of the starboard wing, tearing a gaping hole some four feet in diameter. Dam- age was also sustained to the central portion of the fuselage, however no vital part of the machine had been put out of commission.

F/O W.B. "BILL" LOWTHER
NAVIGATOR R.C.A.F.

W.B. (Bill) Lowther was born in Calgary, Alberta and lived there until moving to Vancouver, B.C., where he attended and graduated from Lord Byng School. After graduation from high school, he worked for the Dominion Bank in two Vancouver branches and in April 1942, joined the R.C.A.F. and subsequently graduated from #5 Air Observer School in Winnipeg as a navigator in September, 1943.

After graduating from A.O.S. and short stays in Halifax and at Camp Miles Standish near Boston, Mass., he arrived in the United Kingdom, to enjoy a short, but most enjoyable time in Bournemouth, before posting to Advanced Flying Unit at West Freugh in Scotland with a dozen Canadian Navigators. These were the first Canadians that this small R.A.F. station had encountered and some most interesting situations developed, as the "establishment" sought to bring these "unruly colonials" around to their way of thinking.

Upon leaving A.F.U., this little band of navigators proceeded to Wellesbourne Mountford near Stratford-on-Avon, where Bill crewed up with a pilot, wireless operator, bomb aimer and two air gunners. The crew was moved to a satellite station at Gaydon, where Operational Training Unit courses were completed in a fairly routine manner. A rather startling event occurred during a sea search over the North Sea in low cloud, when, flying in thick cloud, another aircraft flew over their Wellington aircraft, damaging the fixed antennae on the top of the aircraft and leaving its trailing antennae wrapped around their starboard wing. A close call on their first flight, in aid of bomber operations, as they searched for several crews that had possibly gone down in the North Sea, while returning from a bombing operation the previous night.

Graduation from O.T.U. brought Bill and his crew to Heavy Conversion Unit at Wombleton, Yorkshire, for conversion training from Wellington to the four engined Halifax aircraft and the addition of a Flight Engineer to the crew. Conversion to the Halifax was completed in a rather routine manner, although two of the Navigators who graduated with Bill at Winnipeg A.O.S. died here in separate crashes, and the crew was posted to 425 R.C.A.F. Bomber Squadron at Tholthorpe, Yorkshire, known as the "Alouette Squadron".

The Alouette Squadron was a very successful unit and consisted of many, but by no means, all French Canadian air crews and ground crews. Shortly after arrival on the squadron, the Wing Commander called the crew into his office and explained the French situation and that as there were no French-speaking members in the crew, they might want to be posted elsewhere, but if they wished to stay, they were most welcome. Bill and the crew liked what they had seen so far, decided to stay, made good friends, and soon learned to do things "their way".

Soon after starting their tour of operations, they were on their way to a rocket supply base, when they were attacked on two occasions, by Messerschmidt 109's and a running battle ensued, covering many miles of corkscrewing, during which both gunners scored many hits, resulting in both enemy fighters going down. The Halifax did not sustain any serious damage, apart from numerous holes and Bill was able to chart the probable locations of the crashed fighters, while keeping track of the erratic courses flown during the fighter attacks.

They continued on to the target, bombed as planned, and on return to base a bit late due to the attacks, were greeted by the news that the pilot of another Halifax from the other squadron on their base, had been killed by bullets from an unknown allied aircraft and that Halifax had been flown back by another crew member. The two gunners were suspected of having fired at the other Halifax, but fortunately, Bill's estimated positions of the crashed fighters were proved correct, by confirmation two or three weeks later, from underground sources in occupied Europe, that indeed, the wreckage of the two German fighters had been found in the locations given. Happily the two gunners were credited with the victory, rather than the threatened disciplinary action.

Later in the tour, as they were getting used to their French Canadian comrades and learning a little fractured French or English as the case may be, the squadron was to fly an operation to Brest in very bad weather. The operation was scrubbed and recalled several times and finally a relatively small operation was carried out, by a few of the 6 Group squadrons. On return to England, their base was fogged in, as well as every other base they were directed to, until finally, after flying around the country and almost out of fuel, a break in the cloud revealed an aerodrome. The Squadron, led by their French-Canadian Wingco dived through the clouds toward the aerodrome with the Wingco calling on the radio, " 'ello dis place, where de 'ell

I am?" After several of these transmissions, a "very very English" flying control officer came on the air and commenced a lengthy landing procedure only to have "Joe", the Wingco, take over and give all his "boys" their turns to land, about 30 seconds apart, since everyone was out of gas. After all had landed and the panic and the screaming could still be heard from the control tower, "Joe, the Wingco" became the centre, to "his boys" at least, of a most hilarious international incident.

Towards the end of their tour, their 29th operation, on a raid on Keil, with the huge fires in the city just starting to spread, visibility was still very good and due to the extremely heavy anti-aircraft fire, the night fighters were not operating over the target area, however, they did see an object just above and coming directly toward them, trailing fire. It was one of the new German jet fighters, the first they had seen. The crew was thankful that it did not attack.

Their tour concluded at the end of September and Bill spent the next few weeks instructing new navigators arriving on the squadron and then spent several glorious weeks exploring the south of England and all the good things that London could offer. On returning to the squadron from one of these trips, he was given the task of conducting a small draft of personnel to the Repatriation Depot at Warrington, where circumstances were such, that he was posted back to Canada just in time to marry his fiancee, Kay and spent Christmas, 1944, at home.

Following his leave at home, Bill was posted to Western Air Command Headquarters in Vancouver, where he was stationed until obtaining his release in May, 1945. He received the 1939/45 Star, France/Germany Star, Defence Medal, C.V.S.M. and Bar and the Victory Medal.

After release from the R.C.A.F. Bill returned to banking for a short while, then entered a variety of other endeavours, including management and sales in a couple of wholesale businesses, real estate sales, and for many years has been involved in management of business and ticket operations, until retirement in January 1988, for the B.C. Lions Football Club. Bill was also active in the Canadian Legion and is a Past President of Billy Bishop Branch No. 176 in Vancouver. Bill and his wife Kay and their son, Andrew reside in Vancouver.

F/O DAN C. RYAN

PILOT R.C.A.F.

Dan Ryan was born in Trail, British Columbia and attended primary and secondary schools there. His family then moved to Rossland, where he graduated from high school with honours in art. During his teenage years, he was a keen member of #531 "City of Trail" Air Cadet Squadron and rose through the ranks to Flight/Sergeant. His energetic participation in squadron activities and his enthusiasm for aviation, earned him a flying training scholarship. Soloing after eight hours and fifteen minutes of dual instruction, at the Chilliwack Flying Club on Fleet Canuck aircraft, he went on to qualify and become a licensed pilot at the ripe old age of seventeen. The following year he attended a senior leaders course in Camp Borden and upon returning home, promptly enlisted in the R.C.A.F., realizing an ambition that had been evident as early as grade school.

After enlisting in Lethbridge, Alberta, on October 14th, 1955, Dan was shipped to London, Ontario, the location of the Personnel Selection Unit, (Officers) where the usual aptitude tests were run, to determine whether he was to be a pilot or a navigator. The outcome was never in doubt for Dan, as his previous flying experience allowed him to pass all the pilot's oriented tests with "flying colours", while he took on all the attributes of a semi-illiterate uneducated dunce, when tested for Morse Code or mathematic calculations. Nevertheless, he breathed a sigh of relief, when the chief selection officer shook his hand as a brand new student pilot flight cadet.

There followed two months of rigorous pre-flight training at R.C.A.F. Station Centralia, Ontario. On January 27th 1956, Dan's course (5514) was posted to R.C.A.F. Station Claresholm, the home of #3 Flying Training School. There, Dan learned to fly deHavilland Chipmunk and not to be intimidated by the enormously larger North American Harvard.

On the 9th of April 1956, after a total of one hour and thirty-five minutes solo in the Harvard, Dan set some form of station record. After twenty minutes aloft in Harvard MK II 2817 doing "circuits and bumps", a crosswind manifest itself and Dan wrote off both wing tips and runway lights on all three of the field's runways! Old number 2817 was trucked off to the maintenance depot at Lincoln Park in Calgary and in spite of this Dan graduated from #3 F.T.S. in October and was promoted to Pilot Officer, (one of the last courses to be promoted to this rank) and was posted to Number Two Advanced Flying School at Portage la Prairie, Manitoba.

There, Dan was introduced to the Canadair T-33 Silver Star and the differences between propeller driven and jet aircraft. Upon graduation from A.F.S. Dan was presented with his wings and promoted to Flying Officer. In December 1958, Dan realized a lifelong ambition to fly "the pilot's airplane" ... the Dakota (C-47) and after some time spent as a co-pilot, was finally given a temporary posting to #4 Operational Training Unit at Trenton, where he gained his captaincy on the Douglas aircraft.

In June 1960, Dan was transferred from Training Command to Air Defence Command, Five Air Division and posted to Sea Island, B.C. There he joined #121 Communications and Rescue Flight. He was soon captaining C-47s on the thrice a week Port Hardy scheduled run and then checked out as co-pilot on the venerable old flying boat ... the Canso. This amphibian had been originally designed some years before Dan was born! Because the aircraft was to be withdrawn from service shortly, Dan was unable to gain his captaincy on the type.

On August 10th 1960 in Canso 075, Dan took off for his fifth flight in the lumbering old amphibious flying boat. As they gained altitude, west of Vancouver's Sea Island airport, the Captain explained that they would be shooting water landings at Pat Bay and that it would be good practice as there, the sea conditions were complex. "There's both a primary and a secondary swell running right now after the storm yesterday and the wind shift last night. They are at right angles and on top of that, there's a good stiff wind blowing a fair chop on the water as well. We'll do some orbits over the bay and then drop a smoke marker." he said. Dan had noticed that the burly sergeant who was the flight engineer, had sharpened pencils sticking out of every pocket in his flight suit. He hadn't had time to question the engineer about his pencil collection prior to take-off.

In due course the smoke marker was dropped and they continued to orbit, as the experienced captain studied the surface of the water and the behaviour of the smoke billowing from the floating marker. Eventually, he aligned the creaking Canso up with the smoke and called "downwind check!"

Dan looked out the co-pilot's window and noticed that this downwind leg of the circuit was being flown parallel to the line of smoke and towards the marker! The captain coolly flew the crosswind leg and began his descent calling out his engine and flap settings. The leaden old boat slipped out of the sky towards the choppy water and Dan wondered why he had not been told that they were going to practice "down-wind" water landings.

Just before the hull could touch the water, some sixth sense warned the pilot. The throttles had been cut back completely, but still the speed over the water seemed too fast. He yelled at Ryan to do as he did and grabbed the huge control yoke and with both feet up on the instrument panel and knees locked, he yarded the controls back. By this time Dan's arms were also wrapped around the co-pilot's yoke and holding it back against his chest with his feet braced against the instrument panel. The hull went through the top of a swell and the water threw the Canso back into the air. The next thing Dan knew, the impact had torn both pilot's headsets off and they were headed for the bowels of the cockpit hull.

After six or seven bounces, the aircraft heaved into the water and resigned itself to flying no longer. It was then that Dan found out the purpose of the engineer's wooden pencils. Even before the boat finally stopped in the water, the engineer leaped down from his seat in the pylon and like a flash he pulled up a hatch in the main passageway and disappeared into the dark recesses of the aircraft's hull. Moments later he emerged minus some of his pencils, switched off his flash light and gave the pilot a "thumbs up" sign, who then explained to Dan that he had been concentrating on interpreting the water surface and had mis-read the smoke marker. Dan then asked about the engineer's behaviour. The captain replied, "Oh he just went down there to check for sprung hull rivets. When he finds them, he sticks the sharp end of a pencil in the hole! It's standard operating procedure!"

After that, prior to every Canso flight, Dan checked to ensure that the flight engineer had lots of sharpened pencils.

Undoubtedly, the duties carried out by a 121 KU were the most satisfying of Dan's R.C.A.F.career. He participated in many searches and countless air evacuations, as well as chauffeuring the Lieutenant-Governor, the Hon. George Pearkes all over B.C. in 121 KU's Dakota. It was on a search north east of Stewart, at the head of the Portland Canal, while flying Dakota 692 with his flight commander, that Dan logged a flight of eight hours and twenty minutes. The maximum endurance of the C-47 was given as eight hours and thirty minutes!!

Dan was honourably discharged from the R.C.A.F. on 4th October 1961, and immediately started a new career in commercial art. He moved his family to Edmonton and then progressed from a commercial artist in the printing industry, to an art director in an advertising agency, then to the role of creative director, then an account executive and ultimately to management of two national Canadian advertising agencies. In 1974 Dan moved his family back to the coast, where he worked for a year as the marketing manager of a hotel chain, and then as the advertising manager of a large retail building supply chain. After seven years, he left to join a competing chain in the same industry, again as their advertising manager. Dan is looking forward to another career, which he intends to embark on after retirement from the business world, that of an aviation artist, specializing in Canadian subjects. Dan feels strongly that Canada's aviation heritage should be recorded and recognized. He says, "Aviation played an important part in the development of this country and I hope that in a small way, my art will honour the men and machines who played roles in a part of that development."

Dan is married to Marilyn and has two daughters and two grandchildren by a previous marriage.

F/O ALLAN D. MACPHERSON
NAVIGATOR R.C.A.F.

Allan D. "Mac" MacPherson was born in Revelstoke, B.C. where he took both his elementary and secondary education. While growing up, he took part in hockey, basketball, skiing, swimming, tennis, badminton and track. He was also active in the Outdoor Club and the student's council. He attended the University of British Columbia 1940/41 and enlisted in the R.C.A.F. in 1942 as a candidate for aircrew.

His service training commenced at No. 3 Manning Depot in Edmonton, tarmac duty at No.3 S.F.T.S. in Calgary, No.2 I.T.S. in Regina and then to No.2 A.O.S. in Edmonton, where he graduated as a Sgt. Navigator in August 1943. In September he embarked from Halifax aboard the "Queen Elizabeth", landed at Gouroch, Scotland and proceeded to a Holding Unit at Bournemouth. After a sequence of R.A.F. training at No.1 Advanced Flying Unit in Ansons at Wigtown; at No.30 Operational Training Unit on Wellingtons at Hixon and Seighford; at No. 1662 Heavy Bomber Conversion Units on Halifaxes at Blyton and Sandtoft; and at No.1 Lancaster Finishing School at Hemswell, he was posted to R.A.F. No.12 Squadron, Wickenby, Lincs.

From June to December, 1944, "Mac" flew thirty bombing missions over

160

Europe. His first trips were almost pleasant, compared to later missions. There was a "gardening trip", a mine laying mission in a strait of water with considerable shipping and submarine traffic, between Ile de Re and La Rochelle on the mainland of France. In the act of laying mines, the aircraft was coned by searchlights and it in turn, became the centre of attention of innumerable light flak batteries from both sides. It was an awesome sight, seeing tracers coming at the aircraft, in a horizontal arcing pattern. It was almost as frightening as the time they were coned in the Ruhr Valley on a trip to Gelsinkirchin. At that time, the aircraft had 18,000 feet of altitude allowing it to dive for cover out of the searchlight cone into cloud formations below. Low level night flying over the Bay of Biscay, was a rather risky operation. But low level over the ocean, from Lands End around the Brest peninsula and up the mouth of the Garonne River, then climbing to bombing height, were almost relaxing, even if each trip took over eight hours flying time.

On the crew's twenty fifth mission, the squadron bombing Leader, "Sandy" Mansfield (Lord Sandhurst) on his second tour of operations, volunteered his services. Four hundred and twelve Lancasters participated in the raid, on the industrial city of Russelheim. While the raid lasted only ten minutes over the target, the elapsed flying time was over eight hours. Fifteen Lancasters were shot down. For Mac, the trip was a "shakey do". Their plane "S" for Sugar returned to base but never flew again.

Five days later, the crew, with "Sandy", embarked on a seemingly easy (piece of cake) mission to a V2 Rocket site at St. Recguier, near Abbeville, France. Cloud cover over the target did not allow a good run up. The Bombing Leader requested the pilot to orbit the target, which the Master Bomber had now abandoned, at a lower altitude, in order to visually identify it. THIRD TIME AROUND - UNLUCKY!!! By this time, Radar Predicted Flak, had locked on to their plane, "V" for Victor, and the ensuing flak knocked out the starboard engine. Seven minutes later the port outer had to be feathered. Next, the bomb load had to be jettisoned in order to maintain height to cross the French coast, three miles north-east of Dunkirk. With the continued loss of power and height over the English Channel, the crew decided to try and make it to the emergency landing field at Manston, near Broadstairs, Kent. Indicated air speed was 120 mph. A strong head wind reduced the ground speed to 75 mph. Thirty minutes earlier the ground speed had been 290 mph. Crash positions were taken by the crew. The third engine, starboard outer, "packed up" as the plane approached the runway, going down the funnel. With masterful flying, the skipper pancaked without the expected "prang". After that trip the Bombing Leader decided that this crew had used up all its nine lives and declined to fly future missions with them.

Well, he was right. On the last, thirteenth mission, on Frankfurt, a night fighter raked "V" Victor along its dorsal aspect taking out the mid upper turret and the "greenhouse". With forty miles to target the aircraft, riddled like a sieve, continued on to bomb the target and returned to base with a badly wounded mid upper gunner.

From 12 Squadron, MacPherson was posted to a Repat Depot and after several early morning "health inspections" was homeward bound October 21, 1944 on the "Queen Mary". Submarine watch from the flying bridge during a maximum force hurricane off the coast of North America was an added scarey experience. "Home Sweet Home" for 30 days. Then a posting to Western Air Command, Vancouver. Given the opportunity, he elected to act as adjutant on No. 15 Explosive Depot at Kamloops, B.C. After an administrative course at No. 1 K.T.S., Toronto he returned to W.A.C.to assume the role of Officer Commanding No. 11 Staging Unit at Dog Creek, in the interior of B.C. It was used as a landing field for P-30 Aircobras, P-38 Lightnings, and P-41 Tommyhawks, being flown from California and Washington over the Bering Sea to Russia. After V J Day, "Mac" applied and received his release from the R.C.A.F. in November 1945.

He was awarded the 1939/45 Star, France/Germany Star, Aircrew Europe Star, Defence and Victory Medals and the C.V.S.M and Clasp.

ODE TO A DARK LADY

A beauteous comely maid was she,
Her lovely form a joy to see,
She came as swiftly as the night,
As graceful as a bird in flight,
Into the green years of our life,
Not sweetheart true, nor loving wife,
But dark, mysterious, proud, unknown,
To cherish, love but never own,
Respectfully we learned to pay
Our tributes to her day by day,
And as our lives with hers entwined,
Our joys, our fears, our inner mind
Became a mutual living thing
To take upon our journeying,
She opened wide her arms to share
With us the perils of the air,
Her steadfast spirit, loyal, true,
Was with us always as we flew,
She never faltered, even though
She might be wounded, weak and slow,
We raise our glasses, drink a toast
Remembering a very host
Of things that time cannot transcend,
A gallant mistress, servant, friend,
We loved her to the very end,
My lady Lancaster

AUDREY GREALY

162

Mac attended the University of B.C. in 1946 and was accepted by the University of Oregon Dental School in Portland, U.S.A., the following year. In 1947 he married Barbara, his high school sweetheart and they lived in Portland for the next four years. After graduation, they moved to White Rock, B.C. where Mac commenced a dental practice in 1952 that continued 'till 1981. In 1985 he retired. He still lives in White Rock, has six children and ten grandchildren.

F/LT H.M.MCDONALD D.F.C.
BOMB AIMER R.C.A.F.

Harold McDonald was born in Drumheller, Alberta and the sounds of his childhood were the cacophony of coyote's howls and the steam whistles of a mining town. Some of the sights that memory sustains are of those many freight and passenger trains and the cenotaph that stood near the station.

On Armistice, for a hushed moment, even the great engines were muted to short gasps of steam as the town stood still, until the Last Post severed the silence. The phrase "A war to end all wars" held scant promise. Soon the many of the fidgeting cubs and scouts would have their names chiselled in the memorials' cold gray stone.

After the war Mac was at U.B.C. and graduated in Commerce, worked as a fuel dealer and stock broker. Obtained his Master of Divinity in '76 and had churches in Alberta and the Lower Mainland. He was the former chaplain at Central City Mission and now is "Old Mac" to Longhouse Council of Native Ministry. Mac was awarded the D.F.C., 1939/45 Star, Aircrew Europe Star,

163

C.V.S.M and Clasp and the War and Defence Medals. He is married to Brenda and has four children.

"Mac" as he was called in the service, enlisted in the old post office building in Vancouver, where, but a few years before, the mayor had called out the police and read the riot act to the unemployed. Getting a number was a break for one with a name as common as McDonald. Pearl Harbour had given an impetus to recruiting on the west coast and Mac was soon part of a motley crew of A.C. 2s, entraining for Edmonton. He could not then imagine the anguish of his mother, a First War nursing sister, as she waved him off on the first of many such train trips across Canada.

In Edmonton, Mac's group were not met with the courtesy they had been shown at the recruitment depot. A very miserable sergeant herded them into trucks, not buses, like cattle and THAT, they were to find out, was most appropriate, for they were to be billeted in the old cattle barns at the Exhibition grounds.

There were numerous parades and inspections, some very personal and there were drill parades, church parades, sick parades, parades for inoculations and a thing called a Wasserman test. Big six footers keeled over with this one; Mac was six feet and he keeled over.

Mac received his bomb aimer wing in Edmonton, December 4th, 1942. Some of the songs of the day were "Don't sit under the apple tree", "We'll hang out the washing on the Siegfried Line", while Hitler was taking all to the cleaners. Mac and the rest soon embarked on the "Queen Elizabeth" (93,000 tons) and set sail for England. That night it was announced on the BBC that the "Scharnhorst" had broken through the British blockade and was now out in the Atlantic. That was a Saturday night. The first church parade was a Roman Catholic mass the next morning. Mac and a great many more protestants were present!

England was another world; they spoke English! It is their language, yet Mac found he had to be bi-lingual. You got petrol for your lorry and went to the flicks, there was mild and bitter and Woodbines, barrage balloons that were said to hold London up, pubs, Lyons Corner Houses, huge railway stations and tube stations where people still bedded down for the night.

Coming from training, in the cold of Canada to the warmth and luxury of Bournemouth in the south of England was a trip from agony to ecstasy, but it was short lived and Mac and his colleagues were soon training in Ansons again, in North Wales. This was followed by O.T.U. at Upper Heyford in Wellingtons. "Lord Haw Haw" was supposed to have said at this time "We don't need to kill Canadians; they are killing themselves at O.T.U." Mac was "crewed up" at O.T.U. and was fortunate to be chosen by the very pilot he had hoped for. Their first op was a leaflet raid over the Ruhr, which was silly and poor arithmetic, for Mac had already been informed that one of his old school gang had been lost on such a raid. Then they were off to conversion unit to convert to Lancasters ... and then to the squadron, #57 squadron at Scampton, near the city of Lincoln. It was part of 5 Group and the sister

164

squadron was none other than #617, the "Dam Busters". On August 23rd, 1943 they made their first trip to Berlin ... the first of ten trips. It was the beginning of what became known as the "Battle for Berlin" and although they flew to such places as Munich, Nurenberg, Magdberg and others, they came to feel a sense of familiarity with both the route and the defenses - or at least Mac thought so from his vantage point. After all, they had survived 27 trips - a few to finish and this was the ninth one to the "Big City".

It was January 20th, 1944 when "A" for Annie took off. (The moon was up), which dictated that they would fly the long northern route over Norway and Sweden, then make a dash south for the target and race with lightened load across a darkened sky straight across Germany for home. Had not they done it before? Of course, it was a matter of record.

Mac could see Berlin with the Pathfinders' flares; a bomb aimer was a jack-of-all-trades; a gunner, sometime navigator, seldom co-pilot and the "passer of the pee can". A nervous "pee" was a prerequisite at such a time and after the ritual passing, he stowed it behind him to prepare for what had to be the great moment, a time if ever so short and yet deceptively long, when he gave the orders.

The sight was awesome; a mosaic of the colours of the flares, smoke, black flak puffs, exploding aircraft, incendiary fires all filtered through the prisms of the white and the terrifying big blue searchlights, that could catch them like a moth in their light. Mac's ears were deadened by the roar of the engines and there was no room for idle chatter. Mac saw the target flares and called "Target sighted skipper". "Bomb door open" and for seconds, the skipper flew steady to each command: "Right, left left, left left ... steady ... bombs away ... bomb doors closed."

That was it, that was their moment and old "A" Annie seemed to soar high like an eagle, that had dropped its prey. They weaved and climbed to a greater height and Mac felt higher than the aircraft. Getting home might sound like a piece of cake. "Annie" had shed her burden of bombs and much of her petrol, the moon was down and the lightened aircraft could streak home under the cover of darkness. But bombing Berlin was like busting open a wasp's nest, to augment the terror by night.

Mac totally ignored such thoughts, as he routinely searched the land and sky before him. Hadn't they done it all before? Of course. It was a matter of record. The Germans had many ways of attempting to divert their enemy, such as fake flares, fake airdromes. Mac saw a circle of lights ahead but his wisdom, born of experience, prevailed, as he calmly informed the skipper "Dummy airdrome ahead skipper". "Good for you, Mac" was the reply.

A few moments later, after the circle of light went out "A" Annie was buffeted, blasted and holed with the accompanying death rattle of spent flak on her metal hide. The skipper's instant response was to put his aircraft into a dive to get below the set shell bursts, but Mac was momentarily unaware of this and assumed that this was the moment he had not dared to think of ... they were going for a "Burton". He hadn't much time to think about it, as he was pulled into the nose and bombsight by the centrifugal force of the rapid dive. "A" Annie levelled out with a shudder and the skipper started his routine check of the crew and aircraft. This drill started with the air gunner in the rear turret. Mac, up front would be last. Yet in spite of the pain and the feel of wet blood on his legs, he would wait his turn. That was what discipline was all about and biting his lip and holding back the tears he wondered if he'd get a DSO at least, for WHAT he wasn't sure, but courage counts. At the very least, he would get home on one or two wooden legs. The pilot called the rear gunner. "Are you OK Jack?" "Yes skipper". Then pilot to mid-upper "Are you Ok Vags?" he was OK but reported that there were flak holes in the fuselage. The questioning seemed to move at such a slow pace and Mac felt he was getting weaker and with the pain, could pass out, but he courageously held his silence. His moment would come. At last, the pilot asked "Pilot to bomb-aimer, are you OK?" Mac spoke slowly to stop his voice from breaking. "I've got it in both legs Pat, send Johnny down with a tourniquet and some morphine". Johnny, the navigator forgot the medical requests, but remembered his flashlight and the bright beam fell on the upturned pee can that had dampened the bomb aimers cold numb legs. He called to the skipper, "Mac's OK." Johnny gave Mac a warm hug, and temporarily without oxygen quickly lumbered back to the comforting cocoon of his navigator's tent. Mac continued his search for dummy air dromes and fighters and they soon landed safely.

The next night, Mac had the bar steward give a beer to all in the mess.

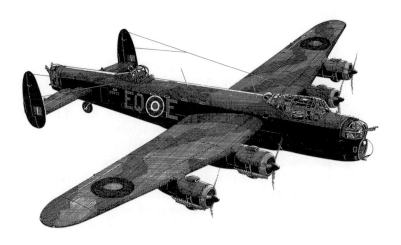

W/CMDR. C.N. MCVEIGH A.F.C.,C.D.

PILOT R.C.A.F.

Charles Norman McVeigh was born in Calgary, Alberta and attended Orlando School, near Craigmyle and then went to St Mary's Boys' School (Secondary) in Calgary and after graduation, attended the R.C.A.F. Staff College and the N.A.T.O. Defence College. During his early days in Calgary he enjoyed riding horses and fishing.

In 1937 he was accepted by the Air Ministry for entry into the R.A.F. on a short service commission at Perth, Scotland and began flying Tiger Moths. He graduated without any problem. On November 6th, 1937 he was given the rank of Acting P/O and sent to #7 F.T.S. at Peterborough, Northants, where he flew Hawker Harts for the first 3 months then Hawker Audaxs for armament training. Again he graduated, the middle of June 1938.

Then followed a navigation course in Ansons, from which he graduated in August of that year. In September, he was transferred to #12 Squadron at Andover, Hants. The Squadron was one of ten, that made up the Advanced Striking Force, which would deploy to France at the outbreak of war and deal with the enemy for a period of 72 hours, when Bomber Command would take over. They were now flying Fairey Battles. They moved to Bicester in Oxfordshire just before war broke out. On September 2nd they deployed to Berry-Au-Bac, France, later moving to Amifontaine. From then on until May 10th, 1940 Mac dropped leaflets on Germany, but nothing of more significance.

However, from that date on and for the next five weeks, they were to lose perhaps 300% of their aircrew. They were given replacements from time to time and then they moved back to Echinens & Souge and then on June 17th to England. On reaching England, they became a unit of 1 Group Bomber Command and they bombed the Channel ports, flying Battles, as support for the Battle of Britain. They also had to give to Fighter Command, most of their pilots and in return, received midshipmen from the Fleet Air Arm. Mac

167

stayed with the squadron as a flight commander and was promoted to F/O and immediately Acting F/Lt.

At Binbrook, Lincolnshire, they converted to Wellington II's and became one of Bomber Command's night bombing units. Mac was shot down on the night of August 17th 1941 and was in hospital for approximately nine months.

Early in May 1942, he was sent to #2 F.I.S. at Montrose, Scotland, where he took instructor training on Magisters and Oxfords and was promoted to S/Ldr on July 1st and transferred to #6 A.F.U. at Little Rissington on Instructor duties. He was made O/C the Satellite at Chipping Norton, instructing on Oxfords.

He was transferred to H.Q. 44 Group Transport Command as Training Officer on 11th March 1943 and was responsible for Accident Investigation, then in January 1944 Mac was transferred to 105 (T) O.T.U. Bromcote for conversion, flying Wellington IC's.

February 1944 saw him transferred to #48 Squadron equipped with Dakota's as "2 i/c". They were located at Down Ampney where they were to become part of the Airborne Force, dropping paratroops, towing gliders and dropping supplies, supporting the 6th Airborne Division. On "D" Day, June 6th, Mac led 48 squadron on the drop ... incidentally, the squadron was the lead squadron for the entire night drop at 1:30 a.m. under very poor weather conditions, as the reader will no doubt be aware.

The Canadian Government asked the Air Ministry if the R.A.F. would be prepared to release two senior officers, Canadian by birth, trained in the Airborne role, to form an R.C.A.F. Dakota Sqdn. Mac was one of the two officers and they formed 437(T) Squadron on September 18th, 1944 and on the same day took part in the operation to cross the Rhine at Arnhem. The R.C.A.F. took him on with the rank of S/L and they formed the squadron at Blakehill Farm where they were based until May 6th, 1945, when they were deployed to Nivelles in Belgium.

Promotion to W/C came on August 26, 1945 and Mac was then appointed O.C.435(T) Squadron at Down Ampney until on September 26th, 1946 they flew the squadron to Canada via Iceland, Greenland, Goose Bay and on to Rockcliffe (Ottawa), where the squadron disbanded.

Several transfers and lengthy flights took place from September 1946, when on November 20th, Mac was sent to England to fly the VIP Dakota. Between October 1947 and July 1948 he attended R.C.A.F. Staff College in Toronto. On July 11th he was posted to the Canadian Joint Air Training Centre at Rivers, Manitoba, to become O/C the Dakota operation. He was transferred in February 1951 to A.F.H.Q. in Ottawa as Staff Officer for Joint and Combined Operations and then transferred again to R.C.A.F. Station St.John's, Quebec as C-Ad-O. On January 3rd, 1957 he was transferred to Training Command H.Q. Trenton as Staff Officer for Organization and Management. From January 'til June 1961 he attended 1(F) O.T.U. for training on Sabres and from September 1961 was a student at the Nato Defence College in Paris, France. On February 9th, 1962, Mac was transferred to #1

Air Division H.Q. at Metz, France as Staff Officer for Organization and Management and he remained there until September 1965 when he was honourably discharged. Mac went into the Collector Plate business with his wife, Peggy, whom he married in 1942. Their daughter, Carol is a nurse.

Mac's decorations and medals are as follows, A.F.C., Mentioned in Dispatches twice, 1939/45 Star, Aircrew Europe, France/Germany Star, Defence Medal, C.V.S.M. and Bar, C.D. and Bar, Tour decoration and Bar and War Medal.

Around the middle of May 1940 the whole of the Atlantic Striking Force had hastily evacuated their bases and re-located some 100 miles to the south in France. They had moved from their base at Amifontaine to Souge. Because the move had been done in such great haste, a lot of equipment and aircraft were left behind. A day after the evacuation, Mac flew a Fairey Battle back to Rheims airfield with a pilot, to fly back a serviceable one if possible. When he got to Rheims, however he found the airfield riddled with bomb craters but still felt he could land and did so safely without damage.

A brief search of the hangar turned up no serviceable aircraft, but they found a tractor and fuel bowser which were badly needed, so the pilot and one crew member took possession of it and set out for home base. The remaining member of his crew helped Mac to load the plane with loot and then they were ready for take-off, except for the fact that Mac couldn't see directly ahead because the nose of the Battle obstructed his view. So his gunner L.A.C. Landon sat on the wing to help guide Mac to a point where a good take-off was possible. He would point to the right for a right turn and to the left for one to the left, but one of them wasn't as quick as they could have been for suddenly one wheel went into a crater and the wing came to rest on the field.

As luck would have it, there was a large number of French soldiers lounging near the edge of the field, and after they were beckoned over, about twenty of them got under the grounded wing and were able to hoist the Battle up and ahead onto even ground; Mac started the engine and using the same direction tactics was able to successfully get off the ground, into the air and away to base. The two man bowser and tractor crew got back a day later, after quite an eventful trip.

On August 16th, 1941 Mac had been on a bombing mission to Cologne, Germany but he lost an engine. The engine was the main part of damage to the Wellington II, but Mac felt he could get home on one engine. However he just couldn't maintain height and was gradually losing it on the homeward leg. When they had crossed the enemy coast they all felt they would make it back to England, but that it would be "nip and tuck". As they were flying over the North Sea Mac decided that it would be suicide to try a ditching because there was no moon and it looked awfully cold down there.

They crossed the coast of Norfolk and sent out an SOS. The searchlight chaps started laying down beams to get them to the nearest airfield as none of the crew wanted to bail out. As they were approaching what appeared to be a clear area, with a black line across the near edge, which Mac thought was a hedge, he attempted to force land.

Unfortunately, the "hedge" turned out to be a railway line and Mac crossed it at a spot where there was a stone bridge, used by farmers to cross the line, and the Wellington struck the edge of it with a tremendous jolt. The nose gunner, co-pilot and navigator were killed, Mac was thrown through the perspex over the pilot's position and landed on the edge of a slope beside the rail line, amongst bushes etc. and the radio op. was concussed but otherwise unhurt in the wreckage, while the tail gunner survived.

Just before they crashed they took the roof and aerial mast off a Home Guard hut, so it didn't take long for the Home Guard to respond and help the crew out of their predicament. Unfortunately one of them stumbled over Mac's legs, one of which was broken and, partly as a result, he was to spend almost nine months in hospital.

The same day that the German Army surrendered their occupation of Norway, May 10th '45, the Supreme Commander of SHAPE ordered that a Dakota be despatched to Oslo forthwith, to bring the German Peace Delegation from Oslo to Scotland. Mac's crew was the crew selected to undertake the trip. He was briefed at their base in Brussels, to the effect that he would find cloud cover over northern Denmark, but it would dissipate over the Skagerrak for a clear flight up the fiord to Fornabu airfield at Oslo. There were no up to date maps available and all they had was a pre-war map and of course, there were no navigational aids, should the weather turn bad.

As it turned out, the weather was broken cloud over Denmark. However, over the Skagerrak there was a low solid deck below, with tops perhaps 3,500 feet, which was certainly not in their forecast. Thinking it would disappear, they pressed on, but with about ten minutes to go before reaching the coast, it was felt that the only way to reach their destination without navigational aids would be to go below the cloud deck, so Mac let down gingerly until they broke below the deck at maybe 200 feet off the water. It was pouring hard at the time.

Soon, some large rocky outcropping appeared in the mist and rain, showing that the Dakota was entering the fiord. Still trusting in the met. forecast, they pressed on, hoping for a clearance. Mac decided to hug the coastline with all crew members up front watching for any kind of trouble, and by this time the rain was pouring heavier and visibility was down to practically zero. However, there was no thought of turning back now, as the fiord was too narrow and just before they arrived in the Oslo basin, they came almost face to face with a huge rock, about 50 feet high, around which Mac was able to swerve. Shortly afterwards they found themselves in the bay and the cloud had lifted 200 -300' and the visibility picked up to about a mile and the rain tapered off quite a bit.

Right in front of Mac, was Fornabu Airfield, a small one with quite high ground on the final approach to it. He went in and landed. There didn't appear to be any other aircraft around and suddenly a German airman beck-

170

oned him to come up to the hangar area and ushered Mac in to see the Commandant.

They stayed the night at Oslo and were greeted by the British Army Commander who had been parachuted in. He was astounded to see Mac, because a U.S. VIP Dakota turned back due to the weather conditions, seven Stirlings had crashed, while a huge number had, like the Dakota, turned back. So, Mac's was the only Allied aircraft to get in that day.

You, the reader, can perhaps visualize the reception they got in the streets of Oslo that night, when the whole city population turned out to celebrate!!

On October 23, 1946 Mac was captain of the VIP Dakota which was to fly Canada's Minister of National Defence - Brooke Claxton - and his wife from Athens to Rome. At the met. briefing, Mac was advised that he would meet moderate frontal cloud to fly through, just off the Greek coastal area, and then reasonable weather for the rest of the way to destination.

They climbed out and after perhaps half an hour, at about 7,000 feet or more they suddenly entered heavy cloud with terrific turbulence, hail and rain and although it was only ten in the morning he had to turn on the cockpit lights. They hit such turbulence that it wasn't a question of turning back, but rather keeping the aircraft in the air.

They would go from highspeed updrafts to equally fast downdrafts and their speed became so erratic that Mac dropped the undercarriage in an effort to try and keep the speed down. They were eventually blown through (what Mac found out later) a front where many isobars converged to a solid black line, and eventually made their way safely to Naples.

After landing and inspecting the aircraft, they found that the hail had stripped all the paint off the undercarriage until it was shining bright. The leading edges of the wings and nose of the aircraft were also stripped of paint and they felt very lucky to have got through that one.

They discovered later, that one other aircraft, a four engine one, was able to turn back because it was flying higher and the pilot was able to see the cloud build up ahead, before going into it.

SHORT STIRLING - No. 1651 CONVERSION UNIT R.A.F.

F/O SIDNEY T. MARTIN
R.C.A.F.

Like so many other young, eager types, Sid Martin joined the Airforce in August 1941. What he didn't tell the recruiting officer, was that he had been born in January 1925 and was just past his 16th birthday—not quite legal size.

He must have spun a convincing story, for he was accepted into the R.C.A.F. as an airframe mechanic. Possibly the fact that he was at the time working as a truck driver for the Commercial Truck Co. of New Westminster, steered him in that direction. Also Sid had been to N.J.Tapp Technical School, after attending Lister Kelvin School in New Westminster.

In any case, the Airforce took three months to declare him underage and put him back in the civilian market. Sid bided his time, until reaching the ripe old age of 17 1/2 plus a few days, and re-enlisted; this time as aircrew. Possibly, because of his rather limited education, or because air gunners were in short supply, he was enrolled as a W.A.G. and promptly sent via #3 Manning Pool, Edmonton to #8 Wireless School in Winnipeg, then on to #8 B & G Lethbridge, #3 A.O.S. Edmonton and finally to #32 O.T.U. at Pat Bay, B.C.

While at #3 A.O.S. at Edmonton, Sid was instructing navigators and nearly ended his career there. The old Mark I Anson lost an engine during a navigation exercise, and although everyone had been assured that the Anson would fly on one, this one didn't prove up to the task, ending up as a crash landing in the badlands of southern Alberta. The kite was a total write off, but the crew was of sterner stuff, (or much luckier) for they all survived.

After that, what could overseas have to offer in the way of adventure? Sid did not have too long to find the answer. From #32 O.T.U. he was posted in April 1944 to Dorval, for advanced training on the old goony bird, to prepare the crew for an Atlantic ferry via Gander, Greenland, Iceland and Scotland. The old DC3 took this all in its stride, although it took 27 hours of flying to complete the crossing. The weather was at its normal worst, making the sight and feel of the solid land of the U.K. especially reassuring. But even there,

there were hazards and Sid landed in London on two weeks leave, to be greeted by the first waves of Buzz bombs.

A posting to the Far East, seemed like a reprieve from doodle bug alley and a trip by the renowned Sunderland, a flight in the right direction. From Tenby in Wales, to #52 R.A.F. squadron at Dum Dum, India, must have been another long grind, but to trade that grand flying boat for the motley collection of airplanes then comprising #52 Squadron - must have been a come down. However, all these work horses had been pressed into service flying "the hump" into Kunming. Sid did 12 of these trips, along with supply flights to the 14th army, which was pushing the Japs down from Imphal to Rangoon and beyond. In all he did 290 operational hours, rose through the ranks to that of F/O and added the Burma Star to the 1939/45 Star, C.V.S.M. and Victory Medal.

Repatriated in September 1945, a long ship's passage to England and a short one to Canada, landed him back home on January 20th, 10 days short of his 21st birthday.

Sid had lost a lot of sports playing time, but unlike many of those who returned, he was able to quickly make up, for during the next 35 1/2 years with the New Westminster Fire Department, he found time to play lacrosse for the famous Salmon Bellies of New West, played world class softball (participating in 4 world tournaments) until 1962 and played senior basketball up to 1960. Not many of the boys can tie that record.

Sid and Esther have been married over 41 years, another good record. Their daughter Jackie also took to the air, signing on as a stewardess with Pacific Western Airlines, while son Wayne works for the Government as a Labour Relations Officer.

"VICKERS WELLINGTON IC Z1572 419 MOOSE SQN R.C.A.F"

173

F/LT G.T.(GORD) PEARCE
PILOT R.C.A.F.

Gordon was born in Elrose, Saskatchewan in 1916. As one might say, he received his education in most towns in Saskatchewan, as his father was with the C N Railway and his job required that he move often. The family lived in the towns of Brock, Melford, Harris, Humbolt, Eston and Gravelbourg. Like many other prairie boys, Gord enjoyed hockey, tennis and badminton—hockey being his first love. He graduated from High School in Humbolt and moved to Vancouver in 1936. Here he found work in Woodward's Department Store in the hardware department and started a career which he was to follow after the war. He also found time to continue his favourite sport, playing commercial and senior hockey.

On the morning war was declared in 1939, Gord and his room mate, were among the first dozen to try to enlist in the R.C.A.F. in Vancouver. They were advised to come back later, when the recruiting would be better organized and they were assured that they would get on an Aircrew draft. After repeated visits, he was finally accepted, but his hopes for an Aircrew posting were dashed, when he failed to pass the medical, due to the faint sign of a varicose vein. Not to be deterred, Gord visited a doctor who did an injection on his leg, which concealed the vein that had caused the trouble. He passed his second medical with flying colours.

It was on to Toronto and Manning Pool in the summer of 1940, where Gord was indoctrinated into the R.C.A.F., learning new skills such as left turn, right turn, about turn, how to salute and how to be brave when getting the needle and the short arm. The most common ailment here, was the Manning Pool Dust Cough. Winter of 1940 saw him in Dunnville, Ontario, on Security Guard Duty. Everyone felt that they had been forgotten and that the war would be over before they got overseas. They were a wild but good bunch of "bods" and they found many ways to relieve the boredom of Guard Duty. One novel way was betting on how many times, one could run around the parade ground "skinny" in the snow, at 10 degrees below zero. Another prank Gord remembers from guard duty days, was one night when a noisy L.A.C. returned from a 48 hour pass, waking everyone up and asking if they felt the call of nature, and finally climbing into his upper bunk and falling into a deep sleep. At this time, some of his victims tied a beer bottle to his arm and set it on the edge of the bunk. You can say that when he moved, he woke up with a start.

After guard duty, Gord was posted to Initial Training School at the Eglinton Hunt Club in Toronto, and from there to No.2 Elementary Flying School at Fort William, where he learned how to "slip the surly bonds of earth" in Tiger Moths. There were no paved runways at this field and during the spring break-up it was a mass of ice and mud. The trainees nicknamed the school No.2 Elimination School. In May 1941, Gord started his Service School Course on Harvards, at No 10 S.F.T.S., Dauphin, Manitoba and received his wings in July 1941. An experience which Gord recalls, that occurred while he was on a cross country exercise, was when his maps were sucked out through the open coup top by the slipstream, and to complicate matters, his Directional Gyro had spun and he couldn't get a course from it. He was lost, low on fuel and felt like filling his pants. After checking over the situation, he remembered an airport under construction which he had flown over, so he backtracked and managed to locate it, and decided to land. There was a steamroller working on the runway and Gord made three or four passes to attract the operator's attention, so he would move the roller from the runway, but nothing happened. It suddenly dawned on him that he had not lowered his undercarriage and when he corrected this oversight, the operator realized that there was a bit of a flap above him and gingerly moved the roller off the runway. After he landed, Gord teletyped Dauphin, to let them know where he was and they expected him to take off right away for base. However, the aircraft had to be refuelled and so did Gord, consequently, when he landed back at base, he found that he was listed as being overdue and as two other aircraft had been lost that day, the Flight Commander was glad to see him back and overlooked the incident. Gord chalked it up to experience!

Everyone expected that after they had graduated and received their coveted Wings, they would then be posted to overseas duty, however, at the time Gord graduated, the Airforce was short of Instructors and instead of the overseas posting, Gord, along with several others, found themselves on a draft to Central Flying School at Trenton, in August 1941, for training as flying instructors. On completing the course, they were told that they would only have to instruct for a few months and then they would get an overseas posting. However, once you were posted to a Command, it was next to impossible to transfer to another Command and the expected "few months" turned out to be nearly three years.

Gord's Instructional Tour started in November 1941, when he was posted to No.7 S.F.T.S. at McLeod, Alberta, where they flew the twin engine Anson. The foothills of the Rockies are noted for the strong winds that occur frequently, and

McLeod is in an area where the winds are the strongest. Airmen tell of the time that the wind was so strong, that they used a logging chain for a wind sock! According to another story, you can tell anyone from McLeod by their permanent lean and by their faces, bruised from flying gravel!

Students were sent solo in 40 m.p.h. winds and they learned to taxi into wind, downwind, and crosswind in these conditions, before they had finished their course; it was like learning to fly at ground level. The instructors worked hard, flying four to six hours, day after day and night after night, in order to get the courses out on schedule. During these hours, many incidents occurred, some serious and some humorous.

All instructors were required to log a few hours of instrument flying each month. On one such exercise, Gord was flying as Second Pilot to F/O Weimer, who was the proud owner of a radio that could pick up commercial airlines and the radio range. In order to do that, it was necessary to let out a hundred feet or so of aerial wire, which was weighted down with lead balls. After completing the exercise, they started for base and for a little relaxation did a spot of low flying between the deep banks of the Milk River, in the area of Butte, Montana. On pulling out of the cut and over some buildings, Weimer said "Did you feel that tug?" Looking down and back they saw chickens flying and people running here and there, wondering what had happened. Needless to say, they had not pulled in the trailing aerial. It had broken windows, pulled down an antenna and no doubt scared the Hell out of them. They must have thought they were being machine gunned. Luckily it did not start a war with the Americans.

On one night flying exercise, with a student, the student flew a wide circuit and was on the final approach, with wheels and flaps down, when Gord asked him if everything was O.K.; the student replied "Yup, should made a good landing sir, I have the flare path lined up this time". "Well you may at that' said Gord, in his laconic fashion, "but it will be on the main street in McLeod!"

McLeod received one of the first postings of the Women's Division in No.4 Command and Gord was "Joed" as their Flight Commander for a parade or two. In recognition of his dedication to duty at all times, he was presented with a tight fitting ladies' corset, which was forcefully fitted and laced on by his fellow Instructors in the Mess.

In July 1942, there was still no posting overseas. Gord and his fiance, Glenn, had decided to get married, and Gord had not yet bought the ring. He remembered that he was due for an instrument flight, under the hood with P/O Rogers as Captain and lookout. They took along a few L.A.C.'s and W.D.'s on leave, to catch a ride to Calgary. It was a bumpy trip, with a lot of cumulo-nimbus cloud around and on the final approach, while he was under the hood, all Hell broke loose. They were hit by a hail storm, the hailstones pounding the Anson with such force, that it felt as if it had exploded. The windscreen on the Captain's side was smashed and ripping off the hood, Gord could see the leading edge of the wings going to pieces, which caused a loss of lift.

Gord jammed the throttles forward and shoved the nose down and just managed to clear a fence and touch down on the grass, short of the runway. He taxied in and let off their passengers who were a bit shaken, to say the least. The aircraft was a mess. The end of the story is that the Captain got the flak and had to explain the incident, and Gord got the important ring, and his bride.

In February 1943, Gord was posted to No 15 Elementary Flying School as Chief Flying Instructor to help revamp the Regina Flying Club to an R.C.A.F. Flying School. This entailed writing the flying orders, organizing flight rooms, course and sequence boards etc. and posting the Civilian Staff Instructors to C.F.S. Trenton for refresher courses. Tiger Moths and Cornells were the training aircraft. Subsequently, No 15 E.F.T.S. won the "Cock of the Walk" Trophy, as the best Elementary School in No 4 Command.

A couple of incidents stand out in Gord's mind, from his time as C.F.I. at Regina. One was the decision that Anthony Eden's son was discontinued as a pilot and reselected as a navigator, a change that he says caused the flak to hit the fan. Another memory is of him giving a student a progress check and some extra dual instruction and finally sending him solo in a Cornell. The student went around the circuit about four times, overshooting each time. Gord stood watching, feeling sick and thinking he should never have let him solo. The student finally landed and it turned out that he couldn't get the throttle to close fully and finally decided that it would be a good idea to cut the switch on the final approach. The student got full marks for using his head and Gord added another grey hair to his own.

In September 1943, he was posted to another course at Trenton, this time, the purpose of the course, was to keep the Instructors happy and they got to fly every type of aircraft at the station, including Harvard, Hudson, Lockheed, Bolingbroke and Hurricane. In October 1943, he returned to Regina and stayed there until the summer of 1944 when the station was closed. Gord finally got the posting which he had been promised in 1941. His first overseas posting after Bournemouth, was to No 1511 Blind Approach Training Flight at Weaton Aston, on Oxford aircraft, then to No. 16 O.T.U. at Upper Heyford and Barford St. John on Mosquitos. He recalls an exercise out of Upper Heyford, with a second tour "bod" as navigator, using the Gee Box. The weather on their return was closed in, which was often the case in England. They tried to get a QFE or diversion from control, but with no luck. It finally sank in, that their radio was u/s and that they could not receive any messages. To make matters worse, they were low on fuel and had two choices - jump or try to get down. The navigator said no way was he going to jump, as he had a heavy date that night and he thought he could get them down with the Gee. Having lots of confidence in the navigator, Gord followed his directions and let down through the clouds and broke out right in front of the tower. Gord was up on the carpet for not obeying orders, but got off the hook, due to not being able to hear the diversion, due to the radio being u/s. On completing the course at Upper Heyford, Gord and his navigator were slated to be posted to 109 Squadron or the Far East, on Mossies. However, the Canadians were pulled off the posting and Gord was repatriated in 1945.

Looking back, Gord says instructors had many Critical Moments which were often thought of as routine scares and all part of their jobs. Instructing had its disappointments, thrills and compensations. Disappointment on being selected as an Instructor and not going overseas with those you trained with. Disappointed and upset, when you had to discontinue a student who had his heart set on being a pilot. Thrilled, when you watched your student's first solo and later proudly receiving his wings. Compensated, when someone would say "I remember you, you were my instructor."

Gord was discharged in October 1945, in Vancouver, B.C. with the rank of Flight Lieutenant. He received the Defence Medal, C.V.S.M. and War Medal.

Gord married Glenn Fisher of New Westminster in 1942, while stationed at McLeod; they have three sons and five grandchildren. After being discharged, they took up residence in Langley, B.C., where he established Pearce Hardware, with his two brothers, Cec and Doug. Gord is now, what he calls, semi-retired, working part-time with one of his sons in Home Hardware in Aldergrove, B.C. He keeps active in flying matters and still holds his flying licence and is a member of the Langley Airport Advisory Board.

F/LT GORDON H. MONTGOMERY D.F.C.
PILOT R.C.A.F.

Gordon was born at New Richmond, P.Q. and attended Rothesay School in New Brunswick, where he obtained his Junior Matric. He later attended McGill University, Montreal, for about six months prior to joining the R.C.A.F. His hobbies included hockey, English Rugby, and skiing and he enjoyed no pre-service occupation, as he joined the R.C.A.F. after University, actually on St. Patricks Day 1942 at Montreal.

He volunteered as a pilot and on the road towards graduating was at #6

Manning Depot, Lachine, P.Q. for 4 months, where he incidentally became a member of a precision drill squadron, then he was posted to #3 I.T.W. Victoriaville, P.Q. for 3 months, thence to #11 E.F.T.S., Cap de la Madeleine, P.Q. for two months flying Fleet Finch aircraft.

In December of that year, Gordon went to #6 S.F.T.S. at Brantford, Ont. until the end of April 1943 where he flew the Anson Marks II and III, (with their cunning yellow camouflage) and he was then posted to #1 Y Depot, Halifax, where he waited to board ship for Liverpool, England. He travelled on the "S.S. Pasteur" arriving ultimately, at #3 Personnel Reception Centre, Bournemouth in July. Early in August he went to #14 A.F.U. at Banff, Scotland and was there for nearly three months, where he again flew Ansons then Oxfords and it was here that he experienced a 6 day course on "beam approach". Following this he was posted to #24 O.T.U. at Honeybourne, flying Whitley Mk V's. This course included an uneventful "Nickel", to an area south of Paris, where a cargo of propaganda leaflets was dropped. Gordon was at #24 O.T.U. until the end of February 1944 and during the next two months was at Group Battle School, Dalton, then Conversion Unit, Dishforth, flying Halifax II and V.

The end of April saw him with #158 Squadron at Lisset, East Yorkshire and he was there, until the end of October, completing his first tour, consisting of 40 sorties. On the move once more, Gordon next was posted to #1669 Conversion Unit at Langar in Nottinghamshire, this time flying a new aircraft, the Lancaster I, staying there for five months, then there were rapid postings to Swinderby, Lincolnshire, Lulsgate, near Bolton, Lancashire, back to Swinderby then to #6 Aircrew Holding Unit, Rufforth, Yorkshire.

At the end of July he was posted to Scotland, but this was just so that he could embark on the "Ile de France" at Greenwich, bound for Halifax. He was originally then posted to Greenwood, Nova Scotia, to instruct crews bound for the Pacific and flying Lincolns, but while on re-pat leave, the bombs were dropped on Japan and the war ended.

Gordon was honourably discharged at #5 Manning Depot, Lachine, P.Q. on Sept 9th 1945, and registered at McGill University a week later, graduating with a B.Eng (Mining). He then went into Mining engineering with Noranda Mines Ltd and served with that firm for 31 years, rising to Vice-President Mining, B.C. He then went to Westmin Resources Ltd. for seven years and retired as Executive V.P. and General Manager, Mining Division on February 29th 1988. Gordon is married to Elizabeth and they have a son and a daughter.

Gordon reported to #158 squadron, April 27th 1944, and made his first trip on May 6th. On reminiscing about his crew, Gord believes they became a good and efficient crew as their experience developed, but they were fortunate, in that they arrived on squadron just as the attacks on major German targets were being reduced and as the "softening up" programme, prior to "D Day" targets, such as marshalling yards, was beginning.

He feels that the risk factor was considerably reduced by this change in policy, even though the trips required to complete a tour, were increased from 30 to 40. Fairly early in the tour, Gord and his crew adopted a philosophy that

179

while they were there to do the job, nevertheless, should any major item of basic equipment become unserviceable, that they would return to base and go another night. This resulted in two aborted sorties, one, when a turret failed before they reached the enemy coast and the other was when an engine failed during take-off. He says this also contributed to their survival!!

Another factor which helped, was that their aircraft was fitted with H2S and Fishpond, another radar device, also a factor in the successful completion of their tour. His wireless operator had some Coastal Command experience in anti-submarine training and he therefore monitored aircraft below them, on his radar, while the gunners concentrated on the sectors level with and above, their own aircraft. If the Wop reported an aircraft converging on them from below, they allowed it to get no closer than a couple of hundred yards and if it was not identified visually by that time they altered course. None of these events ever developed into a fully fledged attack by an enemy fighter, although they were attacked on occasion from level or above, but got away due to evasive action.

On the night prior to "D Day", they attacked a gun emplacement off the Normandy coast. Briefing for the trip, had included a prohibition on jettisoning bombs in the English Channel, but they were not told that the invasion was to take place next morning. Their radar equipment showed concentrated shipping in the area and one member of the crew remarked "There are so many ships down there, that you couldn't get your feet wet if you tried." On their way back from the sortie, they met the first of the glider and paratroop aircraft on their way out; they had their navigation lights on and Gord says it was an inspiring sight, one that he will never forget.

They bombed the railway yards at Dijon, on the Mediterranean coast of France, on the night of the landings, but some of their navigation equipment failed on the way home and they had just discovered where they were, when they flew over Cherburg, which had just been captured by the Americans. It was believed that their anti-aircraft shells had proximity fuses, as they pounded them in spite of evasive action, until they got out of range over the Channel. Fortunately, no-one was injured, the closest being a piece of shrapnel in the rear gunner's boot. Most of the damage was in the rear of the aircraft and as it still seemed to be flyable, Gord took it back to base, where the rear turret and major portions of the tail assembly had to be replaced.

Losing an engine on take-off, with a full load, was a "shakey do", but it worked out well, as Gord always held the aircraft down to build up airspeed, before starting to climb away ... as long as conditions allowed that procedure. On that particular occasion, the main bearing failed on the starboard outer, when they were a couple of hundred feet off the ground. It was a good aircraft, but by the time Gord got the engine feathered and the fuel shut off, flames from the air intake were shooting out, several feet in front of the engine cowling. However, they disappeared once the engine was fully shut down. They then flew out to sea, jettisoned the bombs, in order to get down to a safe landing weight and returned to base. Gord has a green endorsement in his log book for that event.

On another trip, the elevators had been shot up and they landed at a higher than normal approach speed, as Gord did not know what other damage had been done. It was rather a short runway, with a brook not far off the end. It was raining hard and it soon became apparent that they were going to "run out of runway", so Gord released the brakes and opened up the two port engines. This move resulted in a successful ground loop, but with no further damage to the plane, as the undercart did not collapse. There were a few questions asked about why they hadn't followed 'the book' and gone straight ahead, but Gord's decision was proven to be the correct one, when another aircraft which went into the brook was wrecked and there were several fatalities.

Gord's last trip was a daylight op. to Calais, when the army was trying to move the Germans out of that portion of the Channel ports. The decision had been made, to fly in a loose formation, with 9 aircraft in a V, made up of three V's of three aircraft each. They were in the lead aircraft in one of the V's and it was an easy target, with good visibility and little or no anti-aircraft opposition. However, as they approached the bombing point, a straggler from an earlier group was flying 200 feet above and just ahead of them. They went in as far as they could, but eventually broke formation and the straggler's bombs went down, between the two remaining aircraft of the V. Gord did a steep diving turn to get away and this move collapsed the bombsight gyro, so the bomb aimer used his thumb and forefinger as a replacement. The resulting bombing picture showed a good line, but a slight overshoot!!

Typical crew humour was along these lines:- One night during the run up to a Ruhr target, the navigator came up from his darkened position, to see what was going on. All he said on viewing the searchlight and flak was "Jesus" and disappeared back to his position. He never came up for another look!!

Another night, there was a German raid on Hull, when Gord and his crew were just setting out on a trip to Kiel. A voice came over the intercom, "Hey, skip, we should make a deal with these guys. They could bomb Keil and we'll bomb Hull, then we'd all get home a lot sooner."

Very early during the V 1 attacks on London, they bombed at night, a French target, a little in from the coast. From the time that they passed Reading, on their way out, it seemed that every bit of armament larger than a shotgun was firing at the V 1's. There was no opposition over their target, but the "fireworks" display was still going on over England as they turned for home. Once again the voice on the intercom said "Gee skip, I think we should stay over here ... it's safer".

Incidentally, Gordon received his pilot's wing as an L.A.C. and wound up as F/Lt. He was awarded the D.F.C. and also wears the 1939/45 Star, War Medal, France/Germany Star, Defence Medal and the C.V.S.M.

F/LT H.A. MOORE
PILOT R.A.F.

Harvey Moore was born and raised in Glasgow, Scotland. During his secondary schooling he was very active in Air Cadets and was fortunate to gain his glider wings at Edzell (near Montrose) and Private Pilots Licence at Scone, Perth on the D.H. Tiger Moth.

Just before joining the R.A.F. he was one of 25 U.K. cadets to enjoy a two week trip to the U.S.A. through the auspices of the International Air Cadet Exchange.

Pilot training in the R.A.F. at the end of 1957 consisted of 115 hours in a Percival Provost (forerunner of the Jet Provost) at Feltwell and Ternhill. Advanced training on Vampire 11 and Vampire 5 was at Oakington, also 115 hours, with wings awarded in June 1959. The weather was glorious that summer and with a backlog at the O.C.U.'s, three months were spent at Valley, in Anglesey, Wales.

The flying was great and flights were made around the U.K. The Vampire 5 was a delightful and docile little aircraft to fly, because of its forward cockpit and great view. Harvey found it difficult to fly level at altitude because of the nose down attitude required! The next course (four months) was at #232 O.C.U. Gaydon, to train on the Vickers Valiant as a co-pilot for the expanding 'V-Force'. Finally after almost 2 1/2 years of training, Harvey joined #18 Bomber Squadron at R.A.F. Finningley in Yorkshire.

This squadron specialized in E.C.M. and an extra Air Electronics Officer (A.E.O.) replaced the Nav/Radar. The normal crew for all V Bombers (Valiant, Victor and Vulcan) was: pilot; co-pilot; navigator/plotter; navigator/radar and air electronics officer. With the extra E.C.M. equipment carried on the nose and cockpit area, the centre of gravity of the aircraft was forward of the norm and care had to be taken on fuel management, to keep enough in the rear fuselage

182

tank, otherwise a level landing was near impossible!

When the Valiant was designed in the late forties, there were few light zinc-bearing forged alloys available and the one chosen (D.T.D.) was unfortunate. Metal fatigue was encountered with some airframes having less than 3,000 hours and 18 Squadron disbanded in April 1963. Harvey was involved in flying two of the squadron aircraft to St. Athan for eventual break up.

After the Canberra O.C.U. at Bassingbourne, he joined #213 Squadron on the Canberra B(1) 6 (Interdictor) at R.A.F. Bruggen in Germany. 213 was unique, with the only B(1) 6's in the R.A.F. - the predecessor of the B(1) 8. The crew consisted of a pilot, navigator/plotter and navigator/observer. The main role was nuclear strike, but twice a year the aircraft was changed to a conventional configuration, with a gun pack of four 20mm cannon and provision for underwing 1000 lb bombs.

It was in this configuration that he had a 'shaky do' in Cyprus, when flying an S.D.B. sortie out of Akrotiri. The compressor failed and the Avon engine seized solid just as the aircraft was winging over at 3,000 feet for its first bombing dive. Akrotiri airfield was close by, so an emergency maximum all up weight landing ensued, which was complicated by a gusty 25 knot crosswind!

The last tour was on #44 (Rhodesia) Squadron based at Waddington in Lincolnshire, on Vulcan Mark 2 aircraft from 1966 -1969. Some interesting trials flying, were accomplished by Harvey in February 1968 when T.F.R. (Terrain Following Radar) was being introduced. The Vulcan would be flown by the captain at 300 AGL (300 feet above ground level) at 300 KTS on instruments only. The co-pilot would remain visual to look out for aircraft, birds and anything untoward!

One incident remains indelibly in his mind, when climbing out of Waddington over the North Sea one miserable January night. Approaching FL 300 (the aircraft normally operated about FL 450, or flight level 45,000 feet), without any warning, and in quick succession engines 1, 2 and 3 flamed out! Prompt drills; Panic call, descent and heading for land, resulted as the crew tried to analyse the problem. The three engines were relit by 10,000 ft. and no other problems arose. It was discovered that a bomb bay tank had ruptured (due to the failure of two reduction valves) and that almost full pressure engine air, had gone through the fuel system and they were very lucky that one engine kept going and the fuel spilt in the bomb bay did not ignite!

One memorable trip, was when 44 Squadron was chosen to reinforce Singapore by flying 'westabout' instead of the normal route eastwards. It entailed eight Vulcans flying from Waddington to Goose Bay, Offutt A.F.B.(Omaha), McClellan A.F.B.(Sacramento), Hawaii, Wake, Guam and Singapore in eight days. Exercises were carried out in Singapore and also with the R.A.A.F. in Darwin and Perth, Australia. The aircraft were back at Waddington, via Gan (Maldive Islands), Bahrein, and Cyprus, after 29 days and Harvey had flown 18 flights in that time.

The last flight he flew, was as #4 in a demonstration scramble for a visit by the Imperial Defence College, which was uneventful, except for the approach to landing at 1,000 ft., when a near miss resulted, with a Spitfire and Hurricane that were climbing out of Scampton!

Harvey, his wife Laura and two very young children emigrated to Richmond, B.C. in 1969 and have lived there since. Self-employed, he promotes specialized construction materials to architectural and engineering companies.

F/LT NORMAN C. CURRELL D.F.C.
PILOT R.A.F.

Norman was born in the South East suburb of London called Peckham and attended Elementary school, Ramsden Bellhouse in the county of Essex, and later went to Grammar School at Brentford, Essex.

His father had a small poultry farm in Ramsden Bellhouse, which is situated about 30 miles east of London and as Norman was the oldest of a family of five there were always chores for him to do. When he had time he was active in cubs, scouts and then Cadet Corps at Brentford.

He was a bank clerk in London after leaving school and joined the Royal Navy Volunteer Reserve. He also served for two years as an apprentice Deck Officer in the Merchant Navy. In 1934 he joined the Essex County Constabulary, became an instructor in Air Raid Precautions and promoted to Sergeant in 1940. Police Officers were on a "Reserve Occupation" list, but in 1941 permission was granted to join the R.A.F. conditional on being either a pilot or navigator.

Norm applied in July, 1941 but was not called up until Jan. 1942 and reported to Aircrew Receiving Centre, St. John's Wood, North London as a Pilot u/t.

He went through the usual channels of I.T.W., E.F.T.S., S.F.T.S., O.T.U., serving at such stations as Torquay, Devon; Moncton, N.B.; Caron, Sask.; Carberry, Man.; Vulcan, Alta.; Moose Jaw, Sask.; Deseronto, Ont.; Comox, B.C.; Leicester, England; Ibsley, Hants; and flew almost everything including Tiger Moths, Ansons, Oxfords, Harvards, Expeditors and D.C.3's. He also gained experience on Long Range Transport, supply dropping, parachuting and Horsa Glider towing.

His travelling did not stop there as he soon flew out to India with 31 Squadron, to Ramree Island, then to Tilda, Rangoon, Singapore and Batavia, Dutch East Indies (now Indonesia). He was promoted finally in Dec. 1944 to Fl/Lt and earned the following decoration and medals. D.F.C., War Medal, Burma Star, S.E.Asia 45/46 Clasp, Defence and Victory Medals.

Norm was released June 1st, 1946 and emigrated to Canada later that month aboard the Aquitania. He spent two months commercial fishing in B.C. then joined the Western Oil Company as stock auditor and rose to be General Manager in 1949. He moved to Toronto with Gulf Canada in '68 and retired in January 1979.

He is now active in the Lower Mainland Yacht Co-op and other marine groups. One of his three sisters was a W.A.A.F. whose husband also served in the Airforce making two tours on Stirlings. A brother also served in the R.A.F.

He married Marion Archibald of Moose Jaw in 1947 but she died of a brain tumour some years later, then in 1984 , Norm married Bernice MacIntyre. There are two sons from his previous marriage.

The only real problem Norm had at E.F.T.S. on landing a Tiger Moth was that to do so he had considerable assistance from two of his instructors who were determined to show his first instructor that he was wrong when he recommended that Norm be "washed out". At Carberry he had no trouble flying Ansons as his depth perception improved considerably.

In November Norm experienced his first lesson in night flying and on a solo flight had drifted too far downwind before turning in for the final approach, but he did not have the sense to put on more power and he realized that he was going to undershoot, which he did, flying below telephone wires which had suddenly appeared before him. He finally touched down with a gentle "crump" then bounced back in the air before landing on the runway. Next day he visited the scene of his "landing" and found two distinct wheel marks in the light dusting of snow and the top wire of the fence was torn away. He got his wings at Carberry and was posted to #32 S.F.T.S., Moose Jaw where the station was using Airspeed Oxfords.

Norm became an instructor but in the fall of 1944 his tour as instructor was completed and he was posted to #6 O.T.U. Comox, B.C. and after two years on training aircraft the DC 3 seemed to be an enormous plane. At Comox the pilots picked up navigators and W/Op/AGs and crewed up. Norm's crew stayed together a little over one year.

Norm went back to the U.K. in Jan.'45 on a Transport Close Support course, paratrooping, supply dropping and glider towing then to Ibsley in Hants to take the Glider Pick-up Course and finally he was posted to India, first to Karachi where he was introduced to "kite-hawks", flies and camel and cow dung, then to Calcutta, though only for a few days. Then it was on to #31 Sqdn on Ramree Island, 65 miles south of Akyab, where supply missions were the order of the day.

One drop that stands out in Norm's mind was when they had an urgent call for supplies to be dropped to an Army detachment at Sandoway, along the Burma coast. The dropping zone (DZ) was found to be at the head of a deep indentation 70 miles south of their base and so small that they could only get two or three drops out of each pass over it. This necessitated several circuits until all their load had been dropped and consequently they were some three hours overdue at the squadron which had almost given them up for lost. It was a trying experience, but was made worth-while when a signal was received from the Army a day or two later, congratulating the squadron for the persistence and determination shown, to get the supplies delivered.

On another drop, four aircraft were to be dispatched and as Norm's regular crew was on another mission he took the Communications Officer and an Army dispatch crew to push the bundles out. By the time they arrived at the DZ the unit was in danger of being surrounded and had little left with which to defend themselves. The four aircraft crews had been assured that a flight of Mosquitos was on its way to look after the enemy, but no such luck. With restricted space the DZ was barely the size of a football field and the crews naturally wanted to drop the supplies as near as possible to the troops. It took several circuits to complete the drop and the enemy was free to harass them with machine gun fire as they flew over the zone at 400 feet. Fortunately they had nothing heavier and apart from a few bullet holes in each aircraft there were no casualties. Just as they had finished and were leaving, the Mosquitos arrived and proceeded to give a good account of themselves.

The rest of Norm's tour was taken up with supply runs to Semarang, Soerabaja and Bandoeng and other inland towns as specified by the army. Then it was a nostalgic farewell to #31 Squadron personnel and his crew, a fond and passionate farewell to his DC 3 "Molly" and he was flown to Singapore to await transport back to Blighty in one of the Union Castle troopships. After visiting family and friends he headed for Canada House in London to see what the chances were for a return to Canada and four years to the day when he had arrived in U.K. he was back in Canada.

One of the most pleasant surprises he experienced after his arrival was to be advised by the Air Ministry that he was to be awarded the D.F.C. The official citation reads:

"He displayed great determination in Transport Support Operations during the Burma Campaign. Knowing these operations to be vital to the progress of the Army advance, he set a fine example by his keenness and courage. He also dropped supplies to isolated garrisons in Java."

F/LT IVAN J. SCOTT D.F.C., C.D.
PILOT R.C.A.F

Ivan Scott was born in what is now called, Thunder Bay, Ontario, although he claims Port Arthur to be his real birthplace. The family moved further west and Ivan attended public school at King George Elementary in Brandon, Manitoba, followed by Earl Haig Junior High in the same city.

As a youth, he was interested and involved in the Brandon Flying Club and also photography, both hobbies following him during his Air Force service. After his schooling, Ivan became an aircraft engineer (A and C) at Fort William, the other part of Thunder Bay, and had various positions also at Portage la Prairie and Virden, Manitoba, at the air training schools.

In November 1941, Ivan enlisted in the R.C.A.F. and volunteered to train as a pilot. After the usual postings prior to graduation, Ivan received his pilot wings at #19 S.F.T.S. Dauphin, Manitoba in November 1942 and was immediately shipped overseas to England as a sergeant pilot.

Thereafter followed several months of intensive training at A.F.U. on Airspeed Oxfords, O.T.C. on Whitleys at Kinloss, Scotland, where he crewed up with a Canadian navigator, the balance of the crew being R.A.F. types. On completion of heavy O.T.U. on Halifaxes at Rufforth Yorkshire, his crew was selected for an immediate posting to P.F.F. #35 Squadron at Gravely, Hunts, where they completed 20 ops. After this, the crew was posted to #10 Squadron, Melbourne, Yorks for advanced H 2 S radar instructional work. Fifteen more ops were completed here.

On September 22nd, 1943, over Hanover, numberous enemy fighters and light flak were observed, but the most exciting part of the trip, was when the skipper turned around and found most of the crew with emergency oxygen bottles, lined up, singing "Happy Birthday" on the occasion of his 20th birthday, just after completing the bombing run over the city at 17,500 feet.

On October 4th, over Frankfurt, the aircraft was coned by searchlights for

187

about 4 minutes and sustained considerable damage from night fighter attacks and barely escaped, by diving several thousand feet and eventually eluding the master beam and thus returning safely to base.

On November 25th, on a mission to Frankfurt again, the crew were forced to return early, when a constant speed unit over-revved, seized up and tore the port outer engine out of the wing, causing considerable damage to the aircraft. A safe landing was made at Melbourne, where the skipper finally convinced the maintenance N.C.O. that he'd had a little dificulty and that an engine was missing. The N.C.O. just stood open-mouthed when he saw the damage.

Early in January, 1944, after returning from a very exciting and lively operation over Berlin, the crew was met at de-briefing by the A.O.C. and several other senior officers, who praised the captain and his crew, for the outstanding work they had done on this trip. The skipper was quite perplexed for a moment, until it was explained that the navigator and radio officer had been transmitting winds back to base, which had been very accurate and had been used for the main force navigation. Not wanting to worry the skipper, they had neglected to inform him what they were doing. Now, the skipper realized why there had been so much fighter activity in their vicinity, for most of the trip.

An amusing thing happened one day when Ivan and his crew were air testing a new Halifax III, which the squadron had just received. While cruising along at 10,000 feet Ivan gradually shut down three engines, being quite pleased the way the aircraft handled, until a Mosquito flew past, feathered his two engines, did a slow roll and then took off into the distance. Feeling rather foolish, Ivan restarted the three engines and returned to base.

Perhaps one of the most dangerous and exciting trips, was the last trip of Ivan's tour, which almost, in fact, became the last trip anywhere. On April 18th, 1944, the crew was briefed on a long trip, mine laying in Kiel Bay, on what they thought would be a nice, quiet trip to finish off operations. Just west of Kiel Bay, they were attacked by German fighters and a portion of the starboard fin, rudder and elevator was shot away and there were many other holes made in the body of the aircraft. Luckily no-one was wounded and the rear gunner claimed a fighter as probably destroyed. Part of the main problem now, was loss of petrol from several holed tanks, but they completed their mine laying and barely made it back to base, with almost empty tanks.

Upon screening off ops in April 1944, the balance of Ivan's time overseas was spent at #24 O.T.U. Honeybourne, as an instructor on Wellingtons and flying Hurricanes on fighter affiliation. One spectacular event during this period, was on June 6th, "D" Day, when, on finishing a night fighter affiliation exercise early dawn, Ivan suddenly found himself surrounded by all kinds of aircraft and gliders heading south towards the Normandy coast. The only safe course of action was to head for base and land immediately to get out of the way!

It was also during this period, that he met and married an English girl from

Watford, Hertfordshire. In December 1945 he was repatriated to Canada and discharged from the Air Force in January 1946 and his wife and daughter came out to Canada in August, 1946. Ivan attended Brandon College for one year, but in 1947 the family returned to England where they lived in Watford and he ran a successful photography business. However, he sold out the business in 1952 and the family returned to Canada, where Ivan re-enlisted in the R.C.A.F. as an Air Traffic Control Officer.

For the next twenty years he continued to fly, as well as control air traffic and he retired from the C.A.F.(Air) in June 1972 with the rank of Captain. He had been a Flying Officer during the war. Since his retirement, Ivan had been a photographic technician with the R.C.M.P. and retired from that august service in September 1988. He still continues his photography and has been responsible for the photos in this publication.

Ivan now lives in Surrey, B.C., and he and Helen have six children and 10 grandchildren. His decorations and medals include the D.F.C, 1939/45 Star, Aircrew Europe Star, Defence Medal, C.V.S.M and clasp and the C.D., as well as the Victory Medal.

F/SGT GORDON SHAWCROSS
WIRELESS OPERATOR R.A.F.

Gordon Shawcross was born 15th November 1923 at Stockport, Cheshire, England. His life to begin with, was very happy, until at the age of 4 1/2 years, Primary School had to be attended. Great Dismay. "Sit still"; "Don't talk"; "No, you can't leave the room". More dismay, both teacher and pupil. Wet pants, his not hers, of course.

189

He decided at this early age, that academic studies were for the birds, and seeing as he could not fly, not for him. Extra curricular activities such as sports, music, girls, the latter at a much more mature age, of course, were just great.

Nine and a half years later, much to the joy of the teachers and staff, he joined the work force as an apprentice printer. Seven years of work for a pittance and night school loomed ahead, but of course, there were always the extra curricular activities!

Just before Gordon's sixteenth birthday, Prime Minister (Peace in our time) Chamberlain, decided at long last, that Herr Hitler had gone too far. We were at war, "the phoney war" to begin with, but not for long. Airfields, factories and cities in the south were bombed and eventually installations and cities all over the country.

Over a weekend in December of 1940, Manchester got its initiation. When arriving for work on the Monday morning, after spending three hours in a train for a ten mile journey, Gordon found the Printing Company building flattened, along with many more. Nothing but rubble remained.

A new place of work was found and life went on.

In 1941 the Stockport Air Cadets Squadron beckoned, and Gordon consequently became their new physical training instructor and soccer player. On November 15, 1941, he volunteered for R.A.F. Aircrew, much to the chagrin of his parents. Deferrment until August 3rd, 1942, when he reported to Lord's Cricket Ground, Air Crew Receiving Centre, London. In September 1942, he was posted to Brighton for a crash math course and after the course was posted to Ludlow, Shropshire, where he dug ditches.

Three weeks later, after a three day unauthorized leave of absence, he was posted to #10 I.T.W. at Scarborough and then went to Burnaston, near Derby. Flying was carried out at the satellite 'drome, Battlestead Hill, a farmer's field.

Classified for Navigator/Wireless, he was posted to the cradle of the R.A.F., Cranwell, for a three and a half month course in radio, on completion of which he went back to Heaton Park to await overseas draft to Navigation School.

November 1943 saw him on board the "Mauritania" bound for Canada and he peeled a lot of potatoes on that ship. After landing at Halifax they took the train to Moncton. It was marvellous to see lights at night for the first time in over three years, shining on the rivers and lakes.

On December 31st he entrained for #33 A.N.S. Mount Hope, Hamilton, Ontario passing through Montreal at midnight. For the next six months it was graft, classroom, fly, take star shots. Anyone failing the Air Navigation Course who was a wireless op. was sent on an eight week refresher course to one of the radio schools, so Calgary #2 Wireless School was the next posting. Eventually, after two years and seven months of courses and "what have you" he was posted to #5 O.T.U. Boundary Bay, British Columbia.

At Boundary Bay, the two Wireless Ops, Gordon Shawcross and Bill Tennent crewed up with the skipper, Tom Blackburn, and Second Pilot, Ken Watson, for familiarization of the pilots on tricycle U/C; this was on Mitchells (B-25's). At a later date, navigator, bomb aimer and five air gunners formed the

190

crew when conversion to Liberators (B-24) came about at #5 O.T.U. Abbotsford. The course was completed by the end of June and after ten days leave, Gord reported to #45, R.A.F. Transport Command, Dorval.

From Dorval, Liberator KP 140 had to be flown to India, so with a Transport Command skipper and flight engineer, the crew was on its way with many and varied stops: Goose Bay, Gander, Lagens, Rabat Sale, Castel Benito, Lydda, Shaibah, Drigh Road, Karachi, Allahabad and finally Salboni, home of 355 Squadron. At Drigh Road, the bomb aimer, wireless op. and gunners had been left for pick up at a later date, when squadron was known.

When landing at Salboni, the plane was met by the C.F.I. who wanted the R.A.F."bods" all four of them, to stay on strength as he was short of crews. He would fix the paper work.

Nine days later, the first trip was made with a split crew. They were to take off for Jessore to pick up supplies. From Jessore at 0945 they were to fly to Tharkeh where a P.O.W. camp was located. The camp was never sighted and no supplies were dropped, so a course for base was set. Three things went wrong. L.O.R.A.N. went u/s, M/F D/F. couldn't be contacted and some silly so and so transferred the gas from bomb bay tanks, not into the wing tanks, but into the air outside the aircraft. The plane was out of fuel, so a quick S.O.S. was sent with the best D.R. position within a 50 mile radius. Bail out. The second pilot wanted to know how to go through the rear hatch. "Not feet first" Gordon said "Or you will lose your head. Just roll out, balled up, head first, just like this" and away he went.

The first thing that happened was the wind caught his helmet and ripped it off; the phone jack hit him on the chin. No recollection of pulling the rip cord, just gently floating down, desperately trying to remember what to do to stop swinging, how to rotate to get the wind at his back. It was close to 2200 hours and very dark. Nothing could be seen, other than a black meandering ribbon below. A river. Right first time and he was in it! It was a good thing the river was fast flowing as the canopy dropped behind him. Out of harness he didn't think to inflate Mae West, so swimming on his stomach only made the kapok in the collar push his head under the water. On to his back, things were much better, but heading for the outside bank of a curve in faster moving water was stupid. He managed to grab hold of an overhanging branch and pull himself out. Scared stiff. Where were the crocs and snakes? After about an hour of wondering and trembling, he heard voices and the splash of paddles. Natives in a dugout canoe had heard the plane going down and had come to investigate. After picking him up, they took him downstream calling in at each small village, built on the edge of the river, to tell them to be on the lookout for the rest of the crew.

Eventually they reached a much larger village, where he was taken to the head man's hut. A godsend; this man could speak English. It appeared that the plane had gone down in the Sunderbands, the thickest jungle in India, which the common delta of the Ganges and Brahmaputra rivers passed through. Not a very nice place.

He stayed overnight in the village, then downstream next morning to the manager of the lumber company, who all the different villagers worked for. He had a large motor cruiser, so the trip from there was much faster and more comfortable. Khulna was the final destination, an R.A.F. Air Sea Rescue Station, where the exact position of Gordon's pick up could be given. This made it easier for picking up the other crew members. Six arriving in ones and twos, the next day and a half. The navigator was not found for five days. The rest of the crew were back on squadron by this time.

On the 16th September, a supply drop on Saigon airfield was scheduled. Parachute canisters from bomb bays and dead drops from rear hatch. The waist window had been removed for Aldis lamp signals and after the drops, was being replaced by Gordon, when the slipstream caught the edge of the perspex and slammed his arm on the windowledge. The result: a badly dislocated elbow joint. Morphine was injected for pain and the arm put in a sling. He went to sleep in the waist position with the other wireless op. operating the radio.

Awakening, he saw a red light over the tail unit and thought the plane was on fire. It was a flare. Plugging into the intercom, he heard Tom telling the rest of the crew that it was impossible to land at Pegu, as the cloud base was down to ground level. What to do? Bail out? What about Shawcross? Tie a static cord to the rip cord handle and push him out the bomb bay. "Not on your Nellie" was the reply. "We are not far from the coast, let's fly out over the sea and ditch towards shore." This was agreed on.

Fortunately, instead of having to ditch, the plane crash landed on marshy ground. Very lucky because it was 2015 hours and dark. Only the outer port prop was bent. What a pilot!! With daylight, natives from a village close by, came to see what the stuped fliers had been up to now and also what they could get away with.

It was decided after a couple of hours, that Gordon should be taken to the nearest centre of civilization, which was Thongwa. Not a good decision at all. The journey was by river in a single oared boat and took 'till 1900 hours. The place had an R.A.F. Radar Unit and an Indian Army Post. No hospital, just an Indian M.O. who couldn't do anything about the injury. Another shot of morphine. Syriam, across the river from Rangoon was contacted by phone, and it was learned that a Sunderland flying boat had picked up the rest of the crew. The M.O. drove an ambulance the thirty miles to pick up Shawcross and the other crew members who accompanied him.

Arriving back at Syriam, he was told that dislocation could not be reduced there, but 60 M.F.H. in Rangoon could do this the next day. The reason for not crossing the river that night was because the native fishermen put out nets and these got caught in the props of the boats. Another shot of morphine.

Next day, across Rangoon river to 60 M.F.H. where the operation was carried out at about 1330 hours. The elbow had been dislocated for 48 hours and the arm was swollen to three times its normal size, and looked like Popeye's. After ten days at 60 M.F.U. the M.O. decided further treatment was necessary, which couldn't be done at their facility, so a transfer to 27 B.G.H. in Calcutta was arranged.

From 60 M.F.U. a flight was "hitched" to Pegu where Gord spent a night in a hospital tent and next day he was on a plane for Salboni. He then took train for Calcutta where he spent two months in hospital, after which he was posted to Delhi. At Delhi the magic repat. number came up. On to Worli Camp, Bombay for embarkation on the "Georgic", arriving at Liverpool 21 days later. It was hissing down. Monsoons were supposed to be for India. Final discharge from the R.A.F. came in February 1947 after a few medical checks and a lot of leave.

Gord married June in 1947 and they emigrated to Canada in 1957 with three children, number four arriving in 1965. They settled in Brampton, Ontario where they lived for 31 years, 23 of them spent as manager of printing at Ryerson Polytechnic Institute, Toronto. He took early retirement in 1984. Gord's medals include the 1939/45 Star, the Burma Star, the Victory and Defence Medals and the General Service medal and clasp (S.E. Asia).

F/LT C. IVAN SMITH
PILOT R.C.A.F.

Ivan was born in Ancaster, Ontario, just a few miles from Mount Hope Airport. He can trace his family back to John Smith, who came to Canada with the United Empire Loyalists in 1787 and was granted land in Grimsby township. In 1798 he sold this land and settled in Ancaster. His family has seen a lot of Canadian history. He took his public and secondary education in Beamsville, Ontario and took his vocational schooling at Beamsville High & Vocational School. After graduation, he worked as a bank clerk at Vineland, Ontario.

On November 11th, 1941, Ivan enlisted in the R.C.A.F. and was posted to

Manning Pool at Brandon, Manitoba and then to guard duty at Camp Borden and Goderich, Ontario. L.A.C. Smith took his Elementary Flying School Training at # 9 E.F.T.S. at St. Catharines, Ontario, where he learned the joy of flying in Tiger Moths. He took his Service Flying on Harvards at #14 S.F.T.S. and graduated with the coveted Pilot's Wings and received his commission in December 1942. He left Aylmer S.F.T.S. on embarkation leave and in January 1943 was posted overseas to Bournemouth.

From Bournemouth, Ivan took a refresher course on Tiger Moths at #6 E.F.T.S., Sywell, Northants, in March 1943 and in May, he was posted to #17 A.F.U., Wrexham, North Wales on Miles Masters, followed in June by a posting to #4 O.T.U. at Hawarden, North Wales, where he converted to Hurricanes and Mustangs. In October he went to #268 Squadron R.A.F., which was then at Oldham, Hants. The fall and winter was spent on advanced training, Navigation and Air to Ground Gunnery. In January 1944 the Squadron moved to North Weald, Essex and shortly after, Ivan had an attack of appendicitis and was grounded for two months and rejoined the Squadron in April, at Gatwick, under canvas.

Finally, on May 12th, 1944, Ivan made his first operational sortie over France, on a tactical reconnaissance and low level photography mission. On these sorties, the Squadron always flew in pairs, with number 2 watching for enemy aircraft. They flew at between 2000 and 4000 feet altitude and were armed with 4 - 20 mm cannon with which they attacked columns of enemy transportation. If an enemy concentration was seen, they would pinpoint the location and take photographs. With this information, Typhoon rocket squadrons with their heavier fire power, would then come in and finish the job.

On June 6th, 1944, "D" Day, Ivan was over the beachhead at Normandy, with an armada of aircraft directing the fire from the Navy Battleships, to the land targets, to soften up the positions in preparation for the Army landings. During July and August, the Squadron carried out reconnaissance trips all over Normandy and as far east as Paris. For the first part of this period, they flew back to Gatwick for de-briefing, then for a time they would land at B10 near Beny Sur Mer for de-briefing and afterwards return to Gatwick. On August 10th, 1944 they completed the move to France and B10 became their base. The landing strip was made, by the simple process of laying a strip of metal screen over a field, which served its purpose, but in the dry weather, the field was continually covered with a cloud of dust, due to the heavy traffic.

The first night in France was a nightmare. The enemy had brought up a huge gun, mounted on a railway car, and at night, they brought it out of a tunnel, where it was kept hidden during the daylight. It lobbed shells at the airfield all night long and the crews had to bury their cots in the ground for protection. The location of the gun was photographed and these pinpointed the location for the Typhoon Squadron, which was called in and which efficiently sealed the tunnel at both ends. Another cause for discomfort at this airfield, were the terrible attacks of dysentery that almost everyone suffered, and only those who have undergone this torture, can know how they felt.

194

The squadron was getting short of serviceable Mustangs by now and it was converted to Typhoons. A number of their sorties, at this time, were flown on reconnaissance and air to ground, in the Falaise Gap, where they observed the enemy sending in reinforcements in transports, disguised as Red Cross vehicles.

As the enemy retreated up through France, the Squadron also advanced to numerous locations in France, Belgium and Holland to Antwerp. Their sorties included locating and photographing many VI rocket sites. On one occasion, Ivan and a chum were visiting one of these captured sites, when a land mine exploded near to them. Ivan was within thirty feet of the mine. The force of the explosion ripped all the seams in his chum's trousers, but luckily neither one of them suffered any injury.

While the Squadron was stationed at Antwerp, V2 bombs came over quite regularly; one landed at the end of the runway and left a twenty five foot crater. Many poker games were interrupted when the players scrambled under the tables for shelter, when one of these bombs landed.

An article in the *Vancouver Province* on November 1, 1987 reported that Prince Bernhard of Holland had unveiled a monument, to 135 Canadian soldiers who died in the 1944 liberation of the Island of Walcheren. Veterans' Affairs Minister, George Hees, who was wounded during the battle, laid a wreath at the monument. The ceremony took place at Middleburg, Netherlands. Reading the article, brought back memories to Ivan, of an experience he had during this battle.

The Squadron had been doing quite a bit of flying around the Walcheren Islands and on November 2nd, 1944, Ivan was flying in No. 2 position to his chum, Brian Garside. It was Ivan's ninety ninth trip. The Germans blew the dykes as they retreated and most of the land was covered in water. There was flak everywhere from the retreating army. Recalling the event, Ivan said the Honourable George Hees must have been in a real battle. However, on this day, Ivan and his chum flew near the town of Middleburg and his chum was hit by flak. Ivan's aircraft, luckily, had only a few holes. When Garside's plane was hit, he shouted to Ivan. They took evasive action and the two planes turned towards the allied lines and Garside glided inside the lines, picked a small mound of dry ground, and plunked down. Ivan watched him climb out on the wing and wave, then he circled overhead, while the home base got a fix on Garside's location. He was picked up by the Canadian Army fellows and was back at base that evening. Ivan did five more trips, making up one hundred and four all told, and was then sent back to Britain and on an "end of tour" leave.

After this leave, Ivan was posted to #61 O.T.U. where he taught Navigation on Master aircraft. In mid January 1945 he was posted to #56 O.T.U. at Malfield, Berwick-on-Tweed, where he instructed in advanced navigation on Typhoons and Tempests. V.E.Day in May 1945, saw the end of his flying career in Britain and Ivan was put through the process of being repatriated, ending up in Brandon, then Winnipeg. In November, 1945 he was discharged in Toronto, a civilian again. His rank on discharge was Flight Lieutenant. He was awarded the 1939/45 Star, Aircrew Europe and France/Germany Star, the Defence Medal, C.V.S.M. and Victory Medal.

After he was discharged, Ivan went back to the bank until 1947, then he moved out West to Faust, Alberta and became interested in automotive parts. After spending thirty-two years at the work he became a Parts Manager in a G.M. dealership in White Rock, B.C. He is married to Henriette and has six children and thirteen grandchildren, all living in British Columbia.

Ivan has been active in the Royal Canadian Legion for the past thirty-eight years, and has been a member of the Crescent Branch #240, since 1955. He was given a life membership in the Legion a few years ago.

S/LDR RAY F. SMITH D.F.C.,C.D.
PILOT R.C.A.F.

Ray Smith was born in Vancouver the 15th of August 1923 and eighteen years to the day later, he joined the R.C.A.F. as a pilot. He had attended Simon Fraser public school and King Edward High while growing up. The Airforce sent him to I.T.S. at Edmonton, E.F.T.S. at High River, Alta. S.F.T.S. at McLeod.

On the U.K. side it was E.T.O. at Lossiemouth, 1664 Con Unit at Riccal, and his first ops squadron #10 at Melbourne. Ray was to be part of other ops squadrons during his two tours, #102 at Pockington, #77 at Elvington, all on Bomber Command with Halifaxes.

For all this, he earned an ops wing and bar, a D.F.C., 1939/45 Star, Air Crew Europe, Atlantic Star, C.V.S.M and clasp and the C.D. as well as the Victory and Defence Medals.

As the skipper, he was not only the youngest in the crew, but the lowest rank, Sergeant Pilot. He well remembers being interviewed by the promotion board, where a very "pukka" old R.A.F. type asked him why he wanted to be an officer. His reply "To get the same pay as the rest of the crew." drew snorts from several members of the board, but Ray got his commission.

Ray was discharged at Vancouver the 15th of September 1945 and promptly, again became a student, this time at U.B.C. taking agriculture. He later worked for the Parke Davis Company as a traveller and later for C.P. Air as a security officer. It seemed that he just couldn't stay out of the service, for he put in 10 years with the Royal Westminster Regiment, retiring in 1975 with the rank of Major.

Ray and his wife, Marion, are parents of two boys and two girls, also grandparents to five youngsters. Ray was the first president of the Vancouver Aircrew Association and was instrumental in getting this first branch "into the air". He remains an active member.

Ray's aircraft was "X for Breakfast" (not X for Xray) and was well stocked with "Smiths" and "Jones". The rear gunner F. Smith also, the W.A.G. G. Jones, the flight engineer R. Jones, the mid upper F. Jones; to break the monotony, the bomb aimer H. Cork and the navigator R. Page. Skipper Smith was known as "one engine Smith", the crew quite often returning to base on one engine, a railroad locomotive! For instance -

The start of the Battle of Berlin saw "X for Breakfast" off and flying the night of Aug 31st 1943. However, one engine got tired and packed up with a glycol leak just at the target. Bombs were dropped and the crew headed home on three. It was their bad luck to fly over a heavily defended area near Amsterdam, where heavy ack ack fire silenced another engine, which could not be feathered.

They were losing height and fuel at an alarming rate and the crew began to jettison anything moveable. Guns, ammo, chemical toilet, even parachutes were tossed overboard. By this time they were down to 50 feet and still had over half the channel to cross. The W/Op broke radio silence and Caultishall in East Anglia set up a cone of three lights - a welcome sight. No formal circuit here; the east west runway ended right on the beach. It was straight in and lucky too, as the last two engines cut out as they were rolling to the end of the runway!

As the Bard of Avon said "Alls well that ends well." "X for breakfast" was home; one engine Smith and crew were again headed for base by railway locomotive!

The final raid in the so-called Battle of Hamburg was set for the night of July 30th. All was in readiness; the final briefing, dinner, then down to flights, to get kitted up and away to dispersal. After the usual kibitzing with the ground crew, it was start up time. All engines checked out fine. Then it was "Await the order to taxi" - instead, a red flare. The flight was cancelled. After the crew returned to billets, a great electrical storm broke over the station. They were all glad to be on the ground.

Next day, Hamburg was laid on again, only to be cancelled late in the p.m., as the storm was still 50 miles west of the target. The third try on the night of August 2nd. was a "go" as the met. man said the storm was now 50 miles east of the target. On approaching the enemy coast, the storm was still evident on the eastern horizon, but why worry? Was it not well past target? There was cloud and the crew climbed up through it. At about 21,000 feet all hell broke loose. Ice from the props crashed against the fuselage; sparks jumped all around the cockpit and St. Elmo's fire darted about the aircraft. They were taking on masses of ice and were in the centre of a towering Cumulo-Nimbus cloud. When they hit the down draft surrounding the central ascending air column, the craft was flung violently about, ending on its back!

They jettisoned their load, but continued downward at a terrific rate, but were spewed out at about 10,000 feet, just below the cloud base. They set course for home, but by guess and by God, as the gyro had toppled, on their elevator descent and the pilot's compass was highly suspect, as it had been subjected to a great deal of electrical current.

For a long time they headed for what they hoped would be Yorkshire, but landfall E.T.A. passed and still no sign of land. When dawn broke a Beaufighter appeared off their starboard, but he soon left them. Shortly afterwards, they spotted a "Pundit" flashing A., the only difficulty was that there were two locations with that identifier, one in the English channel and the other in the Orkneys. They had no idea which they had intercepted! Heading towards the Pundit they spotted an airdrome occult which verified their position as the Orkneys. The magnetic compass had been knocked out about 50 degrees. Again they landed with only fumes remaining in the tanks!

On yet another trainride to base, the crew was returning from an op. on "Happy Valley" with an engine out, and their aircraft riddled with holes. Ray had decided to pancake at the nearest 'drome, which he did and after debriefing, it was off by train, with an overnight stop at Air Force Transit hotel in London. So the crew was loose in London, in full flying gear, no hats, and badly in need of a shave. They also had a taste for fish & chips and headed out into the blackout looking for a line up that would take them to the nearest source of food.

Well, there were seven grubby airforce men in full battle dress standing in a line. One of the Londoners in civvies asked what the whistles attached to their jackets were for. When he was told they were used in ditching to attract help from other crew members, he said, "Wot does it sound like mite?" The skipper couldn't resist and gave a mighty long blast on his whistle.

Immediately, answering whistles echoed from surrounding streets and as quick as a flash, several large Bobbies were standing beside them. A quick check on their part, found nought amiss and with grins on everyone's faces they disappeared into the night. At least the aircrew whistle had brought help on land and who wants to get the chance to use it from a dingy?

F/O R.J. (BOB) THOMPSON
AIR GUNNER - R.C.A.F.

R.J. (Bob) Thompson was born in Vancouver, B.C., attending Elementary and Secondary Schools there. Following graduation, he went to Vancouver Technical School, where he took courses in sheet metal work. He worked, before enlistment, as a sheet metal brakeman at Western Steel Co. in Vancouver, bending parts for Canso aircraft at Boeings. His early and major interest was flying, and he joined 1601 Air Cadet Wing in 1940. Bob was discharged from 111 Squadron in 1943, and joined the R.C.A.F. in Vancouver in May of that year. His vision was unacceptable for pilot training, so he decided to become an Air Gunner.

He took Ground Training at #1 A.G.G.T.S. in Quebec City, Flight Training at #3 B.& G. at McDonald, Manitoba, and graduated as a Sergeant Air Gunner on December 10th, 1943. He was posted overseas to #22 O.T.U. Wellesbourne, Gaydon, training on Wellingtons, and then was posted to 1659 H.C.U. Topcliffe, the day before "D" Day. He arrived at #426 Squadron in July, 1944, and completed his first 'Op' that month, flying a Halifax VII. Bob was commissioned in September and was posted to #433 Squadron in December. His first operation was done before the Squadron was converted to Lancasters, in January 1945. On February 1st, 1945, he flew on his first Lancaster op, and the a/c was badly hit over Ludwigshaven and his skipper attempted to get back to base. The plane crashed near Dishforth, but Bob and the Bombaimer had bailed out at low altitude, - five crew members were killed on impact.

An evening in September, 1944, started out with an exhilarating wave-top crossing of the North Sea, followed by a climb to 20,000 feet over the north end of Denmark. At this point the aircraft turned south and followed the east coast of Denmark to Keil. About ten miles before the target, an FW 190 was seen crossing over the plane. He had caught the a/c outlined against a searchlight and hit it with one cannon shell that did not explode. This shell entered the top of the Halifax, about four feet in front of Bob's upper turret and passed straight down through the centre section and through the centre of a trusstube. The shell, passing through the floor and bomb bay, between bombs, then exited through the closed bomb doors. After dropping their load, the aircraft avoided a searchlight master beam, with a quick stall and a loss of 7,000 feet of altitude. Having lost the searchlight, it headed for base.

When clear of the target area, the flight engineer checked the a/c. His voice was heard over the intercom "Hey Skipper, there's a funny thing rolling around in the centre section. It's about ten inches long, hexagonal, and painted red". This got an immediate yell from the Bombaimer, "That's an incendiary with no tail, bring it to me fast!" The offending item was then jettisoned from the nose position.

After arriving home, the crew found the trail of the cannon shell, but no other hole in the top of the a/c. However, there was a red paint mark on the side of the entry hole, made by the shell.

One clear day, on their way to base from the Ruhr, at about 6-8,000 feet, they found that all their bombs had not gone. Therefore they decided to find a 'target of opportunity'. To the bomb aimer's delight, a bridge was visible directly ahead. He wanted it. What he wanted, he usually got.

They made the bombing run, but at the last second, the Navigator pulled him away from the release and said, "You can't - there might be Dutch civilians on the bridge."

The next morning, during briefing for another trip, they were warned that they would be crossing over a stream of gliders and paratroops, on their way to take the bridge at Arnhem.

The 26th of December, 1944 required a rush daylight trip to St.Vith, the German Headquarters for the Battle of the Bulge. Being the day after Xmas, there were very few clear heads in the stream that day. Their assigned altitude was 10,000 feet. As they approached the enemy lines, they saw one burst of a box of four flak puffs. A Hally was seen in the middle of the box and it went down. The same thing was repeated a few moments later. The hair on the back of everyone's neck went straight up, because those gunners were so good, then so did they, to 14,000 feet. Bob's crew, however, stayed at the briefed altitude. Strangely enough there was no more flak. On nearing the target, a mass of a/c was seen above Bob's aircraft, and he tried unsuccessfully, to get them into an opening. The bomb aimer did not appreciate the attempt, because it interfered with the bomb run. From the upper turret, Bob could see their bomb doors open and the bombs starting to fall. He sat helplessly, as they came towards his a/c for what seemed like an eternity. One string passed in front of their port engines, and another string passed between the port wing and the tailplane. Bob realized then, how blessed the night skies really were, because one was not able to see what was really happening around the aircraft.

The 6th of December was their last op with 426 Squadron. Flying in Hally OW Y, the crew bombed Osnabruck that night, and headed for home at 6,000 feet. There was a cloud layer below them at about 2,000 feet. All was quiet, until Bob saw a bright ball of light appear below the cloud layer. It was two or three miles to the left and travelling in the same direction as his a/c, at a high rate of speed. He watched this strange light as it raced along below the cloud. As Bob turned his mike on to speak to the rear gunner, the flight engineer spoke up to report the sighting. However, he was too late. The light had suddenly penetrated the cloud and climbed up to their level faster than anything they had seen before. The rear gunner gave the "Port go" as it came up and started in to attack. There was a single half second burst of fire by the rear gunner and the attacker rolled over to the right and dived straight down through the cloud and exploded on the ground. Bob's crew continued their course for home. Eight minutes later another light ball appeared in a similar position. The rear gunner opened fire the same as before, but thought he had missed him on the attack, however, he got him as he broke away. The second attacker had fired a burst as he came in, but did not hit them. This a/c also was seen to dive straight down through the cloud and explode. As both of these a/c turned away from Bob's view he was able to see only one ball of flame behind each one. The crew identified the attackers as ME 163's. Another crew reported seeing a parachute from the second a/c.

Although these aircraft were both claimed as destroyed, they were never accepted as such by Headquarters. In fact it had been stated that no ME 163's ever operated at night. However, the claim had been mentioned in a couple of books published on the history of the Halifax, and in the 426 Squadron history book.

In January of 1945 the Halifaxes were taken away and the Squadron received Lancaster 1's and 3's instead. After three weeks of Conversion, 'A' Flight was supposedly ready for operations, while 'B' Flight converted. The regular rear gunner, because of his size, found the Lancaster rear turret to be very small, so he changed turrets with Bob.

On the evening of February 1st, 1945, the crew started out on their first op, flying their new Lancaster 3 BM-A. They had not flown this aircraft before, so the navigational aids problems had not been corrected, therefore they failed after takeoff. Because of a high cloud cover above, the stars were not visible and the navigator was only able to use Dead Reckoning navigation methods.

They did not locate Ludwigshaven, the target, on schedule but eventually saw it light up about twenty miles to their left and behind them. As they turned towards the target, they realized that they would be late and probably all alone over the target. They were!!

As they made their bombing run, the anti-aircraft gunners and searchlights had a field day with them. The plane was hit just after the bombs had gone. Then a JU 88 came at them head on, firing over them. About then, the skipper considered bailing out, but instead, dropped down to 1500 feet and headed for base.

They were flying in broken cloud all the way and the air seemed rough.

The bomb aimer suggested it was due to something flapping loose around the tail of the aircraft. No one had time to search the dark interior of the fuselage, to find out what was wrong. Nor did anyone call the upper gunner to ask if he could see anything. All the time, Bob was quite ignorant of what was happening up front. He had been told the Skipper had the control wheel right back to keep the aircraft in the air.

They had flown northward for several hours, before the bomb aimer managed to get the H2S working on short range. The picture showed "The Wash" disappearing behind them. This meant they had been over England and were now heading out over the North Sea, towards nothing. They corrected their course to reach the city of York, still in cloud and still at 1500 feet in altitude. When they did not find York on time, the bomb aimer headed for the nose of the aircraft, to try for visual pin-point of their position. He found them to be in the hills near Wombleton. Since the hills there, are 2500 feet, they climbed to 3,000 feet and started a slow turn to the left, while the wireless operator obtained a course to the runway at Leeming. During the turn, the aircraft entered the bottom of a small thunderhead. After holding the aircraft in the air for four hours the Skipper could no longer do so; the aircraft started into a series of three stalls. He gave the order "Bail Out". Bob wasted no time turning his turret, opening the doors, and falling backwards. He found the ripcords and pulled. He did not see the flash or the ship hit the ground, because just at that time his chute was opening. He just had time to glance over his shoulder and see small fires spread over a large area; there were lights on a hangar in front of him as he hit the ground, hard.

Bob met the bomb aimer and they started to walk towards the hangar lights. After walking half a mile, they arrived at the village of Dishforth. The remainder of the crew did not survive the crash.

Bob was awarded the Ops Wing for his tour and returned to Canada for discharge at Jericho Beach in June, 1945. He was awarded the France/Germany Star, the 1939/45 Star, the C.V.S.M.and Clasp, the War Medal and Defence Medal.

Bob worked for Boeing, building B29 parts until VJ Day, then worked with the Aero Club of B.C. to obtain his Engineers and Pilot's licenses. He worked with the Chilliwack Flying Club for two years, before joining Central B.C. Airways in May, 1952. As the company changed its name to Pacific Western Airlines, he remained with the company and served in many positions in Maintenance, including 12 to 15 years as Systems Maintenance Planner. He retired in July, 1984. Bob has three children.

SGT. ALAN STUART
PILOT R.A.F.

Alan was born in Liverpool, England and attended Linacre Council School, Bootle and Bootle Secondary School.

He moved from Liverpool to Crosby, Merseyside and enjoyed soccer, tennis, hiking and model aircraft making. He joined 1128 Squadron, Air Training Corps, became senior N.C.O. and instructed aircraft recognition, morse code and drill. After school he worked in the office of British Railways, which was then called L.M.S. (London, Midland & Scottish)

He joined the R.A.F. at Scarborough, Yorkshire on June 24th, 1944 and applied for pilot training. This process took him to Wolverhampton, where he made his first solo flight in a Tiger Moth, to #6 Air School, Petchefstroom, Transvaal, South Africa, thence to #22 Air School (S.F.T.S.) at Nigel, Transvaal on Harvards and finally, on March 8th 1946, while at Nigel, he qualified as a sergeant pilot. His was the last course to qualify pilots, under the Commonwealth Air Training Plan.

Of the 49 lads Alan had joined up with at Scarborough, only three of them qualified as pilots! One of the three, Colin Taylor, shared the same instructor with Alan at E.F.T.S. and now lives near Portland, Oregon and they keep in touch.

Alan was discharged at South Cerney, Gloucestershire on January 17th, 1948. He married his childhood sweetheart in October that year and then they decided to emigrate to Canada, which they did, sailing from Southampton to Halifax, N.S. on November 8th 1948. They settled in Toronto, Ontario, then transferred to Vancouver in 1957, as sales representative, handling training equipment supplied to universities, hospitals, schools, governments and businesses. Later, he turned his talents to Life Insurance and became a salesman for London Life. He says he will retire one of these days.

Besides his wife Barbara, Alan has four daughters, two of whom are mirror-image twins, two grandsons and two grand daughters. An older sister still lives in England. Alan holds the War Medal and the Defence Medal.

On one occasion at E.F.T.S. at #6 Air School, Alan was practicing forced landings with his instructor, an ex-operational Blenheim pilot. Glancing to the starboard he saw another Tiger Moth about to collide with them and reacting most promptly, he pushed the throttle wide open, stick hard forward and locked his right arm rigidly, to prevent the instructor from pulling them up too soon, into the path of the other aircraft.

Alan could feel the instructor pulling back on the stick, but he waited a few seconds, before allowing the instructor to take over. Only then did he explain to him the reason for his precipitous action and apologised, that he did not have time to warn him of the danger any sooner.

Needless to say, Alan got a thorough bawling out, as only a scared instructor can bawl!! This, Alan accepted, realizing they were both alive to share his remonstrance.

At S.F.T.S. on Harvards, the course included fighter attacks using cine-cameras, low level, cross country exercises, night flying and recovering from unusual positions, on instruments alone. The latter exercise was bewildering at first, but with a little practice, the students could quickly bring the aircraft under control, even if it was on its back or "hanging on its propellor."

One morning, as Alan was taxiing out solo, one of the wheel brakes grabbed hard, causing the aircraft to ground loop viciously and confront another pilot following him. Thinking he must have touched the toe-operated brake on the rudder pedal, he reasoned that if it happened again, he would apply brake on the opposite side.

It did the same thing again and as he felt the swing developing, he applied the opposite brake. The result was instantaneous!! The aircraft's nose went down as the tail came up and Alan balanced there with the airscrew still turning and just missing the ground! He literally heaved on the throttle and stick while trying to lean back to drop the tail down.

After a lifetime suspended between heaven and earth, he was spared any further embarrassment and the aircraft settled down again. Needless to say, he did not attempt a take-off with a brake binding like that.

His last useful Airforce act, was to prevent a Wimpey belly landing, while flying on one engine. Seeing him approaching too low and too close, with his undercart still retracted, Alan gave him a series of reds with the aldis lamp, but the pilot ignored the warning. Not wanting a pranged Wimpey on his record, Alan fired a red Very cartridge across his bows, and, firing up the dead engine, the pilot managed to climb away safely.

Alan Stuart

F/O DOUGLAS THORN D.F.C.
OBSERVER R.C.A.F.

Doug Thorn was born in Abbotsford, B.C. and at an early age moved to Vancouver and was raised in West Point Grey. He attended Queen Mary School and then went to Lord Byng High School, finishing in 1939. After high school he went to work for an electrical engineering company in Vancouver.

Doug joined the R.C.A.F. in 1941 and was sent to Brandon, Manitoba, to Manning Pool. After his time there, he went to Dauphin for a spell, doing hangar duty, before going to Goderich, Ontario to #12 E.F.T.S. for training on Fleet Finches, for pilot training. He washed out on his final air test, for doing too many spins in a snow squall.

His next posting was to #10 Air Observer School, arriving in the worst snow storm in 25 years. On completion of his course he received his observers wing and was given 7 days leave, to go to Vancouver and then to Halifax. Doug purposely arranged to leave four days late, to arrive on a Sunday, when nobody would bother to check on him, as he knew they wouldn't.

Waiting for a contingent of Canadian Airmen, the troopship "Louis Pasteur" had brought over a shipload of prisoners of war. When the airmen went aboard they found very filthy conditions, so repulsive that they organized a disembarkation at three a.m., amid much noise on the streets, as they marched back to the barracks. Four weeks later, they left for England on the "Queen Elizabeth", which had far better conditions and which made a much faster trip, landing at Giffnock in Scotland, and then train down to Bournemouth.

From Bournemouth, Doug was posted to #28 O.T.U. at Castle Donnington, where he joined a crew, all R.A.F. except for a Canadian rear gunner. His skipper, from Glasgow, became a good friend and has remained such, to this day. They finished their O.T.U. on Wellington 1C's in May of 1943. The crew was sent to a Conversion Unit, #1663, at Rufforth in Yorkshire, on Halifax 1A's. From Rufforth they were posted to #77 Squadron, 4 Group, where they flew on Halifax IA, II,III and IV's, mostly the same aircraft, with modifications.

In July, 1943, the crew made its first operational trip to Hamburg and in five days and nights the city was wiped out. After Hamburg, they made three trips to Berlin, on one trip the gunners were credited with destroying an ME 109 that had attacked them. On the first raid to Berlin, Doug went up beside the skipper to see the target area and, having given the pilot a new course out of the target, he noticed he had set the compass black on red, thereby a 180 degrees out, which would have taken them to Russia. He made a quick correction and thereafter he saw every target to set the new course out.

On one trip to Kassel, the Germans knew exactly where they were headed and kindly laid down brilliant flares on either side of the track in, just like street lights, and proceeded to pick off any aircraft that were slightly off course. They lost an engine, due to flak, which filled the area between lights, and they saw many aircraft shot down.

Early attempts to jam German night fighters' ground instructions, were done by our wireless operators, searching the dials, until they found a ground controller talking to a fighter, then trying to garble the information. The practice was soon stopped and a microphone placed in one engine, so that the W/Op transmitted noise, to more effect.

On their tour of 31 trips, Doug's crew returned five times on three engines, all damaged by enemy flak. On one particular trip to the Italian/French border, on the Mediterranean, they were told that they probably would not have enough fuel to return to base. They were again hit with flak, nearing the French coast and lost an inner engine and fuel tank and, probably, the wheel was hit. A quick estimate of the fuel supply, made it worthwhile to try for the English coast. They made it all the way to Reading, where they had to land on one flat tyre, with the aircraft strung across the runway. Next day, there was one angry Station C.O. because they did not have equipment to move the plane and all operations of the day bombers, had to be cancelled. Going through the London underground the next day was an interesting experience, in full flying gear!!

The Thorn crew did 31 trips, including 5 mine laying sorties, one of which required carrying a load so large, the bomb doors could not be closed. Temperature was -40 degrees when they were to make precision drops from 20,000 feet, into a river mouth, but someone 'goofed' and they put the bombs twenty miles inland. Doug's crew was credited with 28 aiming points and he and his pilot were awarded the D.F.C.

Towards the end of their tour, a Free French Squadron was to take over their station at Elvington. Number 77 Squadron was to move to Full Sutton. Thorn's crew were assigned to take the Free French C.O. on three familiarization trips and, subsequently, asked to stay on for a month to instruct the crews. One crew burned out four engines, on their first cross country exercise. At the end of the tour, Doug went to Wellingbourne Mountford (#22 O.T.U.) as an instructor in navigation, until July 1944 when he returned to Vancouver.

Shortly after returning, Doug and Sheila, a schooldays sweetheart, were married. The Thorns now have two successful sons and four grandchildren. They are both very active in the Canadian Power and Sail Squadrons, at both local and national levels.

In 1951, Doug joined #2442 Squadron R.C.A.F. Reserve, working with #442 Squadron which were flying Meteor Jets. He retired in 1954 as a Flight Lieutenant, to attend U.B.C. night school for three years. Doug's medals and awards are D.F.C., the 1939/45 Star, Air Crew Europe Star, Defence Medal, C.V.S.M. and clasp and R.C.A.F. Operational Wings. After his course at U.B.C. Doug went with Crown Zellerbach in sales and was with that company for thirty years. He then worked with Belkin Packaging, again in sales, for about ten years, officially retiring in 1984, although he still runs a small sales agency in packaging. "One of these days" says Doug "I will retire again".

F/O DOUG PRETTY
WAG   R.A.A.F.

Doug first saw the light of day at a place called Tatura, near Victoria, Australia and attended public school there, then secondary school at Kyabram, Victoria. He and his family lived in those places during his youth and Doug says he also lived for football, cricket, tennis and, what else, but swimming, as all Aussies seem to do.

After school, he served his apprenticeship as a meat cutter, in which business he was employed until joining the Royal Australian Air Force in January 1943. He volunteered for aircrew and chose the aircrew trade of wireless operator.

In Australia, his postings were first to I.T.S. at Somers, Victoria, for 7 weeks, then he went to Parks No.2 Wireless school in New South Wales, finally to No. 2 B.A.G.S. at St Pirie in South Australia. Posted to England, he served at the wireless school at Yatesbury, Wiltshire, then had a stint at Hednesford-Halfpenny Green A.F.U., Staffordshire. After a short time there, he was posted to O.T.U. Lossiemouth, converting to 4 engine planes, moving to Wigsley, then Syerston, on to Scampton, thence on to #189 Squadron at Fullbeck, 5 Group Bardney. He was discharged on March 29th, 1946 in Melbourne, Australia, with the rank of Flying Officer. His medals include the 1939/45 Star, France/Germany Star, War Medal and Defence Medal.

After the war he returned to his former trade of meat cutter. He married Joan in 1948 and they have a son and daughter also 3 grand-daughters. They all moved to Canada in December 1967 and now reside in Burnaby.

On Doug's first operational briefing, he noticed a ripple of laughter and amusement among the assembled crews when they were told to "leave the target at one hundred and sixty miles per hour." Being a sprog crew, they flew according to Hoyle. However, leaving the target area at 12,000 feet, at the suggested speed, they ran into intense flak, but luckily no-one was hurt. They were diverted to Lossiemouth, Moray Firth and the skipper, Johnnie Gilmour, complained of flying "right wing low" all the way from the target. As soon as they landed, they discovered a section measuring 8 feet by 2 feet, which was missing from the under portion of the starboard wing, plus numerous flak holes.

Five nights later they flew with a replacement engineer, who had returned two days earlier from leave, in case of a spare bod trip. He had experienced 20 trips already and asked Doug's skipper if he could fly with him, as he heard that he needed an engineer to replace their normal crew member, who was in hospital.

That night, as they were leaving the target area of Houffalize, the engineer, Leo, said "O-kay, skipper, nose down, full revs, full boost." The pilot complied, with the clock showing 300 m.p.h. Then he asked if that speed was alright, to which Leo replied "Of course it's alright, plenty more bloody engines, no more Leo Doyles." So the crew learned a valuable lesson from an experienced airman and from then on, were amongst the front runners leaving flak areas behind. They often wondered how long they would have lasted leaving the areas at 160 m.p.h.

On their fourth trip, returning from Politz, they had left the target two hours behind; Doug was off the intercom, logging the usual half hourly broadcast from base, when the Lanc. suddenly went into violent corkscrews, accompanied by the vibrations of the Wag's guns. Doug switched on the intercom to hear one of the gunners shouting "Come on you sonofabitch, we'll have a go at you". Doug thought he was blowing steam and resumed logging the base broadcasts. Switching back to intercom again, he suggested that the gunners stop playing games, or let him in on them. "Fun and games", yelled one of the lads, "that was a Junkers eighty eight." It had apparently followed them in the darkness by radar and attacked from the rear and below. The gunners raked it with fire power from their six guns and most

208

hit it, as it broke away and did not resume its attack.

Eight holes were later found in one of the turrets, while over forty holes were in the starboard fuselage and there was also a large hole, obviously from a cannon, in the tail plane. The gunner was lucky, as he only suffered a few abrasions on his cheek from splintered perspex.

As their regular engineer was still hospitalized, the Engineer Leader offered to fill in for him .. what a compliment to such a sprog crew!! They took off on February 1st, 1945 at 4 p.m. target Siegen, flying across the Channel at 3,000 feet. From the astrodome Doug counted over 400 Lancs and Halifaxes in the bomber stream - a beautiful sight. The only thing wrong, was that they were all 4 or 5 miles away to the port side.

Doug asked the navigator if they were on the right course and he replied that they were, in fact he said they were bang on. "Well, I've got news for you Bill" said Doug "There are over four hundred of us about five miles off course." The navigator left the seat, scurried over to the astrodome, took a look and then suggested a dog leg to port and soon they were again being buffeted by the comforting slipstreams of other bombers ahead of them, as darkness fell.

On a subsequent trip to Karlsruhe, the controller called up "Drop your load and get to hell out of here. They are up here waiting for you!" There was 10/10 cloud and they had to bomb on floating flares, as a sheet of white cloud covered the whole area, reflecting all the searchlights, with the fighters above. Fourteen bombers were shot down all around them and they narrowly missed a collision, when the pilot nosed the Lanc under another, just twenty feet above, as it emerged from a cloud bank; then he had to leap-frog another in front. They didn't waste time getting out of there - nose down, full revs, full boost!

At their briefing for their 16th trip, to Hamburg, the enemy defenses were estimated to be 700 light guns and 300 heavy and they were briefed to arrive at the target area 13 minutes before "H Hour"(bombing time), then fly around in a certain area to draw the flak away from the Pathfinders. They were at the target by 4.00 a.m. at 15,000 feet and Doug counted 32 searchlights and the sky seemed to be full of flak. Earlier, Doug had suggested the navigator might like to come to the astrodome over the target, as he had never once left his maps, but was always calculating the turn off point, after the bombs were dropped. So, with the sky full of flak and the criss crossing of the searchlights, looking like there were 200 of them, Doug tapped the nav. on the shoulder and asked him to come and have a look. Bill, the nav, took one quick look, then hurried down to his desk, like a rabbit going down into his burrow. He said "If I had known we had been doing this for sixteen trips, you would never have got me up on the second one."....Just so many words, as he was with the crew on the next trip.

Fortunately, they were in the first wave at H plus 2 minutes and it was a relief, to at last feel the bombs leaving the aircraft. Another nine minutes of weaving in and out of searchlights and they were clear of the target area.

They later learned they were actually among flak from 1,000 guns for 26 minutes, carrying a full load of bombs for 15 minutes of that time, so their Patron Saint was working overtime on their behalf.

Doug Pretty

S/LDR. R. M. NEWITT D.F.C & BAR
PILOT R.C.A.F.

Roley Newitt was born in Vancouver and attended Lord Roberts public school, King George Secondary and a year at U.B.C., Vancouver. His youth was spent in Vancouver where he enjoyed swimming, baseball and handball. Immediately after his year at U.B.C. he joined the R.C.A.F. at Vancouver in December 1940, volunteering to become a pilot.

Briefly, his training included flying Tiger Moths at Vancouver airport, Anson aircraft at Claresholm, Whitleys at Kinross then on 35 Squadron on Halifaxes and 103 Squadron on Halifaxes and Lancasters. He rose in rank from Flight Sergeant to Squadron Leader when he was with 550 Squadron, Bomber Command. Number 6 Group requested Roley for a second tour, but he chose to remain with the R.A.F.

His decorations and medals include a D.F.C. and Bar, 1939/45 Star, Aircrew Europe, War Medal as well as the C.V.S.M and clasp and Defence Medal.

Roley was discharged from the Air Force in Vancouver in 1945, then spent four years at the Canadian Memorial Chiropractic College in Toronto and has been practicing ever since his graduation. He now resides in Vancouver again, with his wife Eileen. They have three daughters.

Roley Newitt was a man who loved his pub and one particularly carefree night, his C.O. spoiled everything by telling him he was flying that night, but later, on being called to the C.O.'s office, he was informed that he was to fly a

210

Halifax back to Canada ... to Aylmer, Ontario, for instructional purposes.

Halfway across the Atlantic,with Greenland on his starboard side, and beyond the point of no return, an engine seized up, leaving three, so he hung a right for Bluey West, on the west coast of Greenland. The rest of the crew were 1 and 2 tour men, so he had all the confidence in the world in his wireless op. and his little box, to get them to an aerodrome in Greenland.

The fiords of that country are nothing like the approaches to Maidenhead, Surrey,or the Regent Palace Hotel ... there is nothing but snow and icebergs in inlet after inlet, so when the wop said his radio was out and he couldn't pick up the beam, they were supposed to ride in on, that didn't make his day. They were by this time, down to almost water level, and thus couldn't drop in on them from a great height, so the choice was to pick a fiord, go up it and hope to run into a runway. Luckily, they chose the right one. This would have made a helluva better story if they had not found the right fiord!

The only runway was carved out of a mountainside and on an incline of about 20%, so it meant they had to land up a hill. There was the choice at Bluey West of either coming in low through the fiord, right on to the runway, or dropping down from over the mountains. Most Americans in their Libs or Fortresses, which they flew to a pool in England, opted to come in over the mountains, which were quite high, and then drop very quickly to the runway. Some dropped quicker than "quickly" as there was a pile of Libs and Forts to the side of the runway. Not the best of morale boosters on the way to Blighty!! When those Yankees saw the bomb bays and cockpits without ashtrays or arm rests or windscreen wipers, their immediate reaction was "My God, this ship was built for action only." They were amazed at the size of bombs the R.C.A.F. and R.A.F. carried and the utilitarian make up of the Halifax.

Roley's introduction to Bomber Command was a trip as 2nd Pilot to Trondheim Fiord, after the "Tirpitz". The crew went up several fiords, looking for the ship, but as they were mostly in cloud, they had to come down almost to the deck. The #1 pilot was "hellbent" to find it, but the gunners on the shore, caught them first and riddled them with holes. All Roley was thinking was "What's it like to hit a mountain?" "Good God" he thought, "I have twenty nine more of these trips ahead of me"

However, they landed back at Kinross with the lights of the gas tank gauges shining bright red ... not even enough gas to taxi to dispersal. The powers that be, removed all 2nd pilots for the second attack, the following night, as too many were lost on the first one. Needless to say, Roley's #1 didn't return and Roley turned a shade greener thinking how nice of Bomber command to think up another lovely outing for his second trip to the continent.

From the fiords of Norway to the Bay of Biarritz, near the French/Spanish border, was indeed a contrast in operations and on this occasion, they were to drop delayed action mines (delayed sometimes for weeks, while insignificant boats passed over them and their fear of the area was removed. Then the ore-carrying freighters of the Axis would arrive just in time for the device on the mines to be triggered.) It was learned later, that many were sunk. But, back to the action in the air ... A master beam caught Roley's aircraft and they zeroed in with their Bofars, or whatever, and caught them after they had climbed to a reasonable height to view the beautiful stretch of beach in the bright moonlight.

Roley was oblivious as to what speed Lancaster's wings tore off, but his particular Lanc was doing 400 m.p.h. plus, straight down. The bomb aimer mentioned something about water, when Roley, with the assistance of his engineer, pulled the plane up from the dive, not too far from the very mines they had just laid!! They escaped with a few holes in the wing and tail.

It wasn't long after this, that a notice appeared on their bulletin board, to the effect that Lancasters must not be dived over 400 m.p.h. since that was the speed that wings separate from the body!

Most of Roley's trips were to the Ruhr Valley with the odd diversion to Berlin, Hamburg, Cologne or Frankfurt. His crew knew their job well ... in case of emergency ... see that their pilot got out first!!

F/LT JOHN MOUTRAY D.F.C.,D.F.M.
WIRELESS AIRGUNNER   R.A.F. – R.C.A.F.

John Moutray was born in London, England in 1919 and came to Canada with his parents at a very early age. They resided first on a small cattle ranch near Kamloops, B.C. and John's early education was "being taught at home", on the ranch. He then attended Vernon Prep School and later, Kamloops High School. His father had come from Ireland prior to W.W.1 and started ranching (cattle, horses, with some fishing and hunting).

One day, John aged ten or eleven, sat on his father's lap, while they had a 15 minute flight in a visiting bi-plane and he discovered a new world. In 1938, after a visit to Northern Ireland, he joined the Royal Air Force at the recruiting depot in Belfast. Sent to Uxbridge, 25 miles west of London, England, John soon learned that "biscuits" were to lie on, not to eat!!

Next, came ten thoroughly enjoyable weeks of square-bashing at Cardington, in Bedfordshire, the Balloon Centre and one time home of the British Airships R-100 and R-101. He finally received his beautifully tailored uniform and after one week, was allowed out to Bedford, only to find that many peace time courses had preceded him and no-one paid any attention to this dashing airman!!

Following Cardington, came the Wireless School at Yatesbury, Wiltshire, where he was put on his only "charge" for smoking in the technical section. His punishment? (Due to your fine service record to date ... confined to camp for one week!!)

Awarded his wireless badge, he was posted to 102 Squadron at Driffield, Yorkshire, to #4 Group Bomber Command, about to change over from Handley Page Heyfords to Whitley III's, IV's and V's. Unknown to the R.A.F. (until now) John Moutray lost a Vickers gas operated machine gun, over the side of an open cockpit, into the Irish Sea and was the only air gunner who failed to put any holes in a drogue towed by a Fairey Battle. It was about this time, while changing the accumulator (battery) on a Heyford in the hangar, that the battery was dropped through the lower main plane. He was quickly making his mark in the R.A.F. and he was certainly a man to watch ... but not fly with!!

In spite of all this, he was finally awarded the airgunner's badge, a brass bullet worn on the sleeve above the wireless badge. Later on, the half wing arrived, which at first just read A.G., but was later changed to W.A.G.

So, equipped as he was, John went to war and scared hell out of the Hun by dropping leaflets. He went to Villeneuve, France and dropped them over Prague, Czechoslovakia, a flight of over ten hours, dropped incendiaries on the Black Forest and spent many cold hours in flights up the Norwegian fiords, looking for German ships in the winter of 1939/40 from his bases in Kinloss and Lossiemouth, Scotland.

In those early days they carried no navigator, just two sergeant pilots, one of whom was the bomb-aimer and/or the front gunner. A ground flight mechanic or fitter or armourer, was also the rear gunner and they had to look after their own equipment.

Airmen who flew, received sixpence a day flying pay, on top of their magnificent sum of 2 shillings per day for an A.C.2. Later promoted to A.C.1 and L.A.C., John was posted to Dishforth and 51 Squadron, still in #4 Group. His flight commander was a S/Ldr. "Willie" Tait, later of 617 squadron and "Tirpitz" fame and holder of a D.S.O. four times.

John was promoted to sergeant and was awarded a D.F.M. in June 1940. Shortly after, he was sent on a gunnery leader's course at Warmwell, Dorsetshire and then attended his investiture at Buckingham Palace.

In the early part of the war, there was no limit to the number of trips which would constitute a "tour" and after 47 operations, including 6 trips to Berlin, some to Italy and France, John was posted to 22 O.T.U. in Wellesbourne Mountford, a little place near Stratford-on-Avon, as an instructor on "rest". He flew with a pupil crew, on the second 1,000 bomber raid to Essen, in a "Circuit and bumps" Wellington. He later walked into a lamp-post one night and thought he had finally "bought it". He awoke in Heaven ... actually in the "Black Swan" pub, being revived by his mates with a beer.

Commissioned a Pilot Officer on May 15th 1941, he went back on "Ops" with an experienced pilot and navigator and four very fine expupils. While stationed at Waddington with 5 Group and 9 Squadron, their Lancaster hit another almost head on at 3 a.m. over Lincolnshire as they returned from Berlin. Three members of John's crew were killed, while all the crew of the other Lancaster perished. After a term in hospital, he went back on ops, now at the satellite Bardney, with W/C Burnett D.S.O., D.F.C. as his pilot.

John's last trip of the war, was an interesting finale to operational flying. Returning from Kassel, the aircraft was in the circuit, when it was hit by a M.E.410 intruder and received 67 holes in one burst. The port outer was on fire, port inner feathered, starboard inner on fire and no hydraulics. The undercarriage was lowered by airbottle and with no flaps, W/C Burnett landed the aircraft safely, in pouring rain, down wind on the short runway. Incidentally, he retired as an Air Commodore and still keeps in touch with his wireless operator!

On a previous trip, 7 dummy runs over the "Scharnhorst" & "Gneisenau" in Brest Harbour were exciting, to say the least and great determination was shown by their bomb aimer Jimmy Geach.

John had a very narrow escape earlier in the war, during a leaflet raid over Germany. As an A.C.2 Wop/AG he usually knelt by the flare chute, while dropping bundles of leaflets, but on this occasion, trying to be more comfortable, he sat with his back against the fuselage and spread his legs apart. A time fused ack-ack shell burst through the floor of the Whitley and passed between his legs, exploding somewhere above the aircraft!

John flew with 28 different pilots in 24 different aircraft, beginning with a Vickers Valencia (troop carrier) and finishing up on Lancasters. He completed 65 operations and after the before mentioned D.F.M., was awarded a D.F.C. from King George VI, again at Buckingham Palace, which was truly a highlight of an interesting flying career.

Discharged from the R.C.A.F., (which he had transferred to) at Boundary Bay in October 1945, he became the Art Director at Evergreen Press and was there for 17 years prior to his retirement in 1985.

His hobbies include fly fishing, golf, vintage cars, large and miniature and painting war time aircraft. He lives with his wife Stella, in Langley and has four children, (two by a previous marriage), and four grandchildren.

One interesting family mention should be made, that his father served with the famed 41st Bengal Lancers during the Great War. John's medals also include the 1939/45 Star, Aircrew Europe Star, France and Germany Star, Defence Medal, C.V.S.M. with Oak Leaf, 1939/45 War Medal and M.I.D., Operational Wing and Bar. The Bomber Command Medal (unofficial at this time.)

F/LT KENNETH A. NORMAN C.D.
PILOT R.C.A.F.

Ken was born at Burnaby, B.C. and attended Douglas Road school there. Later he went to T.J. Trapp Technical in New Westminster. He was a member of the school band and his hobbies and sports included softball, soccer, Lacrosse and fishing, also swimming. His only occupation before the war was a Sunday paper boy, but he did spend some time as an Air Cadet and this no doubt was the reason he joined the R.C.A.F. early in January 1942. He volunteered as pilot and first went to Windsor, P.Q. at #3 E.F.T.S. on Tiger Moths, followed by a month at #3 S.F.T.S. at Calgary on Cessna Cranes. He was then posted overseas to Banff, Scotland at #14 A.F.U. Montrose on a BAT course Instrument, thence to Oxford for night flying. His next posting was to Newcastle at #62 O.T.U. flying Ansons, then in quick succession to Grantham, Cranfield and Manston, flying in that order, Blenheims, Beaus and Mosquitos.

Ken had become interested in the military and flying, at the early age of 14, came up before a magistrate of the juvenile court, a friend of the family and a member of the same fraternal order as his mother, who had just about given up on him. He cannot recall any particular event that prompted the action for him to get some military training. Anyway, he was advised to proceed on January 27th

215

1939, to Stanley Park Armouries for the purpose of joining the air cadet squadron to obtain said training voluntarily, or else ...

There were 300 bodies required and 1500 turned up and Ken was not one of the lucky ones to be selected. He was heading out the door, when a call was made for anyone who could play a musical instrument, to report to the band room; up he went and he was accepted. With six other cadets, he spent the next 1 1/2 years in the band of the 111 Auxiliary Squadron. In 1940, Ken was selected for an N.C.O.'s course and he never missed a parade. After joining the R.C.A.F. in 1942 he went to Windsor Mills E.F.T.S.for the great day to start flying, where he had no trouble landing Tiger Moths. The rest of his training was routine through S.F.T.S. and he was posted overseas in June 1943, where, at Bournemouth he was able to convince the selection board that he had tremendous night vision and was selected for Beaufighters ... his dream.

From Bournemouth, Ken went to #62 Ouston, flying Ansons, then to Grantham on Blenheims. He lost a good number of friends there and nearly bought it himself as well, on a Blenheim. Ken finally met up with the Beau at Cranfield and what a thrill that was to feel the power; a beautiful aircraft to fly. Halfway through the course he was converted to the Mossie, which was also a delight to fly. One highlight of this phase, was the air gunnery, where on his third trip he shot off the drogue, the last one, so was told to proceed to the ground target to finish off his ammo, but he came down too low, held the trigger on the 20 mil cannons and suddenly the ground exploded upward and the Mossie flew through a hail of mud. There was no apparent damage and with the ammo all gone, he flew back to base, where he found out that the plane was damaged extensively, the left main spar being completely shattered, in addition to much other damage.

Ken finally arrived at #406 Lynx Squadron at Manston, Kent on January 5th 1945, where he felt there wasn't much more for him to learn about flying, especially as he had a good navigator, Bert Warwick, from the R.A.F. They were given their own Mossie, "E for Easy", and sorties were conducted over the Continent without concern, as they were well trained. On April 24th, at "tea-time", a strange feeling came over Ken. He wrote a few letters, gave a list to the padre, took four packs of cigarettes, prepared for the unknown, took off in E for Easy and settled down. They were heading for the Flensburg area, north of Hamburg; the night was clear, visibility good,maybe a bit too good, full moon ... not good for his eyes. He flew around a bit to let the Luftwaffe know and stay on the ground.

The aerodrome was circled and a likely spot for targets was chosen for an attack. All was quiet on the ground, but as he was about to commence firing, the German ack ack gunners beat him to it and as the Mossie turned away, a heavy thump was felt; moments later, flames erupted from the area of the port main gas tank, with approximately 600 gallons of gas remaining. Ken pulled up to gain enough altitude to bale out when the big guns went into rapid fire on a sure target.

He rolled her over, chopped the power, turned into the moonlight, while the navigator held the flap lever down, until finally, Ken slowed up, saw a long plowed field and set E Easy down gently, made a quick exit when it stopped and made it to the bank of a dike, laid down and watched his fine aircraft come to a sad end. Ken and his navigator were guests of the Luftwaffe until the end of the war.

Note: On arrival back in England, they were informed that out of 77 crews from "D" Day to the end of hostilities in the Second World War, they were the only survivors in Intruder Command.

The major in charge of the Ack Ack was awarded an Iron Cross.

On his return to Vancouver, Ken was taken on as an Air Cadet Liaison Officer, until "R" day, October 1st 1946, when he commenced a career in the Peace time R.C.A.F. as a pilot. He retired happily in November 1970.

Ken was married on February 2nd 1947 to W.D.Corporal Cecile LaBoucane, ex-CAS office, Ottawa, who still rules to this date and will likely continue to the end! They have two sons, one grandson and one grand-daughter and four adopted grandchildren, by his second son. Ken's medals include the France/Germany Star, Defence Medal, C.V.S.M. and Clasp, Victory Medal, 1939/45 Star, C.D., Clasp and pilot's flying badge.

F/O D.A.(DOUG) MOORE
PILOT R.C.A.F.

D.A. (Doug) Moore was born in Vancouver, B.C. on August 25th 1917. He went to school, first at Prince of Wales Elementary, next, to David Lloyd George Elementary, and then to Chesterfield School in North Vancouver until graduation, except for one year at St.George's in Vancouver for grade 10. His favourite sports were, swimming, soccer, rugger and skating.

Prior to joining the R.C.A.F. in March 1941, he worked in his father's factory and at the Vancouver 'Sun'. He joined the field Artillery at age 16, to be allowed out two nights a week and by 1938, when he moved to Vernon, B.C., was a qualified Gunnery Sergeant. He went down to Vancouver in September 1939, to volunteer for the R.C.A.F. and after signing up, he was sent home to wait until called. By the spring of 1940, when he had heard nothing, he went to Vancouver again and found that there had been a fire in the recruiting office and there was no record of him. He again joined up and once more was sent home to wait. While waiting, he went into the Vernon Infantry Camp as an Instructor.

His Air Force call came in March 1941. He reported to Vancouver, thence to Brandon, Man. Manning Depot and from there to Keewaitin Equipment Depot in Winnipeg for guard duty. He achieved some notoriety there, when one night he saw a figure climbing through a window about 2200 hours and yelled "Halt" the required number of times and getting no response, loosed off a round about three feet to the right of the intruder's rump. Things happened very quickly, the officer of the guard and his sergeant came running. He explained the situation and they found a sergeant locked out of his office, to be the culprit.

His next posting was to Initial Training School at Regina, Sask. and from there to Elementary Flying School at Lethbridge, Alberta, where he had his first ride in an aeroplane. It was a Tiger Moth and the flight was made memorable by his instructor throttling back in high wind and flying backwards across the airfield. After one week, the school was moved to High River, Alberta. There, they flew mornings one day and afternoons the next. When he moaned about this, to his instructor - flying last thing in the morning and first thing in the afternoon - his instructor's reply was "that any clot could fly in a smooth air and that some day he would thank him".

After graduation from E.F.T.S., he was posted to #7 Service Training School at McLeod, Alta. This part of his flying training was on Avro Ansons. There, Doug had an American instructor who had been a stunt pilot in Hollywood. One of his favourite pastimes was to visit a girl friend's farm, northeast of McLeod and do stall turns around the windmill, to see if he could get the blades turning. The windmill was between the house and the barn!

After graduating as a Sergeant-Pilot he went overseas to Bournemouth via 'Y' Depot at Halifax, N.S. His only untoward experience in Bournemouth, was in diving over a residential wall, seconds before the street was hosed by a ME 109; he claimed that fear was a great motivator.

His next stop was #6 A.O.N.S. near Gloucester, where he spent 22 months, either there or at the two satellite 'dromes of Morton-Valence and Aberporth. These months were spent flying pupil navigators around night and day, while they practiced what they had learned in the classroom. Some of the highlights of his stay at #6 were - coming out of a cloud one day, to find himself in the middle of the Bristol Balloon Barrage; fortunately they were not all up. Having a pupil lose them one night over the Welsh mountains and finding his way back to Morton-Valence to a safe landing. Had one engine quit while rolling down the runway and the other quit as he turned onto the perimeter track, - out of gas! Another time, losing about two feet off his starboard wingtip while flying on a night exercise. Doug's real claim to 'fame' came one night when he returned to base, after about a three minute flight, with both vacuum pumps u/s. Seeing the C.F.I.'s car coming to meet him, he sent his crew off into the darkness. He had the C.F.I. chew him out for being a pansy pilot, among other things, for turning back, next he suggested what the C.F.I. could do with the aircraft and volunteered to assist him if he experienced any difficulty. What Doug didn't know, was that his application for a Commission had not finished crossing the C.F.I.'s desk -- result was no commission and no promotions, until the C.F.I. was posted about six months later!

Doug was granted a commission, late in 1943, after being posted to the Coastal Command General Reconnaissance School at Squires Gate. After passing the G.R. course, he was posted to the Middle East for O.T.U. His first stop was in Jerusalem; from there he went to R.A.F. Station 'Ein Shemer', a 'Wellington' O.T.U. His navigator, F/L Stewart Webb, had done a tour on 'Baltimores'; his #1 wireless operator was regular Air Force, also on his second tour. The other members of the crew were first timers like Doug. Next came a posting to Aden in Southern Arabia, to #8 Squadron, which had been permanently based there since 1919.

Life was fairly uneventful at Aden. The Squadron's job was ship convoys and to watch for German subs; however, during Doug's time there, none were sighted. They flew patrols out of Rian in Southern Arabia, Bander-Cassim in Italian Somaliland and the island of Socotra off the northeast tip of Africa.

In November 1944, the illness (rheumatic fever) which had attacked his nervous system at the age of eight, started up again. The station Medical Officer heard him moaning while asleep and called him to his office next day. After asking a lot of questions and examining him, he called the C.O. who told him he was grounded. Shortly after, he was on a ship bound for Egypt, having by then been promoted to Flying Officer.

Egypt was fairly uneventful and the next thing, was a ship to England. Back in England, he got some leave and then reported to Warrington for repatriation to Canada. He arrived in Halifax on February 14th 1945 and says it was the best Valentine ever.

His father had died in 1942 so he settled in Calgary, where he married Lily. He moved to Penticton in 1947, where his two sons were born, to sell hearing aids. This was not too successful, so he went on the road for General Foods, who taught him how to sell. After 3 1/2 years, he switched to the Walter M. Lowney Company, regained his health, then went to the Alexander Murray Company, which later became Domtar, Building Supply Division. He stayed with them until a stroke sidelined him in 1978. He retired in 1982.

He is now involved with the Royal Canadian Air Force Association, the Abbotsford Flying Club and through that, with the Abbotsford International Air Show. The medals Doug earned were the 1939/45 Star, C.V.S.M., Defence Medal and the War Medal.

F/LT. LESLIE A. WALKER
PILOT R.C.A.F.

Les Walker was born in Dodsland, Saskatchewan. His father being a clergyman, his schooling was taken at Merryfield, Sintaluta, Carievale and Drinkwater, in Saskatchewan. After completing senior matriculation, he took the Youth Training General Aeronautics course in Regina. His favourite sports were ball, hockey, swimming and skating.

He enlisted in June 1940, in Regina and decided he would like to become a pilot, but on checking with the Recruiting office early in September, he was told he could go with an aero draft later that month, and that when he reached Toronto Manning Pool, he could remuster as a pilot.

After graduating from St. Thomas Aero Engine School, he was posted to #3 S.F.T.S. Calgary, still trying to remuster. Finally, it came through and Les started pilot training at Edmonton I.T.S. in January 1942. He started flying Tiger Moths at #18 E.T.S., Boundary Bay, B.C. but the school was shut down shortly afterwards and a fighter squadron put in its place. He was then posted to #19 E.F.T.S. Virden, Manitoba in April 1942. Late in May, he crashed and after hospitalization, he was pronounced fit for flying duties. He never learned what caused the engine failure responsible for the crash.

After E.F.T.S. he proceeded to S.F.T.S. flying Cessna Cranes and was awarded his pilots wings December 1942 and left Halifax on the "Capetown Castle", on its first run as a troop ship. He arrived at Bournemouth, England, where for two weeks he was with the British Army.

After several other postings, he eventually arrived at Marston Moor, where he flew Halifax Mk I's and II's, but shortly afterwards, he and his crew were posted to Bomber Development Unit at Newmarket, to train the navigator and bomb aimer on H2S (Radar) in Mk II and Mk III Halifax's. Les also had the good fortune to fly Stirlings and Mosquitos. In February

220

1944 he ferried a new Halifax Mk II to join 462 Squadron and on March 9th flew the aircraft to Rabat Sale in North Africa. On new orders, he proceeded to Maison Blanche, near Algiers, then was ordered to fly to Catania, Sicily. Final orders were to fly to Celone, Italy to join 614 Squadron, which incidentally, was totally housed in tents, including the messes.

While on the squadron in Italy, he and his crew were flying a training trip, when Mount Vesuvius erupted. On their final approach to land, the windscreen suddenly became clouded over, as they had flown through hot ash from the volcano and it had burnt the perspex of the windscreen. Les had to land by looking through the little hatch which opened on the side of the windscreen.

(In June 1957, flying among other aircraft, the Canso, on #103 Search & Rescue, Les was practicing water landings when, on this occasion, he made a normal landing, but as the aircraft came off the step and settled in, the tunnel hatch sprang open and water started pouring in. Fortunately, another pilot along for the ride and sitting in the blister compartment, noticed what was happening and called Les through his "mike", which he had plugged in , to get the bird out of the water and "don't ask questions." Les and the co-pilot opened the throttles and with good luck were able to get her airborne, streaming gallons of water from the hull.)

614 Squadron was to be a Pathfinder Squadron, with double the normal compliment of crews for a squadron, but it was decided by Bomber Command, to cut the squadron to normal size and Les, along with others, was selected to return to England. He tried to get back on "ops", but England was loaded with aircrew by this time, (July 1944), so he was posted back to Canada, returning on the "Pasteur". Arriving home in December 1944, he was discharged as W/O 1 to go to Re-hab. School, and placed on Reserve Class E, (Immediate call up if required.)

The School was a good idea, but the young men there were just "brushing up" and those who had been in the service for 4 to 5 years, couldn't keep up with them. Les managed to obtain one senior matric subject he needed, though. Later, he obtained his Commercial Pilot's license and worked at many different occupations, such as spray-gunning appliances at Eaton's, logging on the Thompson River, flew a Tiger Moth north east of Kamloops, landing in a tree (no injuries), worked in an ice plant in Vancouver, ferried the odd aircraft in B.C. and Alberta, then found time to get married in 1948 to Kathleen, known as Kay.

In June 1949 he re-enlisted in the R.C.A.F. as an aero engine mechanic and in 1951 accepted a short service commission and took a refresher pilot training course, at the newly opened Clairesholm #3 F.T.S., on Harvards, and #1 P.R.T.S. Currie Field, Calgary, where he flew Dakotas, Mitchells, Ansons, Expediters, Norseman, Lancasters, Chipmunks, Harvards, C119's (flying box-cars), Cansos, Mustangs and Austers. Altogether Les logged 6,270 flying hours and flew 60 different types of aircraft and still yearns to "get his hands on a Pitts special."

He earned the 1939/45 Star, Italy Star, Defence Medal, C.V.S.M. and clasp and the War Medal. He retired in 1964 with the rank of Flt/Lt.

F/LT A.T.S. FRED WILKINSON
PILOT R.C.A.F.

A.T.S. 'Fred' Wilkinson was born in Grand Forks, B.C. receiving his Elementary and Secondary education there. His spare time activities included hiking, hunting, and fishing, while his participation in sports was in baseball and hockey at city league levels.

In 1941, High School Graduation Ceremonies for Fred were just a principal's handshake, and handouts by Army, Navy and Airforce Recruiting Officers. On leaving school, Fred wanted to join the Airforce, but his dad suggested it might be wise to wait awhile before jumping into things. Mr Wilkinson was a W.W.1 Veteran, who had spent three years in the trenches, serving with the Seaforth Highlanders, had received the M.M. and Bar, as well as a Mention-in-Dispatches. Fred's brother 'Jock' was a signalman in the R.C.A. from 1941 to 1946, seeing much action from Sicily to Germany.

Fred, a painter apprentice in his home town, had worked in the smelter in Trail, B.C., before he applied to enlist in the R.C.A.F. Wearing glasses at that time, he intended getting into a groundcrew trade. Imagine his surprise following the medical, when he was advised that he had 20-20 vision. There was a quick switch to aircrew for Pilot training.

Fred's flying training began at #15 E.F.T.S. in Regina, on Tiger Moths and he received his wings at Brandon, Manitoba in November 1943, having trained on Cessna Cranes. Six months later, at #20 A.F.U. at Kiddlington in England, he was flying Oxfords. He picked up his crew at #86 O.T.U.

222

Gamston and completed operational flying on Wellingtons. Fred finally finished on Halifaxes at #1659 Topcliffe, before being posted to his Squadron in February 1945, at Linton-on-Ouse. It was the Thunderbird R.C.A.F. Squadron, #426 and Fred completed sixteen missions over Europe before the hostilities ended.

As his training neared completion at Topcliffe, Fred and his crew had an experience that was not part of the course. A simple cross-country flight had been scheduled. A proper cockpit check and warm-up were completed, before the aircraft turned onto the runway. With snow banks piled high and the runway clear, the Halifax approached its takeoff speed, when suddenly - the starboard engine backfired. With the rapid loss of power, the aircraft swerved right and plowed into the snowbank, breaking the starboard wheel off. As the starboard wing started to drop, Fred raised the remaining part of the undercarriage, to slow down the aircraft's motion. With much grinding, screeching, and sparks, the Halifax came to rest, at the edge of the bomb dump - completely totalled. None of the crew were injured. Very upset that his aircraft had been totalled, Fred expected a severe reprimand as he stood before his Commanding Officer, Group Captain Avant. He was given a red endorsement "with degree of blame -- carelessness." The C.O. had softened the blow, by telling Fred, whether true or not, that Billy Bishop had had nine such endorsements.

The tendency for Halifaxes to swerve to starboard on takeoff was well known, and some were worse than others. Because of this, Fred and his crew were to experience another close call, on a day raid, with their aircraft loaded with petrol and sixteen 500 pound bombs. Early in the takeoff run, the Halifax swerved off the runway across the grass, stopping just short of the perimeter. The head engineer boarded the plane when it had stopped, and while taxiing back, concluded that no damage had been done. Not enthused, Fred and his crew agreed to a second takeoff attempt. This time he advanced the starboard throttles far beyond the port throttles. The takeoff was completed and the mission successful. The bottom line to the story is, however, that the same Halifax's next trip, was with a different pilot and crew, and the aircraft swerved out of control on takeoff, crashed, and exploded on the airfield. All the crew got out safely.

On his first mission, Fred flew with another crew to gain experience. It was to be a night raid on Chemnitz, close to the Russo-German border, to aid our Russian allies. Fitted with extra fuel tanks, the aircraft carried half the usual bomb load. The raid took eight hours and forty minutes. Although no fighters and only flak were seen over the target, much action was visible around Berlin as the aircraft passed near that area. A line squall at takeoff had caused icing, and their plane had heavy and sluggish going, before the ice broke off when they made it through clouds. Three other Halifaxes from their station were not so lucky, - they had crashed shortly after takeoff because of heavy ice buildup, - only one crew member survived. At the briefing, an interesting directive stated, that if crews were unable to return to

England or France, the chances of survival were greater in Germany than behind the Russian lines.

Fred's most memorable trip, was the raid on Kiel, when his aircraft carried not only a full bomb load, but also, ... a full load of Gremlins. The crew's briefing had ensured high speed winds, but far greater wind speeds were encountered, Denmark being crossed before the mistake was noted. A 180 degree turn to get back on course, had just been completed, when the inner port engine caught fire, -- and the intercom went dead. While Fred and his flight engineer managed to extinguish the fire, feather the propeller, and retrim the aircraft without the intercom, the gunners, seeing only flames, were at a loss to know whether to bail out or not. Fortunately, the fire went out, and the intercom came on, before any action had been taken. Because of the loss of one engine, they had to fly at a lower altitude and at a slower speed than designated. Near the target, their plane was lit up suddenly like daylight, by two searchlights that coned on them. Quick evasive action was necessary, to get out of the beams before the anti-aircraft guns got their range. Fred's prompt evasive action was successful, but somewhat too violent, because his bomb aimer reported that it sounded like the bombs had momentarily lifted off the hooks, and that he hoped none had come loose in the bomb bay. The evasive action had actually moved the aircraft off the proper target run in, so Fred circled around and the target was bombed successfully. Fred's evasive action had also toppled the compass and a few errors resulted. The passing over a very active enemy anti-aircraft battery on the coast made this obvious. It was a slow journey home against high winds, with only three engines, and as they neared the English coast they were diverted to North Luffenham, as their base was fogged in. The approach to the runway was too high, so Fred, amid remarks and groans, made another circuit. After a safe landing, the crew were well looked after by the North Luffenham staff.

Bombing raids provided many incidents, to momentarily startle aircrews and to raise their apprehension levels a bit. Fred's best memory of this, was the thousand plus bomber day raid on Heligoland, as aircraft seemed all too close, in every direction. A Halifax directly above them with bomb doors open, displayed a full load of bombs, while another directly below seemed in danger of receiving their bombs, while over the target. All held onto their bombs until clear, but many must have been held too long to have done much damage to the target. Photographs of Fred's attack showed his bombs hit the edge of the target - a near miss.

During large daylight raids, it seemed to Fred that collision courses were inevitable, while at night this congestion only occurred over target areas, or on the return, as aircraft neared their base. One night a plane was very near their own and the rear gunner reported four fires an equal distance apart. It later turned out to be four glowing manifolds of another Halifax. Evasive action was suddenly necessary.

Fred Wilkinson returned to Canada, as the European war ended and was posted to Dartmouth, Nova Scotia to "crew up" for the war in the East. However, as the Eastern conflict soon ended, he was discharged at Dartmouth.

Fred received the 1939/45 Star, the France/Germany Star, the Defence Medal, the C.V.S.M. and clasp, and the War Medal.

Following his discharge, Fred attended U.B.C., graduating with a BSA degree in 1949. He became an Entomologist with the Research Branch, Agriculture Canada, and retired in 1985 after 39 years employment with the Federal Government.

Fred married Jean Knowles in 1950 and they have two daughters, a son, and three grandchildren. Although he does some consulting, Fred prefers to spend his time fishing, hunting, travelling, and visiting with his children and grandchildren. Fred and Jean live in Vancouver.

F/O DONALD A. WILLIAMSON
PILOT R.A.F.

Born in Victoria, Donald A.("Don") Williamson started school in Hilliers, near Parksville, and then went to school in Sidney, both on Vancouver Island. In 1929, when he was about 10, he and his younger sister moved with their parents to Scotland, where both parents came from around 1910.

There, Don went to school at Rutherglen Academy (Stonelaw) and afterwards worked in Glasgow as a trainee with Brintons Ltd. of Kidderminster, a large carpet-manufacturing firm. In the summer of 1939, he and some friends joined the Territorial Army, after attempts to join the R.A.F. were rebuffed.

A summer camp at Fulwell, in Northern England, was followed before

225

war's outbreak by a posting to Edinburgh Castle where searchlights of the 421st Searchlight (Glasgow) Regiment were set up. Thereafter, the searchlights were moved from site to site across Scotland; and at Roseneath, on the River Clyde, Don was promoted, perhaps laterally, to be a dispatch rider. He daily visited Headquarters at Luss and his deliveries to the various sites included recognition signals called "Colors of the Day". The sites appeared to ignore these colors because, notwithstanding that correct colors of the day were fired by planes that were illuminated or shot at, the sites continued enthusiastically to illuminate or shoot them. In fact, Don claims that the first plane he ever saw being shot down by Allied flak was a Blenheim of the R.A.F.

Requests for a transfer to the R.A.F., the Commando forces or Canadian forces of any sort (where the pay was some 300% higher) were denied until the summer of 1941 when Don was transferred to the R.A.F. (In fact, it later emerged that a Canadian who joined a non-Canadian unit overseas was generally required to stay there until quite late in the war.)

Life in the R.A.F. started well, with a posting to Trinity Hall, Cambridge, where, as it were, other Dons tried to inject navigational and various skills into potential pilots. An early joint meal at Trinity Hall ended quickly in a vigorous bun-throwing contest between cadets and undergraduates, with frank opinions being rapidly and freely exchanged. Unilingual solitudes were soon firmly established. (The fact that this University is one attended by individuals who go on to become lawyers and then judges, may account for, but not excuse, the occasional outbreaks of bun-throwing that have been known to mar some legal functions in Vancouver.) Early flight training began at an E.F.T.S. at Brough in Yorkshire but bad weather and the Luftwaffe severely limited flight time in D.H. Tiger Moths.

The class at Brough was moved later in 1941 to the U.S.A. to be indoctrinated into the U.S. Army Air Corps as part of the Arnold Scheme. The class of 42G, as it became known, was split into two or more parts and trained at various airports in Florida and Georgia and perhaps Alabama on five or more types of planes, including Stearmans and Harvards and graduated in mid 1942, each graduate receiving the usual silver wings, to be followed in short order with R.A.F. wings and in 1945, those of the R.C.A.F.

There were the usual critical moments during training but one night stands out still, when out of about twelve planes, each with a cadet pilot and instructor, six crashed in a violent electrical storm over Georgia, killing all on board.

The class of 42G sailed for the U.K. from Halifax in a New Zealand ship, the "AWATEA", but late on the first night out, there were several loud explosions. Everyone thought that the "AWATEA" had been hit by one or more torpedoes and a rapid general muster took place on the top deck. However, what had happened was that one of the convoy escorts, a U.S. destroyer, had collided with the "AWATEA" and had then sunk. The "AWATEA" limped slowly back to Halifax.

226

Returning to Britain on the "QUEEN MARY", then of course a troopship, Don went in October to an advanced flying unit near Newark and flew Oxfords, at times uncomfortably, when word was radioed that German night intruders were operating in the area. Then on to an operational training unit in Derbyshire to "crew up" and to fly Whitleys, the engines of which at Ashbourne were prone to leak glycol and to become inoperable. Something more serious led to the port engine of a Whitley catching fire in May, 1943 almost directly over Mt. Snowdon and to an emergency landing cross-field at a small training airdrome at or near Sealand.

Don's Whitley crew, consisted of John Callagan (the crew's only Catholic), Tom Moore, Bill Bennett and Bert Davies - respectively Irish, English, English and Welsh. At what were deemed critical or appropriate moments, someone would shout "John, burn some incense quickly".

Allied planners were impressed by the German success in invading the island of Crete in 1941 with airborne forces. A newish R.A.F.Group, 38 Group, needed personnel to train and transport paratroopers and glider pilots to take part in supplying the European resistance forces with materials and some people.

The Williamson crew went next to 295 Squadron at Hurn near Bournemouth, and later at Harwell and Rivenhall, flying Whitleys and the occasional Oxford and, operationally, Albemarles and Stirlings. The squadron claimed (with the forces of the U.S.A. and others opposed) that it had opened the Invasion by dropping paratroopers soon after midnight on the morning of D-Day, in the case of the Williamson crew at a dropping zone at or near Ranville, southwest of Cabourg. Later on D-Day, a Horsa glider was towed over to a landing zone north of Caen.

The night flight in the early morning of D-Day in an Albemarle was uneventful, except for wrestling with turbulence from propeller wash when returning in at 500' to Ranville; but the day flight in the early afternoon as part of a lengthy and massive loft of planes and gliders flying over the incredible number of ships, machines and men off and on Normandy was a quite unforgettable moment.

The Williamson crew (now augmented by Ron Smith as flight engineer for the Stirling) flew on the Arnhem operation on September 17, 18, 20 and 23, 1944. Day one was memorable, with even longer and more numerous lines of planes and gliders and only distant black smoke marking some hasty and involuntary descents. Days two, three and four were different because supplies were carried, to be dropped in daylight from 500 feet. One could look to the left and right and see Stirlings on fire or crashing. With a number of planes in range at any given moment, the German forces apparently did not try to shoot at every plane but instead concentrated their fire on this plane, then on that, with the result that if a plane emerged unscathed, it was simply a matter of luck. The Group suffered by far its heaviest losses at Arnhem.

Donald's medals include the 1939/45 Star, the Aircrew Europe Star and

Clasp, also the Defence and War Medals.

After the War, Don went to the University of British Columbia graduating in 1950 in Arts and Law. He articled as a law student in the summers of 1947 through 1949 with Russell & DuMoulin and continues to practice with the same firm, now B.C's largest and celebrating its 100th birthday in 1989.

MAJOR W.M. (BILL) MOORE, C.D. & BAR
WIRELESS AIRGUNNER - R.C.A.F. - C.A.F.

W.M. (Bill) Moore was born on May 5th, 1925 in Vancouver, B.C. He received his elementary and secondary schooling at the Model and Vancouver Technical Schools.

Prior to enlisting in the R.C.A.F., Bill trained as an Air Cadet and became one of three original sergeants in the Squadron. He joined the R.C.A.F. in January 1943, and completed his training as a WAG at the University of Guelph, Ontario, and #2 Bombing and Gunnery School at Mossbank, Sask. Bill was then posted to the West Indies, for Operational training in February 1944, and was there until August of that year. When he returned to Canada, Bill and his crew were posted to the U.K. in the late summer of 1944.

After attending a two-week Naval course, they were transferred to 1674 Heavy Conversion Unit in Northern Ireland, flying Liberators. Finally, Bill and his crew were posted to #224 R.A.F. Squadron, Coastal Command, at Milltown, Scotland.

The squadron was responsible for submarine and anti-shipping missions in the Atlantic, and along the Norwegian coast. The crew spent most of their flying hours in the monotonous patrolling of the ocean, - "watching water". The trips varied in time from 10 to 11 hours. There were always two enemies to deal with, - raw nature and the ever present U-Boats. Most of the operations were wide ranging, varying patrols, off the east coast of Iceland to the Skagerrak, between Norway and Denmark.

The crew received credit for attacks on two German submarines. The first submarine attacked, was operating with "Schnorkel". This was a breathing apparatus for getting fresh air without surfacing. The schnorkel was picked up on the aircraft's radar, and was illuminated by its Leigh light (a five million candle power searchlight). An attack was made from low-level, dropping 6 - 250 lb depth charges and an extensive amount of wreckage was noted.

Bill homed two destroyers and another Coastal Command Aircraft from Tain to the target and after achieving this with his crew and being low on fuel, returned to base. An interesting sidelight was that the Captain of the aircraft from the base at Tain, Scotland, turned out to be the brother of "Hammy" Hamilton, Bill's skipper. It had been over two years since they had met. Communications between the two aircraft were heavy that night!!

A few nights later, returning from a routine patrol, the bomber crew sighted another submarine. This was attacked from low level, by dropping an acoustic torpedo, which found its mark, as evidenced by an underwater explosion and wreckage, followed by another explosion. Bill, as the wireless operator, homed the 30th Naval Escort Group to the target area, prior to returning to base.

On the night of February 26th, 1945, the crew had completed its first sweep of the Skagerrak, searching for U-Boats without results. A second sweep was carried out and two targets were located by radar. Hammy positioned the aircraft so that the moon's wake was behind the intended target, and he proceeded to attack. The targets were identified as enemy surface vessels in line astern. Hammy selected the rear target; closing to within one mile, the Leigh light was turned on, - and at that moment an enemy aircraft was observed closing rapidly. The pilot immediately put the Liberator into a climbing turn and lost contact with the enemy aircraft. To this day, Bill believes that had the skipper not made that split-second decision to abort the attack, the enemy pilot probably would have added to his score. The Liberator ended up over neutral Sweden, but was soon on a reciprocal course headed for home. En-route, they were again attacked head-on by enemy aircraft. After violent evasive action, another enemy aircraft was picked up on the radar, dead astern. These two aircraft shadowed the bomber for 27 minutes.

Bill volunteered for the "Tiger Force" for the attack on Japan, and was returned to Canada in July 1945. When VJ Day arrived, Bill was shortly thereafter demobilized in Vancouver.

He resigned his commission and rejoined the Regular R.C.A.F. in July, 1946. and served in various ranks, until receiving his commission again in

1961. He retired as a Logistics Officer with the rank of Flight Lieutenant in February 1971. Bill then retired to the Supplementary Reserve, and then in 1971 transferred to the Primary Reserve (Army), serving as a Staff Officer at Saskatchewan District HQ with the rank of Major, until 1972.

Bill received the 1939/45 Star, Atlantic Star, the C.V.S.M. and Bar, the War Medal, Defence Medal and the C.D. and Bar.

In 1970, Bill had joined the C.N.I.B. as their Accountant and subsequently became their Business Manager in Regina. After eight years he transferred to the C.N.I.B., B.C. Yukon Division in Vancouver, as their Chief Accountant. He retired in August, 1988.

Bill and his wife, Doreen, reside in White Rock and have three sons of whom they are very proud. Rand in Calgary, Scott in Regina, and Jeff with the B.C. Forest Service, living in Hope.B.C.

F/O DONALD A. MONTGOMERY D.F.C.
PILOT R.C.A.F.

Donald Allen Montgomery was born in Wilcox, Saskatchewan, November 6th, 1918. He took his schooling there at the Wilcox High School, where he also played all sports, such as baseball, lacrosse and track in the summer and hockey in the winter. After grade 12, Don worked on farms in the Wilcox district, then in an independent gas service station in Regina.

On July 28th, 1941 he joined the R.C.A.F. in Regina and proceeded to Manning Depot in Brandon, Manitoba and then on to I.T.S. in Edmonton. It wasn't until the latter part of the course at I.T.S. that shoes and uniforms were obtainable which excused him from very little parade training and no guard duty. It was in October, 1941 and #5 Elementary Flying School at High River, Alta. that he was able to conquer the manoeuvers on the Tiger Moth. It was then time to move on to the twin engine Cessna Crane at #12 Service Flying School at Brandon, Manitoba in December 1941. In April, 1942 he was the proud recipient of the Pilot's wings of the R.C.A.F. and after a leave, left for England on a Polish ship called the "Batory".

Ten months after enlisting, found him at #15 A.F.U. Leconfield, Yorks - July '42. Then in quick succession came #1516 B.A.T. training at Middleton St. George, #16 O.T.U. at Upper Heyford and 1660 Conversion Unit at Swinderby, Lincs.

It was at #16 O.T.U. where the Canadian pilot being attached to the R.A.F. was teamed up with his English crew - George Grainger, Engineer, Ed Cohn, Navigator, Jack Baker, Wireless Operator, Stan Neil, Mid Upper Gunner, Jack Gardner, Bombadier, Bob Baggs, Rear Gunner. All different, but after 45 operations there are no stronger ties of respect, friendship or comradeship.

December 1942 found the crew at Woodhall Spa, Lincs. on 97 Squadron on Lancasters for a short time and then they moved to Bourne, Cambs. on Pathfinders, where 45 operations were completed. During that time there were quite a variety of trips - the long hauls to Turin, Milan, Spezia, the medium length trips to Berlin, Punemundi, Nuremberg, Frankfurt and then the shorter hotter trips to the Ruhr Valley. The tour was ended by going to Berlin on November 18th, 22nd and 23rd and Frankfurt on the 25th.

Two trips to mention, August 23, 1943 - Berlin, with just a minute either way of the allotted time to drop the load, being early and having to circle for 20 minutes, leaves a very marked remembrance in one's mind. May 25th, 1943 - Dusseldorf, hit with a load of bombs from above on the bombing run in, they lost the starboard inner engine, the end of one wing tip; one jammed the starboard aileron but the engineer feathered the starboard outer prop in error. Ten thousand feet in altitude later, Lancaster ED-875 decided to put things together and take the crew home for a much needed rest.

After ops, with a Distinguished Flying Cross for his efforts "Monty", as he was known, has had a varied flying career. January, 1944 at 24 O.T.U., Honeybourne, Worcs., February and March he instructed at 1659 Topcliffe, Yorks. April #3 F.I.S., May and June back to 1659 Topcliffe while July '44 saw Monty home again on leave with a homecoming reception in the town hall.

After a month's leave, 165 Squadron was the next stop, both in Edmonton and Rivers, Man. where it was parachute dropping at Shilo, Man. flying out of Rivers. Then back to Edmonton on the skid run from Edmonton to Whitehorse. From February to December 1945, it was a Transport conversion course at Pennfield Ridge, N.B. and Comox, B.C. 164 Sqd. Moncton to Goose Bay and Gander. January - March it was 168 Sqd. in Ottawa on Liberators, which brought about a visit to Prestwick, Scotland, again and a new place in Reykjavick, Iceland.

On April 6th, 1946 Monty received his discharge in Winnipeg to start a new life.

After his demobilization, Don started out with Texaco Oil Co. in Regina as a tank truck driver and two years later was transferred to Winnipeg as Branch Manager of the Sales Department. In 1950 he returned to Regina for a few days to marry Marjorie Partridge who was working with D.V.A. at the time.

In 1952, Don was again transferred to the new bulk sales plant in Edmonton and after only two years there he and Marjorie moved to Burnaby where their only child Joanne was born in July that year. Don worked for McGavin Foods Ltd. for 25 years, retiring in 1983 and is now enjoying golf, gardening, travelling and life in general.

His medals and decorations include the D.F.C., C.V.S.M. and clasp, 1939/45 Star, Pathfinders Forces Badge, Defence Medal, Aircrew Europe Star and Victory Medal.

F/O JAMES J. MULVANEY
NAVIGATOR R.C.A.F.

Jim Mulvaney was born in Vancouver, B.C. He attended St. Patrick's Elementary School and then on to Magee High for secondary education. His residence was predominantly in the Kerrisdale district of the city.

In his youth he engaged in a number of activities and his sports included baseball, rugby, Canadian football, tennis, ice skating and swimming. For less rugged activities Jim enjoyed music and collected records.

His first employment was as a clerk in the Postal Director's office, followed

232

by a position of Partsman, Receiver and Shipper with the Finning Tractor Company in Vancouver.

Jim joined the R.C.A.F. in March of 1942 in Vancouver. His first posting was to the Manning Pool in Edmonton, from there he went to #6 Bombing and Gunnery School at Lethbridge, where he was flying on Fairey Battles. He was trained as a navigator, completing his courses at #2 I.T.S. in Regina and at #3 A.O.S - Regina, being promoted to Sergeant, prior to being shipped overseas in January of 1943, on the "S.S. Andes".

Once in England, Mulvaney went to an A.F.U. at Moreton-Valence where, flying in Tiger Moths and Ansons, introduced him to the English countryside. His next posting was to an O.T.U. at Honeybourne in Worcestershire and from there to Conversion Unit at Croft. The crew was assigned to Halifax III's, with Hercules Radial Engines, and they joined #433 Squadron at Skipton-on-Swale.

On the night of February 24/25th Jim's crew were shot down on an operation to Schweinfurt and taken as prisoners of war to Dulagluft at Frankfurt-am-Main, where they were held for a week. They were sent to three other camps, where they were held until they went on a forced march from April 7th to May 2nd of 1945, when they were liberated.

Jim had a unique experience, in that he met a fellow-navigator-to be, Craig Fergusson at Manning Pool and then again, at the A.O.S. in Regina. They were posted overseas together on the same ship, went to the same A.F.U., the same O.T.U. and the same Conversion Unit. Jim and Craig were assigned to the same Squadron, #433 where both crews were billeted in the same Nissen Hut. To add to the coincidence, the two crews were on the same operation on February 24th, when both were shot down and landed 60 miles apart, ending up in the same P.O.W. camp!!

Jim Mulvaney was returned to Canada on the "S.S.Pasteur" and he was discharged on August 22nd 1945. He was married to Marjorie Baguley in August the same year. They have two sons, Richard and John and two daughters Deirdre and Patricia. They have five grandchildren, all of them living in British Columbia. Jim returned to the Finning Tractor Company, in Sales and Branch Management; the firm being involved in heavy industrial logging and construction machinery. His medals include the 1939/45 Star, Aircrew Europe Star, Defence Medal, C.V.S.M. with Clasp and Victory Medal.

One night in September 1943, Jim Mulvaney was a member of a crew from #24 O.T.U. at Honeybourne, that was assigned to do a training exercise, starting from a point in the middle of the English Channel, on a BULLSEYE to the 'target' in Green Park, London. Their Whitley arrived over London when a German raid was in progress and they got caught up in flak intended for the 'Jerries' and they immediately lost their starboard engine!! The skipper asked for a course to the nearest airfield - but no airfield would respond to their request for 'quick assistance', due to the many enemy aircraft in the area. The Whitley was losing altitude down through a "beeping" balloon barrage.

Jim advised the skipper that their descending course pointed them somewhere beyond Uxbridge and Northolt. He was assigned by the pilot to send an

S.O.S. on the downward identification lamp. Being sprogs, they realized too late, that they should have jumped! By now they were down below 1,000 feet; suddenly the skipper noticed a winking green aldis lamp and all else was black. He managed to use the green light to line up the plane and instructed the crew to take-up crash positions. The Whitley hit the ground, bounced and tore itself apart and the crew managed to get out through the remains of the fuselage and then extricate the rear gunner from his turret.

Luckily, there was no fire and soon a 'crash vehicle' arrived and doused the wreck in foam. The crew found out that the Green aldis was in use by paratroopers, flying off Denman field in Tiger Moths, to acquaint them with night flying and the aspects from the air at night for possible jumps. They had actually landed on Denham Golf Course which was adjacent to the airfield. With great flying by the pilot and a good measure of luck - the whole crew survived!

Soon after Jim Mulvaney's crew were shot down over Germany, he was taken prisoner and interrogated in Dulagluft at Frankfurt-am-Main; his interrogator gave him the usual grilling, to which his only answer was his name, rank and number. He casually mentioned to Jim that most of the Canadians he was confronted with, came from Bomber Command in Yorkshire. Somehow Jim's name must have been cross-referenced in his files, because he flippantly told Jim that he had trained in Regina! He was beginning to think the interrogator was away ahead of him. Then he said "I know you R.C.A.F. aircrew hang out at many pubs in Yorkshire and your bunch most likely spend time at the Busby Stoop". Then Jim replied "Your facts are a way out of line. Busby Stoop? never heard of it!" Immediately, the navigator was dismissed.

Later, when Jim was in Stalagluft VI he mentioned his meeting at Dulagluft to some other R.C.A.F. p.o.w.'s from Yorkshire; they, to a man, said "Busby Stoop" *was* a pub at the juncture of the highways and that squadrons in the area visited it regularly. He realized he had visited the pub, but only knew it as the "roundabout", but at least his naivete got him past the Jerry interrogator.

On April 7th 1945, after being moved to Stammlager #357 at Follingbostel, Mulvaney and his section were put on a "Forced March" by the Germans. They understood that the orders to their captors, were to march them to a redoubt area near Berlin. Hitler, it was said, intended to use the p.o.w.'s as a last resort bargaining tool, with the Allies. It was early on the march, that Craig Fergusson and Jim's skipper, George Fielding, and Jim were able to slip away from the barn they were in and from the guards. After considerable difficulty and endeavour, they made it through the German lines to the Allied armies and of course, eventually back to England. Once back to 'Blighty' they were soon shipped back to Canada on the "S.S. Pasteur" and then to Vancouver. In August, Jim was married to Marjorie - with Craig as best man. On leaving for their honeymoon, Craig was given the news that "this was one posting he wouldn't be on!"

W/O 1. W. BERT MORRISON
WIRELESS AIR GUNNER R.C.A.F.

Bert Morrison was born in Saskatoon, Saskatchewan, and received his elementary and secondary education there. After graduation, he attended Vocational School, where he took Special Commercial training. He was raised on a farm and enjoyed most, the servicing and operating of farm tractors. He played hockey, baseball, soccer, hard ball and curling.

In July 1941, Bert joined the R.C.A.F. as a Wireless Air Gunner, taking wireless in Calgary, and training on Norsemen a/c. He attended #3 B. & G. at McDonald. He then trained at #10 A.O.S. in Chatham, N.B., and followed this with training at #7 A.O.S. at Portage la Prairie, using Ansons. He was appointed W.O.2 in October 1943.

To Bert, the training was fairly routine, except for an incident at #3 B. & G. when he did air firing from the rear cockpit of the Fairey Battle. There, two students at a time were involved, and one did his exercise, while the other waited below. Bert had fired first and then signalled to the other student that he was coming down. Usually there was a strong smell of glycol, but something else seemed to have been added. The student had airsickness and the smell was rather overpowering. To his credit, he finished his exercise and Bert was relieved when he landed.

After graduation as a W.A.G., he was posted to IY Depot in Halifax. Shortly after arriving, Bert began to have trouble of a medical nature, with his right elbow, and after examination, was declared unfit for overseas service. However, when the draft was finally called, much to his amazement, his name was on the list. Saying nothing, Bert marched with the others down to the dock, to board the "Queen Elizabeth". He was doing fine, until one of the officers doing the final check, recognized him and the jig was up.

He was finally posted to #10 A.O.S. Chatham, and commenced duties that would last until the end of the war. He flew in Mark 1 Ansons, with a crew consisting of a pilot, a W.A.G., and two student navigators. The W.A.G.'s duties consisted of back tuning the tower frequency, ground station frequency, tuning in range stations, taking loop aerial bearings, and sending a position report every half-hour. Because of the terrain, they carried a life raft with provisions, life jackets, and an emergency transmitter. The W.A.G. also had the duty to supervise the proper procedure, in case of emergency.

One night at Chatham, Bert was to have a flight, the weather was good and he was in the first flight. The route was to be from Chatham to Fredericton, and back to Chatham, which usually took three and a half to four hours to complete. As they approached Fredericton, the pilot advised Bert, that the starboard engine was dropping revs and that he was to send a "return to base" signal. The aircraft continued to lose height, but managed to land safely at base on one engine. About an hour after their landing, fog began to drift in. Some of the aircraft on the flight were able to land with the tower's assistance, and the use of flares. Most aircraft, however, were diverted to other fields. As the time passed, bad news began to come in. One of the aircraft had crashed into a hill near Moncton, and the two navigators killed. Another ditched off Cape Tormentine, and its W.A.G. was drowned. Still another ditched in one of the rivers, with the loss of a student. Bert and his pilot speculated on what their chances might have been, if they had been in the second flight,(which was later) if the starboard engine had conked out during the flight.

Another incident occurred during "sea crawls" which they flew, so the navigators could practice taking drifts. Suddenly, the sound of the engine changed, and after a frantic call from the pilot, Bert found out that when he had switched tanks the starboard engine died. Bert went on the fuel pump and after five minutes, which seemed an eternity, the engine caught, and events turned back to normal. Because of the fixed wooden props on the Anson, which created a lot of drag, the aircraft had dropped close to the water, so it was with relief that a proper altitude was reached.

One flight at Portage la Prairie, a night flight, turned out to be unique. The exercise called for a heading north west to the Saskatchewan border, a short leg south, and then back to Portage. The met. sector forecast thunderheads, which were to be avoided. While they were flying the last leg, the overcast became solid, and the pilot descended to locate his position. There was no sign of Portage, Brandon or Winnipeg. Bert tuned in the Winnipeg beam and determined they were over North Dakota. He found out later, that the wind velocity had increased and its direction changed. They were on an astro exercise, with inexperienced students and accuracy was at a premium. Bert flew the beam to Winnipeg and back to Portage and landed safely. They had put their 'chutes on for the last leg as they were nearly out of fuel.

During Bert's time at Chatham, and Portage la Prairie, he logged just under 1000 hours of flight time, which averages out to something over 300 flights. As there were two students per flight, he was able to observe over 600 young navigators doing practical training. In summer, with its extreme turbulence, one could hardly stand. The students moved around the aircraft when necessary and completed their exercises. During the winter, it was always bitterly cold, and they had to take star shots and do their plotting with cold bare hands. They gained the crew's respect. When Bert was posted to Chatham, quite a number of the pilots were either bush pilots or pre-war licensed pilots. He found them to be "superb and a joy to fly with".

Bert was appointed W.O.1 in April 1944. He was discharged in Vancouver on April 3rd, 1945. He received the C.V.S.M. Following his release, he was employed by the B.C. Electric Co., and remained with them for 37 years. He served 27 years as a transit operator, and 10 years as a student operator instructor. Bert married Claudia, who was an R.C.A.F. W.D. They have a son and daughter-in-law, and two grandchildren.

F/LT WILLIAM E.(BILL) PEARSON D.F.C.
BOMB AIMER R.C.A.F.

Bill Pearson was born at Regina, Saskatchewan in 1922 and attended Connaught Public School there, but when the family moved to Vancouver in 1936 he continued his education at Magee High School, followed by the University of B.C. His sports activities included hockey, football and golf.

He left U.B.C. in January 1942 in order to join the R.C.A.F. and was posted to Manning Depot in Edmonton. He had volunteered as air bomber and trained in Alberta through his I.T.S., Bombing and Gunnery at A.O.S. and was posted overseas in January 1943. His A.F.U. was in North Wales, then at O.T.U. he flew Wellingtons, then was posted to a conversion unit to

237

fly Lancasters. After crewing up, they were posted to #9 Squadron 5 Group, in November that year. Bill and his crew were attached to 54 Base (83 and 97 squadrons at Conningsby P.F.F.) for ten trips as Master Bomber. He continued with P.F.F. 83 squadron and was shot down in August 1944 and was a p.o.w. in Stalag Luft 1.

Bill's decorations and medals include the D.F.C., the 1939/45 Star, Aircrew Europe, C.V.S.M. and Clasp, also the War Medal and Defence Medal. After the war he was honourably discharged on September 28th 1945.

He returned to U.B.C., where later he graduated, with a B.S.A. Honours degree, then joined Labatt Breweries of Canada, with whom he served for 33 years as a brew master, plant manager, director of quality control and production Vice President and General Manager. Bill retired in 1984. He married an English girl from Leicester, Ina, in 1946 and they have three sons and four grandchildren.

From Bardney, Lincolnshire, #9 squadron, in November 1943 he joined in the Battle of Berlin. On Bill's third trip to Leipzig, fighter attacks severely damaged their aircraft and the mid upper gunner was wounded. The pilot, Dave Pearce, successfully fought the controls, to land at an emergency 'drome at Woodbridge, East Anglia, using up the full length of the extended runway, plus the over-run grass. The wounded gunner was rushed to hospital, where, after months of treatment, he was repatriated to his home in Australia.

On the crew's 13th trip, on return from operations and descending through cloud to their base, the aircraft suffered a mid-air collision with another Lancaster. Just moments before, Bill had left the bomb aimer's compartment and the impact with the other Lanc. sheared off most of the front turret and bomb sight area. However, the flying ability of the aircraft was such, that the pilot was able to land successfully. Tragically, the other Lancaster crashed and the entire crew perished.

In April 1944, Bill's skipper completed his tour and was screened, leaving the remaining crew, including the Scottish mid-upper gunner to crew up with 9 Squadron Station Commander and to be posted to P.F.F. at 54 Base, Conningsby, Lincs. This base was the home to 83 and 97 Squadrons, which were the Pathfinder squadrons for 5 Group. The crew completed ten operations as "Master Bomber" on targets in France and the Low Countries.

Early August saw the crew return from leave, only to find with sorrow, that their skipper, W/C Porter along with a pickup crew, were lost on a "gardening trip" to Stettin. An old friend of Bill's became their new skipper, in order for them to finish their second tour on P.F.F., with 83 squadron. On the night of August 29th, Bill joined another pickup crew as a visual bomb aimer and flew with a Squadron Leader who was assuming Deputy I role to mark Koenigsberg. After a successful spot fire being dropped, the aircraft was hit by flak and set on fire. Four of the eight crew successfully bailed out of the aircraft, which was about 4,000 feet. Bill was held in a searchlight and on landing became an instant p.o.w.

The following few days were rough and Bill had to thank a Luftwaffe Oberleutenant for literally saving his neck from a lynch mob, in the burning city. After interrogation, Bill eventually arrived at Stalag Luft 1, to meet many old friends from training days. He remembers a cheery note during the first day of being marched through Koenigsberg, when a rich Cockney voice, coming from a work party, yelled out "Cheer up Canada, don't let the B...... get you down". A friendly voice that was a great lift.

Incidentally, in 1977 Bill returned to flying as a hobby, after obtaining his pilot's license. Since then, he has crossed Canada, visited many parts of the U.S.A. and Mexico and continues to enjoy this freedom. He has also had several meetings with ex-crew members in the U.K. and the warmth of these meetings is memorable.

F/SGT.GEORGE H. PRICE
PILOT R.C.A.F.

George was born at Moncton, N. Brunswick and attended Moncton Elementary and Moncton High School. His introduction to the military came early in life, as his father was the C.O. of the New Brunswick Rangers in the middle thirties and often took George and his brother to camp for a couple of days. The boys looked forward to the Sunday sports of bare-backed horse riding, wrestling, jumping etc. George joined the cadets at age 12 and then the N.B. Rangers at 15, although 3 years under age, having lied about his age.

When the war started, most of the cadets rushed to the Armoury only to be told by the Sergeant-major to go home to their mothers and thus back to school. George's first experience with the R.C.A.F. was as a civilian, working as a waiter at No. 8 Flying School at Moncton, but in January 1942, as he was now 18, he applied for admission to the R.C.A.F. and was sworn in, in June of that year.

His first posting was to Truro, N.S. for a WETP (War Emergency Training) course and he then went to #5 Manning Pool, Lachine, Que., in October. Number 1 Wing was indoctrination, #2 Wing, squarebashing, while #3 Wing was the posting wing.

In February the next year, George was posted to #9 Repair Depot, St Johns, Que., for tarmac duty, until a course opened up. A month later, he was posted to #3 I.T.S. Victoriaville, Que., and now considered "aircrew in training" he was allowed to wear the white flash in his cap. All the trainees were promoted to L.A.C. and after going through a selection board, George was earmarked to train as a pilot. In May he went to #13 E.F.T.S. St. Eugene, Ont., where he was to learn how to fly the Fleet Finch, however, after 5 hours flying he entered hospital, suffering from rheumatic fever.

After a month's convalescence leave, George passed the medical board and returned to #13 E.F.T.S., where he had 73 1/2 hours flying and 10 hours in the Link Trainer. His next posting was to St. Huberts, Que., where he was to fly Harvards, but while on leave, he received a wire to report to #5 S.F.T.S.Brantford, Ont, where he flew Ansons Mk II and III. Brantford was a good training area in winter, because of the smog which blew over from Detroit, so all landmarks had to be well remembered. Even so, some students had to check their compasses and fly I.F.R. (I follow railroads), in order to get back safely to base.

George took off one day, with a student pilot and another student pilot acting as navigator. As they circled to the left the cockpit filled with smoke, but on levelling off, the smoke began to clear. After this had happened several times, he landed and refused to fly in that particular aircraft again. The corporal in charge of maintenance, kept insisting there was nothing wrong with the plane, but several hours later he reported that he had found a tiny hole in the oil line and that every time the aircraft banked to port, the oil dribbled on to the hot engine, causing smoke to rise through the open wing root. If this had not been checked it could have caused an engine seizure.

March 23rd 1944 was the big day. Wings Parade and most of the course graduated as sergeants, then were posted to "Y" Depot Lachine, Que., but were only there two weeks or so, when they moved to #3 A.G.T.S, Three Rivers, Que., on a Commando Training course, consisting of sergeant aircrew only, and they did cliff climbing, unarmed combat, 25 mile night marches etc. On July 7th, George was posted to #1 G.R.S. Summerside, P.E.I. and this was one course he disliked, consisting of advanced navigation, relative navigation, astro nav., coding, ship recce, morse code, meteorology, etc, the aircraft being flown being Ansons Mk V.

He was then posted overseas, on the "Ile de France" arriving at Bournemouth in October. He then had disembarkation leave and spent some time

240

with a pal at Weston-Super-Mare, through the auspices of the "Lady Rider Association." Back at Bournemouth, a lot of time was spent at the Royal Bath Hotel and every time George looks at the beer stein on his rec. room shelf, with the etched bath tap and the initials R.B.H. it brings back fond memories!!

A few days later, going on parade, he experienced pains in his chest and fell on his knees. He thought it may have been the result of his bout with rheumatic fever, but after a session on the "slab" in the examination room and a good dose of castor oil, followed by two hour's sleep, he was as good as new. In December he was posted to a Flight Engineer's Training Unit at St. Athan, South Wales, in preparation for a course as Second pilot/Flight Engineer, on Lincolns for Tiger Force in the Far East. George came second in the course and was promoted to F/Sgt. and in April 1945 he was posted to #1666 Heavy Conversion Unit, Wombleton, Yorks, an R.C.A.F. station, but there was very little flying, as there was an abundance of pilots. Lord "Haw-Haw" was broadcasting from Berlin one night, telling the listening world that Germany had no fear of those gum-chewing Canadians of 6 Bomber Group, as most of them end up in hospital through alcohol related accidents, on their bicycles.

There was some truth in this, as an imbibing F/Sgt, trying to run along with his bike and then attempt to leap on the saddle, missed altogether and went down in a heap on the cinder path. He did this on several occasions and eventually wound up in hospital for a week.

When the war in Europe ended, George was posted to R.C.A.F. Station, Croft, Yorks., there to await embarkation, again on the "Ile de France" bound for Dartmouth, N.S., and in September, when the Japanese war ended, 15 Lancaster aircraft were to be ferried to Claresholm, Alberta, the first leg being to St. Hubert ... a 3 hour flight, while the second leg was to Gimli, Manitoba, a 6 1/2 hour flight.

The weather was clear and the Lancs started up, did their run ups and taxied out for take-off, on the third and final leg for their destination at Claresholm. George, who was flying second pilot, noticed that the skipper, once the aircraft had attained flying speed, was very gently tugging at the wheel but the Lanc would not break ground. The skipper didn't say anything, but George felt there was something wrong with the controls. He looked at the skipper, then at the pine trees at the end of the runway, then reached over to the quadrant, pulled back the throttle, got out of his jump seat, followed the push-pull rods to the back of the Lanc, while the skipper was wrestling the aircraft to a slow down ready for a turn off at the end of the runway. As George expected, the push-pull rods were jammed. Across from the entrance door above the rods was a 3 foot control yoke locking rod, held in place by leather straps. One of the pre-take off checks was to make certain it was secure, so it was always given a tug, but it must have had one tug too much as it had broken loose and was lodged behind the push-pull rods. After an effort the controls were freed.

The other Lancs held back as George's aircraft went down the taxi strip, engines to the point of overheating and allowed them to make an immediate take off.

The 15 Lancs orbited over Winnipeg and then resumed course, for their destination, in formation. A few miles outside Winnipeg, the skipper decided to take the Lanc down and "contour fly" and in no time at all the other Lancs were with them flying just above the deck. Near the Alberta border, they flew over a large roundup of cattle and pandemonium broke out on the ground below, cattle and cowboys going every which way. Imagine the noise of sixty Rolls Royce Merlin engines just 40 or 50 feet above them!!

Over the prairies, they passed over several airfields and they were astonished to see the numbers of parked Libs, Mitchells and Cansos lined up like soldiers.

George was demobbed at Moncton, on November 7th 1945, went back to school and then university. He married Ruth Joan Caddell July 5th 1947, went into the lumber business in Eastern Canada and became Mill Manager. In 1955 the family moved to Vancouver, where George represented a Hamilton wood-working machinery company, becoming West Coast Manager. Later, he formed his own company and worked all over Canada. He retired from the woodworking business in 1985 and continues to fly the second plane he bought in 1969. His medals include Defence Medal, C.V.S.M. with Clasp and War Medal.

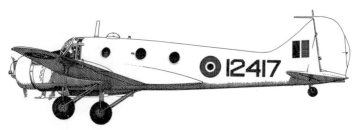

AVRO ANSON MK Ⅴ 12417 R C A F

F/O E.W.(TED) RAWSON
PILOT R.C.A.F.

Ted Rawson was born in Powell River, B.C., but grew up in Kamloops, B.C., graduating from high school in 1942. He started work in engine service with Canadian Pacific. He served with the Rocky Mountain Rangers (Militia) in 1938 and 1939 as a boy soldier. When, in early 1943 the R.C.A.S.C. put out a call for their "Railroad Corps", Ted tried to join, but was told that his railroad experience was inadequate, but his 2 year infantry training was just what they were looking for. Within 6 hours of completing his Air Force medical examination, he was accepted for aircrew.

After a time spent at #3 Manning Depot, Edmonton and three months I.T.S., he was posted to #24 E.F.T.S. Abbotsford, in September 1943 and subsequently graduated as pilot at #19 S.F.T.S. Vulcan, Alberta on May 5th 1944. Next came a commando course in Calgary and O.T.U. at Abbotsford, crewing as a second pilot on B 24's (Liberators). His crew assisted a civilian crew of three, ferrying a Liberator from Dorval to Karachi via Bermuda, the Azores and North Africa, from November 8th to November 13th and arrived at 355 Squadron Sabboni, Bengal on 2nd December 1944.

They made 20 operational trips from December 21st 1944 to April 5th 1945, with 355 Squadron and 16 with 159 Squadron F Digri (Bengal), finishing their last "op" on August 3rd 1945. They took part in bombing and mining missions, as well as dropping supplies to ground troops.

On October 8th 1945, Ted embarked on "H.M.T. Strathaird" in Bombay harbour, bound for England, arriving at Southampton on October 29th. He was then posted to 435 Squadron R.C.A.F.(T) November 1945, flying to various continental destinations, ferrying civilians and military personnel, until April 1946, when the squadron flew the aircraft back to Rockcliffe (Ottawa) via Prestwick, Reykjavik and Goose Bay. Ted was discharged in

Vancouver in June 1946. He is now retired as a locomotive engineer with Canadian Pacific Railway, after 42 1/2 years service (which included time in the Air Force). He had worked on both steam and diesel locomotives out of Kamloops, Vancouver and Cranbrook.

There were no flying entries in his log book from September 24th (Course 89) to October 25th that year (Course 91) at 24 E.F.T.S. Abbotsford, B.C., which can be explained. He was in the "digger" for 14 days. With all of 28 hours flying time, three students decided to have a little "dog fight". It was a lovely September afternoon and 10,000 feet over Chilliwack was their planned rendezvous. They individually made their way to the appointed place and two students formed up, going after the third aircraft. Imagine their horror when doing a half baked formation loop over the intended "victim" to find they had picked an aircraft with two persons aboard, not one. (They found out later, one was an instructor with a student.)

They left the scene post haste, taking as long as they could, to get back to base, but it didn't help. Two hours later, they were on their way to Western Air Command detention barracks at Patricia Bay, Vancouver Island. The charge was "Unauthorized flying". The third student did not get airborne, because of engine trouble.

As any met. man (Cloudy Joe) could tell you ... "Avoid Cumulonimbus clouds as you would the plague." The inter-tropical front in the Bay of Bengal, was a continuous line of cu-nimbus, that built to 40,000 feet, plus, in the afternoon heat.

On May 21st 1945, after a daylight mining operation to the coast of southern Burma, in the area of Mergui, Ted and his crew found themselves south of this continuous line of cu-nim. clouds, so they climbed and climbed until at 30,000 feet they still estimated they had another 10,000 feet to go, which seemed impossible. The only alternative was to get right down to wave top height, almost, and bore through. Not a happy thought. With the radio altimeter set at 50 feet, they flew straight into the worst weather any of them had experienced and what with the rain pouring in every nook and cranny, the aircraft bouncing around as if controlled by a madman, and the Bay of Bengal looking as mean as the North Atlantic in winter, the ten or fifteen minutes boring through this "clag", seemed like two hours. The weather on the north side of the front was calm, but because they used up so much fuel, trying to climb over the top, it left them no alternative but to divert to Akyab, on the west coast of Burma ... and ... a 2 1/2 hour trip to base the next day!

As with most crews he met, because of cramped quarters, the strain of long trips and bad weather, the odd temper "flare-up" was inevitable. Ted's navigator and bomb-aimer, after being cooped up for 15 1/2 hours in the nose of the B 24 on a trip to Siam (Thailand), arrived back at Digri in a picky mood, everything being reasonably under control, till the aircraft was parked. Naturally, all the crew were in a hurry to get out of the aircraft, but unfortunately, the navigator dropped his chest pack on the head of the bomb-aimer, due to his haste to get out. This was the last straw. However, as there were six more of them, they were able to separate the two-some, before any damage was done and after de-briefing, supper and a few double scotches in the mess, all was peaceful again.

Ted's problems with the navigator, developed because his compartment opened where the second pilot's rudder controls were. He would be relieving the skipper monitoring "George", or flying manually, if George was u/s. He found it more comfortable to slip off his mosquito boots, but if his feet were near the navigator's nose and he was a little off course, compass points driven into his big toe, soon got him back on course, with not a word spoken!

Returning from a mining operation in southern Burma, they diverted to Akyab, because of weather and fuel shortage. The next day, they had a leisurely return trip to base over the Sunderbunds, (many mouths of the Ganges) when they spotted a ferry loaded with people which was crying out to be "beat up." After about three passes, the W.O.P. remembered to wind in the trailing aerial. The next day, the squadron Wireless Operator wanted to know where 104 feet of wire with a lead weight at the end had disappeared to, and of course, no-one had the foggiest notion. They couldn't possibly have draped it around that Indian State ferry ... could they? The skipper (first pilot) had a penchant for low flying and this episode wasn't his first run in with authority.

He had completed a first tour on the west coast of Canada, on Stranraers and Cansos, had become a W/O 1 pilot until he returned to Ucluelet with four feet of the mast of the R.C.M.P. patrol boat Uchuck 1 in the bottom wing of his Stranraer. He became an instant Sergeant/Pilot and was posted to Boundary Bay O.T.U. course 5, where he crewed up with Ted. His new crew consisted of four officers and three sergeants ... he being one of them and Ted wondered if A.F.H.Q. had much to do with it. He eventually got his commission 8 months later.

Ted was married to Helen and they have two daughters and two grand-daughters. Ted's medals include the 1939/45 Star, Burma Star, C.V.S.M and clasp, War and Defence medals and Operational Wings.

CONSOLIDATED LIBERATOR MkⅤ 600 - No. 10(BR) SQUADRON R.C.A.F.
GANDER NFLD. - SUMMER 1943

245

F/SGT KEN REID
PILOT R.A.F.

Ken was born in Toronto but received his education at Lord Roberts Public and King George High Schools in Vancouver, where he matriculated. His hobbies were tennis, swimming and softball.

Ken left Vancouver on the evening of October 4th, 1936 as a guard in a C.P. Silk train carrying Chinese to Montreal. He then sailed from Montreal on October 20th on the "Manchester Citizen" arriving in England some 2 weeks later. He bought a ticket for the train fare to London for 24 shillings, which was his total cost from Vancouver to London.

He served as an electrical assembler for a firm making permanent wave machines, for six months, then went to Peel House, the college of the Metropolitan Police of New Scotland Yard for three months training and on July 3rd, 1939 was sworn in by the then Commissioner, Sir Phillip Game. He was then posted to one of the Metropolitan London Divisions, where he served 'til April 30th, 1941 when he was accepted for pilot training in the R.A.F.

Ken's service life included the following stations and aircraft, beginning at #3 E.F.T.S. Shillingford, Berks, on Tiger Moths, then to 32 E.F.T.S. Bowden, Alberta on Stearmans. This was followed by a stint at 37 S.F.T.S. at Calgary on Harvards, 14 A.F.U. Banff, Scotland on Oxfords thence to 10 Radio School Carew, Cheriton, Wales, on Ansons. Still on the move, Ken went next to 29 O.T.U. Bruntingthorpe, Warwicks on Wimpeys and then to 1 E.F.T.S. Panshanger, near Welwyn Garden City, Herts, again on Tiger Moths. His last three postings were 3 G.T.S. Gaydon, Warwicks, 21 H.C.G.U. Brize Norton, Oxfordshire and finally to Elsham Woods, Lincolnshire. These last two stations being on Horsa Gliders. He had his introduction to gliders at Gaydon where he flew the Hotspur glider.

He did not apply for medals, but if he had done so, he would be entitled to wear the 1939/45 Star, War Medal and Defence Medal. He was discharged in Edinburgh on December 11th, 1946.

After the war, Ken returned to Vancouver, in December 1946 and the day after New Years in 1947, began an apprenticeship in Canadian Telephone and Supplies Ltd. and after 37 years as a telephone technician, retired in 1983. His second marriage was to Agnes (Nessie) Reid and he has two boys, Douglas Allan and Keith Austin.

It was the 22nd December 1943 and Ken Reid had the afternoon off from his staff pilot duties at the R.A.F. Radio School, Carew, Cheriton in South Wales. The day was sunny and bright with about 5/10 cloud drifting across the blue Welsh sky, and, he thought, quite good enough to go flying in the Tiger Moth, which was kept at their disposal, but for some unknown reason, rarely used. In the R.A.F. the Tiger Moth was an open cockpit biplane and used in the initial stages of a pilot's training.

Picking up his helmet, goggles, parachute and a map, he climbed into the pilot's seat, and sat there for a few moments mentally brushing up the cockpit procedure; after all it was two years since he had flown one. Feeling satisfied that his recollections were still good, he taxied out to the take-off position.

The Aerodrome Control Pilot (A.C.P.) soon had his green aldis lamp pointing in Ken's direction, denoting permission to move on to the runway, and when he had completed this manoeuver it was quickly followed by a second green, signifying 'Clear for take off!' Upon receipt of this second green he gently eased the throttle forward to its maximum position, and with the Gypsy Major Engine exerting its full 130 horse power, he was airborne in less than 160 yards.

At 4000 feet, he levelled out, but while climbing up to this height he remembered thinking, "This engine does seem a bit ropey" (out of tune). Perhaps it was this odd miss from the engine that suggested the wisdom of staying within sight of the aerodrome.

However, having laboriously climbed up to 4000 feet in the cold December air, which was a little cooler at this height, Ken thought, "Why waste it?". He might just as well do a few aerobatics, as there's always something that needs polishing up.

First he tried a loop, and although there was the odd splutter or two from the engine, the loop itself must have been passable because he hit his own slip stream as he came out of it, indicative of a good loop. Encouraged by the results, he decided to try a slow roll, and while executing this manoeuver, the engine started spitting, coughing and spluttering like it had a bad case of asthma. He wobbled his way out of the roll, but had to work the throttle a little to rejuvenate the engine, and as he did so, got her back on an even keel again. The only sensible course of action open to him, was to return to the airfield; enough was enough, he was calling it a day.

He joined the circuit at the normal 1000 foot level and at the end of the downwind stretch, turned on the cross wind leg, which was then followed by a final turn at 500 feet to line-up with the runway. And then it happened ... the engine coughed out!!

At 500 feet you do not have all the time in the world to study the causes of your sudden dilemma, or its remedial action, but the first check was to make sure the magneto switches were still on ... they were.

Next, he had to give all his attention to landing, because with a scant 500 feet there was no way he was going to make the runway as it was too far away. He could see the nearest field was oblong in shape,but he could also see it had a serious disturbing drawback, and that was a large pond roughly in its geometric centre.

It was a strange field, harbouring a number of unknowns, especially the pond ... how deep was it? Were there any submerged obstructions or pot-holes? He didn't know, but he did know he had a dead engine and that his precious height, space and time were diminishing very fast.

On his approach, it was necessary to slip off a little height, but only enough to clear a hilly rim, and by doing this, it would allow him to make the greatest use of the field for the landing run. This landing run had to include the ground, before and after the pond; and as he was to see later, it was actually a shallow valley. He flattened his glide out,and than sailing along just a foot or two above the ground, the aircraft settled down, like a beautiful bird, for a perfect three point landing, right plumb in the centre of the pond!!

In the next instant, his vision was blanked out by a mountainous wall of water which shot up all around the aircraft. The machine's speed and momentum carried it out of the pond and along the field finally coming to rest within two feet of some trees; the upward slope of the ground acting as a brake (The English Tiger Moth has no brakes).

Stepping out of the aeroplane and taking a closer look at the surroundings, it was evident that the field was rectangular in shape, and with the ground sloping upward in every direction to its boundaries, giving it the definite contours of a saucer.

Within 20 minutes, a rescue party, consisting of four or five vehicles arrived from the station, travelling over a farmer's road and reaching an adjacent field to the downed aircraft. Among the rescue party were airmen, N.C.O.s, six or seven fellow pilots, and a couple of Engineering Officers who were soon appraising the situation and asking some pertinent questions.

The officers made a cursory inspection of the aeroplane and decided she was still airworthy, in spite of her now dirty trampish appearance. One of these officers seemed to possess mechanical knowledge that was both extensive and intuitive, because in less then five minutes he had found the trouble. Perhaps it should be mentioned here, that the engine of the Tiger Moth is gravity fed, and it was some of De Havilland's ingenuity to place the petrol tank as part of the upper center wing section, and shape it like a wing foil.

Climbing up and standing on the seat of the front cockpit he began a careful examination of the petrol tank gauge, and in a very short time remarked, "I think I have found the trouble; whoever worked on this ma-

248

chine, put the float needle in upside down." A spanner was produced and he had it fixed in a jig time. Looking at Ken, he asked "Do you think you can fly her out?" Reid confidently answered in the affirmative, but might have had second thoughts, if he could have seen what lay ahead!

The next task was to push the aircraft to the downwind end of the field, which was easily accomplished, with so much man power available. With this done, the aircraft was swung around, and once more faced into wind. The Technical Officer, taking hold of the propeller himself, turned it a couple of times to ensure petrol was drawn into the carburetor, then with a final glance at Ken shouted, "Contact!" Easing the throttle open one notch, Reid flicked on the magneto switches and gave the same reciprocal reply. With the next downward pull of the prop the engine sprang into life; and almost immediately was purring like a kitten.

To gain a further advantage, the Technical Officer placed four or five chaps on each wing tip to act as anchors, and as Ken opened the throttle, to the point where restraint was no longer possible, he brought his arm up in a prearranged signal, so that they might all let go together, causing the aeroplane to shoot forward as though released from a catapult. In a matter of seconds the aircraft wheels hit the mud on the perimeter of the pond which immediately caused a nose down attitude approaching the vertical.

His spontaneous reaction was to snap the stick back in his stomach, and with the plane's forward motion still fractionally above the flying speed, she responded immediately, sending the aircraft's nose skyward, and at an angle comparable to that of an anti-aircraft gun. When this happened, the plane's speed dropped to the stalling point, and a crash seemed imminent; after all, it was pretty drastic and violent oscillation for an aircraft to be put through.

In the final analysis it was survival, so as the aeroplane hovered at the stall, resulting in the sudden drop of a wing, Ken was able to pull it up again with lightening fast rudder movement. It required the utmost concentration, plus very fast eye, hand and foot co-ordination, but then as one long second followed another, the aeroplane, slowly at first, began picking up speed, and started climbing in a normal manner.

Finally the seesaw take off was over, and although he could temporarily breathe a sigh of relief, there was still no room for complacency because Ken still had to climb fast and hard, to be free of the bowl-like field where he had been an unwilling guest.

He was now low flying up a slope and there were a few long moments as he realized his clearance above the trees had been reduced from feet to inches. He was skimming over an uneven carpet of green foliage, aiming for troughs rather than crests. None too soon, he reached the peak of the ridge, but as he did so he felt some branches brush the lower wing. He caught his breath for a long second or two, than as suddenly as the scratching began, it ceased. Thus it was with a fair amount of relief and exhilaration he realized he was over and clear. He had made it.

Flying homeward, a sprinkling of rain quickly deepened to a heavy shower;

and as everyone knows, flying through a rain storm is most routine, but in an open cockpit plane with no helmet and no goggles (which he had inadvertantly left on the ground after his landing) it became quite another matter. This absence of headgear at speeds of 100 m.p.h. or better, sure clears the dandruff out of the scalp, if it does nothing else. However should this take place during the teeth chattering month of December, the penetrating cold soon makes one feel as if he were flying in his underwear.

Now who would not admire a flying machine capable of violating all the rules of flight in one short afternoon, and then ending the day, touching down with the light hearted grace of a homing butterfly? Taxiing up the hangar apron, it was a sore faced, but thankful pilot who stepped out of the aircraft.

Examination showed there was no damage to the Tiger, and to Ken, that was a welcome relief, because if it had been otherwise, than he would have had to submit a report (providing he was alive), explaining the details of the crash, and the resultant damage to one of His Majesty's aeroplanes.

F/LT GEORGE B. RICKART
WOP/AG – PILOT R.A.F.

George was born at Aberdeen, Scotland, attended public school there and went on to Aberdeen Grammar School. After graduation, he decided to enter the insurance world and became an Associate of the Chartered Insurance Institute of Great Britain.

During his sojourn in Aberdeen, he enjoyed playing rugby, field hockey, tennis and badminton.

In January 1940, he joined the R.A.F. at Cardington, Bedfordshire, where he stayed until the summer of that year, at which time he was posted to radio schools at Prestwick and Cranwell, thence from December 1940 to January 1941 to #10 Gunnery School, Dumfries and promoted to Sergeant. From March to April he was at #20 O.T.U. Lossiemouth and then on to #9 Bomber Squadron, Honington on Wellingtons, from May to July that same year. In the middle of July, he was posted to the Middle East, M.E.D. Harwell, then on July 28th to Abu Sueir, Egypt, via Gibraltar and Malta. It seems George was living up to the Air Force advertisement in pre-war, "Join the R.A.F. and see the world." Still on the move, in August he was posted to #38 Bomber Squadron Shalufa, Egypt, again on Wellington IC's, but before he could settle down almost, off he went again to Malta, the end of August. For a W/Op-Air Gunner he sure travelled!

Towards the end of October 1941, he returned once more to Shalufa. In January 1942, his flight was detached to experiment in dropping torpedoes from Wellingtons. This involved flying at night up-moon, sixty feet above water. In February 1942, he was posted back to U.K. His total number of op flights was 36. To reach U.K. he went by Pan-American Airways Africa, from Cairo to Lagos, Nigeria, thence by the Polish ship "Batory" (which became famous some time later, incidentally).

In May 1942, George was posted back to #20 O.T.U. Lossiemouth as Screen, on Anson Mk I's then on Wellington IC's, and in November he was promoted to Flight Sergeant. Another promotion, to Pilot Officer, took place in January 1943 and in May he was accepted for pilot training and posted to I.T.W. Torquay, England. Then in August 1943, he was posted to grading school at Shellingford and passed for further pilot training, then promoted to F/O.

He then served from November 1943 to January 1944 at #34 E.F.T.S. Assinaboia, Saskatchewan, flying Cornells. From March that year to October he was at #9 S.F.T.S. Centralia, Ontario and received his pilot's wings on October 26th 1944, flying Anson II's.

Further promotion came his way, as in January 1945 he became a Flight Lieutenant ... then the travelling began again ... February to #11 Pre A.F.U. School, Perth, Scotland, flying Tiger Moths ... March to #18 A.F.U. Snitterfield, flying Oxford II's, then April to #1536 B.A.T. Flight, Spitalgate on beam training, again in Oxford II's and then just for a change, in April to Snitterfield #18 A.F.U.

Then from May 1945 to July he was at #3 A.F.U. South Cerney on Oxfords and finally from July to November 1945 he was Staff Pilot at #4 Radio School Madley. George made his last flight on November 26th 1945.

George's medals were 1939/45 Star, Aircrew Europe Star, Africa Star, Defence Medal and War Medal. He was discharged December 1945 at Uxbridge England. He returned to the Insurance company and in 1951 emigrated to Canada and was involved in the insurance world, until he retired in 1985, although he is still involved in part-time work, on behalf of the Insurance Council of B.C. Married to Evelyn in 1943, they have one daughter and two grandchildren.

On December 13th, 1940, the aircraft in which he was WOP/AG, a Whitley, overshot the icy runway and broke up ... no one suffered a scratch!

Taking off from Harwell on the night of July 18th 1941, for Gibraltar, the aircraft struck the top of a tree, damaging the undercarriage and starboard propeller and after staggering around on one engine, made a belly landing. All the crew escaped through the astro-dome and despite a full overload of fuel tanks in the bomb bay, there was no fire or explosion.

On August 14th 1942, on a night cross-country in an Anson I from Lossiemouth, the port engine quit just west of the Hebrides. They turned back, gradually losing height and finally ditching in the Moray Firth. Fortunately, they were picked up by Air Sea Rescue and there were no injuries. Incidentally, the Anson floated for one and a half hours!

F/O ROBERT (BOB) ROBSON
R.C.A.F. BOMB AIMER

Bob Robson was born in Vancouver, B.C. and attended Sir William Van Horne Public School, and later the Fairview High School of Commerce. In his school days he was active in all sports. He was a sales clerk before joining the navy in 1941. Bob transferred to the R.C.A.F. in April 1942.

He graduated from A.O.S. at Winnipeg as a Bomb Aimer, and attended the pre-O.T.U., on the Isle of Man, U.K., training on Ansons. At Harwell O.T.U., Bob was crewed up flying Wellingtons. He completed a survival course at Driffield before being posted to a Conversion Unit on Halifaxes at Marston Moor. Bob graduated and was then posted to #78 Squadron at Breichton on Halifaxes, where he completed thirty-nine operations.

In May, 1944, Bob's crew was briefed for 'gardening' off the Scandinavian coast. On board were two large parachute mines. When reaching the drop zone, one was to be dropped, then after two minutes on course, the other was to be dropped. "N" for Nan reached the drop area and let the first mine go. It was 'corkscrew now' from the rear gunner, Bert Mockeridge. John Wheatley reacted immediately, but not before the aircraft was hit in the belly, by cannon shells from a FW 190. It came in for another attack, when the gunner yelled, "We got him! We got him!" The crew tried then to release the second mine without success, the rear hangar released but the forward one was locked and could not be freed. The mine was hanging half in and half out, consequently, the bomb doors could not be closed. Wheatley decided to turn for home, and eventually landed safely. The next morning they checked out "N" for Nan and were told she was headed for the bone yard. The cannon shell had severely damaged the main spar, and had they done much more evasive action, a wing would probably have been lost. They found also, that the remaining mine parachute was full of unburned tracer shells. The gunners were awarded a probable, but none had seen the FW 190 explode or crash.

In June 1944, the target was to be approximately forty miles south west of Berlin. Robson's crew were briefed to be in the area at twenty-one thousand feet and bomb in descent, releasing bombs at nineteen thousand feet. They encountered much flak on the way, but received no damage. The bombs were released and they turned for home, when suddenly they were 'coned' by search lights. It seemed unbelievable how bright the lights were, at that height and how vulnerable they felt. Skipper John Wheatley put all his skills into evasive action, but the search lights stayed with them. Finally, the skipper called on the intercom for all to prepare to bail out. The crew took the necessary action. Robson opened the escape hatch and was about to climb up to assist the skipper, when suddenly they were in total darkness. They were still apprehensive that a fighter had locked on to them, but nothing happened. The escape hatch was closed and they headed for home. They were now down to one thousand feet. During the de-briefing, Robson was talking to another bomb aimer who remarked that he had seen eleven aircraft coned, but only one got out. Robson put out his hand and said, "Shake hands with lucky eleven!"

Ten crews were selected to bomb targets in Northern France, in daylight, for three consecutive days. They were to fly in a loose type of formation, with the lead aircraft doing the main navigating and the others just keeping check.

Flying Officer Hoffman was chosen to lead. He had previously stated that if he ever had to bail out, he would delay opening his chute until the last minute. He was Jewish and wanted all the advantages on his side in order to escape. They crossed the French coast at Calais. The flak came up and Hoffman was hit by the first salvo. His aircraft fell back and went into a slow spiral. Only four parachutes were seen, but one object that could have been a person falling, fell into some clouds, before a parachute could be seen. Bob was never able to find out if Hoffman survived.

The next day, the remaining nine crews, plus one replacement, took off on the same route. Arriving at Calais the flak came up and again the lead aircraft was hit and went down.

On day three, Bob Robson's crew was selected to lead. As they approached Calais they were very "twitchy." However, the gun crew of the previous two days must have been awarded a forty-eight hour pass because of their successes. The flak came up but was not at all effective. The formation proceeded to the drop zone and all ten crews came home.

Bob Robson was discharged in Vancouver in April 1945 and was awarded the 1939/45 Star, the Aircrew Europe Star, the Defence Medal, the C.V.S.M. and the Victory Medal.

After the war, Bob went into sales and spent the last twenty-two years with Armco Canada Ltd.

Bob married Esther in June 1947 and they have two children, a son and a daughter, also one grandson.

F/SGT. HOWARD (SANDY) SANDERSON
AIR GUNNER R.C.A.F.

Sandy was born in Sault Ste. Marie, Ontario and grew up in that city, taking his public schooling at Northern Road, King George and Sault Ste. Marie Central and secondary school, at Soo Collegiate Institute. Afterwards, at Soo Technical School he took a course in the machine shop. He enjoyed cross country skiing and took a great interest in old cars; his first car was a 1923 Model T Ford, which cost him the huge sum of twentytwo dollars. His second car was a 1932 Model B Ford Roadster, a sporty looking automobile.

254

Prior to joining the Airforce, Sandy worked as a C.P. Telegraph Boy and as a C.P. Express Truck Driver. One day in September 1942 as an R.C.A.F. Mobile Recruiting Truck was driving down Queen Street in Sault Ste. Marie, Sandy followed it and joined up for Pilot duties, but at I.T.S. he found that he hated mathematics and remustered to Air Gunner. He trained at Belleville, Montreal, Quebec City and Mont Joli, Quebec.

In January, February and March 1944, Sandy was stationed at 1666 Conversion Unit, Wombleton, Yorkshire as spare Air Gunner. He was determined to do his tour as a "spare" in spite of numerous attempts to get him "Crewed up," as he somehow felt more in control of his own destiny, flying with a different crew on each Operation. Also, he could avoid a lot of boring lectures and other training drudgery, which other Aircrew types had to attend, as members of a crew.

The Air Force was never able to achieve any appreciable degree of success with Sandy in the area of Discipline and Dedication and as a result, on occasion, he would have discussions with his superior officers. During one of these discussions with a Squadron Leader who had two tours and many gongs, Sandy remarked that his priorities in the Air Force, were wine, women and song and winging his way over Germany by night in a dicey Hally II, was running a hell of a poor fourth in the list. The Squadron Leader suggested that he had plans to make Sandy a hero, which involved issuing him a khaki uniform and a rifle and let him be the first man into Europe on "D" Day.

One time, Sandy and two other like-minded Air Gunners, were on a routine sortie to the City of Leeds, Yorkshire, where their operational headquarters was the Robin Hood Pub. On this particular night, the three errant Air Gunners were rolling a fair sized barrel of beer down the street in the blackout; each one was armed with a pint mug. At each corner they would right the barrel, remove the bung, and fill the three mugs leaving considerable spillage at each location. A local constable of the Leeds City Police, following the wet trail left by the wayward airmen, swooped in from directly astern and scored three direct hits. Sandy explained that they were keeping a good lookout and searching for the rightful owner of the barrel. The Constable listened patiently, then he escorted the three airmen to the nearby Police Station, where he made out his report and took custody of the barrel. Luckily he was a gentleman and a kind and understanding man and he released the three, without charge and without the barrel of beer. During the interlude at the Police Station, Sandy, noticing the beautiful Leeds City Police Badge, on the constable's cap, managed to switch his brass R.C.A.F. cap badge for the P.C.'s chrome badge. (There was an interesting sequel to this incident over thirty years later.)

Being a spare Air Gunner, Sandy was able to get out of a lot of training, parades and inspections and a rear gunner from Ottawa, thought that this sounded good to him and he followed Sandy's routine for forty-eight hours, sleeping in, each morning, skipping training etc. The poor guy was quickly scooped up and spent two weeks in Sheffield, a stiff disciplinary course, for those who defied the regulations.

Soon after this, Sandy was posted to Skipton-on-Swale, 433 Squadron, where he did four trips with a crew, the Skipper of which was obviously destined for high rank and lots of gongs. On a trip over Europe, they were hit by flak and lost the starboard outer propeller; the pilot headed back to England and landed with four or five tons of bombs on board, having refused Sandy's suggestion that they jettison the load in the channel, reasoning that they might endanger shipping. Sandy knew instinctively at that moment, that he was flying with the wrong crew. Later he was posted to 425 Squadron (Alouette), at Tholthorpe and did thirty-two more trips, wearing the Leeds City Police Badge on each trip—a good luck badge, obviously!

On February 9th, 1945, while flying with F/O Mark and crew on his thirty-sixth trip, as spare air gunner in the mid under turret, they were hit by flak over Wanne-eickel, near Duisberg at 6:00 a.m. Sandy was about to take a header out the port side escape hatch, when suddenly, he remembered his R.C.A.F. cap, away up front in the rest position of Hally III K.W.Z. He made his way to the rest position and rescued his cap, with the Leeds City Police badge and started back to the rear escape hatch. While he was squeezing past the mid upper turret, the aircraft suddenly turned over to starboard, with flames streaming from the starboard wing and engines. Sandy looked up forward and realized that he was alone in the aircraft - solo - and he was never that keen on flying Hally's even with a full crew. He made his way back to the rear escape hatch and found that it was now on top of the kite instead of on the side and managed to get half way out when he became caught on something. He thought to himself that this was not a lot of fun - a guy could get hurt in this business. He has no recollection of how he freed himself from the side of the aircraft, maybe he pulled the ripcord on his parachute. He landed in a farmer's field near Zillebeke, Belgium and began hitch-hiking to Lille, France in his electric slippers, having lost his flying boots. A British Army Captain pulled over from his convoy, to the bleeding shoeless Canadian and generously handed over a wad of occupation money and Sandy headed west for Lille. Due to circumstances beyond his control, he was taken prisoner by two French girls and held captive in the Hotel Royale in Lille, for ten days. F/O Mark and the rear gunner A.A. Alger tracked him down and persuaded him to say "adieu" to Lille and return to England by Dakota. (It is understood that he never forgave them for the interruption).

In April 1945, while Sandy was awaiting repatriation to Canada at the Warrington Repat. Centre, he visited a pub one evening and his R.C.A.F. cap with his beloved Leeds City Police Badge went missing - it was believed that a lady of the evening made off with it. Sandy earned the 1939/45 Star, Aircrew Europe Star, C.V.S.M. and Clasp, Defence Medal and the War Medal.

After he was discharged, Sandy went back to the C.P.R. as a Fireman and later joined the Brandon Police Department. In 1949 he moved to Vancouver and in 1950 joined the Vancouver Police Department. The Police Department issues a publication called "The Thin Blue Line" which covers Police matters and Sandy had written the story of the badge incident in Leeds. One day in July 1976, Inspector Bob Rankin of the Leeds City Police, arrived at the Vancouver Police Station and asked to see Staff/Sgt Sandy Sanderson. When he walked into Sandy's office and announced who he was, Sandy said "Statute of Limitations, you can't touch me now." A copy of the publication had reached the Leeds Police office and Inspector Rankin had read the article that Sandy had written and the object of his visit was to bring a badge, identical to the one which Sandy wore, on thirty six operational sorties in 1944 and 1945 and which he had lost at Warrington. He still cherishes this memento of his service days in the R.C.A.F.

Sandy retired from the Police Force in 1979 and still maintains his interest in old cars. He is presently restoring his twelfth vintage car, a 1927 McLaughlin Buick and also a 1915 Model T Ford. Sandy has two sisters and three brothers plus Walter "Irish" McCreight whom his parents took into their family, when he was orphaned. Walter joined the R.C.A.F. and served in 6 Group as an aircraft mechanic. One of his brothers, Ross, served as a Hurricane pilot in North Africa and while stationed at Dartmouth, Nova Scotia, was rescued, when forced to bail out of his disabled Hurricane over the Atlantic. Sandy and his wife, have one son, who followed his father into the Vancouver City Police Force. When asked, how such a free spirit as he was, came to join a Police Force, Sandy replied "If you can't beat 'em, join 'em."

REPUBLIC THUNDERBOLT Mk II KJ154 R.A.F.
#73 O.T.U. FAYID, EGYPT CIRCA 1945

F/LT JACK SCRIVENER
NAVIGATOR R.C.A.F.

Born in Victoria on August 31st, 1922, Jack Scrivener attended the Elementary and Secondary Schools there. He graduated from Magee High School in 1940. Jack completed two full years towards a teacher's degree, prior to his enlistment in the R.C.A.F. in December, 1941. Before joining the Airforce, Jack was an outdoorsman and backpacker, being an active member of the North Shore Hikers. He was very active in youth work - in particular Boy Scouts.

After #1 Manning Depot at Edmonton, Jack went to I.T.S. at Saskatoon, in 1942, and then completed courses in Bombing and Gunnery at Defoe, Saskatchewan. He had further training at #3 A.O.S. at Regina, before graduating as a navigator at Jarvis, Ontario. Posted overseas, he arrived at #20 A.F.U. Millom, Cumberland on the 27th of April, 1943, and then trained at #28 O.T.U. at Wymeswold, completing his training in August of that year. Jack was next posted to #1656 C.U. Lindholme and finally became attached to #156 Pathfinder Squadron on the 22nd of October, 1943.

On the night of March 31st, 1944, R.A.F. Bomber Command suffered its greatest losses of World War II, when 95 aircraft were destroyed over enemy territory, with 545 dead, and a further 152 who became prisoners-of-war, some of whom were badly injured. Jack as a navigator, was flying aboard "Z" Zebra that night.

At 0050, the aircraft was attacked by a German Fighter - went out of control - into a spiral dive, then blew up. From the blazing starboard inner engine the fire quickly spread further back. Philip Goodwin, the pilot, gave the order to his crew to prepare to abandon the aircraft. A call came over the intercom from the mid upper gunner, J.C. Baxter, for the Wireless Operator, H.C. Frost to go back through the hatch door, only to be met by a wall of flames. He closed the door but the call for help was heard again. This time his plea was answered. Frost went through the door and disappeared into the blazing inferno. Meanwhile, Jack had reached for his parachute chest pack and clipped the first lug to his harness. He was sitting next to the first navigator, Eric Sommers, beside his H2S (blind bombing set), when suddenly the lights went out and the aircraft began to spiral and appeared completely out of control. In total darkness, Jack felt himself pressing against the ceiling of the aircraft. Time seemed to have run out, with few options left. In a blinding, searing flash, he was surrounded by a white light. He had the wonderful feeling of floating through space, and being free at last, when suddenly he became aware that he was not floating through space but falling towards ground. Then it came to him - he was still alive! There was another option, the parachute! He grasped for the ring that would open the pack, and found to his dismay and horror, that it was not there. The parachute was clipped to only one harness lug. He found the ring on the pack, level with his head. A desperate tug, a slight jerk, then a welcoming canopy burst forth in the night sky above.

A new realization gripped him; he had been falling through space from the moment the aircraft had blown up. The brilliant light had been the igniting of visual marker flares. He had fallen 10,000 feet, before his head had cleared from the explosion and the disintegration of the bomber.

Jack suddenly had a momentary vision of another parachute canopy not far away. This later turned out to be the pilot, who had also survived the explosion and the long fall.

As Jack glanced down at the ground some 5,000 feet below, a new fear gripped him. A half moon on a landscape covered with snow, revealed a heavily wooded pine forest. Below were the hills of Thuringia, some seventy miles north of Nuremberg - his target for that night. The deep snow would provide a cushion, but not the brittle branches of the pine trees that appeared everywhere below.

Then it happened! He had dropped into a small clearing, rolled over and came to rest. His life had been snatched from an airborne blazing inferno.

Jack's first thoughts after the long fall through space, were focussed on injuries. The threads in the seam of his battle dress jacket in the left armpit, had pulled away. There was a scratch on the palm of his left hand, but it was not bleeding. That was it! A few threads pulled loose and a scratch on one hand. These reflections were interrupted by a clear whistle, that came from the blackness of the woods beyond. A trap or a survivor? Another whistle, and Jack responded. It was the pilot, also uninjured!

His thoughts now turned to escape. He had landed in east-central Germany, some fifty miles from the Czech border - no help there, but 200 miles from Lake Constance and Switzerland beyond. That should be their goal! They would travel by night, hiding in barns and little wooded areas, as they approached the rolling countryside of Bavaria. They would use their small escape kit with the map, compass and Horlicks food tablets, to get underway.

In five hours, the darkness would melt into daylight.

The two of them had travelled only a short distance, when the sound of an approaching truck sounded an alarm. There must have been a forestry road nearby, as a vehicle was heading right in their direction. The rough road provided cover, as they hunkered down. The truck stopped. In the darkness it was difficult to say how far away it was. Voices were heard. Geraus! Geraus! Then shots crackled in four different directions. Then a dog barked. An ominous sound! But luck held. The searchers returned to their vehicle and sped off. Darkness was still with them, but time was clearly running out!

Jack's attention was soon directed to a fire, blazing in the woods beyond, to the remains of the aircraft, and to the exploding magazine rack, that fed 303 shells into the mid-upper and rear turrets. Could there be someone else still alive, thrown clear of the bomber? Jack wondered if someone might be seriously injured, and that it might be better to spend a few minutes searching around the aircraft for possible survivors, even if it meant imminent capture.

The searching was soon rewarded. In the darkness they could make out the webbing of a parachute harness draped over a bush, but had insufficient light to read the name of its owner scratched on the shoulder band. Still, someone else was also alive! So far, apparently, three of them had survived the fall. Prudence suggested that they approach no closer to the burning wreckage. Live ammunition was popping off in all directions, ignited by the burning tailplane.

Having made a search, and with darkness fading into pre-dawn, they knew they must leave the area, or their capture would be inevitable. Little did they realize, in the pre-dawn hours, a wide cordon had been thrown around the wreckage of their aircraft. At first light the noose was tightened. The end came, as they plodded through the snow on a little footpath. There, coming towards them was a small party of the German Home Guard. The leader seemed bewildered on first seeing them. Then he remembered he was carrying a rifle. Jack and the pilot advanced cautiously, hands raised. The babble of voices erupted, then a sign that they should start walking along the footpath. The path soon widened into a road - as they approached a little village - Eisfeld - with its quaint cobblestone street.

The two of them were led into the village police station. Just inside, Ted Isted, the Bombaimer stood with what appeared to be a nasty gash on his left forehead. He had not been quite as lucky in the quick descent to earth. They became aware of another "prisoner." It was Eric Summers, their first Navigator. Four of them survived! Still, four others had not been so fortunate. Their two gunners, J.C. Baxter and V. Gardner had never escaped from their turrets. H.C. Frost, the wireless operator had clearly sacrificed himself, in his attempt to rescue another, before the plane blew up. It appeared that W. Rose, the Flight Engineer, never had time to snap on his parachute.

For the four survivors, a long thirteen months of captivity was about to begin. The long night of death and destruction was at an end. They became prisoners of war in Stalag 1 until June 1945.

260

Jack Scrivener was re-united with his family in Vancouver, on June 14th, 1945. He was discharged from the R.C.A.F. at Jericho Beach in Vancouver in July, 1945. He received the following medals: the 1939/45 Star, Aircrew Europe Star, the C.V.S.M., the Defence Medal and the War Medal.

Jack married Hazel Margaret Troup in Vancouver, B.C. on October 18th, 1945 and now resides in North Vancouver, B.C. He has three children.

He has been active with the Boy Scouts of Canada movement for 52 years, from the day in 1935 when he first became a Scout. Until he enlisted in the R.C.A.F. he served as an Assistant Scoutmaster. On his return from WW II he became a Scoutmaster in Victoria. He then joined Scouting's professional staff and became Field Commissioner for the Okanagan Valley/Kootenay region. He later became Assistant Executive Provincial Commissioner. From 1962 to 1974 he was District Commissioner in Victoria. In March 1986, Jack became Chief Warden of B.C. with the BCFA.

F/O J. DAVID SMITH D.F.C.
OBSERVER R.A.F.

J.D.(Chunky) Smith was born in Southampton, England. He attended public school in Coburg, Ontario and Coburg Collegiate. When he was fifteen years old, his family returned to England, where he spent one year at Tunbridge Wells, Kent and then became an apprentice at Brighton Technical.

He enjoyed his youth in Canada, enjoyed the farm life where they had rifles, became good shots and he was able to use his creative ability. He once built a boat with a Model A Ford engine; that sank! Another time, with some friends, he built a kite plane and one of them jumped over a cliff to try it. It didn't work either. Later,in the R.A.F. he realized the kite's demise was a combination bunt and stall. Back in England in 1940 and seventeen years old, he tried to get a short Service Commission in the R.A.F., became a mobile homeguard, but never did know what he was guarding. He joined the R.A.F. for aircrew training at Lords Cricket Ground in May 1941.

David took his grading course at Carlisle and his flying training in the United States and Canada. At primary school in Tuscaloosa, Alabama, he drew a civilian flying instructor with a wicked sense of humour, training in a PT-17 Stearman. The instructor's delight, was to lull a student to sleep with   THRO-T-T-TLE! NE-E-DLE! A-A-A-L-TITUDE!!! then jar him awake with a snap roll on the downwind leg. He was surprised one day, when he heard a yell and felt a thump, to see in the mirror, his student facing backwards, with hands and feet each side of the vertical stabilizer. He had forgotten to buckle his seatbelt. When the same instructor did it to David in March, 1942 he was all buckled up.

From primary, it was on to basic training at Montgomery Field on Vultee BT-13's and advanced training at Selma, Alabama on Harvards. After 186 pilot hours, David was posted to Observers School at Ancienne Lorette, Quebec. In May 1943, on a navigation exercise to St. John, Quebec, the pilot and David flew at low level up the partly frozen St. Lawrence river. In the middle of the river, David saw a slowly moving periscope sticking two feet out of the water. It was facing away. He reported to the pilot who told him he was dreaming and would not go back for photos. Instead they flew on, under the Charney bridge near Quebec City and kept quiet about their low level exercise. After the war it was found out that German U-boats often made a practice of visiting the St. Lawrence!!

He swung compasses and checked astro-compasses for a month after graduating - they were all wrong. Then took a moving target course at Jarvis, Ontario, before being posted to Harrogate, Yorkshire. A ship recognition course at Jurby, Isle of Man,was put to good use at Scapa Flow, flying in Ansons below the balloons. At Waterbeach, "Chunky" joined 514 Squadron, flying in Lancasters for one tour, 23 trips in 1944. They were warboys for the Night Training Unit for the Pathfinders Flying Force. He volunteered for an additional tour and made a further 23 trips in Lanc's, No 7 Squadron from Oakington.

In the afternoon of April 1945, they were doing a wanganoi marking of Bremen and were about five minutes ahead of mainforce. Altostratus clouds 300 feet below, obscured the North Sea, and, as far as they could see, the whole of Europe. At H minus 10 minutes the sky cleared, as if by magic and fifteen of their pathfinders were alone over a clear and open city. No AA guns fired, and no German fighters were in the air - Germany was shattered and vulnerable. The Master Bomber told them to bomb as they wished. No one did. For each of them, the war was over and they were sick of the killing.

David Smith made 46 trips over Germany. From the Lancasters they flew, they dropped 550,000 pounds of bombs. In reviewing his experiences, he feels the private thoughts of those that flew and gave up their youth, can be summed up by a statement from an unknown tank commander in the western desert, and who, like aircrew, existed in a roaring hell of tortured machinery, doing what the country had trained and expected them to do.

"Only in the secret minds of each of us who had fought, was there a full comprehension of the nature of our own private and combined victories, and each of us was proud, with a quiet pride which rejected praise or sympathy, secure in the knowledge of our achievement."

Dave was awarded the D.F.C. after Dresden, P.F.F. Badge, Aircrew Europe, War Medal, 1939/45 Star and Defence Medal. After Armistice he remustered to Motor Transport, went to Singapore and was in charge of a repair unit with R.A.F. and Malay staff, until his discharge in May 1947 at Blackpool.

In the same year he returned to Canada, did oil survey work in Alberta and in 1948 joined a Consulting firm in Vancouver that specialized in building mechanical services. In 1950 he started a partnership, doing the same work that was incorporated into a limited company in 1967, and David "Chunky" Smith is still hard at work.

He lives in West Vancouver with his wife Robin from Ocean Falls, whom he married in 1951. They have two sons and three grandchildren.

F/LT W.L. (BILL) MARR A.F.C.
PILOT R.C.A.F.

Bill was born in Bramshott, England, on July 5, 1917, albeit his parentage is vintage Canadian. His father grew up in New Brunswick, became a medical doctor and settled down in Fort Langley, B.C. His mother was born in Fort Langley, her parents being among the early settlers of the area. Dr Marr went overseas in World War 1 as a Company Commander, in the First Regiment of the B.C. Horse, a unit which he helped to organize. When it was discovered that he was a medical man, he was re-assigned to the base hospital at Bramshott. Bill's mother followed her husband overseas as a Red Cross Nurse. Two Marrs went to war - three Marrs came back.

Bill grew up in Fort Langley and took his public schooling there and went to high school in Langley Prairie. It was assumed by everyone, including Bill, that he would become a doctor like his father, and he enrolled at the University of British Columbia in the pre-med course. He stayed at the University for three years, but his heart was not in it. He joined the Militia in 1934, the Westminster Regiment Army Auxiliary, which was natural, since his father was a staunch military man. While at U.B.C. he belonged to the C.O.T.C. In the years prior to the second world war, the R.A.F. was recruiting potential pilots, from all over the Commonwealth. Bill volunteered and was about to leave for overseas in 1937, when his mother passed away and he had to remain at home. Again in 1939 Bill was all set to leave for overseas but this time his father died and Bill had to stay at home until the estate was settled.

On September 3rd, 1939, the day Britain declared war, private W.L. Marr was called up for active service with the Westminster Regiment and spent that night in the Drill Hall. In the succeeding months, he made applications to join the Air Force. He had become interested in flying, through a friend and neighbour, Ed Twiss, who was an early T.C.A. pilot, occasionally landing an aeroplane in one of the fields in Langley. Bill was not accepted by the Airforce at first, because he did not have a University Degree, but in 1940 the rules were changed and he became eligible and received a wire telling him to report for duty with the Airforce. By this time he was a corporal stationed at Camp Dundern, Saskatchewan and was about to go overseas with the Army. He says that he contemplated desertion from the Army, but first went to see the second-in- command of his unit, a man who had been a friend of his father. This officer arranged for Bill to be detached from the Unit and sent back to Regimental Headquarters, with a letter authorizing his discharge; the red tape had been cut! Bill was discharged from the Army on June 6th, 1940, and that same night, he was on the train to Manning Pool in Toronto.

One day, while he was at Manning Pool, there was a notice on the bulletin board inviting airmen to a picnic across Lake Ontario at Niagara-on-the-Lake, including a visit to the Niagara Falls. Bill thought it would be a good outing and decided to go. As the airmen boarded the boat that was to take them across the lake, they had to pass by some girls, all with picnic baskets, who were also on a day's outing. As they passed the girls, one of them stuck her foot out and tripped Bill. That was how he met Etta, a delightful Saskatchewan Irish girl, who was working in a Government office in Toronto. They had such a grand time on the peninsula that day, that they missed the boat home and finally arrived home on the midnight boat. Bill spent his last nickel on taxi fare to get Etta home. Etta still looks after him!

From Manning Pool, Bill went to Initial Training School at the Eglinton Hunt Club in Toronto and was posted back to Vancouver for his Elementary Flying School training and from there to Saskatoon, where he did his Service School training on Harvards. Sergeant Pilot Marr, with his new wings, was posted to Moncton on his way overseas, but his orders were changed and he reported to Central Flying School at Trenton, for instructor training. His instructor was John Fauquier, who later became famous in earning a D.F.C. and D.S.O. as Commanding Officer on Bomber and Pathfinder Squadrons.

After completing his instructors' course, Bill was sent back to Moncton, where he instructed on Ansons and since it seemed that he would be there indefinitely, he and Etta were married. Shortly thereafter, Bill was given a check ride by a visiting flight and as a result, he was posted back to Trenton as a Staff Instructor. He did well there, putting in 100 to 120 hours a month flying time, on a variety of aircraft. He received his commission which was backdated, so that his initial rank was Flying Officer.

In the fall of 1942 he had accumulated about 1800 hours flying time and he finally got a posting overseas. He went through Bournemouth and then to an Advanced Flying Unit on Oxfords, to get used to the different terrain of the English countryside. From A.F.U. he did his O.T.U. flying on the Merlin powered Beaufighter Mark 1, crewed up with a navigator and they were posted to 409 Night Fighter Squadron, an R.C.A.F. unit just north of Newcastle. Bill was with 409 Squadron for 18 months, the first nine of which, he was on Mark IV Beaufighters and then they were advised that they were to be converted to Mosquitos. Bill was sent to 410 Squadron at Drem, where he checked out on Mossies and afterwards was sent to the Rolls Royce factory at Derby, where he took a two week course on the Merlin engine. He was put in charge of the conversion, setting up the ground school etc. This took about a week, but only because they were held up waiting for delivery of the new aircraft. One day, three Mossies flew across the field, low and fast in a good beat up; they landed and taxied in; out climbed three girls! The pilots on the squadron figured that if the girls could fly Mossies,so could they. The Squadron became operational on May 24th 1944, just in time for D Day. For his work on the conversion, Bill was awarded the Air Force Cross.

He was in action with the Squadron on two nights before D Day, on D Day and the night after, four nights in a row, during which time they worked over the beachhead. The Squadron was one of the early units to be based in France. Their first airport was Carbiquet, the civil airport for Caen, and they were progressively moved forward, with the advances made by the armies. They were at St. Andre during the battle of the Falaise Gap, than at Amiens and finally at Le Culot in Belgium. They were also involved in the Arnheim do, (The Bridge Too Far) when Bill spent a very frustrating night, trying to defend the Nijmegan Bridge from the Stuka dive bombers. The Stukas were slower but more manoeuvrable than the Mossies and this made them difficult targets. The only thing the Mossie pilot could do was to follow them back to base and try to attack them after they had landed.

Night fighter work had much hit-and-miss and there were a lot of SNAFU'S as there were in most operational flying. Bill recalls an occasion when he was on a low level sweep to sea in a Beaufighter, when they had an apparent engine failure. They finally became aware that one propellor had fallen off and after a rather harrowing flight back to base, (the Beaufighter was not noted for single engine performance), they found that the entire front section of the engine had torn off.

On another occasion, flying a Mosquito, he was vectored in on a target south of Le Havre. They got the target on the radar and made a very good approach to it, eventually getting a visual sighting while in cloud, with visibility of about 100 feet. This was a sure kill, but when they tried to fire the cannon, (Mosquitos had only one cannon for armament), nothing happened. Bill reached down to check the cannon master switch and his mask caught on the gun sight and in the confusion they nearly rammed the tail of the target aircraft. They were saved from collision, then they hit the slipstream from the target aircraft and tumbled out of the way. Bill got on the radio and asked if another fighter could be vectored in on the target. One was and it made radar contact. Bill said "Over to you" and climbed out on top of the cloud. Then he turned for home and in doing so, saw the other Mosquito coming up after him. "Not me" said Bill, turning on his landing lights. The other pilot said "Sorry old boy", but the target was lost forever.

Such things happened frequently. The gun ports in the Mosquito were covered with fabric, to improve the airflow. All of the shells in the cannon were explosive with the exception of the first two rounds, which were standard ball. The first two (Non explosive) rounds were used for the purpose of blowing the gun covers off. Thus the gun could be cocked twice, before an explosive charge would fire. Bill recalls the time when he fired the cannon and the nose of the Mossie blew off - someone had cocked the gun twice when they were arming the aircraft. Bill and the crew arrived back at base safely but he says the aircraft did not fly very well!

Bill finished his tour in November, 1944, having completed 312 hours on Beaufighters and 203 on Mosquitos, a total of 515 operational hours. He does not claim any kills, but he hit three buzz bombs, destroying two of them. After completing his tour, he was sent back to England to an Operational Training Unit at Cranfield. By this time, he had been overseas for three years and wanted to go back home and if possible join T.C.A. as a Civilian Pilot. While he was on the squadron two T.C.A. Captains on the C.G.T.A.S. knew one of the pilots on the squadron and they liked to pay a visit on their stopovers at Prestwick. Bill had got to know them and asked about joining the Airline after the war, so they took Bill's application back to Canada with them.

He was able to arrange a leave home and returned to Canada on the "Ile de France", leaving Britain on V.E.Day. Etta met him in Winnipeg and he had an interview with the airline and was accepted. He was discharged from the Airforce on July 27th, 1945 with the rank of Flight Lieutenant, having earned the Airforce Cross, 1939/45 Star, Aircrew Europe Star, Defence Medal, War Medal and the C.V.S.M. He had accumulated a total of 2,264 hours of Service Flying.

He started training with T.C.A. in September, 1945 and when the training was completed, he went "on line", first flying out of Winnipeg, then moving to his base at Vancouver. Bill was a First Officer on the Mountain run from Vancouver to Lethbridge until 1947 and when the company started the Coast run to Seattle and Victoria, he was made Captain and flew that run until 1951. The working conditions on that run were poor, not giving Bill the time he wanted to spend with his young family (he called it "a bathtub run", not really airline flying), so he asked to be transferred to Toronto. For the next four or five years he flew the route to Cleveland, London, Toronto and Kapuskasing, which was a good run for a family man. In 1969 he moved back to Vancouver and had become senior enough to get on the Boeing 747 and he was checked out on the "Big Bird" at Mirabel.

Bill and Etta have two children, Flynn and Ann and there are now eight grandchildren, six boys and two girls. It was partly the lure of the West Coast and partly the children, that motivated Bill and Etta to leave Toronto, for Bill could have come sooner if he had wanted to. He retired from the Airlines in July 1977 at the age of 60. He became active with the Abbotsford Air Show and became a Director and later President. As his duties wound down with the Airshow, he became a Director in Vancouver's Air Force Officer's Association, an organization that was started in the 1920's by veterans of WW I, and also served a term as President.

As a result of some good investments, Bill was able to clear the mortgage on his house, help his children get set up for life and buy himself a good Cessna 185 on floats, which he used partly for business, but mostly for fishing, until he was 70, when the insurance premiums became prohibitive. Today he is involved in a mining company and had an interest in two other non-mining companies. He had an active and successful retirement, that keeps him young in heart and active in body.

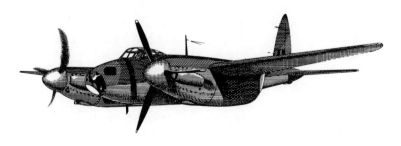

DeHAVILLAND MOSQUITO B.IV

F/LT EMIL THORSON D.F.C.
NAVIGATOR R.C.A.F.

Emil Thorson was born in Vancouver, of Icelandic parents, in 1921. Educated in Vancouver at Tecumseh Public and John Oliver High Schools, he was in his third year Engineering at U.B.C., when Pearl Harbour was attacked by the Japanese. He immediately enlisted in the R.C.A.F. at the old post office, corner of Granville and Hastings streets, Vancouver.

A free train ride, complete with free meal tickets, took him to the snow and sub-zero weather of Edmonton Manning Depot. Frost-bite to the ears and nose were standard fare for most of the aspiring young men. Some of the young American actors from the film "Captains of the Clouds" were awaiting posting to I.T.S. in January 1942. Emil was finally posted to #3 I.T.S. in Edmonton, the next stop being #3 A.O.S. Regina, where he graduated in one of the first straight navigator's courses, in September that year.

After a short tour as an instructor, at #9 A.O.S. St.Jean, Quebec, he was posted overseas in October 1943, but before embarking, managed to persuade his school sweetheart into coming down to Halifax, to be married.

Emil followed the usual route from Bournemouth to advanced navigation school at Staveton, then to #82 O.T.U. at Ossington, #1666 H.C.U. at Wombleton-in-the-Mud Escape School at Dalton. Emil's crew was an "odd man out" crew, as they were the only ones left in the Nissen hut, after everyone else had "made their pick." For a "pick up crew" they had a very successful tour with 408 Squadron at Linton-on-Ouse.

After crashing a Lancaster Mk II, the Skipper was sent to the "glasshouse" at Sheffield and during his absence, Emil flew with P/O Smith who had lost his navigator. One night Emil was replaced by another navigator who had just returned from hospital and wanted to catch up with his crew, so that they would be screened together. Arriving back at Linton-on-Ouse in a damaged condition, P/O Smith tried an overshoot on three engines, failed, and crashed into the M.T.

Section, killing three W.A.A.F. drivers and all crew members.

Emil's most exciting time was when King George VI, Queen Elizabeth and the two princesses, visited Linton-on-Ouse, on August 11th 1944, and it was a special day for both 408 squadron and 426, which shared the base. Emil was awarded the D.F.C. that day.

By mid-August, Emil had completed several ops, with P/O Smith's crew and felt quite at home with them. In the meantime his first skipper, F/O Kennedy had returned from Sheffield and Thorson rejoined his crew in a fresh Halifax Mk VII, with the call sign "Q-Queen." She was ready to do battle. During August she completed many successful ops, mainly tactical in support of the Allied invasion in Europe; targets such as supply depots, marshalling yards, oil refineries, ammunition dumps, dock yards and rocket launching sites, but it was on September 12th, 1944, that the "Queen" would show her true royal blood!!

It was a cold damp morning, so typical of Yorkshire in the Autumn; it had rained heavily during the night and everything was sloppy and muddy. Those crews on the Battle Order had their ops breakfast at 0930 hours and headed off for briefing. The target was to be the oil refinery at Wanne Eikel, situated in the eastern part of the Ruhr valley. The attacking force would run the gauntlet of "Happy Valley", hit the target, zip out over Holland and back across the North Sea to England. The thought of making this attack in daylight, without the support of fighters, was a bit unsettling, to say the least. There were other major attacks laid on, with both the R.A.F. and the Americans, which would dilute the effectiveness of the enemy fighters.

This was to be Emil's 16th operation and the 10th for the rest of the crew and there was a distinct feeling of apprehension for this one, as it was only one day after Thorson's surrogate crew had crashed, killing all members, as related previously. In addition, on the same day, one of the officers on the squadron, in a fit of depression, took his service revolver and blew his brains out. It was indeed a very sad day for the squadron.

Out at the disposal pad, the crew went through their usual checks, while the skipper fired up the big Merlins. As he moved Q-Queen out of the dispersal area, the port wheel suddenly dropped off the tarmac and was well and truly stuck in the rain soaked mud. They were scheduled to be No.3 off, at 14.12 hours, but the Queen, carrying 16 x 500 lb H.E.'s and a full fuel load, watched helplessly, as the rest of the squadron roared down the runway and disappeared into the Yorkshire mist. However, with the aid of a tractor lorry and with full power on the port engines, the ground crew finally eased the Queen back on the pavement and she quickly got into take off position and with less than two minutes to abort time, she was given the green light and with full throttle, the big Merlins roared, as only they could and the Queen quickly gained speed and raced down the runway, headed for the Ruhr.

She had just lifted off the deck and the call for "wheels up" was given, when the mid-upper gunner yelled "Fire in the port outer". The flames were streaking across the wing surface, with the white hot colour of a cutting torch. It looked as though the wing would burn through in a matter of seconds. While the skipper struggled to keep her airborne, the engineer selected the fire extinguisher for the port outer, but nothing happened! The Queen had struggled to 200 feet and was barely clearing the roof tops and trees. Suddenly, she staggered under a terrific explosion in the port outer and miraculously, the fire was blown out! The sturdy Queen was now about 600 feet, with wheels up and in reasonably stable flying condition. The best efforts of the pilot and engineer, were unable to feather the port outer propeller, however, which continued to windmill.

At 3,000 feet, the distraught pilot called the navigator for a course to base, but the navigator replied that he wouldn't do so until they got rid of their bomb load and used up most of their fuel. "Roger, navigator" called the skipper and he headed the aircraft towards the bomb disposal area, near the Wash, off the coast of Norfolk. Surging under the power of the three remaining engines, the Queen was performing admirably and maintaining a steady rate of climb. By the time she was over the disposal area she had reached 10,000 feet and was still climbing. The navigator told the pilot that if he could maintain the speed and rate of climb, he would work out a course to the target and then they could drop the bombs where they belonged! The whole crew endorsed this suggestion.

The main force was following the track laid on by Bomber Command, which zigged and zagged in an effort to confuse the enemy as to the real target. The trick for the lone Queen, was to try and arrive at the target, the same time as the rest of the force, and at the same height. Under the thrust of the remaining engines, which were synchronized into a strong, steady drone, the Queen was able to maintain the remarkable height of 16,000 feet and did in fact intercept the main force, slipping into the middle of the stream of Lancs and Halifax's. The flak was fierce over the target and the Queen shuddered under the jolt of shrapnel, ripping through her fuselage, but the bombs were dropped on the target, the bomb doors were closed and the Queen headed out the back end of the Ruhr Valley. As the flak eased up, the gunners kept a sharp look out for the M.E. 109's, but none appeared.

Unfortunately, however, the valiant Queen was unable to keep up with the main force, which was rapidly leaving her behind, so the pilot felt there was no use in following them. The navigator quickly calculated a new route, to the nearest 'drome in England, but he wondered how long the skipper could keep the Queen airborne. Although the new track passed perilously close to some heavily defended areas, they had no choice but to press on and just north of Rotterdam, all hell broke loose as the Queen was boxed in bursts of flak on all sides. The black smoke puffs whipped by the Queen and the skipper threw her into a violent corkscrew, as once again shrapnel ripped through the fuselage. During the next few minutes the Queen twisted and turned, finally freeing herself from the vicious grasp of the flak, but in doing so, she lost about 5,000 feet of precious altitude.

There were no injuries among the crew, but one wing tank was ripped open, so the engineer quickly swung the three good engines onto that tank, to salvage as much fuel as possible. Nearing the enemy coast, they kept a continuing lookout for enemy fighters, but luck was with them as none appeared; thankfully the Queen headed straight in to Methwold and with one attempt, the skipper skilfully set the broken and battered Queen down on the runway. The crew erupted into boisterous cheers through the intercom to the worn out pilot.

After debriefing and a hearty meal, the crew were bedded down and returned to the squadron the next day in a Stirling, since the valiant Queen had been mortally wounded. The ground crew at Linton were upset, as they felt if the Queen could have landed there, they would have put her into flying condition in no time. They never saw her again, but in due course were assigned a new Halifax Mk VII with the call sign Q-Queen and she served the crew as valiantly as her predecessor, and carried them safely through the rest of their tour.

Emil was awarded the 1939/45 Star, France and Germany Star, War Medal, Defence Medal and the C.V.S.M. in addition to the before mentioned D.F.C.

Emil was discharged on March 9th 1945, went to the University of B.C., completing his engineering degree in 1948. As a professional engineer he was associated with the construction business for thirty-eight years, retiring from his own company in 1986. Still happily married to Kathleen after 45 years, the Thorsons have six children and sixteen grandchildren.

FL/LT F.M."MO" BOTTING
PILOT R.C.A.F.

Frederick Morrison ("Mo") as he was known during the war, was born at Vernon, B.C. However the family moved to New Westminster and "Mo" attended Herbert Spencer and F.W.Howay public schools in that city. Later he attended John Robson Secondary and Duke of Connaught High Schools and took various communication courses afterwards.

He studied piano, enjoyed Fraser River Bar Fishing, swimming, skiing and mountain climbing in the Rockies and after his schooling he became a repeater attendant, swing wire chief with the C.P.R. Communication Department. In October 1941 he joined the R.C.A.F. in Vancouver and went on to No. 3 Manning Depot, Edmonton, No. 16 S.F.T.S. Hagersville, Ont, No.5 I.T.S. Bellville, Ont, No. 13 E.F.T.S. St. Eugene on Fleet Finch aircraft, thence to No. 2 S.F.T.S. Uplands, Ottawa on Harvards. After graduating from Uplands S.F.T.S. he was posted to Trenton as a Flying Training Instructor for S.F.T.S. Schools and it was then, that his fiancee Thelma and he decided to marry and she went back to Trenton with him. However, there were too many on the course and, upon drawing straws, "Mo" was selected (?) to go overseas after two weeks embarkation leave. They were married in December 1942 and have three children and, so far, two grandchildren.

Overseas at last, "Mo" went to No 3 P.R.C. Bournemouth, England, No 6 E.F.T.S. Sywell on Tiger Moths, No 17 A.F.U. at Watton on Miles Masters, then to No 559 Sqdn O.T.U. Millfield, to No 1 Satellite Kinnell, Scotland, to No 1 C.T.W. Tealing on Hurricanes, No 175 Sqdn. R.A.F. Westhampnett, Sussex on Typhoons, to No 175 Sqdn. Holmsley, South England and finally to La Presne, Camilly, France. "Mo" certainly got around, but his travels were halted when he was shot down by ground fire on July 18th, 1944. He was taken prisoner of war and settled at Stalag Luft 1, Barth, Germany until the end of the war. His medals include the 1939/45 Star, Aircrew Europe Star with France and Germany clasp, the Defence Medal, 1939/45 Volunteer Service with clasp and the War Medal.

He was honourably discharged in October 1945 at Vancouver with the rank of F/Lt. "Mo" returned to his previous job as swing wire chief C.P.R. Communications dept. at the main office on Hastings St, then after almost 21 years, resigned and took a position at Lenkurt Electric in April 1956, retiring September 1st, 1981.

The casualty rate of Squadron 175 R.A.F. by early 1944 was extremely high. 175 had a turn-over rate of almost two hundred per cent, not including the C.O. and the two Flight Commanders and of course a couple of lucky seasoned pilots. There were no shortages of green operational pilots, only the aircraft. As the C.O. was ordered to get his squadron up to minimum strength of eighteen planes and twenty one pilots, this was achieved in late March. Obviously it was a build up for the coming invasion. After several hours of local training flights, which concentrated on formation flying, the C.O. requested four new pilots, plus three seasoned pilots to report to intelligence for briefing. He had obtained permission from Group to undertake a "Rhubarb", with a total of eight aircraft, including the C.O. and three seasoned pilots.

"Mo" was one of these experienced pilots. The course was almost a direct line to the south of Paris, sweeping around and returning. This meant long range tanks, two five hundred pound anti personnel bombs, eight rockets and a full load of twenty mil cannon shells for the four cannons. The prime target flying time to a maximum, about two hours and a few minutes. The Squadron was told to refuel at Thorney Island or Tangmere on return and, except for crossing the French coast the entire sweep was to be at ground level. The C.O.'s theory was it would give the new pilots great experience in low level operational flying without the possibility of encountering high level combat with the enemy. On the way to dispersal, the three old timers expressed concern among themselves as it meant they had to protect the new pilots, as well as keep a sharp look out at low levels for targets, which is not easy matter when flying on the deck. Of course there was nothing they could do about it and as such, the "do" was on. It was the custom in the wing, to send a duty met. pilot all alone, to check the weather on the "pond" and the coast of France. He reported that morning, cloud base over the French coast at two thousand feet with intermittent layers up to ten thousand feet, but at times, heavy rain. The weather at this time of year on the south coast of England and the north coast of France leaves much to be desired. The C.O. decided of course, at briefing, to "have a go at it."

One word about formation flying; the C.O. or leader does the navigation. Everyone else flies in cloud, close to the section in front, in order to visibly see one of his section members. This is not an easy task for green pilots, who sometimes lose contact and are on their own, virtually lost, unless they break cloud quickly. They have no choice, but to descend, break cloud base and return home. The Squadron flew across the channel at zero feet, in so called battle formation, that being about two hundred yards apart line abreast. Visibility was good. Three miles from the French coast, the C.O. and squadron climbed in close formation to about eight thousand feet in order to cross the flak belt in relative safety, which extended inland about eight miles at this point. This was, of course, excellent formation operational flying in cloud for the new pilots. The C.O. then let down slowly through cloud, until he broke through the base at about three thousand feet. A miracle happened. All new pilots were with them.

However, what a shock! Almost immediately, the squadron was flying directly into a formation of eight 109's and four 190's, which also had let down through clouds on a reciprocal course. What a coincidence!!! The C.O. knew that the Jerrys would do an immediate 180 degree turn and as such he ordered on the R.T., "turn to port one hundred and eighty, drop tanks, salvo rockets, go on the deck and head for base." Unfortunately, the new pilots were extremely confused and as such were very slow in their turn to port. The C.O.'s red section did a 360 degree turn in order to cover the stragglers, also telling them to "go through the gate" and catch up. A fighter pilot never puts his throttle "through the gate" unless in an emergency. He does not want to wear his engine out. The C.O. knew the novice pilots were very confused and ordered everyone maximum speed on the deck.

In the meantime the Jerrys had made another 180 degree turn on the deck and were not far behind the stragglers. As tail end Charlie, "Mo" found out once and for all, even with rocket rails on, the Typhoon could outdistance the

190's; there was no problem with the 109's. They just could not keep up or get within firing range. Even though the sweep was aborted, the C.O. possibly saved the lives of four novice pilots and also their aircraft (in order to fight another day, when they had gained more experience.) In all "Mo's" operational flying experience, he never again encountered at one time, that number of German fighter aircraft. The novice pilots did not know what really happened, as they attempted to follow orders. But they were certainly enjoying a mild and bitters after their first operational flight, before dinner!!

The following narrative describes a typical Typhoon fighter equipped with rockets and bombs on a sortie over the coast of France. The narrative unfortunately describes the last flight of Jim Cowie, an American in the R.C.A.F. attached to 175 Squadron. His last flight was on May 30, 1944. "Mo" was part of that flight.

Contact time was 13:29 for three minutes to go. The C.O.'s section was already zigzagging to the take off point. Far across the 'drome could be heard the explosions, then the thunderous roar of number two section starting up simultaneously. Puffs of rich blue smoke flew past the start of each Typhoon. The ground crews, ever attentive, and two to a plane, were holding chock ropes and fire extinguishers, watching the pilots for the signal to pull the chocks away. Everything was going like clockwork as they started upon another mission.

At the briefing, intelligence reported haze over the target area and they should run into a few rain squalls going over. All clear! and with the resulting reply from Johnny, Mo pressed the contacts at exactly 13.29. Jim Cowie and Herb Geddes, Mo's number two and three in the section were right on the bit as he saw the blue smoke. A wave goodbye - and Johnny gave a thumbs up signal along with a wide smile. Yes, off again on another nerve wracking flight. No time to check on Jim's position but he was at the starboard wingtip watching every move.

Briefing instructions were, to keep as low as possible on the trip. At 320 miles per hour, the flight plan indicated twenty one minutes to cross the channel. "Mo" glanced at the inked course on the back of his right hand, noticed the W/C was on time for the start of the climb to a safe height, in order to cross the enemy coast with relative safety from the heavy flak. There was no horizon ahead of them. This made it difficult to keep a safe ten to twenty feet above the waves. The Wingco had his eyes glued to the instruments. They continued to search the skies for enemy aircraft, cursing that the dirt was not cleaned off the bubble hood, as each little piece of dirt against the sky looked like a plane. (Until one realizes that it is not moving, one is tempted to shout into the R/T "Bogies above at two o'clock".) However "Mo" restrained himself from doing so, until it was actually established the bogie was a piece of dirt. "Mo" gave a sigh of relief as they would have to dump their heavy load in order to give battle, if it had been a "bogie." The climb started; up went the Wingco on instruments, 500 feet per minute through layers of clouds. They were thin. "Mo" changed the pitch and increased the throttle setting and the

Tiffy responded strenuously. At 8,000 feet they were still in clouds, so they climbed to 12,000 feet, before breaking into brilliant sunshine, where they could now see the coast ahead. They made adjustments for level flight and almost immediately saw Jerry's heavy predicted flak ahead of them. They had their course and the flak was now bursting around them like black puff balls from out of nowhere, a few bursting near their section. "Mo" heard the loud crack and actually saw the puffs explode into a cluster of ever expanding mushrooms, until they went past his eyes. The plane jumped at each crack. They crossed the coast about ten miles west of Dieppe. Their target was on the northern outskirts of Neufchatel so they flew inland a few miles and the Wingco made a slow course change to due east until opposite Neufchatel. As the clouds were only on the channel, the visibility now was perfect. The Wingco dropped to 8,000 feet, "Mo" disengaged the supercharger and prepared for the attack. The Wingco's section on this trip was anti-flak and his section was to fire cannon shells into the target area in order that the flak boys would be forced to take cover and allow the balance of the squadron to concentrate on the target. At the last second he was going to release rockets in salvo and drop his bombs.

The Wingco peeled off to port and was going down fast with his numbers two and three right with him. Mo waited for the C.O. to follow, before winging over and following him down. He throttled back and down they went. Mo was standing on the rudders now, with Jim and Herb right by his side. The speed build-up was tremendous as they flew below the Wingco's section, in order not to encounter his spent shells. The speed was about 525 miles per hour and he was watching the red line on the clock. The Wingco was spraying the ground with anti-flak shells, but it did not seem to do much good as the tracers were coming straight towards them, slowly at first then shooting past at a very fast speed. Between every tracer, there were six or seven shells which they could not see. The Wingco let his bombs go, as well as the salvo of eight rockets which left blue smoke streaks. Next, the C.O.'s section did the same. Their speed by this time was about 550 mph as Mo swung in to the left a little, as he did not want to run into the debris from the Wingco's and C.O.'s attacks. They let everything go and pulled up to level flight at about 3,000 feet. There was, of course, the usual blackout, due to heavy G/S. Unfortunately they flew through the debris and smoke momentarily, but continued on, following the Wingco and the C.O. The Wingco hit the deck and headed at a very fast pace towards the coast and they reformed but Jim was no-where to be seen. Herb slipped into the number two position and signalled to Mo by passing his hand over and across his throat, indicating that Jim had had an accident.

About a quarter of the way across the channel the airspeed dropped to cruising, so they adjusted pitch, throttle and coolant flap controls to normal. Approaching the English coast Mo switched on the I.F.F. control and crossed the coast at 500 feet, setting course for home base, Holmsley South. The landing was uneventful. At debriefing, Herb reported that Jim's tail seemed to break off and he flew right into the deck. It was unlikely that he was hit by flak at the angle he was diving, so they assumed it was structural failure, due to the speed encountered in the dive. Jim was the only loss on this flight and intelligence stated that it appeared their op was very successful and they would not have to return. They went to the mess and had a silent drink to their lost comrade in arms.

F/O KENNETH ROSS SPRATT
PILOT R.C.A.F.

Kenneth Spratt was born at Brandon, Manitoba the 22nd October 1916. He attended King George public school and Earl Haig High School, both in Brandon.

To graduate in the dirty thirties, meant working whenever and wherever one could, at any job available, and Ken covered a lot of territory. Pitching sheaves at harvest; pumping gasoline; shovelling snow in the C.P.R.'s extra gang; cutting cord wood; selling for T. Eaton Co.; working as a mechanic's helper and finally as a bridgeman on the B.& B. gang of the C.P.R.

When in 1938, the R.C.A.F. began to expand and recruit, Ken was quick to apply. He took a trade test and was accepted as an Aero Engine Mechanic "C" group; his first steady job. His first posting was to #2 equipment depot in Winnipeg, where he graduated just as war was declared.

With the outbreak of hostilities came guard duty. The closest Ken got to an aircraft for some time, was to see Wapiti, Siskin and Hurricane fighters being shipped to the east coast, to bolster our maritime defenses.

Early in October, 1939, the Airforce gave him a change of scenery, posting him to Jericho Beach. There were few aircraft there, a motley collection of Blackburn Sharks, Vancouver Flying Boats, Stranraers and even two Vickers Videttes. Most of the mechanics again drew guard duty, but by this time, Ken was getting service wise and wangled a driving job in Motor Transport. No more sand bag details for him!!

A fleet of Hurricanes stored at Jericho, were brought out of mothballs, readied for flying and were on their way to be towed to Sea Island, when a change of orders called, to ship them by rail to Halifax, for trans-shipment overseas. It must have been a rush order, for in less than 24 hours, they were loaded aboard the train, despite the fact that some of the crates had yet to be bolted down. (The job was finished en route, the last of the work party being detrained at Coquitlam freight yard!)

From Jericho, K.R. was posted to the new station of Coal Harbour on Vancouver Island. The base had yet to be completed, but was being used as a refuelling stop, for Coastal Command aircraft. Shortly afterward, Corporal Kenneth Spratt was on his way to #3 S.F.T.S. in Calgary; now he was doing full time maintenance and swears, to this day, he can top overhaul a Cheeta IX blindfold.

December 1941, when the Japs attacked Pearl Harbour, found Sergeant K.R. on his way to Prince Rupert, to look after Blackburn Sharks. About this time there was a drive on, to get men to remuster to aircrew and as N.C.O. in charge of engine maintenance, it was Ken's job to rule on recommendations for transfer. He himself had been trying for some time to remuster to aircrew and told all and sundry, how unfair it was to keep him as essential. In fact, he was sounding off, when the orderly sergeant brought in a sheaf of re-muster forms for him to sign. He took scant regard to the names included and signed them all, still bitterly bemoaning his lot.

However, when two weeks later, the re-musters came back to the station, Spratt's name topped the list of those accepted for aircrew. The orderly Sergeant had pulled a fast one. What a send off the station gave six new airgunner hopefuls!!

At the end of I.T.S., the prairie airdromes were all flooded, so this group was sent as Wireless Operators to the Navigation School at Edmonton. There, they drove the Air Controllers to distraction, pulling many tricks to get priority landing at that busy airport. But soon it was flying for training; first at Virden, Man., for elementary, second to service school at Yorkton, Sask. On graduation, airman K.R. Spratt became P/O Spratt.

When word of postings leaked out, Ken found himself slated for Stanley, N.S., a place he did not really want to visit. Being wise in the ways of the service, he presented himself very early at the adjutant's office and somehow got signed orders to report to High River, Alta. With the precious paper in hand, he quickly vacated the station prior to 9 a.m. and could not be located to correct his destination, so staff conveniently changed his posting. It pays to get time in!

When things slacked off at High River, he was posted to Instructors' School at Pearce, Alta. and from there got an overseas posting. However, on arriving at Command in Winnipeg, after leave, he was informed that now, he was slated to return to Vulcan, Alta, to instruct. He and a buddy lucked in at this time, running into a Squadron Leader whom they knew, and had their postings changed to Brandon, K.R.'s home town.

When the last course went through Brandon, Ken was sent to Yorkton, where he remembers helping to wash out an entire course of English students. (They were not ready to go solo, after fifteen hours of instruction.)

It looked as if Ken would finally get overseas, for his next stop was back to Brandon for a survival and commando style course, to prepare for a journey to the Pacific. At Brandon, the army took their training seriously; they used live ammo "to pin people down" but Ken was not fated to see live Japanese bullets, for ceasefire in the Pacific brought the training to a halt.

Then it was back to Yorkton, where the Commanding Officer was doing a good job of collecting all the non-public equipment he could, to turn his station into the best equipped, for hobbies, crafts and sports for the personnel, who were returning p.o.w.'s, receiving check outs, to again become current with aviation.

Spratt, at this time, wore several hats; C.F.I., Fire Officer, S.F.O., and chief scrounger for the C.O.. All this activity came to an end, just prior to Xmas 1945, when the Officers Mess burned to the ground, with the sad loss of a huge stock of liquid spirits, which had been hoarded for a record Christmas bash.

Next posting was to Centralia for an administration school, then on to Penhold to instruct Polish Aircrew, who would be returning to face their continuing problems back home.

Of all his students, Ken remembers most vividly, a large man who had been a truck driver and carried over his habits to the aircraft, hitting the brakes or rudder pedals with all the force he could muster. To tone down his movements, Ken had him fly in bare feet, but this proved rather hard on his shins, as, to unlock the flap handle on the Cornell, one usually hit the lever with one's heel.

On a simulated engine failure, right after take off, the student reached down to unlatch the flap lever with his hand, rather than his bruised heel. He pushed the stick full forward, so he could see, and the aircraft nosed towards earth. Ken took over and attempted to pull the stick back, but the student resisted, only force engendered by sheer terror overcame the resistance of the student's hand. The aircraft hit the ground just as the nose came up and bounced into the air, wings dropping. A straight ahead landing was impossible because of the terrain. Spratt had to do an extremely careful, slow circuit, bringing the craft down for his most gentle landing, where the wings drooped to earth; the main spar was cracked diagonally right across its full width.

The student was gouged by the stick from his eye to his ear, but survived, to become a Lancaster pilot.

Ken decided that he had had enough of the service, but since he was permanent force, he had to buy his way out, forfeiting all his pension money. He retired with the rank of F/O in January 1946.

In civvy street, Ken first went back to the C.P.R., but shortly, went out on his own, buying a service station. Later he worked for Bristol Aeroengine, Vista Lite, Eher Gearmatic Co from which he retired in 1981.

Ken has been very active in community volunteer work, a good deal of his energies going to help the Lower Fraser Valley Cerebral Palsey centre. He had twice been named volunteer of the year.

Doris and he were married in October, 1942 and have a family of three girls and a boy. On Legion parades he wears his C.V.S. medal and the Victory medal.

F/LT WILLIAM DOUGHTY
PILOT R.A.F.

Bill was born in Carlisle and received his elementary and high school education in that northern England city.

At the age of 18 he volunteered for aircrew in the R.A.F. and went to Scarborough for I.T.W. Later he solo'd in a Tiger Moth at Sywell, Northampton. His Elementary Training was at Bowden, Alberta in 1942, with Service Flying Training at Estevan, Saskatchewan, later that year. In 1943 he was posted to Flying Instructor's School in Vulcan, Alberta and he was also an instructor at Carberry, Manitoba and Debert, Nova Scotia.

After his training at O.T.U. Boundary Bay, B.C. he was posted overseas, where he flew Liberators on 159, 160 and 356 squadrons, based in Bengal, India, the Cocos-Keeling Islands in the Indian Ocean and Kankesanturai on the northern part of Ceylon, now Sri Lanka. His operations were over Burma, Siam, Sumatra and Malaya.

In his Airforce career he flew many types of aircraft including the Tiger Moth, Stearman, Anson, Cornell, Crane, Oxford, Bolingbroke, Harvard, Hurricane, Hudson, Mosquito, Mitchell and Liberator.

His most persistent memory is the dichotomy of emotion between controlled fear en route to the target, and supreme euphoria on the homeward track, while his most harrowing experience, was on V.E. Day plus one, when the aircraft suffered multiple strikes from anti-aircraft fire over Port Blair, Adaman Islands. This resulted in the aircraft being written off completely, on return to base.

Bill's most satisfying experience was on V.J.Day, flying as slowly and as low as possible over Changi, Prisoner of War camp, Singapore and seeing the exultation of the just liberated prisoners of war, as they waved at their aircraft.

Bill was discharged in London in 1947, after taking an extra year in the Royal Air Force. He then attended the University of Manitoba, where he obtained a medical degree and has had a general practice, with emphasis on aviation medicine on the West Coast.

His medals include the 1939/45 Star, War Medal, Defence Medal and the Burma Star.

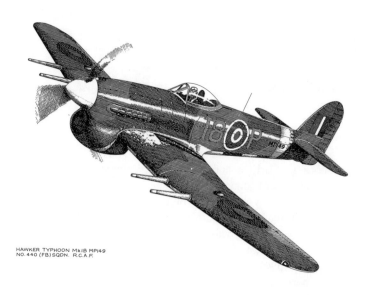

HAWKER TYPHOON MkIB MPI49
NO. 440 (FB) SQDN. R.C.A.F.

F/LT ROBERT L. TODD
PILOT R.C.A.F.

Robert was born in Hamilton but grew up in Brantford, Ontario. He attended Central Public School and then Brantford Collegiate.

Robert's military career commenced in the summer of 1936 when his uncle arranged for his enlistment, as a boy soldier, in the Royal Canadian Horse Artillery. Being short of signallers in that section, as they prepared to leave for summer camp at Petawawa, Ontario, the 54th Battery of 4.5 Howitzers took along two young teenagers, to fill out their ranks to Militia standards. Upon returning and starting High School, he joined the Cadet Corps and the following year, he earned his gun layer's badge and later still, was promoted to the rank of Lance-Bombardier. High School cadets were always in demand by the local regiments, for summer camp replacements and hence, Robert did a stint in the cavalry, with the Tenth Brant Dragoons and also with the Dufferin and Haldimand Rifles. With the advent of war, in September 1939, he tried to enlist for overseas service, when his battery mustered to wartime strength, but alas, one had to be nineteen years of age to be shipped overseas. Robert was granted an immediate discharge and the 54th Battery left with the First Division, without him.

After his battery left, Robert joined the Dufferin and Haldimand Rifles of Canada, thinking that they would eventually be sent overseas, but after one year of military service parades and field training, he became restless and applied to enlist in the Royal Canadian Navy. While waiting to be called up by the Navy, Robert joined a school chum, who was going to Hamilton, Ontario, to join the R.C.A.F. and they applied to become air gunners. In the fall of 1941, the Air Force called him for another interview and asked if he would consider being a Pilot, or Navigator. Robert jumped at the chance and then went to Wentworth Teachers College and finished his Senior Matriculation. In the spring of 1942 he became L.A.C. Todd R.L. 152449. He escaped the normal guard duty stint, by volunteering for high altitude tests in the pressure chamber, at #1 I.T.S.

Eglinton Hunt Club in Toronto. Then on to #12 E.F.T.S. at Goderich, where he learned to fly the Tiger Moth and he obtained his Pilot's Wings at #16 S.F.T.S. Hagersville.

Along with eighteen thousand other Canadian and United States servicemen, Robert sailed for overseas on the "Queen Elizabeth" and arrived in Bournemouth, just in time to become involved in a raid by twenty-two F.W. 190's which dropped some five hundred pounders and strafed the garden park, in the town centre. Several airmen were killed and many, including Todd were wounded. After he recovered, Robert was posted to #15 A.F.U. at Ramsbury, #1 Blind Approach Flying School at Watchfield, #15 O.T.U. at Chipping Warden, on Wellingtons, where he put together his crew that flew forty five operational sorties during 1944.

The crew converted to Stirlings at #1657 Heavy Conversion Unit at Stradishall and was posted to #149 Squadron (Special Duty) on Number Three Group, Lakenheath and subsequently #199 Squadron of 100 Group at North Creake. His operational tour consisted of daylight bombing, night bombing, low level mine laying and a dozen trips across France, at five hundred feet, dropping badly needed supplies to the French Underground.

Asked which of his sorties he considered to be the most memorable, Robert recalls the night of July 7/8, 1944, when they were returning from a drop to an underground cell at Gondolier 14, (code name) near the Alps.The Bomb Aimer was lying in the nose of OJ-K for King, and calling ground fixes to the navigator, by which he could plot the course on the way home, when they flew across the centre of a German airfield that was shut down for the night and was in darkness. Suddenly, they were surprised to see the ground defenses' anti-aircraft guns popping off at them. Both of the Gunners were disappointed that they did not have a chance to return the fire, so Robert started a 360 degree turn and came back with the guns firing from all three turrets, at their "friends" on the ground. After one pass, they resumed their course for home, however, by this time the Bomb Aimer, who had been firing from the front turret, had become disoriented and could not pick up and identify any ground fixes, so the Navigator resorted to using dead reckoning and they continued on their way homeward. After a period of time, they spotted lights on the ground, than doors and windows opened up and people ran outside the buildings and were waving lights, white cloths and what have you. Suddenly, a river loomed up and there was more concentration of houses and buildings. The crew realized that they were over Paris, not in April but on July 7, 1944! The order was "Alter course and get the h___ out of here, fast. Real fast."

Another memorable occasion occurred in December, 1944, when they blew a tyre upon landing, after a spoof raid with R.C.M. equipment. When the tyre blew, Robert put on full throttle, raised the undercarriage and started praying "Our Father, who art in heaven.....". He raised the flaps and set course to Woodbridge, an emergency landing field on orders from flying control. "It is going to be a wheels up landing, crew, you had better bail out". The six man crew, tried and true, returned, "We are going in with you". Right, Robert did

282

his check, altitude three thousand feet, gas off at all engines, switches off, feather props. They were committed to a dead stick landing all the way in. Robert drew on all his skills and brought the plane in smoothly, only scratching the belly and bending the prop tips, although the plane was a write off.

The crew was screened finally and Robert was posted to a tour of instruction, at #24 O.T.U., Honeybourne and Long Marston on Wellingtons. The thought of doing circuits and bumps with green crews in Training Command, was too much for Robert and he volunteered for the Tiger Force Pacific Draft and was returned to Canada and attached to 425 Squadron at Greenwood, N.S. When the Japanese heard that the R.A.F. Bomber Command was joining the Super forts at Okinawa, they up and quit!

Robert's medals include the 1939/45 Star, Aircrew Europe, France/Germany, C.V.S.M. and clasp, War Medal and the Defence Medal. He was demobbed on September 8th, 1945, at Greenwood, Nova Scotia and after the war, he worked with a tyre manufacturer, who also made recreation vehicles. He was in this work for 19 years and had five years in the consulting field. Bob was also a Justice of the Peace for four years. He married Margo in 1975 and has four children from his first marriage.

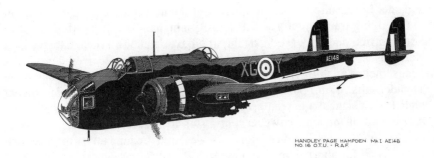

HANDLEY PAGE HAMPDEN MK I AE148
NO. 16 O.T.U. - R.A.F.

F/O TONY WILSON

PILOT R.A.F.

Tony was born in York, England and through encouragement from an uncle, who had served in the Royal Flying Corps in WW 1, soon developed an interest in aviation and aircraft modelling. Secondary education was received at Nunthorpe Grammar School, in York and when the Air Training Corps was established and a school squadron was formed, he was one of the original cadets to join.

From Grammar school, Tony went on to Leeds University, to start a course in architecture, but as soon as possible he joined the Leeds University Air Squadron, volunteering for flying duties with the R.A.F. Volunteer Reserve, passed his medicals etc. and was sworn in, on November 11th, 1942 at Padgate, Lancashire. After completion of the university course, he went on to full flying training, at #14 E.F.T.S. Birmingham, on Tiger Moths, out to South Africa on Tiger Moths again, at No.6 Airschool, Potchefstoom, then Harvards at #22 Air School, Vereeniging, where he received his pilot's wings, thence on to Egypt for operational training at #73 O.T.U., at Fayid, on Thunderbolts. From there, he went to India, where he flew Thunderbolts at #8 R.F.U. Yelahanka in readiness for posting to a squadron in Burma.

The end of the war, however, put a stop to squadron postings, so Tony, together with about 20 other pilots, was declared "redundant", grounded and interviewed for alternative use to the R.A.F. Tony was subsequently posted to Kandy in Ceylon, for an equipment course, returned to India, posted to Agra and was surprised and pleased, to be recalled for flying duties as a pilot, with 20 squadron, which was at Agra, converting to Hawker Tempest II aircraft. Flying with 20 squadron did not last very long, however, as the squadron disbanded, due to lack of pilots, in mid 1946 and the five pilots left, were transferred to 30 squadron, which was also there, flying Tempests.

In December 1946, Tony became "Tour expired" and was duly repatriated to England, where, after an interview at H.Q. Fighter Command, he was posted to Flying Control at R.A.F. Church Fenton in Yorkshire (nine miles from his home). This lasted only a few months, before he returned to Leeds University, to resume his studies. He graduated as an architect, moved to Northampton and joined the staff of the County Architect's Dept. Tony was married to Audrey, an ex-Wren at Hull in 1952 and they have one son and three grandsons. His medals are the War and Defence Medals.

As one of the founding members of a gliding club, he was invited to be an instructor with the Air Training Corps, under the Training Branch of the R.A.F.V.R. and following a refresher course at H.Q. Training Command R.A.F., was assigned to #5 (F) Squadron, A.T.C., Northampton. He later transferred to #487 Squadron in Birmingham, when he moved from Northampton, and finally, he resigned his commission (R.A.F.V.R.) in 1965 prior to emigrating with his family to Canada. In Canada, Tony found employment in his pre-war occupation and has been an architect ever since.

It was early in 1944 and Tony had one more flight to complete the night flying course on Thunderbolts, at #73 O.T.U. Fayid, Egypt. With no set exercise to carry out, he decided on an altitude climb, checked his oxygen supply, took off and climbed up over the Great Bitter Lakes, Suez Canal and the Sinai Desert. Breaking through the dust haze, that hangs over Egypt to about 10,000 feet, he continued his climb to his target altitude of 35,000 feet and levelled off, flying north over the Sinai Desert. From this height, he could see Egypt spread out below him, like the maps he remembered at school, the city lights of Alexandria, Port Said, Port Suez and Cairo, with hundreds of small towns and villages, lighting up the shape of the Nile delta, the coastline of the Mediterranean and city lights in (then) Palestine and to the south, the coastline of the gulf of Suez into the Red Sea.

In his own words, "The night air was very still at this altitude and crystal clear. The huge engine throbbed away quietly, yet I had no feeling of speed or movement, and in turning, the aircraft seemed to fly in slow motion. It was as if I was hovering under a huge blue-black dome, the colour changing to light blue-grey at the horizon all around. (Flying a Mark II Thunderbolt with the bubble canopy, gave him 360 degree vision by turning his head). The cockpit lights gave a soft glow to my own little world, suspended between the stars above and lights on earth below, enhancing my feeling of complete isolation, tranquility and peace, over 6 miles above the earth ... just me and my aeroplane as a boyhood dream come true."

"As I was descending, the peace and quiet were broken by the Control Tower, calling my call sign. "Cordite Forty-five, report your position and return to base". I reported that I was at twenty-eight thousand feet and would call back when I was ready to join circuit. One very un-radio type question followed "What the h... are you doing at twenty-eight thousand feet, Cordite Forty-five?" Fayid Tower, this is Cordite Forty-five, I am descending. Over and out".

Tony duly joined the circuit and landed after an hour and a half flight, in a beautiful aeroplane that was to be one of the most exhilarating and memorable flying experiences of his life. "Years later", recalls Tony, "I read F/O Magee's poem 'High Flight' and I too, knew what he meant, when he wrote:- 'Oh I have slipped the surly bonds of earth'"

It was October 1945 and Tony, like many other Thunderbolt pilots, who were at Bangalore in South India, waiting posting to squadrons when the war ended, were declared redundant, together with several aircraft. He and four others were assigned to fly five old Thunderbolts up to Lucknow, in North India, for disposal in the "scrap yard" there.

The day before leaving on this 1,000 mile trip, the aircraft were test flown and Tony found that his aircraft had soft brakes, no compass, port elevator trim not working and the radio would receive but not transmit. The wheel brakes were "pumped up" and the aircraft declared fit to fly ... with escort only!

The next morning, 5 aircraft taxied out for take off, when one of the pilots had a burst tail wheel and had to be left behind, when the others took off on the first leg to Hyderabad, for lunch and refuelling. During lunch, he arrived with a new tail wheel fitted and all 5 once again taxied out for take off. While revving up against the brakes, Tony had to pump one brake to prevent the aircraft swinging, but decided to take off with the others. This time, however, another pilot had a problem with his propeller C.S. Unit and he was left behind ... to catch up later.

The next leg was to Nagpur, for a night stop and on arrival they did the usual line astern beat up, peeling off to land individually, when the one who was leading, misjudged his approach and went round again. This was lucky for Tony coming in second, as he found he had no wheel brakes and at 130 m.p.h., a Thunderbolt needs a long runway, to stop without brakes. He used up the runway, went on further and finally stopped with the aircraft nose over a 5 foot deep monsoon drainage ditch. Not proposing to go further, he shut off the engine and waited for a truck, to tow him back to the flight area, where mechanics found several leaks in the hydraulics, to brakes and flaps and a damaged undercarriage leg door, that was cutting an ominous groove in the main wheel tyre.

The following morning, 5 aircraft, once more prepared for take off; Tony had to pump brakes, despite repairs having been done, another pilot had propeller problems, so 4 aircraft took off bound for Allahabad. Upon arrival, control was informed that Tony would land first, with faulty brakes and would they have emergency trucks ready?

He landed "just over the fence" and by leaving the flaps down and fishtailing the rudder, managed to stop, before the runway did. He did not dare to touch brakes at speed in case he ground looped and damaged the aircraft.

Only 3 aircraft were able to take off the next morning, on the final leg to Lucknow where, upon arrival, they closed up in tight formation and gave a display of beat-ups, in various formations, before the final line astern and peel off, with Tony as leader, to come in first. He once again used the full runway, before the three aircraft taxied away, with a jeep leading them to the area in the "boneyard", where the aircraft were parked proudly in line at their final dispersal.

With everything switched off, Tony took a final look around the cockpit, pulled the screwdriver from the leg of his flying boots and quickly unscrewed the zippered first aid case and then the black hand grip, off the control column, with its bomb and gun buttons. Souvenirs of what was to be his last flight in a Thunderbolt; an enjoyable one, though a bit shaky in places, delivering an old aeroplane to its final resting place, never to fly again.

Back at the control tower, the three pilots were thanked for their "airshow" before going aboard the Dakota, that had been sent from Allahabad to collect them and return to Allahabad for three day's leave. Three days later, another Dakota flew them to Madras, from whence they were flown by an Expeditor back to Bangalore, completing a memorable and eventful flying experience.

F/O G.H. "BOB" TANNER
R.A.F. WIRELESS OPERATOR/AIR GUNNER

G.H."Bob" Tanner was born in Croydon, Surrey, U.K. He attended Woodside Public School in Woodside, Surrey and then attended Heath Clarke Secondary School at Thornton Heath, Surrey. Bob also took a course in polytechnics at S.E. London Technical Institute and became a member of the Association of Professional Engineers of B.C., after he emigrated to Canada.

He grew up in Croydon, Surrey and his favorite activities were hiking, cricket, soccer and cycling. Prior to his enlistment he was a Lab. Assistant to a power company, the London Electric Supply Corp.

Bob enlisted in the R.A.F. at Victory House, Kingsway, London, in July 1939 for 6 years Regular Service and 6 years Reserve. He was sworn in at West Drayton, Bedfordshire, in July 1939 and started "square bashing" at Cardington, Beds, in August 1939.

He completed his radio course and air gunnery in England. Some of the aircraft in air gunnery were Westland Wallace, a biplane with an open turret, Fairey Battle with open rear turret and Whitley Mk I with manual turrets.

In March and April, he completed O.T.U. on Ansons Mk I, Wellingtons Mk I with Vickers turrets and Wellingtons Mk IA with F.N. turrets. In May, 1940, Bob, as a Sgt. W.O.P./A.G. was posted to No.3 Group Bomber Command to 99 Squadron, R.A.F. Newmarket, Suffolk. He completed 30 operations over Germany flying on Wellingtons Mk IA, IB with F.N. turrets, including a mid under turret.

On August 25th, 1940 on a Wellington I"B" he made his first bombing raid to Berlin, accompanied by 42 other Wellingtons, Whitleys and Hampdens flying at 10,000 feet, 115 knots with a flight of seven and a half hours duration. They made two more Berlin raids in August and early September, notwithstanding Goering's negative attitude. On the third trip, they were caught in the searchlights (coned) which they could not avoid. The pilot put the aircraft in a very steep dive and unable to jettison the bomb load, they stood by to bail out. Finally, with three men pulling on the stick and standing on the dash, the bombs left the aircraft, the plane at this time was leaving Berlin at about 330 knots and below 1,000 feet.

In September, 1940, during the Battle of Britain, they were headed for Leipzig. Takeoff was at 2230 hours with 10/10 cloud from the Dutch coast onwards. Unable to sight the ground at E.T.A., they turned and bombed an unknown airfield through a break in the clouds, unfortunately they were now lost and with daylight approaching at 10,000 feet, low on fuel and still above clouds, they suddenly broke into the clear with bright sunshine. They were flying west down the centre of the English Channel and at 0730 hours they recognized the Isle of Wight on the starboard bow. Their aircraft was rapidly approached by fighters (R.A.F.) and they identified and the fighters took them into Tangmere through the balloons and they landed. Both engines stopped on the runway; they were out of fuel and had to be towed off the runway. They returned to Newmarket at 1030 hours and the Commanding Officer was "pissed off". Apparently their drift south was accounted to a wind reversal over Europe, during the night.

Bob was then transferred in October, 1940 to 214 Squadron at Stradishall, Suffolk and still with 3 Group. He made two operations at that base.

On November 25th, 1940, flying a Wellington I"C" with takeoff at 2200 hours, he left for Luqa, Malta to join 148 Squadron. E.T.A. at 0800 hours. The aircraft was loaded with spare parts and freight. At 2200 hours, 1,000 feet and climbing, the second pilot went back down the fuselage, behind the main spar to turn off the main fuel tanks and use up the overload fuel tank in the bomb bay, then returned to his seat. Both engines stopped; the overload tank had not been turned on. When that happened the aircraft stalled, nose up and then went into a steep dive. Very quiet but windy.

The second pilot returned at Olypmic speed down, (or up) the fuselage to open the fuel cocks. Both engines were windmilling and fortunately, started up. Otherwise there would have been no story. They were very close to the ground and it was also very dark. Since they did not hit anything, the crew returned to breathing. The aircraft climbed back on course and they arrived at Luqa at 0800 hours.

The second pilot was a Squadron Leader who shall remain nameless, (skipper was a Pilot Officer) who had flown Valencias in the Middle East and was returning to the M.E. with them, just for the ride.

While at 148 Squadron and flying a Wellington, they took off at 1615 hours on a daylight raid on Castel Benito, south of Tripoli, Libya. The squadron was on full strength of 9 aircraft in 3 vic formations of 3 aircraft at 2,000 feet. They were attacked by Fiat CR 32 and 42 fighters, but they backed off in face of turret crossfire.

The Wellingtons attacked the airfield at about 1,200 feet, with the aircraft in line astern, on a left hand circuit. They silenced the ground guns with turret fire and bombed and strafed the airfield at low level. Bob's group damaged and destroyed 86 enemy aircraft (info. obtained from enemy reports). All their aircraft returned safely, but had some damage from bomb splinters. Subsequently they had two more raids on Castel Benito, but not so successful, as the enemy were waiting for them.

On February 2nd, 1941, they left at 0240 hours to Comiso, Sicily. 148 were requested to carry out multiple bomb runs at 20 to 30 minute intervals, to give the impression of a carrier force (string bags), operating west of Sicily. All aircraft ran in singly from the west and dropped two or three bombs, (they had 18 - 250 pound bombs on board) then retired to the west for 15 minutes, then back again, for another go. They had seven bomb runs over the target, both high level (10,000 feet) and dive bombing (in a Wimpey!). It was nerve wracking after three hours on and off the target.

Operating out of Malta was a different "kettle of fish" from U.K. operations. Malta was a hot spot and the object of constant attack, on relatively small targets, such as Luqa.

Typically, the airfield was attacked sometimes daily by forces of 50 to 150 enemy aircraft, mostly Ju 87 dive bombers with screamer bombs, Ju 88s, Me 109s and 110s and Do 111s. On some occasions they were bombed four and five times in twenty four hours. Similarly, other targets were the dockyard and Hal Far fighter airfield. From November 1940 to January 1941, they had 8 Hurricanes (used ex-Battle of Britain) and 3 Gladiators (biplane fighters) as the total fighter force opposing the Luftwaffe and Regis Aeronautica, out of Sicily and Castel Benito, Libya. The fighter boys did a heroic job, but most did not survive.

By April 1941, Luqa was becoming untenable as a bomber field, as the enemy concentrated on the repeated destruction of 148 Squadron aircraft. They had lost about 36 aircraft in six weeks, on the ground and though their total strength was 9 aircraft, replacements could not be maintained. Perhaps this was a tribute to the effectiveness of 148 as a bomber force.

In any event, squadron personnel were finally evacuated by the Royal Navy, via H.M.S. Bonaventure, a high angle anti aircraft cruiser to Alexandria, Egypt. Forty-eight hours after they left the ship, she was hit by four torpedoes off Crete and went down in seven minutes.

The Squadron was re-equipped in Egypt, at Kabrit and returned to Luqa on a shift basis, with 70 Squadron of Kabrit. Two weeks at Luqa and two weeks operating out of Kabrit into Libya. There was always activity at and around Malta. By this time, Bob had 20 operational flights into Italy, Sicily and Libya, to bring a total of 52 raids against the enemy.

In July, 1941, Bob was on rest, seconded to R.A.F. Burg El Arab, Western Desert, as temporary cipher officer. Subsequently, he suffered from a poisoned leg, was hospitalized and contacted diphtheria, while in hospital. He returned to the U.K. in January, 1942 on "S.S. Duchess of York" and acted as anti-aircraft gunner en route.

Bob was an R.A.F. instructor during 1942 to 1945 on Training Command. It involved air and ground duties, including wireless and gunnery. He moved to various stations during this time and was promoted to Flight Sergeant in June 1942, Warrant Officer in June 1943, Pilot Officer in August 1944 and his final rank of Flying Officer in January 1945. In November 1945, he was posted to R.A.F. Empire Air Armament School at Manby, Lincs. and was seconded to Flying Control duties as Flying Control Officer.

In 1946, he was posted to St. Athan, South Wales on a special radio course. Bob was demobilized in March, 1946 at Air Armament School at Manby, Lincs. U.K. He received the 1939/45 Star, Air Crew Europe Star, Africa Star, Defence Medal and the War Medal.

After leaving the service, Bob continued night school and had a certificate in Mechanical Engineering, U.K. 1946–1951. He became a draftsman, designer, division engineer and petrochemical engineer. Bob emigrated to Canada in May, 1957 and entered the consulting engineering industry. He moved to Vancouver in February,1969 in the consulting business and started his own company in 1986, Tanner engineering Corp., Member of the Association of Professional Engineers of British Columbia.

Bob and his wife Hazel Mary, were married on March 25th, 1944 and have three children, Anthony R., Adrian V. and Jill M., all living in the U.S. and Canada, married and with families.

F/O I.R.G. TODD
PILOT R.C.A.F.

Ivan Todd was born at Vulcan, Alberta, raised on a farm and completed his high school at Champion. He worked for a road construction company, for eight months, before joining the R.C.A.F. in Calgary, and was then sent to Manning Depot in Edmonton. Accepted for aircrew, he took his I.T.S. at Saskatoon, Saskatchewan, his E.T.S. at Davidson and then returned to Saskatoon for his F.T.S. After receiving his pilots wings he was sent to Maitland, N.S. for a Commando's course. This course became a little extended, before being posted to a Royal Navy Fleet Air Arm training school at Yarmouth, N.S.

At Yarmouth he flew telegrapher air gun trainees, in Anson and in Swordfish aircraft. Two hours in the morning, two hours in the afternoon - weather permitting. After getting airborne, fog was always welcome, as a legitimate excuse to low fly. But some operations were more carefully organized.

A popular fellow pilot was being married in Annapolis Royal, an hour's flight from Yarmouth, on the west coast. While the Royal Navy pilots understandingly flew up the east coast, the Canadian pilots delayed their morning take off and carrying as much armament as available to them - rolls of toilet paper, took off at 0900 hours to arrive for the 1000 o'clock wedding. Formations of Ansons and Swordfish buzzed and dived on the church from all directions and heights. All planes returned to base, the mission was a success - the wedding had been delayed an hour!

From Yarmouth, Todd was sent to Torbay, Newfoundland, to fly for No. 1 Composite Squadron, that was often referred to as a flying club. There were Tiger Moths, Harvards, Norsemen, Grumman Goose, Hudsons and Venturas. The Hudsons had a sixteen foot boat, fully stocked, strapped underneath their bellies, that could be parachuted to crews that had ditched in the North Atlantic. Other duties included communication, mail and supply drops, drogue towing and low level flying for army practice. Special unauthorized interests were navigational familiarization flights to the French Islands of Saint Pierre and Miquelon. Imported rum could be purchased in five gallon wooden casks for ten dollars a gallon. From Torbay, his last flight was ferrying a Hudson to Summerside, P.E.I. where the aircraft were being mothballed. Then a posting to Moncton, N.B. for either Pacific duty or discharge.

At Moncton, Ivan was honourably discharged, received the C.V.S.M. with Clasp and met the girl who would later become his wife.

In September 1946 he registered at the University of British Columbia and graduated with a Commerce Degree in 1950. He married Catherine in Dec. 1946.

While attending U.B.C. he continued his interest in flying, obtained his commercial pilots license and joined, through the R.C.A.F., what was called Operation Chipmunk. This required flying fifty hours per year in Chipmunks, to provide a nucleus of immediately available instructors.

Since graduation, Ivan had been associated with the lumber industry as a buyer and as a wholesaler. Prospecting and mining have provided some diversions.

Ivan lives in Langley, B.C. His wife, Catherine, died in May, 1989 after a brief illness. He has three children and nine grandchildren. Although retired, he still maintains his lumber contacts and is involved in some mining ventures.

F/LT JOHN WATERS
BOMB AIMER R.C.A.F.

John was born in Vancouver, B.C. and raised in the west end of the city, overlooking English Bay. He received his public and secondary schooling at the Vancouver Preparatory School for Boys, graduating with senior matriculation. He was active in sports, of which his favourites were swimming, football, tennis, mountain hiking and skating on Lost Lagoon, when there was sufficient ice.

Prior to joining the R.C.A.F. in June 1940, he worked as a junior accountant. He failed his medical for aircrew and settled for ground crew. Some thirty months later, he again applied for aircrew and was accepted for Pilot training, but was "washed out" at Thunder Bay (then Fort William). He successfully completed bombaimer training in Canada and was posted overseas, arriving in the United Kingdom in the early summer of 1943. He was posted to the operational training unit at Chipping Warden, where he ultimately crewed up.

At the conclusion of his tour, John was repatriated to Canada, returning to the U.K. six months later, for purposes of crewing up for the Far Eastern Theatre, but shortly afterwards, the war ended and he was posted to Oldenburg, Germany, as Paymaster of the Air Disarmament Wing. He received his honourable discharge in Vancouver, in May 1946. He was the recipient of the 1939/45 Star, Aircrew Europe Star, Operational tour wing, Defence Medal, C.V.S.M. and bar and the War Medal.

Incidentally, John's brother Ken, a Flying Officer navigator on 119 R.A.F. Squadron, Coastal Command, flew on Sunderland Flying Boats. He was killed in action in 1943.

After discharge, John was employed by the B.C. Electric Company and its successor B.C.Hydro, in their Marketing Division, on Dealer Services and Sales Promotion. After taking retirement, he carried on, in a consultative role to Hydro, for a short period. Married after the war, he and his wife Catherine have two sons and three grandchildren.

One of the most memorable trips his crew ever took part in, was on June 5th on the eve of "D" Day. Five Fortresses from 214 Squadron and 24 Lancasters from 101 Squadron, flew ten hours on a rectangular course, from Beachy Head to Dungeness, then across to the line of the Seine in order to disrupt enemy radio communications, jamming and dropping enormous amounts of "window", to give the impression of a massive bomber stream heading in that direction. After patrolling for ten hours, they left the French coast and headed back towards England, just before daybreak.

They met a most tremendous aerial armada of troop planes and gliders, going in for the main assault near Caen. This armada seemed to stretch for miles. It was a fantastic sight. The crew's thoughts were all on those brave men going in to fight on "D" Day.

On another occasion, they were briefed to go to the heart of the Ruhr, to the Nordstern oil plant in Gelsinkerchen, but as they approached the target area, the rear gunner reported seeing a Lancaster about 200 yards astern. The Lanc suddenly dived away, leaving a Messerschmidt 410, which had been stalking the Lanc, in perfect position to shoot at them. The rear gunner shouted a warning, but the next moment they were raked from stern to nose by gunfire from the 410.

The starboard engine burst into flames and the intercom became dead and soon they were losing height, the pilot struggling to keep the aircraft airborne. To worsen matters, they were also attacked by a Ju 88, the wireless operator was wounded and there was further damage to the aircraft.

At this time, John realized that the wireless operator needed help, as he was covered with blood; remembering some of the medical lectures he had gone through, John injected him with morphine and he eventually rallied and between the two of them, managed to get the intercom working again. At this point, the pilot decided to turn back and obtained a course for Woodbridge, the crash 'drome on the English coast, however, their troubles were still not over, as when they landed, the right hand undercarriage wheel, which had been damaged by the enemy fighter, caused the aircraft to swing violently to the right, into the path of a stationary Lanc, whose crew had luckily just vacated.

John's Lanc cut the other in two, just missing the bomb bay, which still contained a 12,000 pound bomb. Fortunately, they were not carrying bombs on this trip, which was a special anti-jamming mission. Again, happily, only one of his crew had to go to hospital.

They learned later, that the demolished Lanc had been on the same mission as themselves, but had been unable to drop bombs, due to the bomb bay doors not being able to open. The wireless operator went to hospital in Ely and eventually recovered. The crew returned to base the next day. A sad end to this episode was that the decimated Lanc's crew went missing, on their very next raid.

During May 1943, John was doing circuits and bumps, bombing exercises, map reading etc. with various pilots and crews at Chipping Warden O.T.U., while waiting to pick up a crew. One of the pilots with whom he flew, (in a Wellington) was a very likeable and cheerful fellow, with a good sense of humour. However, he always landed on the grass instead of the runway, resulting in some fearful bumps. Eventually, John asked with all respect, why he always did this and the pilot smiled and said that any fool could land on the runway, but it took skill to land on the grass... Needless to say, that answer did not impress John very much and he decided immediately to look around for another crew!!

One of John's worst trips, was an op. to Stuttgart, in July 1944. The city had on two successive nights been visited by bomber command and by flying the same route. At briefing the crews were told they were going to use the same route once more because, according to "Intelligence", the enemy would not expect Bomber Command to fly the same route 3 nights in a row. None who flew that night were very impressed by that logic!

They had hardly crossed the enemy coast, when they witnessed a terrible sight of aircraft blowing up in mid air. It took them nearly 4 hours to reach Stuttgart and whereas they had been promised cloudy weather by the "Met" office, it was a clear, moonlit night ... a bonus for the enemy night-fighters. Happily, they reached and attacked Stuttgart and returned to base safely. All agreed that it was a terrible strain on the crew.

P/O J.W. "BRICK" BRADFORD D.F.C.
PILOT R.C.A.F.

'Brick' Bradford was born in Hamilton, Ontario, his education beginning in the Adelaide Hoodless Public School and his Secondary Schooling at Delta Collegiate. From Secondary he went on to Hamilton Technical Institute for vocational training. From his early childhood, he avidly followed aviation and while in high school, he began to take flying lessons. From 1938 to 1940 he continued taking lessons and progressed from Private Pilots License to Senior Commercial License and on to an Instructors Endorsement.

Bradford joined the R.C.A.F. in June 1940 and served at #7 E.F.T.S. as an instructor. At this stage of the Commonwealth training plan, none of the pilots had been to Manning Pool, nor had drill and kit instruction in the R.C.A.F. Before being posted overseas, or other duties, it was necessary to do a short course on Harvards to get 'wings.' "Brick" went to #6 S.F.T.S. in Dunnville, Ont. and a Wings course before going to the "Y" Depot in Halifax, where he boarded the troopship "Andes" enroute to Glasgow.

His first base after arriving in England was Bournemouth, on the south coast, where he became oriented to the countryside and like many others, had occasion to select his choice of action. His preference was to Photographic Reconnaissance on Spitfires and so, in March of 1943, he was posted to #17(P) A.F.U. at Watton, Norfolk.

Five weeks of flying on Miles Master II craft were followed by two months at Squires Gate in Lancashire; that involved intensive classroom instruction, plus 30 hours of "hands on" navigation in the Avro Anson, around the Irish Sea.

A posting to #6 O.T.U. Dyce in Scotland, increased the proficiency on handling the aircraft, as well as proficient skill in photography, in fighter tactics and convoy escort. Brick received his commission in early September 1943, becoming a Pilot Officer, after some time as an exalted W.O.1.

In October of 1943 he left England for India, in a Mark XI Spitfire and from November 11th to April of 1944 he was with #21 Ferry Control in Karachi. Brick joined #681 Squadron (Photographic Reconnaissance) with Mark II Spitfires. After one year, he had 306 flying hours and 60 trips completed and was posted to a P.R. O.T.U. in Tel Aviv for a rest tour. In April of 1945 Bradford was aboard the troop ship "Winchester Castle" to Egypt.

When V.E. Day arrived, the troops were in a Tent Camp near Cairo where, the R.A.F. wisely decided, that the airmen had better be confined to camp. The word came that all Canadians were to be repatriated immediately.

On May 28th the Canadian airmen were back in Bournemouth, awaiting transport back to Canada. They were accommodated in the Royal Bath Hotel, which served as the Officer's Mess and accommodation for R.C.A.F. personnel. The prisoners of war were given priority on the first boats to leave England and they were followed by volunteers for the Pacific Theatre. On July 30th the "S.S. Ile de France" prepared to sail to Halifax with 10,000 or so troops on board. Brick Bradford arrived at #1 Repatriation depot in Lachine, P.Q. on August 6th and was at #4 Release Centre at Toronto, ready to seek a flying position with Trans-Canada Airlines on September 14th 1945.

The decorations and medals that were awarded to Brick are the D.F.C., the 1939/45 Star, the Burma Star, the Defence Medal, the C.V.S.M. and the Victory Medal. He was honourably discharged in September 1945 and continued flying as a professional pilot with T.C.A. now Air Canada until 1988. He and his wife Mary, whom he married in 1946, have two sons, Scott and David and two grandchildren, Emily and Andrew.

While at Benson, Oxfordshire, the H.Q. for P.R., Brick was asked to volunteer to go to 681 Squadron in India. The carrot dangled under his nose, was that he would have a brand new Spit Mark XI to ferry from England to India.

After the aircraft was checked, he took off from Port Reath, near Land's End, not knowing that the trip would take 21 days. He had no baggage, so all his gear was stowed at Benson. His flight plan indicated he was to fly right across Spain at 40,000 feet then land in Gib. Thirty minutes out, the oil pressure dropped to zero, so he had to return.

While waiting for the Spit to be repaired, he was sitting in the Officer's Mess, when he was asked if he would care to make a fourth hand at bridge. His bridge partners turned out to be three Generals, General Crerar, General Carton De Wyart and another, whose name he has forgotten. General Crerar was from Brick's home town and knew his father.

Two days later, with the Spitfire now in first class order, Brick was on his way to Algeria and a night stop in Tripoli. The following day he was off for Cairo where, upon landing, he was informed the Spit was due a 25 hour inspection and that he could expect to be there for a week. On November 6th, and this was 1943, he took off for Lydda in Palestine, then to a staging

296

post which is assumed to have been Shaibah in Iraq. Here he was held up by a sandstorm, but was able to take off the next day, for Bahrein Island in the Persian Gulf. Here, he met another Spit pilot, also ferrying a plane to India. They travelled together from there on.

The next morning they took off for Sharja in Oman where, on landing, it was 110 degrees in the shade. Their next stop was Drigh Road airport, Karachi. Little did Brick know that he would be flying this route years later as an airline pilot! It had taken him 25 hours to fly from England to Karachi!

All the pilots there, were to be sent to a pilots pool at Poona, but Brick suggested to the C.O. that they start ferrying Spits around the country where needed. The C.O. agreed and Brick and the others were soon flying aircraft all over India. Brick even had opportunities to co-pilot Dakotas and Libs and the highlight of these delivery flights would be the return journey to Karachi, #21 Ferry Control, riding in the Imperial Airways Flying Boats, which were still operating at that time. Five months later, Brick was posted to 681 Squadron in Calcutta, to begin a tour on Photographic Reconnaissance.

There was a bridge on the Salween River in China, which was the Japanese supply route to the Burma Road. Intelligence and Photo Reconnaissance had been unable to acquire any recent information.

It fell to Brick to take off early in the morning of June 7th. His Spitfire was equipped with two vertically mounted cameras of 36" focal length and 1000 exposure magazine. The fuel 'stop' for the mission was close to the front line in North-East India and as such, it was required to fly over the signals area, to ensure the correct signals of the day were displayed, in case the airport had been over-run by Japs during the night. The signals were O.K. so Bradford landed, re-fuelled and was on his way to the Salween River. He spotted it and began following the river and recognized some bends from his map. He had been flying at 30,000 feet and began a rapid descent and at 14,000 feet, observed his target and had enough time for a straight and level run over the bridge.

Brick realized he was at the limit of his range, nor could he afford extra climbing, because of fuel consumption. His heading of W.S.W. to the fuel stop, was taking him toward a black and ominous looking sky. Around 22,000 feet, it began snowing and he was in cloud and turbulence. He noticed the wings and the windshield began to pick up icing; the airspeed, altitude and vertical speed and static port were totally iced over. To add to his 'joy' there was violent turbulence hail and lightning. He dropped the nose and reverted to 'turn needle' and 'slip indicator' and used the sound of the slipstream, as an indicator of speed. He began to wonder if he would make it back that day!

Bradford advanced the power to maximum "take-off", hoping he could climb out of the weather. After what seemed like an eternity, he broke out of the cloud, with towering thunderstorms on either side. The horizon gradually erected and the ice began to dissipate. He was at 42,000 feet; it had been a long climb out of that weather. The fuel gage indicated 30 gallons of fuel left; he could see the Bay of Bengal off on the left, with the mouth of the Ganges and he realized he was well past the fuel stop and set power for a long descent and headed for his home base in Calcutta. On landing, the fuel tank was empty as he had been in the air 3 hours and 45 minutes!!

Brick's photographs taken on the mission, indicated that the bridge had been rebuilt, after previous bombings and was again operational. A few days later it was bombed again and made u/s. Brick makes a brief overview of Photographic Reconnaissance in the China - Burma - India theatre.

There were three photo squadrons based at Alipore on the south side of Calcutta. Photo labs. and Interpretational Centres were close by. Number 681 Squadron, with Spitfires, covered all targets up to 450 miles behind enemy lines, such as airports, railroads, towns, harbours, and any other items considered important. This was done on a daily basis. The United States Army Air Corps, 40th Photo Group covered all medium range targets with P-38 (Lightning), and 684 Squadron covered long range targets as far south as Singapore.

F/LT H.E.J."ED" AVELING
PILOT R.C.A.F.

Ed Aveling was born in Saskatoon, Sask. He attended the Simpson Elementary School in Yorkton and continued his secondary education at the Yorkton Collegiate Institute. From 1918 to 1937 the Aveling family lived in Yorkton, where Ed's father was a Ford Dealer and the life was generally 'comfortable.' Ed had woodworking as a hobby.

In 1937 the family moved west to Vancouver, establishing the family

298

home. Ed was employed, first as a service station attendant and later, he moved to a job as an automotive parts clerk. On December 5th 1941 he joined the R.C.A.F. in Vancouver.

Aveling began his training as a student pilot, on Fleet Finches, at #13 A.F.T.S. at St. Eugene, Ontario, followed by his Service Flying training on Cessna Cranes at #11 Yorkton, Sask. Ed's next posting was to #1 G.R.S. Summerside, P.E.I. on Ansons.

It came time to leave Canada and on arrival in England, he was posted to #20 A.F.U. at Croughton, Northants., to master the Airspeed Oxford, before going on to Wellingtons at #6 O.T.U. Silloth, followed by preparation on Halifax's at Longtown, Cumberland and from there, Ed was posted to #517 Squadron, flying Halifaxes at Brawdy, Pembroke, South Wales.

Ed was engaged in long range meteorological sorties for Coastal Command, 700 miles south from Brawdy, over the Bay of Biscay. Two flights a day were scheduled - one at noon and the other at midnight - a flight was never cancelled and while they always took off, they were frequently diverted to Gibraltar, Ireland or Scotland.

On June 5th 1944, Aveling's crew was to fly the midnight trip. At briefing, the Intelligence officer gave a complete picture of shipping, convoys etc. around the British Isles and on to the Atlantic. On this night, about midnight or before, the Intelligence officer revealed a large map and there was not a ship or convoy on it. His comment was "anything you see out there, consider it to be ours! "THEY KNEW D-DAY HAD ARRIVED!!

At about the same time as the troops were landing on the Normandy beaches, Ed and his crew were ditching their Halifax in the Bay of Biscay. At an altitude of 18,000 feet and 700 miles from Lands End, a mechanical failure in the constant speed unit in the port outer engine, caused the propeller to go into full fine pitch and 'windmill' at a terrific speed. The vibrations set up by the windmilling were so sharp and severe, all the instruments and maps on the navigators table disappeared.

In a few seconds, an oil line was cracked in the port inner and all the oil was lost. The prop on this engine was feathered and the engine stopped. About this time the port outer caught fire, adding considerably to the dismay of the crew! Fortunately they were able to extinguish the flames but, with two good starboard engines, one port engine windmilling and the other port engine dead, Ed was unable to maintain altitude. The aircraft slowly lost height and was successfully ditched.

The nose of the aircraft broke off at the wing posts and sank with Ed still at the controls. Somehow he managed to get out, swallowing salt water and gasoline in the effort. The rest of the crew got out of the aircraft and released the "J" type dinghy and all managed to get in. The 'skipper' was so sick for six hours from the salt water and the gasoline, that he didn't care what happened.

When the trouble first began, the Wireless Operator had been in communication with home base, sending back a weather report. Without hesitation, he sent the code signals for "Engine Trouble" "Returning to Base.", followed by latitude and longitude. The signal was sent three times. Later, it was found that base received the message once, but half way through the second transmission all contact was lost and nothing further heard. The vibrations had shaken the radio apart - it was fortunate that the W.O.P. had acted so quickly.

The following morning - June 7th - at about 8.00 a.m., a Catalina from Air/Sea Rescue Squadron #202 was sighted flying in the general direction of the dinghy. The crew released in succession, "3 Star Red " rockets, and while the first stars were still in the air, the Catalina was seen to bank slightly towards the crew. Its nose came down and moments later the Catalina roared over the dinghy at 25 feet. Close enough to count the rivets in the hull!!

The seas were too rough for the Catalina to set down, so it stayed overhead, while an American destroyer was directed to the dinghy. Another aircraft relieved the first and maintained a constant cover. Twenty four hours later, the destroyer arrived and the survivors were taken aboard - ending 24 hours in the dinghy.

The destroyers were part of a task force of one escort carrier and four destroyers on anti-sub patrol. The following day, the crew were transferred to the escort carrier and the next three weeks were spent stooging around the Atlantic. While aboard the carrier, a signal was received from the British Admiralty, advising that a Japanese submarine and a German sub. were to rendezvous at a certain position. The task force intercepted and sank the Japanese sub.

The carrier eventually docked at Norfolk, Virginia, and Ed Aveling was flown to Washington, D.C. The rest of the crew entrained for Dorval Airport. At the R.A.F. delegation in Washington, a sympathetic R.A.F. officer, after hearing all the details of the ditching and rescue, arranged leave for Ed, as well as transportation to Trenton, Ontario.

He then boarded the train, for a journey across to his home town of Vancouver, to spend three weeks with the bride he had married before going overseas. He returned to England from New York, aboard the "Queen Elizabeth" - arriving back at his station, ten weeks after he had successfully ditched the aircraft.

Flight Lieutenant Ed.Aveling was discharged in September 1945 in Vancouver and received the following decorations: 1939/45 Star, Atlantic Star, C.V.S.M., War Medal and Defence Medal.

His occupation after discharge centred around real estate. He was a real estate salesman and then a house builder. In the last twenty-five years he has been the owner/operator of a real estate company. Ed's first wife died some years ago, and he re-married last year. He and his wife Beverley, live in West Vancouver. He has two sons, Brian and Bill.

p

W/O H.W. "HERB" WILLIAMS
BOMB AIMER R.C.A.F.

Herb W. Williams was born in St. Vital, a suburb of Winnipeg, Manitoba. He took his public schooling on the Prairies and later his secondary education at Brandon Collegiate. He became interested in aviation and aircraft modelling at an early age. The Brandon Flying Club annually played host to the touring barnstorming pilots who, for a small admission, put on an air show of dare-devil aerial aerobatics, as well as offering plane rides to the public at $5.00 a flip. To a teenager growing up in the depression of the 1930's, this was always a dream - to fly!!

One day in 1941, a friend of his, Bob Rosenberg, said to him "Why don't we join the Air Force Herb?" The city of Brandon was filled with aircrew trainee personnel, from every part of the Commonwealth, participating in the British Commonwealth Air Training Plan. Billboards and posters everywhere, encouraged one to "Join the R.C.A.F. and See the World" and "Be a World Traveller at 21." So, early in 1942, when both had attained the minimum age requirement of 17 1/2 years, they applied at the R.C.A.F. Recruiting Centre and were duly sent off to Winnipeg, for aircrew enlistment examinations and medicals etc. Naturally, they both had envisioned becoming pilots; after all, the Air Force needed them! However, they were soon to discover the R.C.A.F. had other ideas, Herb was to become a Bomb-Aimer and Bob a Wireless Air Gunner.

Herb commenced his flying training at #5 Bombing & Gunnery School, Dafoe, Sask. where he had to overcome his proneness to airsickness, if he was to remain in aircrew. To see his name on the Flight Flying Schedule, was sufficient to send him out behind the hangar "calling Hughie"! However, he was to overcome this problem and went on to #1 Air Navigation School at Rivers, Manitoba, where he was to receive his Bombaimer wing. After spending some time at #1 O.T.S at St. Marguerite, P.Q. he was finally sent overseas, arriving at Bournemouth early in 1944.

After completing the Operational Advanced Flying Unit training at Staverton, Gloucester, it was on to #24 Operational Training Unit, Long Marston, Warwicks. where "crewing up" took place. While on a night exercise, the aircraft suffered a double engine failure. The pilot, Gord Retallack, unable to extinguish the engine fires, ordered the crew to abandon aircraft. Fortunately, all crew members got out unharmed. The crew was posted to 1664 Heavy Conversion Unit, Dishforth, Yorks., the #6 Lancaster Finishing School, prior to being sent to 419 Moose Squadron, Middleton St. George, Durham, being part of No 6 R.C.A.F. Group, Bomber Command.

Part way through their tour, they were briefed for another heavy raid into Germany, this time to Hanau, a city of 40,000, lying ten miles east of Frankfurt. The target was the Dunlop Tyre Works. Taking off with a full bomb and gas load, the aircraft airspeed not yet up to take-off speed when suddenly the starboard tyre blew under the strain. With a prayer from every crew member aboard, the aircraft lifted off the runway, the undercarriage barely clearing the fence at the edge of the field. Someone up above was looking down on them and smiling! After successfully bombing their target, they were directed to change course and to land at Carnaby, an emergency landing field on England's east coast. Gord, the pilot, skilfully landed the aircraft with the port wing low and they were quickly lifted off the runway by a huge crash-tender.

On many of their bombing operations over Germany, the crews would jam enemy radio communications, drop thousands of propaganda leaflets printed in German proclaiming "DIE EST DE ENDE" as well as enormous amounts of "window" (fine strips of aluminum), to give the impression to the enemy ground radar defenses of a massive bombing raid.

Early in 1945, Bomber Command changed their tactics, from principally night operations only, to also hit the enemy in daylight as well. This support of the advancing ground forces, who had done so well since D-day, in their determination to eventually take Berlin, brought them closer each day to achieving that goal. In these daylight raids, the bombers usually flew in "gaggles" - loose formations of aircraft grouped behind a Vic of three leaders. Upon these few crews, rested the navigational responsibility of the whole gaggle. Their course and timing must be perfect, if the bombers were to reach the target at the correct time, with proper concentration, and with the planned fighter cover.

Having completed a goodly portion of their tour, they were chosen to be deputy gaggle leaders on two raids, both of which were successfully completed. The next daylight raid, led by "Rattleshack's Crew", was to the Engeldorf marshalling yard at Leipzig. Along with seven other Canadian Lancaster squadrons, they were to block the main rail lines passing through the large Saxon industrial and communications centre. They did that and more. Operating in perfectly clear weather conditions, 419's raiders easily pinpointed their way to the specific target, obtaining beautifully clear pictures of the aiming point. The accurate and highly concentrated nature of the bombing, was only too evident in the excellent bombing photos. Rail lines, rolling stock, sheds, and round-houses were engulfed in a steady torrent of high-explosions. A number of great explosions were triggered and voluminous smoke clouds churned up to 12,000 feet. Little did they know that this was to be one of the most successful attacks of the war, against Germany and was to complete a tour of operations for this crew, in the European Theatre of war.

Even before hostilities ended in Europe, plans were being made for R.C.A.F. #6 Group's participation against Japan. 419 was one of eight heavy bomber squadrons, detailed for "Tiger Force" and prepared to fly home to Canada. On June 1st, the Moose Squadron left Middleton-St-George, on the first leg of the homeward bound flight to Nova Scotia via St. Mawgan, the Azores and Gander. Air Chief Marshall, Sir Arthur Harris, K.C.B., O.B.E., A.F.C., Air Officer Commanding-in-Chief, Bomber Command, came to Middleton-St-George to see the first squadron depart and to wish the aircrew "bon voyage" and good luck, in future operations. In paying tribute to No.6 Group he said:

"You leave this country, after all you have done, with a reputation that is equal to any and surpassed by none. We, in Bomber Command, have always regarded our Canadian Group and Canadian Crews, outside the Group, as among the very best."

In Canada, the personnel of the eight squadrons, went on leave, preparatory to re-organization, re-equipment and training for the Pacific theatre. Before their re-formation became effective, however, the atom bomb blasted Japan out of the war and early in September the squadron disbanded. Herb was honourably discharged in September '45 and was transferred to the R.C.A.F. Volunteer Reserve. He received the 39/45 Star, Aircrew Europe Star & Clasp, Defence Medal, War Medal, C.V.S.M. & Clasp, Operational Wing, Caterpillar Pin and Bomber Command Medal (unofficial at this time).

Subsequent to his discharge, Herb chose a career in the automotive parts wholesale business management field. Ultimately, he operated his own transportation business, for a decade, prior to spending ten years as a real estate broker.

Herb served as a Field Artillery Reserve Army Officer at Brandon and Shilo, Manitoba, for a period post-war. He and his wife, Fran, a former Officer with the Royal Navy, were married after the war. They have one daughter and two sons, one of whom is an N.C.O. with the R.C.M.P. They also have five grandchildren.

Many years later, in June of 1981, Herb and his wife, holidaying in the U.K., were able to return to Middleton (now known as Tees-side Airport). The Ground Services Supervisor, Brian Champley, certainly 'rolled out the red carpet' for them, assigning one of his staff and a vehicle, for a two day tour of the old station. Coincidental to this, a flight of four R.C.A.F. helicopters, visiting from their home station of Lohr, West Germany, arrived. Needless to say, that evening, many old memories of wartime events were recalled over drinks in the hotel lounge. In the a.m., before the departure of the flight crews, Major Lyle Adams, O.I.C., and his men, all autographed Herb's flying log book as a memento. Herb and his wife, were then invited to accompany them to the flight tarmac, for an inspection of one of the 'choppers.' One of the junior officers then asked if they could do a fly-past for them before their departure.

This was one of the proudest moments of Herb's life; when four R.C.A.F. helicopters in formation flew past the control tower of Middleton, and each bowed their noses in turn, in recognition of someone else who had served many years before.

FLIGHT SERGEANT ALEX. S. BLAIR
AIR GUNNER R.A.F.

Alex Blair was born at Alloa, Clackmannanshire, Scotland and attended schools at Sunnyside Elementary and Alloa Technical and Commerce, Alloa. He studied to be an engineer and enjoyed cricket and was an ardent football and soccer player.

At eighteen he joined the R.A.F. at Edinburgh, Scotland, in January 1944, to be trained as an Air Gunner. Initial training at A.C.R.C. St. John's Wood, London, I.T.W. at Bridgenorth and then onto A.G.S. at Andreas on the Isle of Man. The training aircraft were Avro Ansons. Now, Alex felt they were getting somewhere. Twelve weeks and many rounds of ammunition later he became a qualified sprog A.G. and a brand new Sergeant. Then after a "so-called" commando course, Alex and his fellow A.G.s were sent to Canada on the "Queen Elizabeth". Standing beside some repatriated American service men going home, many of them seriously injured, all with tears in their eyes as they passed the Statue of Liberty, was a moment that Alex will never forget. From New York, they travelled by train to Montreal, then on to No.5 O.T.U. at Boundary Bay, B.C.

It was springtime in British Columbia, the weather was beautiful, they were flying in B-24 Liberators with turrets, equipped with two 0.5 inch machine guns - what more could you ask for? There were five A.G.s assigned to a crew, four turret gunners and a waist gunner. Each A.G. was able to state his preference for a turret position. Alex chose the Ball turret. There was no opposition from the other air gunners. From Boundary Bay, Alex went to Abbotsford, where crewing-up took place. The air gunners met the skipper and other members of the crew. Until the end of the course they flew together as a unit. When O.T.U. and a 14 day leave were over, Alex reported to Lachine, Quebec where the crew collected a new B-24 at Dorval to fly to and join a squadron, in India. With a compliment of ten crew members KP 136 left Dorval, via Gander and the Azores to the Far East. From the Azores to Rabat to Castel Benito to Lydda in Palestine. Flying over Egypt would not have been complete without seeing the Pyramids and the crew had the added thrill of a couple of low passes over the Sphinx and the Pyramids. After a further stop at Shaibah, they reached Karachi, their destination. Flying time 45 hours, actual time 17 days. Two stops over were necessary, to allow individual crewmen to recover from dysentery.

The original plan was to fly the B-24 direct to a squadron, but arrangements were altered and it was flown to Allahabad,with the crew and Alex flying back to Karachi in a Dakota. Alex never did see KP 136 again nor did it appear at Salboni where he was to join 355 Squadron a few days later. With the end of hostilities the squadron was being cut back and with the prospect of being totally disbanded, he transferred back to the R.A.F. station at Mauripur as an Airfield Controller. Alex spent the next two years at Mauripur. Off duty he played soccer,travelled, swam and enjoyed the Sergeant's mess. When de-mob orders came through he returned to England to be discharged at Kirkham, Lancs in July 1947.

Alex was awarded the Burma Star (Pacific Clasp) Defence General Service decoration.

After discharge he resumed his Engineering trade, got married in 1951, had two sons and in 1965 emigrated to Canada and moved to Vancouver, B.C. He continued his work as an engineer at Vancouver Burrard Dry Docks until his retirement in 1986.

Alex and Nancy have three sons Sandy, Colin and Alan, also four grandchildren, all residents of British Columbia. Alex keeps busy and maintains his airforce contacts as Secretary of the Vancouver branch of the Air Crew Association.

F/O HARVEY KYLE
AIR GUNNER R.C.A.F.

Harvey Kyle was born in Regina, Saskatchewan in the year 1924. His first schooling was at Richardson but he was back to Central Collegiate in Regina when he graduated into the working world; getting a job as a clerk with the Saskatchewan Wheat Pool.

One of his favourite boyhood pastimes was shooting gophers, a sport that made him a very good shot and no doubt contributed to Harvey receiving a Proficiency Award at #3 B.& G. at MacDonald, Manitoba, where he had been posted after Manning Pool Brandon and I.T.S. at Winnipeg.

After a short stay at Pennfield Ridge O.T.U., Harvey was posted to 145 Squadron, Dartmouth, N.S. His record on accurate shooting led to his appointment as squadron Gunnery Leader before the squadron was posted to Torbay, Nfd.; at that time he was the ripe old age of 19.

He completed a tour of operations in Atlantic convoy patrols and was posted as gunnery officer to the new #5 O.T.U. at Boundary Bay, B.C., flying on Mitchells and Liberators. However, Harv wanted to get overseas and somehow wangled a posting as rear gunner to one of the crews under training. Many of these men were tour-ex, as was his skipper. The time was the fall of 1944.

All graduating crews were supposed to pick up new aircraft on the East Coast and fly them to India. However, the normal airforce S.N.A.F.U. saw them heading east by boat. First to England and then by one of the slowest old tubs left afloat, the S.S. Orduna, finally arriving at Bombay, India early in 1945. There followed two sessions of O.T.U.s one at Poona and the final one at Kolar Gold Fields in central, southern India. Then it was on to 356 V.L.R.H.B. squadron at Salboni, Bengal, India. Salboni was a delightful place in the boiling Bengal jungle. It had been a prison camp and it was said that life term prisoners had been sent there, for no-one lasted long in that heat. Such details didn't seem to bother the R.A.F.and as entertainment they arranged very long flying trips over Burma and the Kra Isthmus.

As the Liberators were the only aircraft with sufficient range to get well behind the Japanese lines, they were used for all types of work. Mine laying, high and low level bombing, train bashing and bridge destruction, the bridge on the river Kwai being a favourite target. They also ranged far into Thailand and French Indo China, sometimes airdropping supplies to insurgent forces.

When 356 Squadron was posted to Cocos Islands, Harvey and crew were sent to 159 Squadron at Digri to finish their tour.

Several trips stand out in Harvey's memory. In May 1945, one of his first trips was to Point Blair in the Andaman Islands, a well defended navy base of the Japanese. Number 4 engine packed up just short of the identification point, but they elected to continue until #3 engine also started to give trouble; at that point the skipper elected to jettison his bombs and thus endeavour to return to base on two, via the Andaman coast and the Cocos and Preparis Islands. These uninhabited atolls had been supplied with emergency supplies by submarine and were visited regularly to check for any crews that might have ditched and survived to beach on the hard white sand. On the way up the coast they flew over a flotilla of native war canoes. Andaman Islanders were still cannibalist head hunters. Falling into their hands was listed in R.A.F. survival rules, as a hazard!!

Years later Harvey was to read that it was not until 1953 that these people had turned to Christianity; one of their first missionaries after conversion was a young Scot whose grandfather had disappeared while on mission work in the same area. When he asked the old chief if he had any memory of a red headed MacIntosh, a tall highlander, the chief replied, "I remember him well. He was delicious." It was a good thing that they were able to remain airborne and get back to base.

June 17th found the crew searching an area of the infamous Singapore to Bangkok railway looking for targets of opportunity. They located a train which promptly stopped, the crew abandoning their rolling stock to the airforce. Harv had a field day shooting up the goods cars and the locomotive.

Harvey celebrated his first wedding anniversary, July 10th, 1945, in a rather unusual way. They were en route to Bangkok flying at 100 feet over the Gulf of Siam, low to avoid radar detection, when they suddenly found themselves in the midst of a large Japanese fleet. They were given a very warm reception on their bombing runs on the ships. Number four engine was put out of service and several ventilation holes ripped in the fuselage.

On return to base the starboard gear would not lock down. The skipper tried for a go around with the object of a bail out at a safe altitude but could not coax the machine airborne again, the gear collapsed. The craft cartwheeled on its right wing, spinning down the runway towards a storage area holding many gallons of aviation fuel. In Harvey's words, "During the crash, oxygen bottles, sanitary toilet and much other loose gear hurled through the fuselage like balls at a bowling alley. We travelled on our belly for over half a mile while the under belly was being torn off. When we finally came to a halt the aircraft was full of smoke, flames and mist from hydraulic and oxygen systems. We were unable to get to or out of the rear escape hatch; those of us in the rear managed to smash our way out by breaking the starboard window."

Although everyone got out, it was next morning on their way by flat deck truck, to the crash scene, that almost did them in. The truck driver came to a very quick halt at the runway intersection (He later claimed that someone had shouted that an aircraft was approaching), a following truck travelling at about 40 miles an hour, plowed into their rear hurling most of the crew onto the concrete. Harvey never fully recovered from this crash; he had received some injury the night before. After returning to civilian life he was forced into early retirement due to severe back problems. If the Japanese don't get you the R.A.F. will! Harvey thinks that the ground crew were out to get them as they had been flying the newest KN series craft - the pride of the fleet.

In civilian life Harvey worked as a salesman. He, his wife Hazel whom he married in 1944 and their four sons called many places home. Regina, Cleveland, Ohio, Calgary, Penticton, Minneapolis, Minnesota, and finally coming to rest in Burnaby where Harvey retired in '76. They also have 3 grandchildren.

Harvey proudly wears the Atlantic Star, The Burma Star as well as an ops wing and bar along with the 39/45 and War Medals.

H P HALIFAX MkII W7710 405 VANCOUVER SQN

W/O H.E.(BUD) ROBERTSON
PILOT R.A.F.

Bud Robertson was born in Detroit, Michigan, to British parents. His parents returned to England and he was raised at Stroud, Gloucestershire. He attended Marling Secondary School in Stroud.

He was employed by the Sperry Gyroscope Co. as a scientific instrument assembler, prior to volunteering for pilot training with the R.A.F., in August 1941. He started flying training, on Tiger Moths at Fairoaks, Surrey, before being posted to the Southern United States, for training under the American Army Air Force.

Training on Harvards, he received his pilots wings at Craig Field, Alabama.

Returning to England, he gained considerably more flying experience on Masters and Hurricanes, before joining an operational squadron - No. 193 - 2nd Tactical Air Force, flying Typhoons in April 1944.

Weather permitting, the operations were conducted daily, dive-bombing railyards and strong points and low level bombing and strafing trains, road convoys and troop concentrations, then returning across the channel, to their field near Bournemouth. Shortly after D-Day the squadron moved over to Normandy, operating from a former wheat field, upon which wire mesh had been laid.

This closer proximity to the actual fighting, allowed individual pilots to make several short trips per day, attacking vehicles and troops on the roads and strong points, designated by army intelligence officers.

The operations most vividly remembered, are those when the aircraft was severely damaged. One such occasion on August 18th, 1944, involved a low level bombing operation to close a railway tunnel, north-east of Port Leveque in Normandy. The Germans had mounted a naval gun on a railway carriage, which was concealed in the tunnel. This gun was then rolled out after dark, to shell ships anchored offshore, unloading supplies. The Typhoons for the first time, were carrying 500 lb. bombs with eleven second delays. Bud was flying No.2, spaced back far enough he hoped, to allow the leader's bombs to explode. The tunnel was very well defended, the tracer shells were just a solid wall of golden chains continually rising. He really wondered how it was humanly possible to get through this withering fire and was saying silent prayers for the leader's bombs to explode. At the last minute, the bombs exploded right in the mouth of the tunnel. Coming in right on the deck he released his bombs and immediately was hit. A cannon shell pierced the wing where the aileron joins, flipping the aircraft on its back and at the same time freezing the joy stick. Wrestling for control, for what seemed an eternity at very little height, the controls miraculously became free and the plane righted, landing safely, after an anxious flight, at base.

Friday, April 13th, 1945, will always be remembered. The Typhoons were now carrying a 1000 lb. under each wing. The operation was to dive bomb some 194 mm coastal guns, that were shelling shipping off Den Helder in the north of Holland. Pulling out of the dive, a shell exploded in the wing fuel tank. Gasoline streamed out, in a long cloud. Why the plane did not explode, as Bud had seen several others do, he will never know. Fortunately there was enough fuel in the reserve tank to just make it back.

He was the recipient of the 1939/45 Star, Aircrew Europe Star and Clasp, Defence Medal and the Victory Medal.

After the war, he covered the south of England and Ireland as a commercial traveller, until emigrating to Canada in 1956. He continued in sales in the Vancouver area until 1961. He then formed his own company, manufacturing aluminum greenhouses and sun rooms. He sold the company and retired in 1986.

He and his wife, Gail, have many interests and commute between their homes in West Vancouver and Victoria.

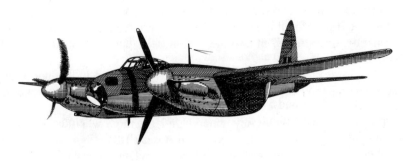

DeHAVILLAND MOSQUITO B.IV

F/LT W.D. THOMSETT
PILOT R.C.A.F.

Wally, as he has been known, (and still is) was born in Vancouver and attended Lord Byng High School, after the usual public school experience at Bayview and Queen Mary. He joined the R.C.A.F. in August 1941 in Vancouver, leaving behind, occupations such as banker, sawmill labourer and logger.

His training began on Tiger Moths, at Portage la Prairie and then on twin engine Cessna Cranes at Yorkton, where he graduated as a Pilot Officer. Shortly afterwards, he went overseas, where he began further training at East Fortune, Scotland, flying Blenheims and Beaufighters. After some time at #2 O.T.U. at Catfoss in Yorkshire on Beaus, he was posted to 404 Squadron at Wick, Scotland and it was there, that he commenced his operational tour. His tour commenced in April 1943 and ended in July 1944. His final rank was that of Flight Lieutenant.

After his tour, Wally became a test pilot for the new Beaufighters, from Bristol and when he passed them as being fit for service, he delivered them to 404 squadron, stationed at Banff, Scotland.

During his tour with the Beaufighters, he estimated that he flew nearly 35 trips, lasting an average of 3 hours and a half. This squadron had approximately 10 to 12 planes at any one time, including several torpedo Beaufighters. The Beaufighter was designed in 1938 as a high performance long range fighter, but it was found to be more useful for night fighting and strike duties. It was a two seater and a very dangerous aircraft, according to Wally; if the pilot had to bail out, the chance that the other crew member would ever get out was zero.

Most of Wally's tour trips were towards Norway, where the enemy had plenty of trouble keeping the iron ore ships and the German naval units as safe as possible. The Germans hated the Beaufighter, calling it "The Whispering Death," but it was not all one sided. Wally's 404 squadron moved to Banff in February 1945, where 6 Beaus were lost during an operation against destroyers and minesweepers, the unit's worst casualties of the war.

One day at East Fortune, Wally was flying a Blenheim Mark IV, practicing single engine landings. On the downward stretch, he cut the starboard engine and lowered the flaps, with wheels ready to turn for the final leg. He realized that he would have to use more power and gain a little more speed, if he was going to finish the exercise and land safely.

He pushed the right throttle forward, to activate the starboard motor, but nothing happened. Apparently it had seized up, as it was very cold that particular day. He then gave full throttle to the port motor, forgetting to pull up the wheels and flaps and at this point, nothing seemed right. If he had let go of the wheel, the aircraft would have immediately flipped upside down, as there was a tremendous pressure being exerted.

He realized, with his heart in his mouth, that he would have to cut the port motor and regain some control of the aircraft and then dive to keep up the airspeed and crash somewhere. This all was happening at 1,000 feet and needless to say, he had still omitted to pull up the wheels and flaps. The ocean looked too ominous to ditch into; the woods in the distance looked quite soft, but he had heard that they weren't quite as soft, when they were crashed into, so he decided on a farmer's field and managed to glide the plane to it. Still forgetting the wheels and flaps, he announced on the radio that he was going to crash. He figured he wanted to die with a bit of a fanfare and just before crashing, he hoped he would be knocked out, as he didn't want to feel a hunk of steel through his body.

At the last moment, he remembered the wheels and flaps and he grabbed the lever to release the locking mechanism and when he eventually hit the ground, the wheels were pushed partly into the aircraft. No doubt he would not have been able to recall this, if he had not released the lock. As it was, the plane was a real mess, but he was fortunate enough not to be injured. To top it all, he also forgot to switch off the ignition switches, which, of course, is one of the first things one learns to do, in case of crash landing.

In June 1943, Wally was escorting a motor torpedo boat from the Norwegian coast; he was flying a Beau Mark II and heading back to the Orkney Islands. The Norwegian boat crew had sneaked into a fiord and hidden there for a few days; at daybreak they had slipped out, sunk a ship and then were heading home. On such occasions, they usually asked for an escort, particularly if they had suffered any damage. Wally escorted them out of range and headed back to the Islands from where the flight had originated.

He was flying just above the waves, when he spotted an aircraft heading for the Norwegian coast at about 500 feet; the cloud base was about 800 feet. Wally knew it must be an enemy aircraft as their own squadron planes, flying to Norway, never flew higher than 50 feet, so he flew up into the clouds and turned to follow the plane, which turned out to be a JU 88. As Wally crept closer he would drop out of the clouds and then climb back up

312

again, until, finally he was in a good firing position and he opened up for 12 long seconds, his four 20 mm cannons. The enemy was soon aware of this and their turret gunner opened fire on Wally. The JU 88 also began to climb up into the clouds, however, before reaching the safety of the cloud cover, black smoke was seen, also flames from the engines. Wally did not wait to see the result of this encounter and turned for home. Air Ministry gave him a "probable" for this episode.

With all the excitement of the chase and guns going off and smoke in the cockpit etc., Wally didn't notice, until on the way home, that something almost funny had happened. Very close to the right side of his head in the cockpit was a familiar necessity. This was the metal cup, attached to a rubber bag, just in case one had to relieve oneself during flight. He could never imagine trying to use it at 50 feet above the North Sea, especially with the parachute and seatbelt straps criss crossing him like a tight girdle!!

This is what had happened. A bullet from the JU 88 had entered the windshield and severed the rubber bag from the metal cup and the bag had fallen on his shoulder. He still has the dented cup and the bullet, as a reminder of how close he came to being knocked off by one stray bullet!!

Wally had gone overseas on the liner "Queen Elizabeth" (93,000 tons) late in 1942, landing at Greenock, Scotland. He and the rest of the passengers took all night on a blacked out train, to reach the seaside resort of Bournemouth, on the south coast of England. They were then billeted in a hotel, which had been taken over by the R.A.F. The first night, as they were trying to figure out what the little bits were, floating in the warm beer, the radio was playing. Soon a voice which grew familiar to them announced "Jairmany calling, Jairmany calling" (Yes, it was the notorious 'Lord Haw Haw'). He then said "We know you arrived in Bournemouth today and we suggest you go back where you came from." This seemed rather strange and uncanny, since they had been very secretive about their whereabouts. However, trying to swallow the warm beer and not the little bits floating about,seemed more important at the time.

Later in the spring of 1943, on the squadron at Wick, Northern Scotland, they were again flying Beaufighters armed with the 4 x 20 mm cannon and four high explosive rockets, as well as four armour piercing rockets. Their task was to sink German ships off the Norwegian coast. After hours, there wasn't much to do, except sit around and booze it up, or play pool or bridge, or listen to the radio. Around 10 or 10.30 p.m. the B.B.C would wish everybody, in a very British fashion, a very goodnight and then sign off.

Within moments, the swinging sounds of Tommy Dorsey, Glen Miller and others would hit the air waves. In between the songs, the announcer would say "This is Germany calling" and he hoped they would enjoy the music. Then came the news report about an attack made by enemy aircraft that day, off the Norwegian coast. Invariably, they would indicate there was no damage to their ships, but always that several R.C.A.F. planes had been shot down. The facts always seemed to be distorted in favour of the Germans.

Wally would listen to this garbage and realized that the Germans must be believing they were breaking the R.C.A.F. boys' spirits, with their apparent ability to tell them all about what was happening.

However, this had quite the opposite effect, for instead of getting upset, they considered the Germans to be stupid, arrogant and lacking a sense of humour.

For his services during the war, Wally earned the 1939/45 Star, Atlantic Star, C.V.S.M. and Clasp, War Medal and Defence Medal. He was discharged in Vancouver in 1945.

Wally was married, but divorced and has two children and 2 grandchildren.

In civvy street again, he worked in the parts department for General Motors, then as a car salesman, neon sign salesman and eventually was in real estate.

W/O WILLIAM (BILL) CARROLL
WIRELESS AIR GUNNER R.A.F.

Bill Carroll was born in London, England, receiving his early public education there, and later attended Borough Polytechnic and Westminster Technical College where he received vocational training. During his early years in London, Bill was an enthusiastic player in soccer and cricket. He became employed in the engineering field.

Carroll joined the R.A.F.V.R. in London in October 1940. He completed his wireless course at Yatesbury in Wiltshire and his gunnery course at Dumfries in Scotland in May 1941. Two months later he finished his O.T.U. training at Chivenor and was posted to #217 Squadron in September 1941.

He joined the crew of Flying Officer Arthur H. Aldridge whose aircraft was a Beaufort. Two other crew members were Sergeant Vincent Aspinall, the navigator, and oldest at thirty years, and Sergeant Alan Still, a wireless operator/air gunner who with Bill Carroll was twenty-one.

Number 217 Squadron had been posted to Ceylon to counter the threat of the Japanese Navy in the Bay of Bengal and the Indian Ocean. En route, however, the squadron was asked to defend two British convoys being attacked by ships of the Italian Navy. The Beaufort squadron had left Portreath in Cornwall, equipped with long range fuel tanks, and on leaving Gibraltar had flown across the Mediterranean, one of the aircraft was attacked by an Me 109, and one of its wireless operators/air gunners was killed by a cannon shell. It was in the middle of June 1942 that its fifteen Beauforts finally arrived in Malta.

On June 15th, nine Beaufort crews including that of Bill Carroll's were ordered to take-off and attack the Italian ships. The aircraft left base at 04.00 hours on a dark and starry morning. As F/O Aldridge was taxiing out of the dispersal area his plane became blocked by another Beaufort having engine trouble. Carroll's crew had to wait twenty minutes before being cleared for take-off. This unfortunate delay meant that this plane could not fly as planned in formation with the others. Once airborne, the navigator suggested that they head straight for the approved point of intersection by themselves. As day dawned, a line of four ships was barely visible ahead, with four smaller vessels protecting their flanks. The pilot decided to move in from the dark side of the sky and dropped down to one thousand feet and altered his course accordingly. Since none of the other Beauforts had arrived it was decided that an attack should be made. Gunners were asked to hold their fire temporarily as they had not been seen by the enemy ships. As he turned into the attack the pilot decreased height further to eighty feet and cruising at 140 knots swept across the bow of the first destroyer. Carroll said later that they came so close he could have thrown a bottle on its deck. Eight hundred yards out from the cruiser, the pilot released the torpedo. After the aircraft was swung across the bow of the cruiser, the aircrew observed a great spout of water with fire and debris shooting up from the bow of the stricken vessel. Carroll watching the plume rise from the ship shouted, "We've blown the bows off her!"

Suddenly aroused, the warships opened up with a heavy barrage of tracer fire towards the Beaufort. Evasive action was taken and because of this skillful action, the Italian ships did not score a hit on the aircraft. Looking back at the damaged ship, Carroll thought the ships suddenly seemed to be firing in all directions. He had not seen that the other Beauforts had just arrived on the scene. The Italian ships were turning sharply to avoid torpedoes and were firing at the aircraft. The pilot now turned and headed for base and eventually made it safely back to the airdrome.

Maintenance crews were anxiously awaiting for news of the attack when they landed and became excited to hear that a cruiser had been hit. Carroll walked with his crew back to the Operations Room; all were feeling satisfied with the attack. The crew, however, were shocked to hear that they had to take off again that same day for another operation.

In spite of the attack on the Italian fleet, the westbound British convoy could not complete its journey to Malta. With two of their merchantmen bombed and sunk, three destroyers and a cruiser lost from aerial or U-Boat attacks, the plans for refuelling at Malta were fading. The convoy turned back to Alexandria, and the Italian fleet to Taranto. Nine Beauforts took off at 19.30 hours on the same day, the 15th of June, to hunt for the retreating Italian fleet, but the search proved to be in vain. The Beauforts returned to their base after five and a half hours of night flying. It is to be noted here that the Italian Navy never again put to sea as a fleet.

The convoy from Gibraltar continued to Malta in spite of losing three of its five merchantmen. Number 217 Squadron could at this time have continued to Ceylon but because of the conditions at Malta stayed for a few weeks, being detained at Luqa.

An enemy convoy had left Naples in Italy bound for Tripoli in Libya with war materials for Rommel's Afrika Korps. At 11.15 hours, nine Beauforts of #217 Squadron took off from Malta to attack this target and were escorted by six Beaufighters of #235 Squadron. Bill's pilot, with his own crew and aircraft, Beaufort I, was flying on the left side formation and carried an eighteen inch Mark XII torpedo. The Beauforts flew very low over the sea but at differing heights. As they came into sight of the ships, heavy fire surrounded them. At one point, Bill Carroll shouted to his pilot to dive to starboard as they were on a collision course.

His skipper took violent action immediately, just as another Beaufort slid beneath at water level just missing them. As they turned again they had to fly through a wall of flak, but their torpedo run was made in spite of the heavy fire from the ships.

As they flew across the bow of a merchantman and released the torpedo from a distance of seven hundred and fifty yards, the Beaufort was struck by four cannon shells. The 20mm shells severed the starboard aerilons cables and both the navigator and the pilot were wounded. In spite of this, the pilot managed to check the aircraft's descent before it could hit the sea, by increasing the throttle setting. The Beaufort gradually climbed and began to fly straight and level. The wireless operator opened a first aid kit and tended to the wounded.

A few minutes later a Beaufort was seen being attacked by a Junkers 88, and Aldridge, in spite of wounds, shouted that he was going in to help out and asked Carroll to be ready with guns. Carroll opened fire and saw black smoke pouring out from the port engine of the Junkers, when suddenly another Beaufighter swooped down and sent the enemy plane crashing into the sea. It was now time to head for base. With the ASI damaged, the pilot called for help from his navigator, who then read out the airspeeds, and the Beaufort, though crippled, landed safely and soon rolled down the runway at Luqa.

Bill Carroll went on later to Ceylon and finished another tour of operations with #203 Squadron on Liberators in the Far East.

Carroll was discharged in London in April 1946. He received the 1939-45 Star, the Atlantic Star, the Africa Star, the Burma Star, the Victory Medal and the Defence Medal.

In 1947, Bill Carroll married Brenda, a W.A.A.F., and has two boys and two girls, with eight grandchildren.

Bill emigrated to Canada later and became president of an engineering company that bears his name. He now resides in West Vancouver.

F/O GRANT MCDONALD
R.C.A.F. AIR GUNNER

Grant McDonald was born in Grand Forks, B.C. He attended Elementary and Secondary Schools in Grand Forks and Penticton, B.C. Upon leaving school in 1940 he enlisted in the Canadian Army where he served until June 1941, when he re-enlisted in the R.C.A.F. in Toronto, Ontario.

He was sent to #21 E.F.T.S. at Chatham, N.B. flying in Fleet Finches, but was unsuccessful in pilot training. He completed an air gunners course at #4 B & G school in Fingal, Ontario. Following a refresher gunnery course in the U.K. he was posted to #19 O.T.U. at Kinloss, Scotland, where he crewed up with the pilot Ken Brown, whose profile appears elsewhere in this book. On completion of O.T.U. the crew were posted to St. Eval, Cornwall, for anti-submarine sweeps on Whitley V's. Following conversion to Lancasters at Wigsley, the all N.C.O. crew was posted to #44 Squadron, R.A.F. Bomber Command, #5 Group, at Waddington, Lincs.

On an extremely cold night in March 1943, while on a trip to Berlin, the pilot who was in the target area, checked on the intercom with the rear turret and failed to get any response. The wireless operator went back to check and discovered that McDonald had not fallen asleep but had passed out from want of Oxygen. Condensation from breathing had frozen solid in the oxygen mask supply hose cutting off the supply of oxygen. This resulted in a severe headache for several days afterwards.

In late March 1943, McDonald and the crew were posted to #617 Squadron, R.A.F., which was being formed at Scampton, Lincs, for the purpose of destroying the Ruhr Dams. After six weeks of intensive low level flying, navigation, bombing and gunnery exercises, the operation took place on the nights of May 16/17, 1943. Nineteen planes under the leadership of Wing Commander Guy Gibson carried out the attack on the three dams, which had held back hundreds of thousands gallons of water, needed for the German industry.

The very special bombs which had been designed by B.N. Wallis, a Vickers Armstrong scientist, were to be dropped and bounced or rolled along the surface of the water until they hit the dam wall, then sink, to explode against the dam. Many experiments had been carried out by Gibson and Wallis, but these showed that the casings of the bombs, which were ball shaped, broke into bits even if they were dropped from as low as one hundred fifty feet. Two weeks before the operation, however, further experimentation revealed that if the bombs were dropped from sixty feet, they would not disintegrate. The Lancaster with bomb load weighed over sixty thousand pounds and it required the greatest skill to keep the aircraft this low over calm waters, in almost total darkness.

The Ministry of Aircraft Production installed miniature searchlights on the fuselage of each Lancaster, and set them at an angle so that the beams would intersect at exactly sixty feet below the aircraft. This meant that the pilot had to fly the plane by making certain the crossed beams lay on the surface as he made his bombing run.

The first wave of planes led by Gibson attacked the Moehne Dam and it was breached. Gibson then led his three other planes, which each had a bomb load, to the Eder Dam, which also was successfully breached, although one plane dropped its bomb on top of the dam and the resulting explosion destroyed the plane itself.

The Sorpe Dam was the objective of Grant McDonald's crew, in the second wave, and considerable damage resulted, although the dam was not breached. On his return to base from this operation Gibson was awarded the Victoria Cross. Grant saw two aircraft from his group, hit by anti-aircraft fire explode and burn. There was little chance of survival at this low altitude in anti-aircraft fire that was so close and intense. His aircraft was flying so low, that it was possible to see trees horizontally silhouetted against the searchlights. The front gunner, (no mid-upper turret on these aircraft), and McDonald, fired continually at the searchlight and gun positions.

Of the thirty Canadians who took part in this operation, Grant McDonald is one of nine still alive. He concluded his tour with #617 Squadron with attacks on specific targets such as factories, viaducts, power stations, and rocket launching sites. Also included was temporary assignment to Tempsford for two operations of a different type, the dropping of arms to resistance fighters in occupied territory. At the end of March 1944, he was posted to #29 O.T.U. at Bruntingthorpe for instructional duties. He was repatriated to Canada in the spring of 1945, and received his discharge at Vancouver, B.C. in June 1945.

He was the recipient of the R.C.A.F. Ops Wing, the 1939/45 Star, the Aircrew Europe Star, the Defence Medal, the C.V.S.M. and Clasp, and the War Medal.

Grant was married in 1948 to Marge and has worked for many years in the Customs Department of the Federal Government. He took early retirement in 1976 and lives with his wife in Vancouver. They have no children.

FL/SGT R.B. "RON" SIMPSON
NAVIGATOR R.A.F.

Ronald Bell Simpson was born in London, England. He still has early memories of watching tug boats and shipping along the Chelsea embankment on the River Thames. The family moved to Wembley, Middlesex where he attended public and secondary schools, which he remembers as five miserable years, with no personal success either athletically or academically.

For religious views, when the second world war started, he registered as a conscientious objector, but in 1941 gave up his pacifism and tried to join the Fleet Air Arm. He was rejected for inadequate education, but was accepted for flying duties with the Royal Air Force and was called up in August 1942. With his large feet, the R.A.F. had to get footwear, including "escape" boots custom made, which resulted in him being excused marching duties. In Ron's opinion, the R.A.F. could not afford shoe leather, nor the lag time in replacing worn out shoes, so with the exception of attending pay parades, he went everywhere by bicycle.

He went through the usual courses, I.T.W. and E.F.T.S. in Cambridge, then to Heaton Park for Navigator/Wireless training for Mosquito aircraft. At Heaton Park he contacted measles, which delayed posting until July 1943, but since he never could take Morse, he failed radio school and was reclassified as a Navigator. In March 1944 he was sent to St. Jean, P.Q., Canada to take his navigators course at No. 9 A.O.S. He caught athletes foot, was hospitalized for six weeks, but eventually graduated in September 1944.

Most of the R.C.A.F. instructors at No. 9 A.O.S. were bi-lingual, and students included Free French, Norwegians, Poles and other non-commonwealth allies. Ron remembers in training how they were never lost, since the staff pilots flying Ansons knew the country well and track crawled everywhere, despite navigating students' instructions.

After graduating, he returned to England, just before Christmas 1944 and was posted to Dumfries and to other stations for familiarization courses in Wellingtons, Lancasters, DC-3's and Yorks. Ron did not see Squadron or Operational service at any time. His principal memory of R.A.F. life was humping kit-bags through main-line railway terminals.

He emigrated to Canada immediately upon discharge and worked on various engineering projects across Canada, principally Hydro-electric developments and Defence construction.

In December 1977, Ron married Carla Carlsen (Australian), then secretary to the Australian Trade Commission in Vancouver. He retired at the end of 1982 and moved to White Rock, B.C. in 1985 where he still resides. Ron's interests and hobbies are golf, fishing and outdoor sports, listening to classical music and playing contract bridge. He brews his own beer and keeps busy as secretary of 804 (Semiahmoo) Wing R.C.A.F.A. and maintains membership in other associated airforce clubs.

F/LT RICHARD A. CONLIN
WAG & PILOT R.C.A.F.

R.A. Conlin was born in Trail, British Columbia on August 31, 1917. He attended Drumheller Public and High Schools in Alberta. He studied to be an electrician taking an international correspondence course to do so. Con was active in sports and was a hockey player for the Drumheller Rockets and the Drumheller Minor teams. He also coached Little League baseball for eight years.

Can you imagine a young fellow who was an apprentice in Drumheller, Alberta travelling the big highway to Calgary and hearing on his car radio all about the war being declared in Europe? He immediately turned his car around and drove to the nearest recruiting office.

As a result, one year later he was on guard duty in Dartmouth, Nova Scotia, standing in the rain making funny motions with his rifle! He then attended the British Empire Training Scheme and graduated as a Wireless Air Gunner.

Time passed and eventually he was on a ship to England, full of expectancy of what the future held for him. By the time they landed in Scotland he had lost all his money in a poker game and was forced to spend his leave in Bournemouth, hanging around the barracks due to lack of funds. The Commanding Officer (bless his soul) determined that this Conlin fellow must be a keen type and therefore posted him directly to an operating squadron, along with nine others, bypassing O.T.U.

He was then posted to 407 Squadron at Bircham Newton, England. His first operation was mine laying in the North Sea, a very scary job and "Con" in his ignorance reported to the captain of the aircraft that the port engine was on fire! This caused much consternation but turned out to be only the exhaust. So much for his first operational flight!

The task of 407 Squadron was shipping strikes, which they excelled at.

321

The Hudsons would go in at mast height and skip bomb, always with the element of surprise, where possible.

On one operation, arriving at the German coast, they spotted a large ship, through the mist and rain at about 8 p.m. A standard run was made on it and at the last second they noticed a large red cross and decided it was a hospital ship and refrained from dropping their load. The price for this mistake proved costly, as after passing over the ship, ten or more flak ships greeted them, lighting up the sky and really "peppering" them. The aircraft was full of holes and barely made it back, landing at a "Q" site which completely destroyed their "S" for sugar.

On a cloudy, rainy day at 10 a.m. on February 12, 1942 they were rounded up and told to report to Operations room where they learned that the "Scharnhorst" and "Gneisenau" had departed from their port and were escaping up the English Channel into the North Sea. Instructions were given to head them off and act as a decoy so that the "Swordfish" aircraft could attack with their torpedoes. After much milling around and false starts they were finally off and headed to a point where the battleships might be.

A layer of cloud at 1,000 feet hid their formation of three Hudsons and they made contact through the use of A.S.V. (Anti Submarine Viewing). Many aircraft were above them, friendly and otherwise. They were in the middle of a formation of three with heavy flak all around them, when the aircraft on the right took a hit and disappeared. The aircraft on their left suddenly left the formation and they dropped lower, releasing their 4 - 250 pound bombs (which couldn't even dent a tugboat), then scooted back into the clouds and made it back to base.

Bob's two good friends, flying alongside of him were posted as missing.

The Hudson, though a converted civilian air liner, could, and did, take a lot of punishment. Their Hudson "S" for Sugar had 27 shrapnel holes in it.

At the end of ten months and thirty five operations later, only eight of the original members of 407 Squadron survived. Shipping strikes had taken a heavy toll.

In spite of all of this, "Con" survived and was posted back to Canada as a Radar Instructor, airborne, on mid Atlantic sweeps. These were performed flying in Hudsons, Digbys, Venturas and Cansos. He saw his share of sinkings and hardships by these boat crews, which left an unforgettable impression.

During the last year of the war he applied for pilot training, graduated and joined Transport Command in 1945. He made many friends throughout the years and they remain so to this day.

"Con" received his honourable discharge at Calgary, Alberta in September, 1945. He received the 1939-45 Star, Atlantic Star and Clasp, Aircrew Europe Star and Clasp, Defence Medal, Canadian Volunteer Service Medal and Bar and War Medal.

After his discharge he became the owner and manager of an electrical contracting company in Vancouver, British Columbia. "Con and his wife

322

Rita (nee Tuffley) have been married for 47 years and have three sons, Rick, Bill, and Leigh and one daughter Jo-Anne.

KARL W.KJARSGAARD
PILOT

Karl is the only associate member of the Vancouver branch and is such by special authority of the Branch Executive. Karl was not wartime aircrew and of course is not entitled to full membership in the A.C.A. He is very interested in research and restoration of WW II aircraft and is currently investigating the crash of a Halifax in a loch in Ireland. He has been a valuable asset to the branch in programming of videos, many of these unavailable to the general public. For his service to the Branch, the Editorial committee asked Karl to submit a profile, which we are glad to include.

Karl was born in Moose Jaw, Sask. and educated at Queen Elizabeth School, Prince Albert, thence to Semiahmoo Senior Secondary School, White Rock, B.C. He then attended Selkirk College of Aviation Technology at Castlegar, B.C. and had two years flight training (Private, Commercial, Instrument, Licenses).

He was always interested in antique aircraft of W.W.II and spent some time on research and restoration of aircraft such as the Halifax, Hurricane and Spitfire. His interest also included antique cars. Other than those fascinating hobbies, hockey and curling kept him fit. In 1971 he graduated from College, had two years of bush flying in the Arctic and North West Territories and was hired by Canadian Pacific Airlines in 1974. His father, James, was a trucker, also an antique aircraft pilot, while his mother was a Doctor of Education (Music).

Ever since Karl was three years old, he was fascinated by aircraft flying around and during the ten years he spent in Moose Jaw, the craft he saw more of, were Harvards, the primary trainer of the '50's and he remembers the snarl of their props and engines as they passed overhead.

When he was sixteen, he drove to Vancouver Airport and there found a B25 Mitchell abandoned in a far corner of the tarmac. It was going to be scrapped, according to some people Karl talked to, so he wrote a letter to "Air Classics" in the hope that someone might have influence to save the WW II bomber.

Some months later, Karl had a letter from Oregon, in which the sender indicated he would like to purchase the Mitchell and would Karl like to help prepare the B25 for a ferry flight? Karl was very keen and spent many hours helping to get the aircraft ready. He even found the log books of the Mitchell in downtown Vancouver, which were most helpful in the preparation of the proposed flight. Finally, after months of work, the aircraft was pronounced fit to fly and it took off from Vancouver Airport and Karl felt that he had helped save a fine old bomber for others to see and appreciate.

During his flight training years, he worked the summers of 1970/71 for the B.C. Forest Service and then was based at Castlegar and Cranbrook in Grumman TBM Avengers, where he worked as a loader of fire bombers, (pumping fire retardant into each bomber) as each Avenger would pull up to the loading point. They were dry summers and the seasoned pilots taught Karl a lot even though he was a "sprog" pilot.

Karl received his private pilot instruction by one of "The Few", Sqdn.Ldr. Allan J.A. Laing, an honour he will always cherish. Laing was a Flight Commander with 64 Squadron at Church Fenton, Yorkshire.

During the Spring of 1972, Karl received his multi-engine rating from an inspector by the name of Ken Brown. Flight Sergeant, later Squadron Leader, K.W. Brown (whose profile appears elsewhere) who had piloted Lancaster "F for Freddie" when it dropped the famous Wallis bomb on the Sorpe dam in Germany. During Karl's short time with Ken Brown, in the training aircraft, he felt the strong influence of Ken's character and gained insight as to what it takes to be a good pilot and have the drive to complete a mission.

Karl felt that to be in the company of, and receive the flying knowledge from such a man, has been one of the greatest gifts a pilot of his generation could obtain.

He now flies Boeing 727's and 737's for Canadian Airlines International.

F/L ART (EDDIE) EDWARDS
PILOT - R.C.A.F.

Art, or "Eddie" as he was known during his airforce days was born at Sandbach, Cheshire, England in 1918, but was brought to Canada by his widowed mother in 1920. His mother married again to a C.P.R. station agent who couldn't seem to live in one place for long. As a result Art attended eight different schools in Manitoba and northern Ontario, getting through elementary and high schools. Art tried to follow the lead of several friends who had gone to England on cattle boats to join the R.A.F. Although he applied for admission to the R.C.A.F. immediately after the outbreak of war, it was December 1940 before he was finally accepted for aircrew training at Winnipeg.

There followed the usual sequence of pilot training: guard duty at Mossbank, Sask, then I.T.S. and elementary flying training in Regina, then graduation as a sergeant pilot after a course on Cessna Cranes at Saskatoon.

Following wings award, the next posting was to Summerside, P.E.I. for a General Reconnaissance course in D.R. and astro navigation, and sundry other subjects to fit a pilot for flying long range anti-submarine patrols. At the completion of the course the chief instructor advised Art that as his navigation marks were low, he was only considered fit to fly Beaufighters, and would so endorse his records. As this was exactly what Art had been hoping for, he found it rather hard to appear properly humble.

From Summerside everyone went to Halifax "Y" Depot and then in an overcrowded transport to Liverpool, then via sealed train to Bournemouth. From there, after two weeks of lectures and "shots", he was posted to the first of two Beaufighter O.T.U.'s. It wasn't a single engine fighter, but with two big engines, four 20mm cannon and six machine guns it was, at least, a fighter. The first O.T.U. at East Fortune in Scotland let him fly Blenheims for a while, a beautiful, docile aircraft, followed by ten hours in Beaufighter Mk IIs with Merlin engines. Because of the design of the Beau and its lack of operational equipment, the tendency to swing on takeoff was frightening, particularly to sprog pilots. Indeed

325

when the student pilots were sent out for their first solos on type, the whole station turned out to watch, and had they been filmed, these first solo takeoffs would have made some of the most exciting film footage of the war!

Following completion of training at the advanced O.T.U. at Catfoss in Yorkshire, he was posted to 404 Canadian squadron, then doing fighter sweeps into the Bay of Biscay out of Chivenor in Devonshire. This was an interesting combat area as R.A.F. long range patrol bombers hunted German submarines, Ju 88 fighters hunted the bombers, Beaufighters hunted the Ju 88s, and long range FW 190s hunted the Beaufighters. Soon 404 squadron was transferred north to Tain and then to Wick to convert to the new Mk X and XI Beaufighters, and search for German convoys along the Norwegian coast. Soon afterwards, three all-Canadian crews arrived on 404 squadron which meant that three mixed crews with Canadian pilots and English Navigator/Wireless Ops had to be transferred elsewhere. Art, with his English navigator, Ted Pope, was transferred to North Coates in Lincs, to 236 squadron which was part of the shipping strike wing composed of 236 and 143 fighter Beaus, and 254 torpedo Beaus.

The wing was going through a series of tactical changes to try to find the way to do the most damage to the huge German convoys that were bringing Swedish iron ore down the coast, and at the same time keep Beaufighter losses to an acceptable level. A typical wing strike had 143 squadron armed with cannon, 236 squadron armed with cannon and 8 rockets, and 254 squadron armed with cannon and torpedoes. The wing was escorted to and from the convoy by Johnny Johnson's Canadian Spitfire wing which was responsible for eliminating the convoy's fighter escort of Me 109s or FW 190s. Losses incurred, averaged 2 aircraft out of 36. Unfortunately, these losses represented only part of the casualties incurred as the squadrons had to fly 3 sorties per day searching for convoys, and a high attrition rate ensued. This campaign which lasted from early 1943 until the end of the war, is studied by staff colleges, and played out by War Games buffs. It has been well researched and written up by Roy Nesbit in his book called "The Strike Wings".

Early in 1944, an incident occurred that affected Art's character for the rest of his life. While leading an aircraft section in a diving attack on a German escort ship, a 20mm shell hit the aircraft armoured windscreen leaving it totally opaque, while another hit a propeller blade, making it necessary to shut down the starboard engine. The Spitfire escort lost him, so it was necessary to fly home alone, at low level without being able to see forward. He decided during the next hour, that if he ever got the aircraft back to base, and on the ground in one piece, that nothing that could ever happen after that would be worth worrying about. Whenever anything unpleasant occurred in later years, this memory always recurred.

In April of 1944, while taking off for a training mission, an engine failed. The aircraft hit a seawall at the end of the runway, and Art spent the next six months in various hospitals and rehab centres. At the end of this period he was declared tour expired by 236 squadron and posted to Bircham Newton, Beaufighter and Mosquito Unit as a test and ferry pilot, and six months later was repatriated to Canada. The last few months of the war were spent flying student navigators out of Rivers,

Man. and taking an armament officer's course at Mountainview, Ont. Eddie was discharged after the war in Vancouver, September '45 with the rank of F/Lt and earned the following medals;- 39/45 Star, Atlantic Star, C.V.S.M. and clasp and the War and Defence Medals. He attended U.B.C. for one year and became a sales manager.

In 1951, following the outbreak of hostilities in Korea, he was back flying again, first a refresher course on Harvards, followed by three years in Winnipeg as station test pilot for the C-45 fleet. This was followed by another three years on 435 squadron out of Edmonton on C-119s (Boxcars). At the end of the tour with 435 squadron he was able to satisfy a long standing ambition and fly jets for a while.

Out of the R.C.A.F. in 1958, and through with military aviation for good, he spent the next six years establishing a new career in manufacturing, while keeping a senior commercial pilot's licence current. With a civilian career well established he spent the next eight years giving private flying lessons, and teaching aerobatics in a Chipmunk at Pitt Meadows airport, finally retiring from flying altogether in 1972.

He married his wife, Lee in 1945 after returning from overseas and they have two children, Terry and Michele.

MALCOLM F. (BILL) GRAY D.F.M., C.D.
PILOT R.C.A.F.

Malcolm, or Bill as he was known, was born in Edmonton, Alberta and graduated from Daniel McIntyre High School in Winnipeg where the family had moved to earlier. His hobbies were golfing, model building and gardening, and after graduation he became a salesman.

Joining the R.C.A.F. in May 1942, Bill volunteered to be a pilot where he was posted to several stations including #8 E.F.T.S. Sea Island, B.C. on Tiger Moths, #3 S.F.T.S. Calgary on Ansons then to England to #12 A.F.U. Grantham on Oxfords. By now it was July 1942 and he was posted to Wellesbourne/ Stratford on Wellingtons 1C; then to Topcliffe, Yorks on Wimpey Mk3's where the squadron converted to Halifax Mk 2's and they moved again to Middleton-St-George, Durham where 419 squadron became operational again as a 6th group squadron. Bill finished his tour in July 1943 completing 28 ops, after which he had a "Cooks tour" of stations too numerous to list. He then went back to Canada in Nov 1944 for a month's leave, returning to England in Jan 1945 to take training for "Tiger Force". However, the war was ending and he returned to Canada being discharged in Dec. 45 at Vancouver.

He rejoined the R.C.A.F. in Jan 1952 with rank of F/O and was posted to #3 F.T.S. Calgary for a refresher course on Harvards. Bill was then sent to Trenton, then to Claresholm spending the next two years instructing N.A.T.O. students on Harvards. After a jet course he instructed again, on the T-33 jet aircraft at #3 A.F.S. Gimli and in Oct. 1957 he was posted to #1 P.S.U.(0) London, Ont.

In Oct. 1961 Bill received his last posting in the R.C.A.F. to Lincoln Park, Calgary where he ferried various aircraft in use at the time, such as the T-33, C-45, C-47, Harvard, Otter etc., mostly around western Canada with the occasional trip overseas. He finally retired from the R.C.A.F. in Jan. 1964.

His medals include the D.F.M., '39/45 Star, Aircrew Europe Star, War Medal, Defence Medal, C.V.S.M. & clasp and the Canadian Forces Decoration (C.D.) He retired as F/Lt. Since his airforce retirement Bill has been self-employed as a Manufacturers agent.

He married Nancy, who died in 1976 and married Eileen in 1977. He has three sons and four grand-children from his first marriage, also one step-son, two step-daughters and five other grand-children.

Just after midnight on Sept 15, 1942, Bill and his crew took off on a raid to Bremen flying a brand new Wellington 1C, carrying four 500lb bombs. They were part of a course of 15 bomber crews, under training and this was their second op, having gone to Dusseldorf two nights before, bombing the target and managing to return in one piece. A third of the way home, 8000 ft above the North Sea, they ran into trouble as a German night fighter got his chance for an attack unobserved. From very close dead astern he fired a two to three second burst from about 4 guns then passed about 20 feet over Wellington "E" for Easy, slightly to the port side and the silhouette clearly showed it to be a Ju 88. Gray commenced evasive action, going into a steep diving turn and the Ju 88 pilot probably was certain that he had a kill. However he destroyed the port tailplane and the hydraulic system in the port wing. The Wimpey was badly damaged but the engines were O.K. and it was still flyable, although much slower and harder to control. With the help of the W.O.P. Gordie Low and Nav. Chuck Hancock they arrived back at base about 5 a.m. and, with no hydraulics, Gray made a wheels up landing on one of the runways, but the Wellington was a write-off.

Several days later the crew was posted to 419 Sqdn. at Topcliffe, Yorks to fly Halifax's. In Feb. 1943 the squadron was ordered to send 8 aircraft on a mine-laying trip to the Frisian Islands, off the N.W. coast of Germany. This was to be Gray's 12th op. with three members of his original Wimpey crew plus 3 new members. Descending from about 6,000 feet they flew directly over a Flak ship at about 1,000 feet, which opened fire and hit their aircraft "P" Peter in the port wing with light anti-aircraft red and green tracer shells. They stayed on their mine laying run, however, dropping the two mines on target, but climbing away from target, on a heading for base it was soon obvious that the port inner engine was badly damaged and in fact no longer serviceable, so it was feathered. It was then discovered that the hydraulic system had also been damaged, and it was not possible to either close the bomb doors or open the radiator shutters on the 3 remaining engines. Fifteen or twenty minutes later the port engine (outer) failed and was shut down. At this time at 3,000 feet, in order to maintain height with the bomb doors open the two starboard engines had to be opened up to almost full power and they began to overheat. Losing altitude rapidly, and flying below 1,000 feet and just above stalling speed, Bill gave the order to take up ditching positions and ordered the W.O.P. to send out an S.O.S., with their position. They successfully ditched at 9p.m. about 100 miles east of Hull. Gray discovered that the landing light in the vertical position was a great help in judging the height above the water, just before touching down.

At the last minute, Gray jettisoned the escape hatch at the same time closing the throttles and cutting the switches to the starboard engines. The Halifax hit the water in a tail down wings level position at about 100 mph, catching the tail wheel first.

The second impact a few seconds later was much more severe, but brought the aircraft to a stop. Bill lost consciousness for several minutes from the shock of the landing and coming to, was sitting in ice cold water, waist high. Climbing out of the top hatch he saw that the dinghy had inflated successfully and the crew had already managed to climb out and on to the semi submerged wing and were preparing to board the dinghy. After they got aboard and were drifting away, the aircraft was still floating. They settled down for a long, wet night but they actually spent 22 hours in the dinghy before being picked up by 2 R.A.F. Torpedo Boats at 7p.m.

After a short stay in the Naval Hospital at Grimsby, Gray and his crew were back on their way by train to the squadron at Middleton-St-George to continue their operational tour.

Nine months later they evened the score. Returning from a raid on Bochum at night, they encountered an enemy fighter in the early morning hours near the Dutch coast; this time they had the advantage and the enemy pilot did not see them. Gray's rear gunner F/O Russ Harling shot it down in flames. It was later confirmed as a Ju 88 night fighter.

F/O C. ROBERT JONES D.F.C.
PILOT R.C.A.F.

Bob Jones was born in Regina, Sask, on November 12th 1921. His family moved to Vancouver in 1928 and lived directly across the road from the Vancouver Airport which was situated on Lulu Island. There, Bob witnessed the first airmail service, Vancouver to Seattle, and fell in love with aviation. He attended schools on Lulu Island and in Vancouver.

In 1939 he rode a freight train as far as Saskatoon and went to work on a farm not far from Regina. When war was declared he applied to join the R.C.A.F. in Regina but was told to go to Vancouver to enlist. In June 1940 he tried to enlist in the Seaforth Highlanders but was told to go home as he was under age. A bit wiser, he went a few blocks up the street and enlisted in the Royal Canadian Artillery and in 1941 he transferred to the R.C.A.F. and enlisted as pilot/navigator.

From Manning Depot, Edmonton, he did guard duties at Claresholm and then did I.T.S. at Regina and after being processed as a pilot, he was sent to E.F.T.S. in Regina, flying Tiger Moths. Next came service flying at Claresholm on Cessna Cranes and after graduation in October 1942 he was sent to England, then to Dalcross, Scotland (19 A.F.U.) on Oxfords. In January he was posted to 23 O.T.U. Pershore on Wellingtons and on completion to Conversion Unit at Topcliffe to fly Halifax aircraft. The courses were full so he was posted to 427 Sqdn Croft, but as 427 was about to convert he was sent to 426 Sqdn Dishforth.

His first operational flight was in May 1943 as second pilot to Duisberg. The aircraft went u/s over the enemy coast and returned to England. After two more ops, where his was the only aircraft to return to base, he applied for North Africa. After a familiarization course in Portreath, England, eleven planes took off for Rabat Sale, Morocco via the Atlantic ocean to avoid night fighters over the Bay of Biscay. A severe hailstorm was encountered and at 6 a.m. the navigator reported that they were lost. Jones flew east towards land and they pinpointed their position on the coast of Portugal. The navigator was then able to give a new course for Rabat where they arrived safely. It took three days to repair the fabric of the aircraft and to give some idea of the ferocity of the storm, one of the aircraft was hit by lightning and had its nose turret knocked off!! From Rabat they flew to Zena in Tunisia, where they joined 425 Sqdn..

Bob's second op to Italy brought more adventure, as when heading for home, they had engine failure over the Mediterranean. After the second engine failed, Jones put the plane in a glide and after frantic efforts, managed to cough life into one engine. About that time the Wag. informed Bob that all radios were dead, including the intercom. A red Very cartridge was fired when they reached the coast of Tunisia, in the hope that they could obtain landing clearance into Tunis. The cartridge set fire to the lining of the fuselage, so now on fire and on one engine, the real drama began. However, someone out there knew of their distress. Using a system of searchlights, whereby the lights were shone parallel to the ground and then raised to 45 degrees in the direction of heading, then having the aircraft change course by the direction the lights pointed, they were led for over 50 minutes through the mountains of Northern Tunisia at night.

But the aircraft was losing altitude and Jones advised his crew that they could bail out, but because he had more faith in his aircraft than the parachute, he would stay. About that time he heard a voice saying "Bob, you don't need to be afraid, no-one is going to be hurt." It was a voice as plain as a person sitting next to him, and from then on he was free of fear. Well, almost!! They emerged to the desert short of fuel, on one engine and with no means of communicating, also two crew members with hands burned while attempting to put out the fire. Almost as if on cue, a flare path lit up, the good engine faltered and the bomb aimer bailed out at 500 feet (and survived). Bob headed for the flare path but on the final approach the engine failed again and he landed wheels up at the end of the runway of an American air base. The flare path lights came on at that precise moment only because there was one aircraft arriving.

They were back in England for Christmas and conversion to the Halifax aircraft. Bob's crew was assigned "D" Dog and his English engineer, Sgt. Morris was quick to paint a British bulldog on the nose of the aircraft, then they were ready for ops once more. Their first trip to Berlin was followed by most major centres: Leipzig, Schweinfurt, Augsburg, Stuttgart, Frankfurt and to Nurenburg where Bomber Command suffered its worst losses of the war (96 heavy bombers lost). For most of the time they were in bright moonlight and there were many goofs on the raid by both Pathfinders and bomber crews. Jones was caught in flak over Stuttgart, but the flak burst kept leading him, so he managed to get out of its range and back to England, where he landed at Middle Wallop, a fighter base.

Jones completed his tour in July 1944 having had only one abortive trip and that as a result of engine failure shortly after take off. Amazingly, during the tour he never received a hole in his aircraft; at the completion of his tour, to his knowledge, "D" Dog was the only original aircraft of the sqdn still on operations and he credits this to his crew and a "bit of luck". On its 77th op "D" Dog failed to return, however.

A posting to 24 O.T.U. Honeybourne was followed by one to Long Marston, where he instructed until after the end of the war with Germany. During this period he attended 3 F.I.S. at Lulsgate Bottom and the Bomber Command Instructors' School at Finningly, then he was discharged at Boundary Bay on October 10th 1945. Bob would like to have it noted that he gives a lot of credit in his completion of a tour to the fine ground crew of "D" Dog.

He was awarded the D.F.C., 39/45 Star, Aircrew Europe with France & Germany bar, Italy Star, Defence Medal, War Medal and the C.V.S.M.

After the war, Jones moved to California where he instructed for a while, then he crop dusted for several years, including one season in Ontario. He flew for several years in Canada as executive pilot, water bomber pilot on forest fires, charter pilot and instructor. He helped organize an Experimental Aircraft Association chapter in Squamish. In 1974 he and a friend started an Air Cadet Squadron and Jones was the C.O. for the next four years. He married Verna, a math teacher in 1960 and they reside in Squamish, B.C.

F/O REG. H. LEWIS
RAD/NAV R.A.F.

Reg was born in London, England in 1923 and after attending various elementary schools, he graduated from Chelsea Secondary School. He enjoyed swimming, cricket and soccer, was on the school gymnastics team and in his spare time fished. He took articles as an accountant and shortly after the outbreak of war was transferred to an essential occupation. He volunteered for the R.A.F. and was placed on the P.N.B. (Pilot, Navigator, Bombaimer) Scheme and did his basic square bashing at A.C.R.C. in London, on completion of which he was posted to I.T.S. Torquay. After passing out, he was posted overseas to East London, South Africa under the Empire Air Training Scheme, to No. 48 A.S. and after successfully completing this course was posted to No. 43 A.S. Port Alfred.

He graduated from this course, was awarded a wing and a commission and then posted to a holding unit at Durban awaiting posting to U.K. After arriving in U.K. he was sent to Harrogate, Yorks, where he volunteered for a Guinea Pig training course for night fighters. This course was taken on Wimpeys fitted out with a blacked out cabin amidships, rigged with radar and using Spitfires for targets. At the completion of this course he was posted to a Mosquito fighter O.T.U. where it was found that he had not done any "Beacon bashing", so he was sent north to a small airfield outside Durham, accommodation courtesy of R.A.F. in Quonset huts. After putting in the required time he was posted to 151 Squadron (Fighter) at Bradwell Bay.

The squadron was on the east coast and after two night cross-country exercises, Reg was on ops flying a Mosquito Mark 30 with a modified nose to take a radar scanner; armament was four cannon mounted in the belly and in addition to the standard fuel tanks, the aircraft was equipped with wing drop tanks, for the extended range of ops.

To get to the operational area they had to exit England through two routes; one north of the Wash, the other west of Beachy Head. The corridor in between was known by the code name "Diver Belt", the divers being German pilotless planes nicknamed Buzz-Bombs by the civilian populace. On one of the support sorties over the Polish Redoubt, just in front of the Russian lines, the aircraft took some heavy flak and the starboard engine was hit and put out of commission along with their R.T. (Whilst flying over this area, crews had to wear plastic coated Union Jacks around their necks to identify themselves as allies, also an incendiary bomb was carried in case of forced landing so that the aircraft which had bags of hush-hush equipment on board, could be destroyed.) Bearing this in mind they decided to attempt to get back to U.K. and headed for a "crash" airfield at Manston on the Isle of Thanet; this field was in the middle of "Buzz Bomb" alley, so on approaching the field, Reg frantically tapped out the letters of the day on the wing lights and fired off, what he hoped, were the right sequence of colours through the Very pistol; fortunately for them, both the ack-ack gunners were up to the mark on night silhouette recognition and did not have itchy fingers. The tower must have realized that their R.T. was out and at last switched on the runway lights and thanks to the skill of the pilot, W/O H. (Lofty) Hymas, they landed safely. This episode gave them a record for the longest distance on one engine. Shortly after this, incidentally, Lofty lost his life in a flying accident during air to ground firing practice; some 15 minutes earlier the pilot had dropped off Reg.

The squadron was posted to Predannack airfield on the Lizard, Cornwall and Reg crewed up with a "sprog" pilot, W/O Phil East and on their first trip together the aircraft sprang a leak and all the coolant drained from the port engine which promptly caught fire. This happened right after takeoff and there was not enough height or airspeed at this time to get the undercart down; the pilot showed great skill in belly landing a plywood aircraft with a full war load of fuel. The quickness of the fire tender crew was instrumental in saving their lives.

In early 1946 after another mishap, Reg was grounded and became a Link trainer instructor for budding Rad/Navs; from there he was posted to R.A.F. Uxbridge to await demobilization. He was in receipt of the '39/45 Star, France & Germany Star, War Medal and Defence Medal.

Returning to civilian life after discharge at Uxbridge in March 1947, Reg was Assistant Clerk of Works at Chobham airfield in Surrey, then entered the Inland Revenue Branch of the Civil Service. He emigrated to Canada in 1957 and worked in sales for Finning Ltd in Vancouver and in various branches in B.C. He is now retired and lives with his wife Marlene in North Vancouver. He has a married daughter from a previous marriage, living in Prince George and Reg also has a grand-daughter Kimberley and grand-son Bradley. Reg's spare time is taken up with his garden, exercise, walking, camping and trying to understand his camera.

 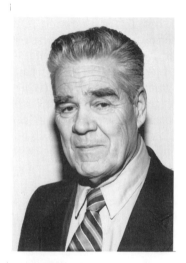

F. JACK McMAHON
AIRGUNNER/PILOT R.C.A.F.

Jack was born in Edmonton, Alberta and attended Gradin Grade School, then St. Joseph's High School where he got his senior matric. Moving to Vancouver, he attended U.B.C. for one year in Engineering. He then spent three years in a sales management course. His hobbies included tennis, skiing, swimming, badminton, hockey, football, baseball and boating. After university he worked as a sales clerk surveyor's chainman.

He joined the R.C.A.F. in 1937 at Calgary and was posted to Camp Borden for the usual square bashing and basic training and this was followed by a succession of postings to Trenton, then to 6 T.B. Squadron, Jericho Beach '39, 6BR Squadron Alliford Bay, then Patricia Bay 120 Squadron. He remustered to aircrew in December 1941 then went to I.T.S. Edmonton and to 16 E.T.S. in the same city and then after a sojourn at S.F.T.S. McLeod, Alberta, received his wings in September 1942. He was then posted to Sheperd No 2 Wireless training, as staff pilot and was posted overseas early in 1944 to O.T.U. Wellsburn Mountford then to heavy conversion Dishforth to 425 squadron in December 1944. He returned to Canada in August 1945 and was posted to communication squadron Winnipeg.

Jack's medals include the 39/45 Star, Aircrew Europe Star, Defence Medal, and CVSM & clasp. His promotions had been to corporal in 1940, sergeant in '41, F/sgt in 1942, W/O2 in '43, P/O later that year, F/O in '44. He was discharged at Dartmouth in 1946 and continued with his engineering at UBC in 1947, 1948, 1950 and 1953. He then became a charter pilot on the west coast of B.C., Associated Air Taxi and then incorporated Western Airmotive (1952) Air Charter & Maintenance Company, which he sold in 1963. He then incorporated Transwest Helicopters (1965) Ltd in 1964 and converted to Helicopter Commercial license and flew and managed this company for 20 years. He is presently Operations Manager Can Arc Helicopters. Jack was married in London, England to Patricia in 1945 and they have 4 children, all teachers.

One day in the fall of 1940, at Alliford Bay, Queen Charlotte Island, B.C., an aircraft which appeared to have been designed to spend its life on wheels arrived, equipped with float gear. The five occupants stayed the night and next morning took off for Pat Bay but it stalled and crashed in the sea, all five being lost. Not long after this incident McMahon and two officers were told to report to Pat Bay and take delivery of the aircraft which was a Northrop, the same type mentioned above. They were to bring it back to Alliford Bay. McMahon was at that time a tradesman air gunner with the rank of sergeant.

When they arrived at Pat Bay the aircraft was waiting for them straining at its mooring, obviously eager to go. The first leg of the trip was uneventful and they landed at Bella Bella. The following day, although it was overcast with a slight drizzle a decision was made to proceed. After sufficient warmup, the pilot headed the aircraft into the wind and they took off. At about 500 feet a turn on course was made and at that point the engine spluttered, caught for a while, then quit. Silence reigned supreme. Needless to say, all hell broke loose in the cockpit as the pilot desperately attempted to get the aircraft from an untenable position well over the trees to a position back over the water in order to secure a chance of a water landing. In the meantime McMahon was busy tapping out an SOS which, in retrospect seemed the ultimate act of futility. Afterwards McMahon grasped two rails running the length of the cabin and shut his eyes. Later on he couldn't remember what happened until he climbed out of a very bent Northrop Delta which was now upside down in about 7 feet of water. All crew members survived with just a few bruises and McMahon was pleased to get three weeks sick leave. However, upon Jack's return to Pat Bay, there, patiently waiting, floating serenely at its mooring was another Northrop Delta, eager and ready to go. The next day with S/Ldr Fred Ewart again at the controls, they soon headed for Alliford Bay. Once more the flight was uneventful until near Alert Bay they ran into a blinding snow storm, so making a 180 degree turn they retreated to Pat Bay which they reached safely.

The crew proceeded to shore after securing the aircraft to the mooring buoy, however, just as they reached the dock and turned for another look, an amazing scene was taking place. There, before their eyes, incredulous as it may seem, they saw the Northrop slowly sinking below the surface of the water!! One of them was noticed displaying a satisfied grin for whatever reason no-one will ever know. Jack was later recommended to remuster, got his wings, and eventually was fortunate enough to serve with the Alouette Squadron stationed at Tholthorpe in 6 Group.

On March 10 1945, F/O McMahon flying Halifax "S" for Sugar experienced his first daylight raid in a gaggle formation.

A Halifax directly in front of him literally blew up and various bits and pieces flew by including parachutes. Also present on the scene were ME 262's which travelled at tremendous speeds. At last McMahon was over the target area, the marshalling yards at Leipzig. After dropping their load it was the usual "Let's get the hell out of here" but at this time things began to happen which were not planned. For one thing a 1,000 pound bomb hung up, then almost at once the outboard starboard engine propellor went into flat pitch. They were at 16,000 feet at this point and every possible effort was made to feather the prop without success. To make matters worse the electrical system packed up which meant that no navigational aids were available.

Jack's excellent navigator, Ron Neilly, resorted to dead reckoning and a course was set to land at Ipswich in Suffolk where an emergency field was in place. After firing a Very cartridge to attract Mustang fighter assistance, no fighters appeared so they were on their own.

Due to the rapid advance of allied forces, bombs were not to be jettisoned over any area where those forces might be in action and as the bomb now seemed to be loose and rolling around in the bomb bay McMahon decided to hang on to the bomb until over the channel. In the meantime, because of the incredible drag caused by the runaway prop they were losing altitude and at 6,500 feet they were directly over Cologne and subject to hostile gunfire. Taking evasive action, they lost more precious altitude. Shortly afterwards the channel came into view, the bomb doors were opened and the bomb jettisoned. Their height was now around 1,000 feet and even with the 3 active engines going full bore, the plane was still losing altitude. At last Ipswich was close at hand and Jack was given a straight in approach as he was now down to 500 feet and they landed safely.

F/O R.H. PREBBLE
PILOT R.C.A.F.

Bob Prebble was born at Tugaske, Sask but six years later the family moved to Vancouver where Bob attended Nelson Avenue and Kingsway West elementary schools, followed by South Burnaby High School then Inglewood High in West Van where he matriculated. His hobbies were flying and science. After high school Bob went to Fort William, as it was called then, and was employed by the Canadian Car and Foundry Co in the manufacture of Hawker Hurricanes.

He joined the R.C.A.F. on November 12th at Fort William and volunteered to be a pilot. He was at the following stations in the course of his training:- Brandon, Regina, Vancouver flying Tiger Moths in Feb 1941, then Dauphin, Man. in April on Harvards. He then went overseas to 53 O.T.U. at Llandow, South Wales in August flying Spits, thence to Biggin Hill on 401 Sqdn. in October again on Spits, thence to Hendon in Jan 1942 flying Lysanders and on to Grangemouth 58 O.T.U. on Spitfires. He was then posted to Digby 402 on Spits in '43 and to Upavon #7 F.I.S. in February 1944.

Bob saw action over the coasts of Holland and France in 1943 and had the privilege of flying with 402 Sqdn R.C.A.F. with four aces in the war. :- W/C L.S. Ford D.F.C., W/C L.V. Chadburn D.S.O., D.F.C., W/C J.D. Mitchener D.F.C. and Bar and G/Capt G.W. Northcott D.S.O., D.F.C.

On the morning of July 4th 1943, 3 E boats were reported moving in line astern down the coastal waters of Holland. 402 Sqdn, in anticipation of an early morning strike, had flown down to Coltishall on the east coast, near Norwich. The plan of attack figured out by leaders Ford and Chadburn was that 6 Spits were to go towards the Holland coast and four south towards Dover, to attack enemy shipping. One of the six had engine trouble leaving 5 for the attack and at 5,000 feet and about 5 miles distant, the enemy opened fire with cannon fire enhanced with tracers.

The 3 "E" boats, about 50 ft in length and heavily armed with cannons and machine guns, were approached in line astern. Chadburn flew directly in line with the boats and received a lot of cannon fire which smashed his perspex windscreen, causing it to become opaque and so after having initially fired his cannons, he turned away, not being able to see. Ford flew over all 3 boats firing as he went but the cannon fire was so intense that he crashed in the sea and was lost. Another Spit received a cannon hole in the fuselage behind the pilot's head and had to turn away. Prebble and the remaining pilot turned slowly towards the boats and were able to fire, the latter pumping shells into the second boat from the side finishing his run. He was not hit. Bob now opened up with cannon and machine guns at about 500 feet and avoided cannon fire from the boat by side slipping pressure on the rudder while keeping the guns pointing to the middle of the boat. He kept on firing to zero feet, so close that the small lifeboat on the "E" boat showed up in the 8mm film. Prebble claimed this boat as probably sunk.

In July 1943, on a ramrod withdrawal escort for U.S. Fortresses an incident took place which proved to Bob that some pilots really did have eyes like eagles. 402 Sqdn had just been engaged in a down to earth series of dogfights with 109's and was broken up into small groups of Spits. Chadburn, after destroying a 109, headed home with 3 more Spits behind him and gained altitude to 8,000 feet, when a call came over the R/T for assistance. "For God's sake somebody get down here and help me. I have two of them on my tail."

Chadburn immediately reversed direction and headed for the deck in a screaming dive of close to 500 mph. Prebble had to blast his throttle wide open to keep up. Approaching ground level, Bob, immediately behind Chadburn saw smoke from his guns at the same time that he saw the 109 Chadburn was firing at. And now, before Bob could blink an eye, Chadburn pulled severely back on the control column and climbed again while Bob was quietly blacking out, but still conscious and holding his position until he could see again. When he could, there was Chadburn right in front of him, still climbing vertically and arriving right back where he had started from. The pilot who needed help got it!!

Bob's medals include the pilot's flying badge, operational wing, '39/45 Star, War Medal, Aircrew Europe Star, Defence Medal and C.V.S.M. and he attained the rank of Flying Officer in 1944. Bob was discharged in Vancouver in 1945 where he started his own manufacturing business, Capilano Metal Products Ltd which he operated for 35 years. He was married to Mary at Weston-Super-Mare, England in 1943 and they have a son, Scott and daughter Jan. His brother F.N. Prebble did tours in Halifaxes and earned the D.F.C.

F/LT N.I. (NORM) TYCHO
WIRELESS AIRGUNNER R.C.A.F.

Norm was born in Smithers, B.C. and completed his public and high school education there, qualifying for university entrance. He was interested in sports, playing hockey, baseball, basketball as well as being an avid skier.

Prior to joining the R.C.A.F. in Sept. 1941, he worked as a surveyor's assistant. He was accepted for pilot training and was sworn in at Vancouver. After completing manning pool, guard duty and Initial Training School he was posted to E.F.T.S. (#19) at Virden, Man. and commenced flying training Feb. 25th 1942. He did not qualify to solo and was "scrubbed" because of poor depth perception on his landings.

He remustered to wireless airgunner and attended #4 Wireless School at Guelph, Ontario. From there he was posted to #7 Bombing and Gunnery school at Paulson, Man., receiving his wings January 25th, 1943. Norm was now posted to #111 Operational Training Unit at Nassau in the Bahamas, for training on B25 Mitchells and B24 Liberators. During this part of the course one of the WAGs had to stay on the ground. It was during Norm's turn on the ground that the entire crew went missing. No signal was received from the aircraft.... it vanished and to this day Norm wonders if there is anything to the "Bermuda Triangle". Norm was immediately advanced one course and crewed up with another pilot, Ian Jeffery.

From Nassau the crew was posted to R.A.F. Transport Command at Dorval for further training. The crew was then posted overseas to #1 (C) O.T.U. at Beaulieu, Hampshire, arriving on July 24th 1943. Here the crew picked up another skipper W/C Drapper and a seasoned WAG "Tapper" Daley, both R.A.F. types. Having completed the course the crew was posted to #53 Sqdn, Coastal Command at Thorney Island on the south coast of England and had its first op on Sept 6th, an anti submarine patrol in the Bay of Biscay. Norm completed 7 sorties in this area, enemy aircraft being spotted on three occasions, but they did not press home any attacks.

339

Norm and the crew were now posted to #83 VLR Sqdn at Ballykelly, Northern Ireland, where they concentrated on convoy escort work in the North Atlantic. The patrols were from 14 to 16 1/2 hours duration and took them well into mid-Atlantic. The weather was usually very bad and icing a real threat and Norm remembers on two occasions when "ditching" was a strong possibility as ice was building up and the skipper was having trouble maintaining altitude. The pulsating rubber de-icers would not keep the leading edges of the wings, tailplanes and fins clear of ice. He ran through the ditching procedure with the crew and just as they had given up hope, the ice broke away and they felt the aircraft come to life again. What a tremendous feeling of joy and thanks to the "Man upstairs".

Fuel consumption was very high under these conditions and on one patrol the flight engineer advised the skipper he didn't think they would make it back to base. However, they made a landfall over Southern Ireland and there was a possibility of landing there, but this would have meant internment in Southern Ireland, so they decided to return to Ballykelly where a successful landing was made. The tanks were dipped and the flight engineer reported "We just made it."

It was time to move on again and Norm and the sqdn moved to Reykjavik, Iceland and continued with North Atlantic patrols, sometimes above the Arctic Circle. These were long, cold and tiresome patrols and flying in these Northern latitudes played havoc with the aircraft compasses. The navigators were continually getting fixes from the sun or stars. From Reykjavik they then moved on to Tain on the east coast of Scotland, where patrols were carried out just off the coast of Norway and at an altitude of approximately 100 feet.

Norm completed his tour while at Tain, on Feb.14th 1945 and was then posted to R.A.F. Station Leuchars, Fife, Scotland to fly with a test flight and he crewed up with former members of #86 Sqdn. This involved air testing and acceptance testing for 206, 547 and 224 Squadrons and it came to an end on June 27th, '45 when another posting followed to 426 Transport Squadron (R.C.A.F.) at Tempsford, Bedfordshire. 426 sqdn. was involved in transporting British servicemen to and from India.

Norm was repatriated to Canada and received his honourable discharge in Vancouver June 3, 1946. He was the recipient of the '39/45 Star, The Atlantic Star, the War Medal, CVSM & clasp and was Mentioned in Despatches. After discharge, Norm was employed by C.N. Telecommunications as Installation Inspector, Plant Extension Supervisor and Project Co-ordinator. He was married in December 1945 in Leuchars and he and his wife Doris have one daughter, four sons and six grandchildren.

340

Epilogue

WHITE CHRISTMAS - BLACK ANGEL

There were only three of us who entrained that winter's night bound for Edmonton, Bill and Old Harry and myself. Harry was dubbed "Old Harry" because he was twenty-four, most aircrew were under twenty. We were awkward and shy in our new officers' uniforms, recently purchased at Spencers on Hastings Street and if an army private saluted us, we hardly knew how to return the salute. Mothers, fathers, brothers and sisters tried to hide their true emotions pressing their Christmas presents upon us. The hissing steam, the "All Aboard", and the tolling of the bell was a welcome cacophony of sound, that released us from youth's remembrance and heralded us on our way. A way beyond all imaginings and for most, a way of no return.

Army personnel crossed the country in the congenial company of their units on troop trains. Senior officers would provide a climate of security, as well as control. We three were quite alone, located at the end of the pullman next to the black porter's cramped cabin. Loneliness soon lashed us into the beginnings of friendship, and the porter, Amos Bones, did his bit to befriend us.

"Leave your shoes under the curtains Gentlemen, I'll shine them in the night."

Wearied from our sad leavetaking, we welcomed the suggestion and were soon abed. The train rocked us gently, yet the mournful whistle was an ominous sound, for some, they were rushing to their Valhalla.

The first call for breakfast, found us united for comfort, self conscious in our still so new uniforms. The table was resplendent in white linen and silver and our waiter served us with a flair, that belongs to the past. Billy mistook a gleaming service jug and poured coffee over his pancakes. Before anyone dare question the ways of an "officer and a gentleman", he announced in stentorian W.C. Fields fashion, "the only way to eat hotcakes, boys", and gulped the sodden mess, with convincing gusto. Christmas Eve we were together again, for the traditional turkey dinner, but something was sorely lacking. We were supposed to be men, strong men, yet short months ago we had been boys. We needed a parent; poor Old Harry tried, but he was in need of one too. Our answer was very near to us. In the darkened evening, our train screeched to a stop, blocked by a snowslide.

The coach lights were turned off, to conserve energy and our attempts at humorous bantering, totally failed to dispel the dark moods of my soul.

Then the deep baritone of a Black Angel: "Gentlemen, please join me in my quarters!" It was a command, yet the most welcome of invitations. In a matter of days we would be aboard the "Queen Elizabeth", but I am fully persuaded, that the captain's commodious cabin could not compare with the comfort of the cramped quarters of Amos Bones. He produced a bottle of rye; Mom had made me a Christmas cake, the other two had similar offerings; it was a feast!

The snowfall had stopped and we could see Mount Robson, the moon over it like a glorious star on this snow stilled eve. And then our dark host started softly singing "Silent Night." I was grateful that the darkened coach hid my tears. His strong arms were around me and halted high in the mountains, granted a pause in our fearful journey, I felt the love that is Christmas.

In our bunks we were awakened by the gentle jolt of the released train, as bell and whistle heralded its long descent. As we left the mountains, we seemed to be leaving all those Christmases past. Amos Bones left us at Edmonton, as if part of youth and its security was passing away.

It was Christmas and the last one for Old Harry and twelve more of our class of graduates. The engine steamed, whistled and smoked, as if impatient to deliver us to Armageddon. Christmas would never be the same again, but somehow that Advent Eve had prepared me to accept it.

Harold McDonald D.F.C
Padre A.C.A.

HAWKER HURRICANE Mk IV LD 973
NO 438 "WILDCAT" SQDN. R.C.A.F. MAY 1943

Glossary

A.A.	Ack Ack, anti aircraft gunfire
A/C	Air Commodore or aircraft
A/C 1	Aircraftsman 1st class
A/C 2	Aircraftsman 2nd class
A.F.C.	Air Force Cross
A.F.M.	Air Force Medal
A.M.	Air Ministry or Air Marshall
A.V.M.	Air Vice Marshall
Ace	Star performer in the air
Ammo	Ammunition
Bag	Secure or shoot down
Bail out	Leave aircraft by parachute
Bank	Dip a wing
Base	Home air station
Beat up	Attack
Beau	Beaufighter plane
Beetle home	To return to base
Bind	Depressing job, boring
Binders	Brakes
Black, a	Performance bringing discredit
Blackout	Momentarily lose consciousness
Blockbuster	Very heavy bomb
Blood wagon	Ambulance
Blower	Telephone
Bogey	Unidentified aircraft
Bomber boy	Crew member in bomber squadron
Boob, to	Make an error
Boost	Extra pressure, supercharge engine
Bought it	Dead
Bowser	Gas tender that refuels aircraft
Box barrage	Concentration of A/A fire in space
Briefing	Crews being told about forthcoming op.
Browned off	Fed up
Burton, go for a	Go missing or be killed
Caterpillar	One who jumps from a/c by chute & lives
Ceiling	Highest level of cloud layer or max. height a/c can climb to
Cheesed	Very miserable
C.F.I.	Chief Flying Instructor
Chiefy	Flight Sergeant
Chop, get the	Be killed
'Chute	Parachute
Circuits and bumps	Flying around field and landing
Civvy	Civilian
Clock	Airspeed indicator
Cloud 10/10	Sky completely covered by cloud
Cloud 5/10	Sky half covered by cloud
Cockpit	Space for pilot to sit
Conk out	Cease functioning
Coned	A/c lit up by enemy searchlights
C.O.	Commanding Officer
Cookies	Heavy bombs
Corkscrew	Take evasive action
Crack up	Accident causing damage only, to a/c
Crate	a/c
Dead stick landing	Landing without use of engine
Deck	Deck or airfield
Ditch	Force land in water
Dogfight	Aerial combat
Drink	The sea
Drogue	Target towed by a/c
Dual	Flying with instructor
Duff	No good
Duff gen	Incorrect information
Dummy run	Bombing run but no bombs dropped
D/F	Directional finding bearing
D.F.C.	Distinguished Flying Cross
D.F.M.	Distinguished Flying Medal
Erk	Airman
E.T.A.	Estimated time of arrival
E.T.D.	Estimated time of departure
E.F.T.S.	Elementary Flying Training School
Evasive action	Avoid an encounter
Fan	Propellor
Fido	Fog investigation & dispersal op.
Fighter boys	Fighter command pilots
Fitter	Aero engine mechanic
Fix	Visual fix by ground recognition
Flak	German a/a gun fire
Flap	Any sort of sudden excitement
Flat out	Full speed
Flat spin	Running around in circles, a/c nose high
Flight	Six aircraft
Flip	Joyride

F/Sgt	Flight Sergeant	Mae West	Life saving jacket for use over water
F/Lt	Flight Lieutenant		
F/O	Flying Officer	Maggie	Miles Magister aircraft
Fuselage	Body of a/c	Milk run	An easy, short operation
Gaggle	Flight of aircraft	Milling around	Defensive circling of a/c in combat
Gardening	Sea mine laying by aircraft		
Gee	Radio navigational aid	NAAFI	Navy, Army & Air Force institute canteen
Gen	Reliable information		
Gong	Medal or decoration	Natter	Talk to
Gremlins	Mythical creatures invented by R.A.F.	Nickels	Leaflets
		Nissen Hut	Corrugated iron hut
Grounded	Confined to ground for discip. reasons	N.B.G.	No bloody good
		N.C.O.	Non commissioned officer
Ground strafe	To machine gun from low level flight	Oboe	Ground controlled radar system
Group	Number of stations or wings	On the clock	On the airspeed indicator
G/C	Group Captain	Ops	Operations
G.P	General purpose bomb	Ops room	Operations room where information is given and air raid planned
G.C.I.	Ground control interception		
Hallibag/Halley	Halifax bomber		
Happy Valley	Heavily defended German Ruhr Valley	Orbit	Circle around
		O.T.U.	Operational training unit
Hare after	Pursue	Overshoot	Go beyond destined stopping point
Heavies	Large aircraft, bombs or guns		
		Pack up	Give up
Hedge hop	Fly low	Pass the buck	Pass the responsibility
H.E.	High explosive	Pasting	Punishment
H2S	Airborne radar navigational aid	Pathfinder	a/c in Bomber Command in front of main force to mark target with flares
Hurri	Hurricane fighter plane		
I.F.F.	Identification friend or foe	Pattern bombing	All a/c in formation bombing at once
In dock	In hospital		
Intercom	Intercommunication in a/c	Peel off	Turn away from formation
Intruder	Night ops to impede enemy in use of his airfield	Perspex	Glass-like material for windscreens etc
Irons	Knife, fork and spoon	Piece of cake	Easy, a cinch
I.T.W.	Initial training wing	Pinpoint	Locate place or target exactly
Jankers	Extra duty		
Jerry	German	Plastered	Well covered (bombing) well oiled (airman)
Kite	Aircraft		
Kitty, in the	In the bag	P/O	Pilot Officer
Knows his onions	Competent	Pond	Atlantic Ocean
L.A.C.	Leading aircraftsman	Popsie	Girl friend
Lanc	Lancaster bomber	Prang	To damage, destroy, wreck
Lay on	To provide	P.R.U.	Photo reconnaissance unit
Leg	Stage between landings on long flight	Prune, Pilot Officer	Ficticious character who behaves as every officer should *not*, appearing in magazine TEE EMM
Let up	Throttle back		
Lib	Liberator bomber		
Line	Story of personal achievement	Pukka	Genuine
		Press the tit	Press the button
Line astern	One behind the other	Pull the plug	Release the bombs
Line bombing	Bombs dropped in a line	Pull your finger out	Stop slacking, get going
Lizzie	Westland Lysander aircraft	RDF	Radio direction finding
Loose off	To fire	Recce	Reconnaissance
Lowdown	Inside story	Rhubarb	Offensive ops by fighters to make enemy retain strong
Luftwaffe	German Air Force		

	forces in Western Europe	Tail end Charlie	Rear gunner or rear a/c in formation
Rigger	Airframe mechanic		
Run up	Aiming attack by bomber	Tally ho	Enemy or target sighted
Scramble	Fighter pilots hurrying to aircraft	Tannoy	Station public address system
Saturated	Complete bomb coverage	Tarmac	Airfield runways surfaced with macadam
Second dickey	Co-pilot		
Serviceable	Ready for use or action	Thro' the gate	Place throttle for maximum power
Sgt	Sergeant		
Shakey do	Occurrence with serious consequences	Three pointer	A good landing on all 3 wheels at once
Ship	Aircraft	Ticking over	Engine idling
Shoot up	Dive onto, as though attacking	Tiger	DeHavilland Tiger Moth training bi-plane
Shot down	Beaten, whether in air fight or arguement	Tinfish	Torpedoes
		Touchdown	To land
Shot down in flames	Hopelessly beaten at anything	Tracer ammo	Ammunition that traces its path
Shot up	Attacked by gun fire	Twirp	Simple minded soul
Skipper	Captain of a/c	Undercart	Legs or wheels of a/c
Sling one up	Salute	U/S	Unserviceable
Soggy	a/c when controls are slow to react	VLR	Very Long Range
		W.A.G	Wireless Air Gunner
S/L	Squadron Leader	Weave	Meander flight path so as to see behind aircraft
Solo	Fly alone, generally for first time		
		Whack	Attempt
Spin in	To crash, failing to recover from spin	Wimpey	Wellington bomber
		Winco/Wingco	Wing Commander
Spill the beans	Give or leak information	Window	Metallic strips dropped by a/c to confuse enemy radar
Spit	Spitfire a/c		
Sprog	New airman or airman under training		
		Wing	Number of squadrons
Squadron	12 or 18 aircraft	Wizard	Star performer
Station	Air base	W/C	Wing Commander
Stick	Line of several bomb bursts	W.O.P	Wireless operator
Stooge around	Idle about on ground or in the air	W/O	Warrant Officer
		Written off	Killed; crashed, beyond repair
Strafe	Attack, usually with machine guns on ground targets		
		W/T	Wireless telegraphy
Stuka	German dive bomber	You've had it	You have missed it

"DeHAVILAND DH-82C TIGER MOTH '438B'"

THE GROUND CREW

Always there, all the time ......

..... a job well done